Introduction to Governance, Government and Public Administration

Aimee L. Franklin • Jos C.N. Raadschelders

Introduction to Governance, Government and Public Administration

palgrave
macmillan

Aimee L. Franklin
Department of Political Science
University of Oklahoma
Norman, OK, USA

Jos C.N. Raadschelders
John Glenn College of Public Affairs
The Ohio State University
Columbus, OH, USA

ISBN 978-3-031-32688-2   ISBN 978-3-031-32689-9 (eBook)
https://doi.org/10.1007/978-3-031-32689-9

© The Editor(s) (if applicable) and The Author(s), under exclusive licence to Springer Nature Switzerland AG 2023

This work is subject to copyright. All rights are solely and exclusively licensed by the Publisher, whether the whole or part of the material is concerned, specifically the rights of translation, reprinting, reuse of illustrations, recitation, broadcasting, reproduction on microfilms or in any other physical way, and transmission or information storage and retrieval, electronic adaptation, computer software, or by similar or dissimilar methodology now known or hereafter developed.

The use of general descriptive names, registered names, trademarks, service marks, etc. in this publication does not imply, even in the absence of a specific statement, that such names are exempt from the relevant protective laws and regulations and therefore free for general use.

The publisher, the authors, and the editors are safe to assume that the advice and information in this book are believed to be true and accurate at the date of publication. Neither the publisher nor the authors or the editors give a warranty, expressed or implied, with respect to the material contained herein or for any errors or omissions that may have been made. The publisher remains neutral with regard to jurisdictional claims in published maps and institutional affiliations.

This Palgrave Macmillan imprint is published by the registered company Springer Nature Switzerland AG.
The registered company address is: Gewerbestrasse 11, 6330 Cham, Switzerland

We would like to acknowledge the support of our academic institutions and professional colleagues at universities all around the world. We are also grateful to our undergraduate and graduate students who provided input about the book (when we used earlier versions in Introduction to Public Administration classes).

Thanks to Stewart Beale at Palgrave for his support for our project and assistance through contracting and publication. And, special recognition and gratitude goes to Julie Raadschelders, Ph.D., who provided valuable insights and technical support to us through the development, writing, and editing process.

Foreword

The study of public administration and policy in the past half-century has made great steps toward understanding, among other things, how policy originates; how it is made, developed, and implemented; the roles that different institutions play in developing and managing policy; and the impact of different organizational forms and models on how policies work. To make such achievements scholarship in the field has of necessity become a series of specialisms focusing on, for example, the role of interest groups, parties, parliament, courts, and different spheres of public management such as coordination, regulation, and human resource management, among many other fields. In this book Aimee Franklin and Jos Raadschelders go beyond exposition of these main specialisms and offer a survey of the nature of public administration from the perspective of helping students as citizens make sense of the world. This is what they describe as the "civics education" aims of the book.

Franklin and Raadschelders manage to offer a superb integration of these different strands of knowledge by making "government" and "governance" the focus of their work. "Government" as a name for a field of study was, until recently, regarded as a somewhat old-fashioned academic label that lived on in the names of university departments that for one reason or another did not choose the more modern "political science" or "politics." The term "governance" and its relatively recent popularity have focused attention once more on the connections between a range of social, administrative, economic, and political processes, and the relationship between them and the institutions and procedures connected with public authority, that is, with "government." In doing so, terms such as "government" and "governance" highlight the importance of understanding the relationships between these different strands of knowledge. These are the key underlying themes of the *Introduction to Governance, Government, and Public Administration*.

The perspectives covered in this book draw from political science, political theory, economics, social psychology, as well as history and law. The different disciplinary perspectives are used to develop answers to the key questions they raise in each of the 13 chapters. The questions and the answers matter to us all as citizens and the book is written for a much wider audience than those studying for final-level examinations in public administration. It is, as the authors say, designed to appeal to citizens as well as aspiring public officials. It will, of course, be of great value to public administration finalists too, mainly because it explores connections between the range of different features that are often discussed separately.

London, UK   Edward C. Page

Preface

Almost all public administration textbooks are nationally anchored: American textbooks are written with an American audience in mind; English textbooks with an English audience; Dutch textbooks with a Dutch audience, etc. This textbook is written by an American scholar (Franklin) and a Dutch scholar (who has lived and worked in the United States since 1998). It will be no surprise, then, that several of the references in our book are to American literature and scholarship. Still, throughout the text, mention is made of political-administrative systems in and of other countries. Thus, we hope this textbook is helpful for students and instructors in African, Asian (e.g., China, India, Japan, and South Korea; to name the four countries in Asia with very sizeable PA programs), European, and Latin American countries, as well as those who teach in Australia and New Zealand. When it comes to the institutional arrangements for governing, there are a variety of ways that countries have developed these: presidential or parliamentary system; monarchy or republic; democratic or authoritarian; one-party, two-party, multi-party, etc.

The normative reason for this book is that civics education, so standard in secondary school curricula in the 1940s–1970s, has been disappearing, at least in Western countries. Consequently, secondary or high schoolers come into college without basic knowledge about the position and role of government in society. For better or for worse, and whether people like it or not, the government in many countries is the only social actor that can make authoritative decisions on behalf of the entire citizenry. Other social actors influence the steering of society (such as labor unions, churches, specific issue interest groups, sports associations, non-profit organizations, corporations, businesses, etc.). Still, none have the formal authority to make binding decisions for a country's population. This has only been established relatively recently, that is, in the past 200–250 years. As much as we may speak about collaborative management, private-public partnership, contracting-out, privatization, hollowing out of the state, and so on, the state (and its government) remains the single, sovereign actor.

Contemporary government, so different from its historical predecessors, has been multiplying in response to the combined effects of industrialization, urbanization, and population growth. Indeed, people living at the turn of the twentieth century would not recognize the scope and intensity of government activity and services today. It is no wonder that the emerging social phenomenon of a government that is deeply and in various ways intertwined with society has attracted the attention of scholars in political science and law since the late 1800s. Public administration emerged on both sides of the Atlantic as a study independent from political science or law between World War I and World War II. The earliest general handbooks of public administration date back to the late 1920s. After World War II, the number of public administration programs slowly, then more rapidly, increased in Western democracies. The same growth has happened in other countries where industrialization, urbanization, and population growth coincided (such as in the past 40 years in Asia and South America).

Our book is not an introduction to (comparative) political systems but an introduction to public administration. That means that this textbook is applicable in many different national settings since the challenges of administration and management are very similar everywhere. Just consider that public bureaucracies everywhere have a personnel system, that government is financed through taxation, that policy is developed in collaboration with a variety of stakeholders and implemented based on strategic and tactical plans, and that government performance is increasingly measured in terms of ranking or of monies.

This textbook provides an overview of the various substantive areas that comprise the study not just of public administration but also the way it is related to and embedded within the conceptions of governance and government in a particular society. In the first six chapters the focus is on the position and role of government in society and how government is embedded in the larger structures of governance. In Chaps. 7–12 we deal with main public administration topics. The concluding chapter offers some thoughts about the nature of the study of public administration. We present this in a manner that fosters an understanding of government in society in ways that are accessible to both undergraduate and entry-level graduate students. We believe this is important because faculty and students need to be able to connect through literature that is written with an eye on pedagogy rather than on scholarship.

Norman, OK Aimee L. Franklin
Columbus, OH Jos C.N. Raadschelders

Acknowledgments

We would like to acknowledge the support of our academic institutions and colleagues, of undergraduate students who provided input about the book (when we used it in introduction to public administration classes), and of Steward Beale, publisher at Palgrave, and greatly supportive of this effort.

Contents

1 The Characteristics of Public Administration   1
When Did These Two Subject Areas Emerge?   2
How Was This Achieved?   2
Developing Curriculum: For Democracy and for Efficiency   3
How Did They Pursue That Goal?   3
The Interdisciplinary Study of Government in Society   7
The Pedagogical Approach of the Public Sector and This Book   8
Practical Applications   9
In-Class Instructional Suggestions   9
References   9

2 Governance Through Government and Public Administration: Is Governance A Nuisance, a Necessity, or a Blessing?   11
What Are Common Metaphors for Government?   13
What Is Government?   14
How Are Governance and Government Related?   19
How Does Government Unite the People?   23
How Do People Connect Outside Government?   24
Why Does Government Exist?   28
Practical Applications   30
In-Class Instructional Suggestions   31
References   31

3 The Sovereignty of Government   35
What Is Sovereignty?   35
What Is the History of State Making?   40
What Are the Theories of Sovereignty?   43
Why Is Sovereignty Necessary for Society?   46
Practical Applications for Students   54
In-Class Instructional Suggestions   55
References   55

4 Government Culture and Climate — 57
- Why Do We Refer to The Government As a Bureaucracy? — 58
- How Do Culture and Climate Differ? — 60
- What Are the Different Layers of Culture and Climate? — 62
- What Are the Dimensions for Comparing Culture and Climate? — 69
- How Is Culture Reflected in Expectations for Public Servants? — 72
- Examples to Test Your Understanding — 77
- Practical Applications for Students — 79
- In-Class Instructional Suggestions — 79
- References — 80

5 Government: Institutions, People, Interactions — 83
- How Does Government Appear to the Public? — 83
- Who Provides Government Services? — 86
- What Are the Stereotypes of Interactions with the Government? — 89
- How Do Elected Officials and Civil Servants Interact? — 92
- Why Do We Want Participation? — 95
- What Are the Interactions Between Citizens and Civil Servants? — 97
- Practical Applications — 102
- In-Class Instructional Suggestions — 103
- References — 103

6 The Services and Size of Government — 107
- Elephantitis *in Government*? — 107
- What Services Does the Government Provide? — 109
- What Are the Types of Government Policies? — 112
- What Theories Explain Government Growth? — 115
- What Are Demand-Side Theories? — 115
- What Are Supply-Side Theories? — 118
- What Are Bureaucracy-Internal Theories? — 119
- Practical Applications — 123
- In-Class Instructional Suggestions — 124
- References — 124

7 Setting the Course of Government — 127
- Who Sets the Course of Government? — 128
- How Does the Intergovernmental System Set the Course of Government? — 129
- What Is Intergovernmental Relations and Multi-Level Governance? — 130
- What Are Metaphors for Intergovernmental Relationships? — 132
- What Is the Judiciary's Role in Intergovernmental Relations? — 133
- What Is Policy Analysis? — 134
- What Are the Limits of Policy Analysis? — 135
- What Other Policy Analysis Tools? — 137

	How Are Decisions Made in Government?	137
	What Are the Purposes of Strategic Planning?	140
	Who Makes Government Rules and Regulations?	141
	Why Do We Want Regulatory Reform?	143
	What Is the Value of Risk Assessment and Scientific Standards?	146
	References	149
8	**Administering Government Programs**	155
	What Is Included in the Strategic Management Cycle?	155
	Why Is Stakeholder Engagement Important?	156
	When Do We Want Participation?	157
	What Are Important Components of Strategic Plans?	158
	How Do We Transform Strategic into Tactical Plans?	160
	What Makes Planning Processes Successful?	161
	What Are Benchmarking and Best Practices?	162
	How Does Implementation Turn Decisions into Actions?	163
	Who Are Street-Level Bureaucrats and What Is Implementation Discretion?	164
	What Are Common Implementation Problems?	165
	What Can Organizations Do to Leverage Advances in Information Technology?	167
	Chapter Summary	169
	Practical Applications	169
	In-Class Instructional Suggestions	170
	References	170
9	**Designing Government Organizations**	173
	What Are Theories of Organizational Structure?	174
	When Are Hybrid Organizational Structures Valuable?	176
	What Do Organization Charts Tell Us?	177
	What Are Organizational Design Principles?	178
	Is There One Best Way to Organize?	182
	What Organizational Designs Foster Collaboration?	184
	What Organizing Structures Encourage Interorganizational Collaboration?	185
	What Is Important for Interorganizational Collaboration?	188
	Practical Applications	190
	In-Class Instructional Suggestions	190
	References	191
10	**Managing the Human Assets of Government**	195
	What Is Involved in Human Resource Management?	196
	How Has Human Resource Management Evolved?	198
	What Are Different Types of Personnel Managers?	201

What Are the Core Functions of Human Resource Management? 202
Why Is Creating a Representative Bureaucracy Necessary? 207
How Do We Encourage Innovation? 209
Can Organizations Document and Manage Employee Knowledge? 212
References 215

11 Managing the Financial Assets of Government 219
What Is the Budgeting Function? 219
What Are the Purposes of Budgets? 224
Why Is Budgeting So Complicated? 227
How Could Government Budget Processes Be Reformed? 227
What Are Different Intergovernmental Funding Relationships? 230
What Are Capital Projects? 231
How Do We Manage the Finances of Government? 233
References 240

12 Controlling the Activities of Government 243
How Do Performance Measures Promote Accountability? 244
What Are Performance Management Systems? 247
What Challenges Are There in Performance Monitoring? 248
What Are Organizational Controls? 251
How Can We Design Adequate Controls? 258
References 261

13 What Is Public Administration? The Nature of the Study 265
Why Is Public Administration a Science, a Craft, and an Art? 267
What Are Public Administration's Wide-Ranging Interests? 268
Why Do We Have Principles for the Study of Public Administration? 269
What Is the Nature of the Study of Public Administration? 271
How Does Public Administration Promote Civic Duty and Trusteeship? 272
Why Is Studying Public Administration Challenging? 274
What Are the Ways We Can Improve Public Administration? 275
References 277

Concept List 279

Index 297

LIST OF TABLES

Table 1.1	Table of contents. Public administration	6
Table 2.1	Four types of goods and services	27
Table 2.2	Public and private ownership and funding	28
Table 4.1	Types of maladministration and corruption	74
Table 4.2	Definitions and examples of corrupt actions	77
Table 5.1	Stereotypes about politics and elected officials	90
Table 5.2	Perceptions about and reality of government and civil servants	91
Table 5.3	Stereotypes about and reality of citizens	92
Table 5.4	Citizen and administrative participation in government	100
Table 6.1	Matrix of Government Policies or Service	115
Table 7.1	Costs and benefits for a community park	136
Table 8.1	Participation in the policy process stages	158
Table 8.2	Things to consider in Internal/External Assessments	160
Table 10.1	Features of three personnel management labels	198
Table 10.2	Phases of civil service development in the United States	199
Table 11.1	Stages of budgeting	226
Table 12.1	Performance measure characteristics	247
Table 12.2	Three classes of evaluation and the life cycle of an organization	252

CHAPTER 1

The Characteristics of Public Administration

Governance, government, and public administration (PA) are global phenomena. While these three concepts are strongly interrelated, there are also significant differences in the scope and function of each within a society. We outline, define, and describe these three concepts in Chaps. 1 and 2. The flow of chapters in this book mirrors the ordering of the three concepts in the book title. How government, governance, and public administration are expressed describes the institutional arrangements that circumscribe the position and role of government in a society that also vary from country to country. Combined, they reflect the movement from abstract ideas about what it means to live as a collective comprised of individuals to specific information about administering public programs that function only by the authorization of one specific government jurisdiction.

Writing an in-depth comparative study of government, governance, and public administration is impossible. What we have done is provide a high-level description of the institutional arrangements with examples from various countries (Chaps. 1 to 5). This is followed by a more detailed description of how governments function (i.e., personnel, planning, policy, finance, and evaluation) (Chaps. 6 to 11). The book title conveys the reality that all sedentary societies have formal institutional arrangements for *governance* through various social institutions (e.g., governing dynasties, aristocracies, religion, merchant and trading associations, and memberships in social groups). From the High Middle Ages on, that is, around the tenth to twelfth centuries, slowly but surely, the institutional arrangements of *government* have become the most important formal institutional arrangement in the governance of society.

Public administration provides the administrative expertise and experience that shores up the structure and functioning of governments today. The study of public administration focuses on two major areas: a) the relationships between society and governance structure, and b) the structure and processes in and ideas about government. These two emphases make the study of public administration challenging because you must differentiate the role of government from the role of people, as a collective, who have formed a society. In this book, you will learn about the administration of government programs and how to manage the delivery of government goods and services, even when they are not directly provided by government organizations (Durant, 2020). In addition to these functions, you will find out how public administrators play a vital role in learning what governance structures are desired by *The People* and how to facilitate the creation and implementation of public policies that reflect those preferences.

When Did These Two Subject Areas Emerge?

The study of the relationships and structures and processes of today's methods of governance goes back to the late nineteenth century. It is important to note that there are two general types of government: *authoritarian* and *democratic*. In authoritarian government systems, the study of public administration is limited to administrative skills and techniques and serves those in power. Authoritarian government systems are not particularly interested in education for citizenship and desirable civic behaviors; diversity, inclusion, equity, and justice; and relations between political officeholders and career civil servants. Democratic governance systems and its public administration, on the other hand, are grounded in the expectation that government serves the need of the people and the combined preferences of individuals become the preferences that should be fulfilled as a collective.

Another difference is that in authoritarian systems, power is concentrated within the leader, or a small elite, who are not constitutionally responsible to the body of the people. In democracies, authority and power are fragmented across the legislature, executive, and judicial branches.

During the late nineteenth century, the combined effect of urbanization, industrialization, and population growth resulted in the demand for more public services. Many times, these services were provided by people appointed based on friendship or kinship, and not on the basis of merit. At the same time, in industrializing countries, civil servants and citizens pressed for a more professional public service. As a result, civil service laws passed between the 1880s and 1940s established merit systems in Western Europe and the United States. People wanted a government that was responsive to public needs and professional in its service delivery; they needed professionally trained civil servants who were not subject to political control.

How Was This Achieved?

Until the 1880s, government was reasonably small, with few services provided to the public. However, as demands for government services increased, so did calls for making government workers more accountable for providing services efficiently—just like for-profit organizations. In addition, there were calls to ensure that government workers, called civil servants, were hired based on merit. Hiring based on merit meant workers were selected based on a pre-established set of knowledge, skills, and abilities, and/or prior relevant experience, making them eligible for hire. Before that, many government workers got jobs through a patronage system, where a political official hired family or friends.

As mentioned above, civil service laws were adopted that assured a professional civil service. These laws and other changes in the number and size of government organizations led to the formulation of principles to guide a new area of study called public administration. It also led to a curriculum of study that increasingly emphasized efficiency as the cornerstone of the study of public administration.

Developing Curriculum: For Democracy and for Efficiency

Both civil servants and academics influenced the curriculum for studying public administration (Stillman II, 1998). Top civil servants, especially at the municipal level, developed training programs for their civil servants. The need for immediate and successful reforms in the delivery of public services was most felt at the municipal level. At the time, national governments were comparatively small and mainly involved in making laws and regulations, not direct service delivery. Municipal governments provided actual services, and it was their job to meet the burden of providing increasingly efficient public services.

How Did They Pursue That Goal?

Reformers traveled to other countries to learn about best practices. They learned about city planning, public transportation, health care, postal services, and municipal economic activities (Saunier, 2003). These reformers tapped into the knowledge and interests of young academics who also traveled abroad and brought back knowledge of rational and efficient administration. Higher-level municipal civil servants were also very active in reforming their cities and developing programs to instruct their employees. These municipal reformers organized themselves into professional associations. This tradition of sharing best-practice knowledge continues through profession-based associations such as a national society for public administrators and organizations for police chiefs, public works, government finance, economic development, etc.

One of the earliest curricula in public administration was developed at Johns Hopkins University in the 1880s and 1890s (Hoffman, 2002). That curriculum included courses in politics, economics, history, law, and ethics, emphasizing government as a global phenomenon while simultaneously recognizing its activities are conducted in a specific cultural context. In addition, classes were offered on the history of municipal government, the quality of municipal administration, economic and social ethical principles to guide civil servants, and city government as the best level for providing a wide range of services.

Woodrow Wilson was an assistant professor at Johns Hopkins. He insisted that municipal power ought to be expanded and its administrative organization made more efficient. This early curriculum was unique because it emphasized a historical and comparative method that encouraged searching for and borrowing usable organizational structures and practices (Raadschelders, 2002; Raadschelders et al., 2015; Wilson, 1892[1889]). It also emphasized *participatory administration* and *organic government*. Participatory administration changed government from an institutional arrangement that imposed rules and policies upon people to one where it actively invited input on policies and rules. An organic view of government suggests that the state is a living organism that consists of citizens and government, working together in perfect cooperation through continuous dialogue.

In that spirit of participation for collective action, civil service reform became a significant item on the public administration reform agenda. As a result, two very different approaches emerged for reforming government. One group embraced the idea of an organic state, where democracy was shaped through continuous interaction between citizens and government officials, which would facilitate the professionalization of municipal administration for a better democracy. Woodrow Wilson's early writings can be placed within this group.

The other group pointed to the concept of an efficient state, where the cause of democracy could be advanced by design and engineering for efficiency. That second approach quickly dominated the reform movement (Karl, 1983). An efficient government was a government that pursued its policies and justified its choices based on hard facts such as those collected through surveys and presented as statistics.

That kind of government prompted the creation of research organizations and consulting firms. Some people emphasized budgetary and social control; others embraced the idea that municipal government should develop a policy to enhance economic fairness and social welfare (Schiesl, 1977; Stivers, 2000). This emphasis assumed that there was a correct way to (re)solve any governmental and organizational problem. An example of this approach in Western Europe was Henri Fayol's work on efficient organization. In the United States, Frederick W. Taylor's *Scientific Management* (1998 [1911]) is a good example.

Public administration scholars have argued that the origins of public administration in the United States were quickly assuming the masculine feature which assumes that the correct answer to any problem must be based on facts, complex data, and measures (Grimmelikhuijsen et al., 2017; Jilke et al., 2016; McSwite, 1997).

Frederick Winslow Taylor, the father of Scientific Management, was a prominent proponent of these ideas. Taylor's conception of efficiency was getting things done by optimizing human effort and materials. Doing so would remove the value judgments of political science and focus on the business-like objectives to be reached by the government through the introduction of a science of administration (Pfiffner, 1946 [1935]).

A desire for a science of administration (often called Scientific Management) emerged as the study of public administration was being formally recognized. In the words of Pfiffner (1946 [1935]):

> ...specialists in public administration have achieved a considerable degree of uniformity in their thinking of those problems of administration which tend to exist irrespective of the subject matter of the service or function being performed. Suppose a considerable degree of uniformity in the approach to solving problems among the specialists is characteristic of science. In that case, public administration has some right to the claim of being one. (p. 9)

This approach to public administration, dominated by striving for efficiency and the application of business[1] management principles, would go unchallenged until the late 1940s. It was expressed as a search for universal principles of organization, such as the unity of command, the span of control, and through an emphasis on management activities. Luther Gulick is the creator of the acronym POSDCORB, describing the functions of the executive, that is, planning, organizing, staffing, directing, coordinating, reporting, and budgeting. He argued for finding techniques and structures that would facilitate efficiency. Gulick's approach included an awareness of the importance of worker morale, health, and social and economic status. Indeed, the famous papers he co-edited with Lyndal Urwick in 1937 included an essay on why it was efficient to pay attention to workers.

Taylor emphasized optimal workflows, while Gulick focused on identifying universal management principles. Both tried thus to contribute to the development of a science or administration. The science aspect of public administration is reflected in the textbooks of the time and, thus, in public administration curricula (Lee, 2011). In the table of contents of Pfiffner's 1935 book, for example (Table 1.1), we can see public administration's preference for a clear-cut, no-nonsense way of running the business of government. This book primarily focuses on organizational activities in parts two to five. The influence of the external environmental context of the organization is limited to discussions of administrative law and public relations in parts six and seven.

Pre-war public administration instruction focused on serving the practice of administration by presenting universal principles of organization and management. As a result, scholars were confident that a science of administration could be developed. However, by the end of World War II, the pre-war optimism about the science of administration had already been challenged.

---

[1] We use the term "business" as a generic term to describe any organization or organized group that uses business management principles for efficiency in organizational operations. We use the term for-profit to describe an organization that operates specifically to make a profit and is required to pay taxes on those profits.

Table 1.1 Table of contents. Public administration

Part One: Introduction
1. The New Public Administration
2. The Study of Public Administration
3. Public Administration's Role in Modern Civilization and Culture

Part Two: Organization and Coordination
4. Organization
5. Principles of Administrative Organization
6. Staff and Line
7. Proper Use of Boards and Commissions
8. The Organization of Business Enterprises: The Government Corporation
9. Relation Between Levels of Administration
10. The Administration of Field Services
11. The Administration Machine in Motion
12. Voluntary Coordinating Devices

Part Three: Planning and Research
13. Planning, Research, and Standards
14. Standards and Measurements

Part Four: Personnel
15. The Personnel Program
16. The Federal Personnel System
17. Recruiting
18. Classification and Compensation
19. Placement and Employee Evaluation
20. Employee Relations
21. In-Service Training

Part Five: Finance
22. Financial Organization
23. Federal Financial Organization
24. Budget Planning and Enactment
25. Budget Execution and Post-Audit
26. Purchasing and Procurement
27. Collection, Custom, and Disbursement of Receipts

Part Six: Administrative Law
28. The Legal Basis of Administration
29. The Structure and Procedure of Regulatory Agencies
30. Judicial Review of Administrative Action
31. The Rule-Making Process
32. The Law Office as a Staff Agency
33. Officers and Remedies

Part Seven: Public Relations
34. Administration and the Public Interest
35. Administrative Public Relations
36. Day-to-Day Contacts Between Employee and Citizen
37. Publicity and Report

SOURCE: John M. Pfiffner (1946 [1935]). New York, NY: The Ronald Press Company

Two fundamental approaches dominate the post-war development of public administration. In 1947, Herbert Simon forcefully argued that public administration had to study observable facts from which it ought to develop theories about decision-making in organizations. In his view, a true science of public administration should steer away from the more impressionistic approach so characteristic before the war. Values, while important, belonged to the realm of the politician and decision-maker. They were not a concern for scientists. Thus, the method of the investigation had to be objective and rational, resulting in valid knowledge at any time and in any context (Simon, 1957 [1947]).

The contrasting figure was Dwight Waldo. His 1948 book could not differ more from Simon's. Waldo lamented that in striving for efficiency and organizational perfection, public administration scholars had forgotten the fundamentally political nature of any public activity, choice, and decision. As a result, one could not distinguish between values and facts, as Simon did, without the risk of embracing a mechanistic view of government.

More importantly, the modern state had become an *administrative state*, one where the bureaucracy of public administration programs and employees wielded enormous importance in the execution of policies and provision of public services (Raadschelders & Lee, 2005). Indeed, Waldo argued, there is no historical parallel for the unprecedented expansion of bureaucracy in the past half-century. He advocated for the study of public administration to center its efforts on analyzing the relationship between democracy and bureaucracy from a historical and comparative perspective (Waldo, 1984 [1948]). This view is reminiscent of the Johns Hopkins curriculum in the 1880s.

To what extent do these two approaches continue to be represented in public administration? The jury is likely to be forever out on this question. Indeed, there may never be a consensus answer. A sizeable group of scholars in public administration advocate for a scientific approach that works with mathematical formulae, quantitative methods, and statistical evidence. Some research in public management and bureaucracy is an example of that approach (Krause & Meier, 2003). At the same time, plenty of public administration scholars side more with Waldo in their emphasis on the degree to which administrative action is value-laden and thus influenced by political theory, public sector ethics, gender perspectives, historical development, and collaborative government (Emerson & Nabatchi, 2015). One thing both approaches have in common is that idea that public administration draws from many knowledge sources including academic disciplines.

The Interdisciplinary Study of Government in Society

Since the 1960s–1970s, the scope of the study has increased to the point that we can now say that the study of public administration is the interdisciplinary study of government in society (Raadschelders, 2011). Recent handbooks still contain chapters on organization, planning, decision-making, implementation, public budgeting and finance, human resource management, etc. In addition to these topics, they include chapters on the political nature of bureaucracy, leadership, the constitutional structure of government, organizational culture and change, ethics and integrity, as well issues of diversity, equity, inclusion, and social justice.

The comparative and historical perspectives are seldom used to clarify to what extent government and its administration are unique to a particular country and how they are comparable to other countries (Raadschelders et al., 2015). However, the study of public administration is comparable across countries since it studies organizations using a wide variety of theoretical and conceptual approaches that are not country specific. Indeed, the body of knowledge for the study of public administration is not determined by methods, theories, or geographical locations, but by the object of knowledge: government.

The Pedagogical Approach of the Public Sector and This Book

This book is written for first- and second-year university students, which is unusual. As a field of study emerging in the late 1800s, the topic of public administration has typically been an upper-level or graduate-level undertaking. Bachelor's degree programs in public administration, policy, and affairs did not start until the 1960s in continental Europe and in the 1990s in the United States.

After graduating from high school/secondary education, one can study public administration as a college major in many countries. However, textbooks are not written specifically for students who have little knowledge about what it means to be a citizen (instead of a subject), the position and role of government in society, civics, and public sector ethics. This is because civics education has dropped out of many secondary school curricula (Raadschelders & Chitiga, 2021). This is a critical oversight our book attempts to fix. With this book, we hope to give you knowledge for becoming a fully engaged citizen, if not a public servant. Unlike graduate students, few undergraduate students have experience with government or have worked in the public sector. Recognizing the lack of an experiential foundation, we provide supplemental material for each chapter with suggested activities to learn more about how governance works, the societal problems for which government intervenes, how government activities impact people, and the organizations and people that provide government goods and services.

After graduating with a bachelor's degree in public administration, any employer would expect you to have some theoretical understanding of public administration combined with applicable skills. This book emphasizes how to translate concepts and theories into practice for the governments that serve us. Through this type of learning, knowledge can be transferred to real-life situations. In Chap. 1, we begin by learning about the dynamic exchange of public administration wisdom between theory and practice and how this impacts us as members of society in ways that are different from how government impacts us in our daily lives.

Practical Applications

1. The concept of the administrative state dates to the 1940s (Dwight Waldo). Look around you: What examples do you see of the administrative state where you live? Can you identify examples where the administrative state has no influence? We'll give you one example: the color of your hair.
2. Is it possible to separate facts from values in public policy discussions and decision-making? Elaborate on how you reached your answer.
3. Why is it important to know about the political-administrative systems of countries other than your own?

In-Class Instructional Suggestions

1. Provide students with knowledge about government development and its study of public administration in your country. Encourage them to look at public statements by elected officials from different political parties to identify differences in desired trajectories of change and the potential underlying reasons for these calls.
2. Demonstrate how the government of your country differs from a nearby country to show how a comparative perspective of public administration is important for the education and training of future public servants.
3. Provide information on the history of trust in government in your country or geographic region. What factors may contribute to declining trust in government in your nation or geographic region? What can be done to restore citizen trust in government?

References

Durant, R. F. (2020). *Building the compensatory state: An intellectual history and theory of American administrative reform*. Routledge.

Emerson, K., & Nabatchi, T. (2015). *Collaborative governance regimes*. Georgetown University Press.

Grimmelikhuijsen, S., Jilke, S., Olsen, A. L., & Tummers, L. (2017). Behavioral public administration: Combining insights from public administration and psychology. *Public Administration Review, 77*(1), 45–56.

Gulick, L., & Urwick, L. (1937). *POSDCORB*. Institute of Professional Administration.

Hoffman, M. C. (2002). Paradigm lost: Public administration at Johns Hopkins University, 1884-1896. *Public Administration Review, 62*(1), 12–23.

Jilke, S., Van de Walle, S., & Kim, S. (2016). Generating usable knowledge through an experimental approach to public administration. *Public Administration Review, 76*(1), 69–72.

Karl, B. D. (1983). *The uneasy state: The United States from 1915 to 1945*. The University of Chicago Press.

Krause, G. A., & Meier, K. J. (2003). *Politics, policy, and organizations: Frontiers in the scientific study of bureaucracy.* The University of Michigan Press.

Lee, Kwang-Hoon (2011). *The knowledge evolution of American public administration: A concept, content and historical analysis of introductory textbooks.* University of Oklahoma, unpublished doctoral dissertation.

McSwite, O. C. (1997). *Legitimacy in public administration: A discourse analysis.* Sage.

Pfiffner, J. M. (1946 [1935]). *Public administration.* .

Raadschelders, J. C. N. (2002). Woodrow Wilson on the history of government: Fad or constitutive framework for his philosophy of governance? *Administration and Society, 34*(5), 579–598.

Raadschelders, J. C. N. (2011). *Public administration: The interdisciplinary study of government.* Oxford University Press.

Raadschelders, J. C. N., & Chitiga, M. (2021). Ethics education in the study of public administration: Anchoring to civility, civics, social justice, and understanding government in democracy. *Journal of Public Affairs Education, 27*(4), 398–415.

Raadschelders, J. C. N., & Kwang-Hoon Lee (2005). Between amateur government and career civil service: The American administrative elite in cross-time and cross-national perspective. *Yearbook of European Administrative History.* Nomos Verlagsgesellschaft, 201-222.

Raadschelders, J. C. N., Vigoda-Gadot, E., & Kisner, M. (2015). *Global dimensions of public administration and governance: A comparative voyage.* Jossey Bass/Wiley.

Saunier, P.-Y. S. (2003). Les voyages municipaux amériqains en Europe 1900-1940. Une piste d'histoire transnationale. *Yearbook of European Administrative History, 15,* 267-288.

Schiesl, M. J. (1977). *The politics of efficiency: Municipal administration and reform in America 1800-1920.* University of California Press.

Simon, H. (1957). *Administrative behavior* (2nd ed.). Macmillan.

Stillman, R. J., II. (1998). *Creating the American state: The moral reformers and the modern administrative world they made.* University of Alabama Press.

Stivers, C. (2000). *Bureau men, settlement women: Constructing public administration in the progressive era.* University of Kansas Press.

Taylor, F. W. (1998 [1911]). *The principles of scientific management.* .

Waldo, D. (1984 [1948]). *The administrative state: A study of the political theory of American public administration.* Holmes and Meier Publishers.

Wilson, W. (1892 [1889]). *The State: Elements of historical and practical politics.* D.C. Heath and Co.

CHAPTER 2

Governance Through Government and Public Administration: Is Governance A Nuisance, a Necessity, or a Blessing?

We may not see it often, but the decisions about the kind of governance society wants are all around us. In Chap. 1, we suggested how government authority is used through institutions, organizations, and people to provide governance. The government organizes society and regulates our lives from birth as an articulation of governance. First, the hospital registered your birth with a government agency. Next, your parents had to get a social security number for you. Later, your parents took you to the playground. As a toddler, you did not know that every playground is subject to various government safety rules. After a few years, you started going to school. Still, you did not know that government regulates schools by prescribing what must be in the curriculum and how many hours you must take to get credit. When learning how to ride a bike, you had to learn the rules of the road, such as stopping at stop signs and obeying traffic lights. These are all examples of government structuring our lives—even though we may not realize it.

Sometimes government is a nuisance, especially when you are waiting to get your driver's license or going through paperwork to get a federal student loan. Sometimes government is a necessity, especially when we want it to deal with anything from potholes to criminals. The government can also be a blessing, especially when responding to natural and human-made disasters. Consider how government coordinates responses to natural disasters such as earthquakes, floods, tsunamis, volcanic eruptions, and major storms like hurricanes, tornados, and polar vortexes. The government must also respond to human-made disasters such as domestic terrorism, school mass shootings, and economic distress caused by a contaminated water supply. Think about the governments' response to the 2008 economic recession, the COVID-19 virus that caused a pandemic, and in recent decades, the massive migrations of people across the globe. People look to the government for assistance when

© The Author(s), under exclusive license to Springer Nature Switzerland AG 2023
A. L. Franklin, J. C.N. Raadschelders, *Introduction to Governance, Government and Public Administration*,
https://doi.org/10.1007/978-3-031-32689-9_2

confronted with challenges that no individuals, groups of individuals, non-profit and for-profit organizations can manage. Indeed, the government is the only actor in society that can make decisions for everyone living in the country. We always have a relationship with the government; even though, at times, it is not pleasant.

One example is being pulled over by the police for driving at an unsafe speed and getting a traffic ticket. As Wills observed: "…all human relationships grate or gall at times—which does not make us call the parent-child relationship, the husband-wife bond, or friendship mere necessary evils. They are necessary goods that do not uniformly please" (1999, p. 305).

As with any relationship, relations between government and its citizens are sometimes strained. Whatever the case, having basic government knowledge will benefit you as a citizen. This is not just for some seemingly exalted reason, such as the civic duty to participate, but because government constantly influences your life. Knowing how, why, and what you might do to change it are valuable tools. The study of public administration (PA) provides the knowledge you need to navigate government successfully.

People reading this book for a class may aspire to a public sector career as a politician or civil servant (someone who helps implement government programs). Over the years, we have met many students who pursue these careers. We have also taught many in-career professionals to advance their public sector careers by studying for an undergraduate or graduate degree. Many others work in the for-profit or non-profit sectors. The government regulates the for-profit sector, so becoming an expert on public administration can be beneficial for navigating the maze of regulations or advocating for policy change. In addition, the for-profit and non-profit sectors often partner with government organizations to coordinate service provision to vulnerable persons such as the elderly, veterans, or the unhoused. You may not know your career aspirations, but if you plan to work or live in a community with anyone on earth, this course will be helpful.

You are, first and foremost, a citizen. This means you should know not only about your rights but also about your civic duties and what it means to be a citizen based on the form of government where you live. The government is a system of legal and political institutions created to distribute authority in society and regulate relationships among members of that society and between societies. As an institution of the people, authority is delegated to the government to make decisions on society's behalf. These decisions are carried out through policies that define how the order will be maintained, when the government (instead of individuals) will be responsible for achieving society's goals, and how and with what resources those goals will be achieved.

We can categorize forms of government into two general forms: ruled by one person or an elite versus ruled by the many. Aristotle distinguished between good and bad forms of government: monarchy v. tyranny, aristocracy v. oligarchy, and polis v. democracy. Differences in these three general forms of government are reflected in choices about the role of the citizens in governing, how state leaders are selected, the number of people who can act with the authority of the state, the legal powers given to them, and limitations placed upon government leaders.

Whether you are a citizen or a government leader, you must know the law. You also will benefit from knowing how to function when the law influences you, you want a permit or license, need information about toxic waste or a rally permit to protest private or public actions. In addition, for-profit and non-profit organizations, because they are (highly) regulated by the government, benefit when their employees are knowledgeable about government laws, rules, and processes.

Knowledge about public administration will help you navigate the system of government where you live. All around the world, no matter the form of government, a common complaint is that government is unclear, impenetrable, and unaccountable. Yet, as we know it, society is lost without active, engaged, and knowledgeable citizens just as citizens would be lost without government. Therefore, government and its citizens need each other to help determine what can best be done to secure a brighter future, what actions are expected from the government, and what actions are expected from individuals.

What Are Common Metaphors for Government?

You can think about government in various ways. It helps to do so in metaphors. For example, we can imagine that it is like a family reunion. Some people love to go to these. Others are reluctant to go because they will see many people they do not know. Either way, you will learn about family relationships, histories, and even secrets at a family reunion.

The study of government can be like going to a family reunion. You learn about many organizations that you have never heard of before. You find out more about organizations with which you are already familiar. You get a sense of history about how the government has developed and learned theories about government and how government should operate. Also, you learn some secrets about how government works and the challenges and choices that those inside government continually face.

What happens when you go to a family reunion? Usually, you already know some people there, such as aunts, uncles, cousins, and grandparents. However, there are many people you do not know. Your close relatives often take you around and introduce you to other relatives. When they make introductions, it is common for them to also talk about familial relationships. For example, this is Bob, your second cousin by marriage. As the family reunion progresses, you meet more people, some of whom you are instantly attracted to and others with whom you have no desire for further interaction. At the end of the reunion, you may find yourself exchanging contact information with some of your relatives to contact them in the future. When you go home, you may share information with your close relatives about stories you heard and relationships you were not aware of.

This might happen as you read this book. There are some topics that you already know about or are familiar with. You will also learn about many new topics. As you learn more about government, some areas will be fascinating, others downright dull. When you finish the book, you may find other courses you want to take to get in-depth information. Throughout your studies, you'll share information with other students about the stories you read and the relationships we described.

At a family reunion, you will often identify shared values, attitudes, and patterns of behavior that we learn as family members to interact with each other. The same happens in government as people work together and develop a shared history. It is not uncommon for them to simultaneously promote shared values, attitudes, and behavior patterns. Although part of it is influenced by where we come from, it can also be affected by those we interact with and our roles as part of an organization. One of the big reasons for having a family reunion is to keep the family tree alive and preserve the collective memory of family history. Thinking about government as a family reunion that nurtures the family tree is a metaphor that emphasizes social relations between people. If anything, government nurtures and protects social ties.

The individuals you meet at a family reunion are like trees, and the extended family is the forest. In a way, the government can also be thought of as a forest of organizations, with trees at the international, supranational, national, regional, and municipal levels. You will learn that government consists of thousands upon thousands of organizations. True, people often speak of government as one big organization. But it is not. It is more like a forest, and this book will help you recognize the various trees in that forest. However, while this book focuses on government, it is not the only actor involved in governing society. In the following chapters, we will consider the role and influence of other organizations in the for-profit, non-profit, and voluntary sectors and individuals on how governance occurs in society.

What Is Government?

This book introduces you to government and the study of public administration. Public administration studies how government carries out what is desired by the people for the governance of society. This is accomplished through the three branches of government.

We assume you are taking an Introduction to Public Administration class as the beginning of an undergraduate degree program to study government. Therefore, we have designed this book to introduce you to many topics relevant to you as a citizen, which will be valuable when you study PA as a major. The contents of this book represent what is called a survey of the study. This means that we emphasize breadth over depth, describing many topics in an introductory fashion rather than describing a few topics in detail. To get the depth of knowledge, you might take courses covering public policy, public values, public management, public finances, political-administrative relationships, and so on.

If you have never taken a class about the government, many of the topics in this book could be challenging to understand because they seem very complicated. Part of the reason is that most people are somewhat familiar with what governments do. However, few are aware of how much government activities influence their daily lives. Most of what we know about government comes from personal experiences, from reading and listening to commentary about government actions in the media, and, perhaps most importantly, from hearing opinions from family and friends. These information sources are unreliable since they are not comprehensive and can be biased to make you agree with their conclusions and opinions. In this book, we focus on defining public administration, providing descriptions of activities in government organizations, and presenting many perspectives on government that are, at times, conflicting. Knowing a range of perspectives and the logic supporting these perspectives allows you to determine your view about the government's proper position and role or functioning in society.

Understanding of government can be overwhelming at times. This can be because of the tendency to use a specialized language (with many acronyms, such as PA for public administration) to talk about government policies, organizations, and activities. Like other organizations, government organizations have subject matter experts with degrees in the professional area in which they work, such as meteorology, for those employed by a national weather service. The specialized language they use is a sort of shorthand reflected in the frequent use of acronyms. Abbreviations are not limited to organizations and positions. Much of your learning about government and public administration involves learning about the major policy areas, people, and lingo.

Government constitutes a massive portion of society's activities since it operates at the municipal (city, county), regional (state, province), national (federal), supranational, and even international levels. Public servants also have titles and acronyms identifying their rank. When people hear the word "government," they quickly and often think of the national level. However, municipal government is far more critical for direct service delivery in many countries. People also tend to think that each level of government has distinct activities demarcated from activities of and at other levels of government. However, each level of government has organizations in the same *substantive policy area*, such as public health, environmental protection, education, public safety (military, law enforcement, prisons), public transport, etc. As you will learn in Chap. 7, there are very few policies and areas of activity where the responsibility solely lies with one level of government. Instead, government activity is highly intertwined, as is indicated by concepts such *as policy field, network analysis,* and *multi-level government.*

In this opening chapter, we focus on the importance of multi-level government and the fact that these levels of government are highly intertwined. In Europe, this is generally referred to as central-local relations, commonly known as intergovernmental relations in the academic literature. The concept of multi-level government refers to the functional relations between different levels of government and even between various levels within a country and supra- and international governance organizations. This is because there are very few policy areas that do not involve two, if not all, levels of government (Tatham et al., 2021).

Deil S. Wright distinguished intergovernmental constitution, intergovernmental relations, and intergovernmental management 1990. The intergovernmental constitution (IGC) involves all formal institutional arrangements foundational to a governmental system. One can say it serves as the soil and the fence around society's garden. It also includes the value-laden foundations not expressed in a constitution or other formal documents created at founding a governance regime, including values, customs, expectations, behaviors, and histories that people in a country share (cf. Lane, 1996). Intergovernmental relations (IGR) refer to the relations between various levels of government and between those and international and supranational organizations. Finally, intergovernmental management (IGM) focuses on the operational level of governing, rules and regulations, and day-to-day activities. The *New Public Management* (NPM) movement that developed in the late 1980s focused almost exclusively on the IGM level, particularly seeking to improve efficiency, effectiveness, and economy of public service delivery. This has been successful in various Anglo-American countries but less so in African, Asian, European, and Latin American countries (Raadschelders & Vigoda-Gadot, 2015).

These three distinctions for multi-level governance can be used as levels of analysis. They are relevant to both federal and unitary systems of government. In a *federal state*, the subnational or regional level shares sovereignty with the national level of government to some degree. In a *unitary state*, the municipal or local level is subordinate to the regional (province, state) level, and the latter, in turn, is subordinate to the national level.

The levels of government are not only highly interwoven, but they also are deeply connected with the for-profit and non-profit sectors. In many Anglo-American countries, these three prominent institutional actors collaborate to provide, produce, and govern collective services (see ACIR, 1987, for the distinction between these three activities). An excellent example is the United States, where, even during colonial times, the public sector relied on for-profit and non-profit actors for various public/collective services. In other words, for-profit and non-profit actors often provide what government cannot do or wishes not to do. Durant has called this the *compensatory state* (2020). In many countries, especially democracies, public sector development and implementation of policies and services are augmented by non-profit and for-profit activity. The extent to which this is done varies from country to country.

Public Administration (Government) or Public Affairs (Governance)?

The course for which this book is prescribed is most likely offered by a public administration or public affairs department, school, or college. Classes to complete these degrees are offered in various organizational settings: as a section in a Department of Political Science, as an independent Department or College of Public Administration/Affairs, as part of a Business or Non-Profit Administration program, and even as part of a Law college. What is common is that most will include the "public" designation to denote courses that are specific to public action and public organizations. In this textbook, we refer to all the different kinds of degrees in this area as *public administration*.

Until the 1960s/1970s, public administration was generally defined as (a) the implementation of government policy and (b) the academic program that studied this implementation and prepared (future) civil servants to do this work. The term "public" affairs was used to describe anything or anyone involved in the governance of society. For simplicity, we shall consider public administration, public policy, public affairs, and governance to be synonymous terms encompassing government and other societal organizations.

Well into the 1960s, politics and policymaking were considered the responsibility of political officeholders. At the same time, the actual planning and implementation of policy fell within the purview of career civil servants. As a result, public administration was viewed mainly in technocratic terms, including a study of leadership, organizational structure, and administrative skills (planning, managing personnel, overseeing budgets, evaluating policies, etc.). Since then, the study has expanded to include instruction on topics like administrative culture and ethics; political-administrative relations; government reform and administrative change; public service motivation; and diversity, equity, and inclusion. There has also been growing attention to public policy as a process and as substantive areas of policy knowledge and (which used to be more identified with political science). It has also increasingly included international and comparative perspectives (which used to be addressed in international relations and comparative politics).

To better understand how public administration and public affairs are related, we must first differentiate between these terms: governance and government. The term governance has been used for government-controlled activities and regulations. It is more commonly used to denote the various organizations involved in governing society, such as government, labor unions, interest groups, professional associations, for-profit, non-profit, religious organizations, etc. More particularly, it concerns the governments' links to the broader political, economic, social, cultural, demographic, and geographic environment (Kettl, 2002). Governance, though, is a somewhat fluid concept, prompting some to say that defining it is like trying to "nail a pudding on the wall" (Bovaird & Löffler, 2004, 2016).

Nevertheless, words like governance and public affairs point to the fact that government is nested in society. *What differentiates the government from other societal institutions and organizations is that it is the only actor with authority to make decisions binding for all residents in the jurisdiction.* This statement emphasizes how government organizes society to protect the interests of everyone. Governance provides a set of rules for governing the behavior of individuals, groups, and organizations to benefit society.

Government is the function in society that serves to protect and advance the sovereignty of the citizens. Government is both a legal structure as well as a social phenomenon. Government is a legal structure separate from other social organizations such as labor unions, industries, and religious, for-profit, and non-profit organizations. Government has certain obligations and authorities not assigned nor granted to any other organization. From a social phenomenon view, government is a social organization that seeks to protect and advance the interests of people in society, especially those in need. But here, the difference between government and other social organizations is unclear. After all, religious-affiliated groups and non-profit organizations also help people in need. Still, they are not part of government and do not have the same authority and obligations to the people they serve.

To make things more complicated, both perspectives of government as a legal and as a sociological phenomenon capture something essential about government. They are like two sides of the same coin. Although the legal definition emphasizes the distinct position and role of government in society, the sociological definition shows that government performs functions comparable to other organizations. A good definition of government emphasizes the distinctiveness and comparability of government. Drawing from the work of others such as Easton (1953, 1965), Blondel (1990), and Crick (1992), we use this definition. *Government is comprised of those organized elements in the public sector that jointly produce an authoritative allocation of values to rule a divided society without undue violence.*

Let's more closely examine this definition, to gain a better appreciation for the meanings of and relations between the use of these words—authoritative allocation of values, divided society, and undue violence. First, only government holds the authority to make binding decisions on behalf of society at large. No other organization can decide on behalf of all people living in the jurisdiction in most societies. Second, only public officials, including politicians or civil servants, decide how financial and human resources will be obtained and used. Spending one penny more than the budgeted amount or exceeding hiring caps can lead to termination. Finally, government officials determine which policies and activities have top priority, lower priority, or no priority through laws and budgets. Every time an organization submits a budget, the people preparing the budget have valued some policies and activities over others. Every time a city council talks about spending money to improve a water plant or a highway overpass, they must weigh what is more important: an improved water plant or a bridge. These are ways we allocate values in government. The *authoritative allocation of values* involves elected officials and civil servants. To say that elected officials make all major policy decisions and that civil servants simply carry out these decisions is a gross misrepresentation and simplification of reality. In practice, elected officials work closely with civil servants since they have the detailed and expert information necessary to inform decisions about what government can do, how it can be done, and at what cost. In other words, both are involved in the authoritative allocation of values.

Ruling divided societies, the second element in our definition, is vital in democracies and protected by the right to freedom of speech. Nowhere are government operations as challenging as in democracies because every citizen is entitled to voice their opinions and express their needs. In Western societies, interest groups consolidate and amplify individual citizens' voices to be better heard. After all, there is power in numbers. For every policy issue, there are many interest groups with different preferences that government officials must continuously weigh. For each of these questions, you can easily think about groups that would have a preferred answer: Should we drill for oil in the Arctic Wildlife Refuge? Should we legalize marijuana? Should the government support stem cell research? Should the government support physician-assisted suicide in the case of terminally ill patients? And what should we do about things like protecting the rights of women and other historically marginalized groups, requiring universal health care, or committing to climate and human sustainable development goals?

These are fundamental issues that can divide society deeply. The first part of our definition of government suggests a center of power in society, namely the legitimate government authority that most people will accept. The second part of our definition emphasizes the government's mediating role between different societal interests. In other words, the first part of our definition is more legal, and the second part is more sociological.

Finally, good governments rule without excessive or undue violence. This means that government is not just the only actor who can legally punish anyone in society for collectively defined unacceptable behavior: more than any other actor in society, government must demonstrate the wisdom or necessity of its policies as well as the usefulness and reasonableness of what it proposes. It cannot force people to accept whatever it wants.

How Are Governance and Government Related?

Our definition of government is highly abstract because we want to capture its political, policymaking, and administration activities as well as include the legal and sociological elements. We find this necessary because, initially, an authoritative allocation of values was presented as a definition of politics, clearly suggesting that politics was separate from administration (Easton, 1965). In a legal sense, that is correct. Elected officials are elected by the people (or appointed by elected officials) and are directly accountable to the people. Since civil servants are not elected, some would argue that they should not influence policy and politics. However, putting on a sociological lens, we can recognize that separating them from the political process is impossible since elected officials cannot be influential without the expertise of civil servants (Page & Jenkins, 2005; Page, 2012).

Is this partnership between elected officials and civil servants important? You bet. To study government, you must include both politics and administration. They are distinct concepts. The idea of distinguishing politics from the administration was first proposed in early nineteenth-century France. It was adopted in the United States in the late nineteenth century (Martin, 1987). Politics was concerned with the functions of the legislative and executive branches. Administration was involved with the execution of the political will. Using a dichotomy of (or strict separation between) politics and administration, the original study of public administration concerned the activities and processes necessary to execute political will.

Nowadays, public administration contributes to political decision-making by setting and structuring government action, organizing government programs, and administering government activities. Moreover, when government is tasked with directly providing goods and services, public administrators must manage government's human, physical, and financial assets, and control operations for accountability. These topics are presented in Chaps. 6 through 12. However, when adopting the idea that, in practice, politics and administration are highly intertwined, we need to pay attention to the government's role and position in society. We first present these ideas in chapters on sovereignty (Chap. 3), culture and climate (Chap. 4), and political-administrative-citizen relationships (Chap. 5).

The concepts of government and governance are similar because they share the same root: "to govern." However, three issues define the difference between government and governance: the role of government, the position of the government, and the nature of government (Rhodes, 1997). We expand on the differences in the following paragraphs.

First, the role of government concerns ideas about the appropriate size of government and the definition of good government. Some embrace the idea that small government, or a minimal state, is good government and then assume that other societal actors will deliver public services. You could think of charity-based, non-profit organizations offering services to needy people without government help, such as religious organizations that are present in nearly every country. Good governance focuses on the balance of political and administrative efficiency, effectiveness, and economy on the one hand and fairness, due process, and equity on the other. This is relevant to all governmental or non-profit organizations.

Second, we need to consider the position of government in relation to profit and non-profit organizations, and as a mediator in social interventions. Whether we see government as a partner with other organizations in program service delivery or as a mediator between organizations and individuals, the result is the same: governance needs government, and government needs governance.

Imagine a society with no organization but government. In many countries, people organize themselves into organizations more like social affiliations, such as religious organizations, sports clubs, homeowners' associations, professional or parent-teacher associations, labor unions, and so on. While these organizations differ from the government, they are also indispensable in the "entire" universe in the protection of society and delivery of public programs and services.

At this point, we need to pause and draw your attention to the fact that societies and governments are continuously changing. Hence, our perspectives on the position and role of government change. Since the late nineteenth century, the dominant perspective on government was Weberian, emphasizing the rule of law, the importance of hierarchy, and the necessity of clear divisions of labor. Max Weber was a German jurist and social scientist whose work on bureaucracy has influenced the study to a great extent. In the later 1970s, this Weberian approach came to be called *Traditional Public Administration*.

This was followed by a period, labeled *New Public Management* (NPM), where business management principles were perceived as applicable to the public sector. Some consider NPM to be a transitory phase between traditional public administration and government and governance. This change is well captured in two relatively recent developments in the study of public administration: called *New Public Governance* (NPG) in Europe and *New Public Service* (NPS) in the United States. Both emphasize the importance of looking beyond the traditional Weberian perspective on government which is regulatory and hierarchical.

New Public Governance stresses the importance of interdependencies between public, non-profit, and for-profit actors in delivering collective services. Provisions of these services do not operate like a hierarchy because they are self-governing, autonomous networks of actors to a smaller or larger degree (Osborne, 2010; Stoker, 1998). In the introduction to his edited volume, Osborne observes that: "NPM has actually been a transitory stage in the evolution from traditional Public Administration to what is {...} called the *New Public Governance*" (2010, p. 1).

New Public Governance is also presented as a sequel to traditional public administration and as a contrast to NPM, emphasizing that governments exist to serve the people. In the new public service perspective, communities are fundamental to advancing citizenship, society, and its members (Denhardt & Denhardt, 2000). Both NPG and NPS find networks between institutional and organizational actors vital to the health of societies and their governments.

Imagine a society without a final and neutral arbiter to settle disputes between people. Would we accept regulations from a Buddhist, Catholic, Hindu, Methodist, Mormon, Jewish, or Muslim government that are biased against any other religion? Would we accept a government that provides services and makes policies for Muslims only? Of course not. Government serves all citizens irrespective of ethnicity, race, age, sexual orientation, religion, political affiliation, etc. Since no organization has a more extensive clientele than government, the government is an organized network and is linked to other organized networks. More than any other organizational network, government mediates conflicts between members of different organizations and associations because only government has the authority of the people to do so.

Third, there is the nature of government to consider. Is the government just like a for-profit organization? *Or* should it operate using business-like practices? The distinction is subtle. When you assume that government is just like a business, you manage with a profit motive and seek customer satisfaction. If that is possible, Microsoft and the tax collection agency are no different. Both are big organizations that deal with money: Microsoft seeks money from its customers and government gets money from the taxpayers. Instead, you could suggest that we run government *somewhat* like a business. In that case, some government operations and activities could benefit from business-like practices (such as public utilities) and still recognize that government differs from for-profit organizations since profits are not the primary motive.

Taking these three categories together, government is a core actor in the governance of society. In a democratic society, government wants other actors to participate in the governance of society. Indeed, if you have lived in a pluralist political system (called a polity), imagine the horror of living in a society dominated solely by government, a religion, or the military. In polities, the government actively invites the governance of other societal actors and people can question and contest the way the government governs. Thus, government is nested in society. This is illustrated by the fact that it is not the only actor involved in direct service delivery to citizens. That is, collective services can be provided by a range of public, for-profit, non-profit, and voluntary sector actors, as we describe next.

Public Administration and Public Programs

Above we noted that government is one type of organization and there are many other types of organizations. Government develops policies that guide the delivery of public services, whether provided only by the government or in partnership with other organizations. Government also provides services directly to citizens, but it is not the only provider of services. For instance, through the police, the government contributes to maintaining order and safety in society. However, there are also for-profit security organizations that do the same. Government provides health care, but there are also for-profit health care providers. Government can contract out the delivery of services for public programs to other organizations while—ideally—maintaining oversight over the cost and quality-of-service delivery. Two examples of this arrangement are when a for-profit organization runs prisons based on a contract with the government, or when a non-profit organization contracts with government to provide supportive services to abused children. In most Western countries, the government is the only actor allowed to use force to make citizens comply with the law. The word "force" includes quite a range of actions: writing a speeding ticket, arresting people, incarcerating people, and in some nations executing people. However, government and its partners in other sectors can, and do, provide a wide range of programs and services provided through government funding.

We use the term public administration as the organizing concept for this book. This is because it identifies the government as the object of study in this book. For all organizations providing public services, the work is done only through the authority granted to government.

How Does Government Unite the People?

We have seen that government fulfills many roles and functions. Still, it could not do this without people who feel connected to and as a part of the government. What connects people, of course, is the fact that biologically they are all human beings (*Homo sapiens sapiens*). But we are not alike. Everyone has their own unique life experiences. Their self-identity reflects a combination of their gender, race, class, sexual orientation, physical ability, etc., reflecting an intersectionality of multiple identities. However, there is one social characteristic that most people in a society share: they are citizens. So, all people share that they are human and citizens. Is that what holds us together?

Well, yes and no. Yes, in the sense that legally all citizens are equal under the law (unless they have forfeited their civil rights because of criminal activity). No, in the sense that government relies upon people to connect. Government can declare us to be a community in a legal sense, but that does not mean that we are willing to care for one another. In the large-scale imagined communities of today, the people at large can mainly be heard through their elected representatives. It is thus that political parties can unite people of very different backgrounds. Authoritarian political systems generally have one party, where people can become members and climb the ranks based on personal relations and even *nepotism*. Then, there are two-party and multi-party systems. Arend Lijphart (1968) distinguished between *majoritarian democracy* (also referred to as the *Westminster model*) and *consensus democracy*. The former is often a two-party system where one party gains the majority in elections and forms the government/cabinet. The latter is a multi-party system where no party can get an absolute majority in the legislature. Various parties must form a coalition with majority support in parliament. Both types of democracy can be seen as ideal types since reality is far more dynamic, as Patapan et al. showed in their study of developments in so-called Westminster systems after independence (2005, p. 245). The multi-party systems of continental Western Europe are also different, varying along various dimensions (federal–unitary; centralized–decentralized; presidential–monarchical), and change is the normal situation (compare Page & Goldsmith, 1987 to Goldsmith & Page, 2010).

How Do People Connect Outside Government?

This section describes how government and governance thrive when people connect without being told to do so. In the pursuit of a good society, a division of labor exists between the three main sectors of organizations in society: the public sector, the for-profit sector, and the non-profit (and voluntary) sector. The public sector addresses issues vital to all in our role as citizens. The for-profit sector responds to the demands and desires of people in their role as consumers. Finally, the non-profit sector helps individuals with specific needs in their role as clients. Each of these three sectors is important. In the end, however, it is the government, known as the public sector, that provides the legal and organizational framework for society. That framework consists of politics, policy, and administration. However, government (and governance) would be impossible without other mechanisms such as social capital and the varying organizational sectors that foster voluntary relationships between people.

Social Capital: The WD-40 and Superglue of Society

To govern is easiest in societies where people bond with one another. When this connectedness exists, we are willing to accept that few among us will govern the many. Elected officials and those who support them (political appointees and civil servants) are drawn from us. In a polity, those who govern are representatives of those who live in the government's jurisdiction or are citizens living within or outside its geographic boundaries. They do not belong to a different class of people. They are not "higher" than anyone else in terms of citizenship. Governments are most potent when people agree on the government's proper role and functioning in society. Agreeing on these requires a shared sense of what government is and what it does. Robert Putnam (1994, 2000) calls this social capital.

Social capital does not exist without effort. In a family, we feel a connection based on having grown up with mom, dad, grandparents, and siblings. In society, people are not connected based on blood relations but instead based on consciously pursued cooperation. Social capital is created through connections between people that build trust, goodwill, fellowship, and neighborliness. A strong social capital society is one where one individual helps another without expecting something in return from that individual. But, and that is the beauty of social capital, in a healthy society the helping individual knows someone will be there to help when in need. So, how would we define social capital? Social networks or associations support us and provide connections to accomplish our goals (Page, 2012). For example, when you are looking for a job, you contact people you know, and you may ask your friends and family if they know other people who could help you get a job.

Social capital cannot be taken for granted. It is something that can connect as well as divide us. When it connects very different people, we speak of *bridging social capital*: bonds that connect people across political ideology, race, ethnicity, intersectional identities, etc. Examples of bridging social capital are organizations involved in civil rights movements. Having social capital that bridges our differences is vital. It is the WD-40 that greases the wheels of parts not necessarily connected (Putnam, 2000).

Bonding social capital is much more exclusive by nature since it provides identity and community with like-minded people who share similar ideas and interests, such as in religious groups, country clubs, and college fraternities and sororities. This type of social capital functions like a Superglue between people, bonding them firmly together.

A healthy society has both bridging and bonding social capital. It is people's nature to connect with those they consider comparable (bonding). Still, in the broader community of people in modern society—where we do not and cannot know everyone personally—we need bridging just as much. Bonding teaches people the value of personal connection; bridging teaches people that we must learn to live with people different from us. In a stable society, bonding with people who are familiar leads to bridging with others who are different.

When bonding leads to bridging, it creates an atmosphere of trust and cooperation. Government cannot be effective and helpful to people without it. When bridging stops and people are excluded, sectarianism, ethnocentrism, discrimination, and corruption may occur. In that situation, the government is not trusted by the people. It is forced to be the harsh judge rather than the benevolent mediator in conflicts between people. Western societies are built upon the notion that it is possible to protect collective interests through high levels of social capital.

Government and the Determination of the Public and Private Spheres

Another way to think about the connections between people in our daily life and how this influences the functioning of government is to consider this question, "What is government?" It is not as easy to answer as it may seem because government is very pervasive in our everyday life. We can define government as those working in and for it, including elected officials, political appointees, and civil servants. It can also be defined in terms of its regulations and law or in terms of its policies and programs. In these definitions, government is everything that concerns and relates to the *public sphere*. The relationship building activities described above occur in the *private sphere*, meaning they are not forced, or enforced, by government. In these definitions, government is everything that concerns and relates to the public sphere and how it is informed by and influences those who are governed.

Government is the public sphere mainly, though not exclusively, and it is involved with issues that people find essential for society. Its clientele are the people as citizens plus all people who are not citizens and have come from another country as an immigrant or refugee (Raadschelders et al., 2019), visiting students and scholars, and illegal aliens. Some services benefit everyone, including defense, public safety, environmental protection, and diplomacy.

Other services help groups of people whom citizens believe deserve government support, such as children (education), the elderly (social security), the sick (health care), the unemployed, and the disabled (social services). Thus, government caters to the needs of the people as a collective.

The private sphere is mainly, though not exclusively, involved with issues that people take care of by themselves with no government intervention. Consumers of products such as cars, soaps, carpets, houses, airplanes, clothes, food, and entertainment and services acquire these in the private sphere based on their individual preferences. Non-governmental organizations cater to people's needs, and private consumption is based on individual preferences and ability to pay.

The public and for-profit sectors are not only highly intertwined, but they also dabble in each other's activities. For-profit security agencies provide public safety, as do the military, police forces, and fire departments. Education is offered through public, for-profit, and non-profit organizations. Public and for-profit utility (gas, electricity, water) companies exist as do public health organizations at the county level and for-profit health management organizations.

Graham Allison provided an interesting comparison of the characteristics of the public and for-profit sectors. He wrote that public and for-profit organizations are alike, especially in the challenge of integrating various managerial functions. However, the differences, he thought, are more significant. One difference concerned environmental factors such as a lower degree of market exposure (e.g., less focus on prices and profits). A second difference was about the nature of organization-environment transactions that included, for instance, the fact that government has unique sanctions and coercive powers. Finally, the third difference focused on internal structure and processes, such as, e.g., the fragmentation of authority and power across branches or government.

Allison (1987) concludes that the major difference between public and for-profit organizations is, in many democracies, the distribution of power in the document forming the organization. General management functions are concentrated in the Chief Executive Officer (CEO) in a for-profit organization. However, the government does not have a CEO since general management functions are dispersed across the three competing branches of government: legislature, executive, and judiciary.

There is also a sizeable non-profit sector that provides services to those in need, just like the government, and these organizations do not strive to make a profit. Examples of non-profit organizations are the International Red Cross, the World Bank, and all sorts of religion-based services. Finally, various supranational and international and voluntary organizations are deeply involved in the governance of collective interests. The best-known example of an intergovernmental, supranational organization is the European Union; an excellent example of an intergovernmental, international organization is the United Nations; an excellent example of a non-profit, international organization is the International Organization for Migration.

We can further illustrate the distinction between what is in the public and private spheres by considering types of goods and services on the one hand and ownership and funding on the other. First, a range of goods and services is available to citizens and people. These range from purely individual goods to purely public or collective goods. An individual good can only be used or consumed by one person. When you purchase a loaf of bread, no one else can buy that same bread. In other words, your purchase excludes others from consumption.

On the other hand, a public good is available to everyone. No one can be excluded from its use. In Table 2.1, you can see that exclusion and jointness of use result in four types of goods and services.

Each of these types of goods can be provided in various ways. For instance, the government can maintain and operate a toll road or find a contractor to do so on its behalf. Generally, pure public goods are not contracted out (Weimer & Vining, 2005). From this table, you can see that government provides pure public goods. Moreover, it does so whether we like it or not. In Table 2.1 coerciveness is a feature of public organizations. This means that government can do things even when you are against them. For instance, pacifists may not like weapons and military action. However, citizens must pay taxes and accept that some of these funds are spent on national defense.

Another way to distinguish between the public and private spheres is by focusing on ownership and funding. Some organizations are owned and funded by the government. Other organizations are owned and financed by private actors. And as you can expect, there are privately owned organizations that are publicly funded and publicly owned organizations that are privately funded (Table 2.2).

A final way of distinguishing between public and private spheres is by focusing on the mix of economic and political authority exercised by an organization (Bozeman, 2004 [1987]). Tables 2.1 and 2.2 infer that an absolute distinction between public and for-profit organizations or goods is straightforward. Sure, there are pure public and pure private goods and organizations. Still, there are many more types of organizations and services in-between. Also, the functions of these organizations tend to overlap to varying degrees. This is, for instance,

Table 2.1 Four types of goods and services

Degree of jointness of use		Alternating or rival uses	Common or non-rival uses
Degree of exclusion	High	Private goods: bread, books, shoes, cars	Toll goods: swimming pools, toll bridges, and roads
	Low	Common goods: water and natural parks	Public goods: peace and security, national defense

Source: Ostrom, V., and Ostrom, E. (1977). Public goods and public choices. In E. S. Savas (Ed.), *Alternatives for Delivering Public Service: Toward Improved Performance* (p. 12). Boulder, CO: Westview Press

Table 2.2 Public and private ownership and funding

	Public ownership	Private ownership
Public funding (taxes, government contracts)	Department of Defense, Social Security Administration, Police departments	Defense contractors and Corporation Oak Ridge National Laboratories
Private funding (sales, donations)	U.S. Postal Service, Federal Home Loan Bank Board	General Motors, IBM YMCA, Walmart

Source: Rainey, H. G. (2003). *Understanding and Managing Public Organizations* (p. 68). San Francisco, CA: Jossey-Bass; Rainey adapted and revised this from Wamsley, G. L., and Zald, M. N. (1973). *The Political Economy of Public Organizations*. Lexington, MA: Heath

the case with the many non-profit and quasi-governmental organizations that function similarly to government.

Why Does Government Exist?

There is substantial literature about how and why the government emerged and why it exists. This section focuses on government origins and why the government continues to exist. Thousands of years ago, few human beings were on our planet. Their lives were very different from ours, and they roamed from one area to another in the continuous pursuit of food and shelter. They were never sure when or where they would find these in their nomadic existence. Also, they depended upon the seasons to gather fruits and roots. They had to move with the migration of animals upon which they fed. They were hunter-gatherers who seldom killed more than they would eat. Early humans lived in small groups that you could call bands that gathered in tribes now and then. They generally had a chief who fulfilled other functions, such as priests and war leaders. But then, some 10,000 years ago, something changed the history of humankind forever. People stopped being nomadic and started planting crops, domesticating animals, and building permanent residences. When this happened, the government emerged as people began to live together in ever-increasing numbers in relatively small areas (Diamond, 1997; Raadschelders, 2020).

Once you have domesticated plants and animals, you can produce a surplus. That is, you do not consume everything yourself because you can produce plenty. This surplus can be traded for products produced by people nearby. A surplus allows for trade and creates a situation where some people do not have to work the land and can specialize in other activities, such as being a soldier, priest, administrator, or king. The earliest specialized professions in cities were those of kings and clerks. As surplus and specialization increased and population size and density increased, the tribal bond disappeared to be supplanted by a system of law and administration. This was necessary since, in large communities, people no longer knew everyone.

A system of law and administration provided the discipline and order necessary for survival on an impersonal basis. The evolution of sedentary communities started some 10,000 to 12,000 years ago. That was a period mainly of self-governing arrangements among people. City-states emerged about 5000 to 6000 years ago in the area known as the Fertile Crescent. It is then that formal institutional arrangements for government are developed. The government evolved from being a self-governing mechanism to being situated above the people and under the control of a small and influential political and economic elite. This area stretched from the Nile Delta to Euphrates and Tigris rivers in present-day Iraq.

Through trade and conquest, these city-states gradually formed into empires. From then on, law and government became necessary elements in structuring society. They bind people together *in imagined communities* (Anderson, 1995). People are no longer tied by the tribal bonds of old but by government and other social identities such as those provided through customs, religion, language, and history.

In this society, leadership functions are broken apart into multiple positions. Initially, most, if not all, leadership functions were performed by one person; in city-states and empires, specialized leaders such as politicians, generals, priests, and judges emerged. They did so because a single individual could not oversee everything needed to protect society from internal threats, such as crime, and external threats, like military conquest. Defense, police, judiciary, and taxation are the oldest functions for which the government assumed responsibility (Finer, 1997; Raadschelders, 2017a). Also, early governments took up the task of building public infrastructures such as water irrigation systems, roads, and public buildings.

Today government still exists for the protection of society. However, other rationales for the government's existence have been added. A political rationale for the government's continued existence is identifying and serving the public interest at large through the election of top officials. In most nations, government exists to serve and protect all people, especially those who cannot help or defend themselves, such as children, senior citizens, the unemployed, and the disabled. This is a social rationale for the existence of government.

Government, as most world citizens know it today, represents a third stage in the development of collective actions in human society: the first stage is that of self-governing arrangements in sedentary societies, the second stage is that of government above the people, and the third stage—and only in democracies since the late eighteenth century—is that of government for, by, and of the people (Raadschelders, 2020).

Early governments did provide some services to these groups of people. You can think of granaries in ancient Egypt that provided basic staples in the case of a bad harvest or prolonged drought. It was not until the twentieth century that the social rationale for the existence of government led to the systematic redistribution of economic resources through direct taxation. Of course, some of the taxes we pay still go to traditional government functions. Nevertheless, in most societies, government now is tasked with redistributing large sums of money to those in temporary or constant need.

If there is any way today's government differs dramatically from previous governments, it is the welfare state. Over time, government has increasingly been asked to protect people and serves as a guardian against anything in society or the economy that potentially harms us. More specifically, the economic rationale for our need for government is to protect us against negative *externalities* and provide for the protection of pure public goods that the market cannot or will not provide.

Externalities are unwanted byproducts of, for instance, industrial production. Many industries make products in ways that are or can be harmful to humans, animals, and the environment. While the product is good or valuable, its production can pollute our air, water, land, and atmosphere. During the twentieth century, for the first time, governments took responsibility for protecting us against the externalities of industrial production. In doing so, government became responsible for correcting market imperfections.

Chapter Summary

In this chapter, we considered common metaphors for government and how they reflect our feelings (often like a love/hate relationship) toward the role of government in society and our personal lives. The metaphors reflect our lived experience of government as an institution with many programs—some of which we may not use or even want—but that have been determined to be necessary to promote society's shared values. When we think about government like this, we are considering the meaning of shared governance and our philosophy of how the government is a means to unite people in society as they identify a shared purpose and a way to guide collective action for public, more than private, goods and to promote the values of the civil society we desire in our imagined community. In Chap. 3, we tackle the definition and question of the sovereignty of government over the governed and all within its borders. Historical and contemporary theories of sovereignty are presented to set the stage for understanding how and why government operates the way it does today.

PRACTICAL APPLICATIONS

1. How are governance and government related in your country?
2. Learn more about why the different sectors often work together by examining partnerships with the International Federation of Red Cross and Red Crescent Societies to enhance resilience.
3. How important are the non-profit and for-profit sectors in your country for delivering public services? Some countries, such as the United Kingdom and the United States, have privatized or contracted-out many

services. Other countries have done so much less. What is the situation in your country in this regard?
4. Look around where you live, in newspapers, social media, and so on, and find examples of common goods (also known as common pool resources). This is also an area where countries vary.

In-Class Instructional Suggestions

1. Invite students to research how many bills are annually issued by the legislative body of national or subnational governments in your country or how many regulations are issued annually by government departments and agencies to implement delegated authority from the legislature. See also Raadschelders (2017b) on the balance of primary and secondary legislation in the United Kingdom and the United States.
2. How many departments and agencies does the national or a subnational government have in your country? You can have students analyze an organizational chart to see what is communicated about the role of government in society, and the types of goods and services provided for the collective.
3. Provide examples of how political-administrative systems can be and are structured. Then, ask students to compare and to contrast these systems to better understand the political-administrative system of their own country.
4. Provide links to websites of non-profit organizations in your country that are vital to the provision of government in society. Then, let students look for other examples.

References

Allison, G. T. (1987). Public and private management: Are they fundamentally alike in all unimportant aspects? In J. M. Shafritz & A. C. Hyde (Eds.), *Classics of public administration*. The Dorsey Press.
American Commission on Intergovernmental Relations, ACIR. (1987). *The Organization of local public economies*. Advisory Commission on Intergovernmental Relations, A-109.
Anderson, B. (1995). *Imagined communities: Reflections on the origin and spread of nationalism* (2nd ed.). Verso.
Blondel, J. (1990). *Comparative government: An introduction*. Routledge.
Bovaird, T., & Löffler, E. (2004). Understanding public management and governance. In T. Bouvaird & E. Löffler (Eds.), *Public management and governance* (1st ed., pp. 27–38). Routledge.
Bovaird, T., & Löffler, E. (2016). *Public management and governance* (3rd ed., pp. 27–38). Routledge.
Bozeman, B. (2004 [1987]). *All organizations are public: Comparing public and private organizations*. Beard Books.

Crick, B. (1992 [1962]). *In Defense of politics*. The University of Chicago Press.
Denhardt, R., & Denhardt, J. (2000). The new public service: Serving rather than steering. *Public Administration Review, 60*(6), 549–559.
Diamond, J. (1997). *Guns, germs, and steel: The fates of human societies*. W.W. Norton and Company.
Durant, R. F. (2020). *Building the compensatory state: An intellectual history and theory of American administrative reform*. Routledge.
Easton, D. (1953). *The political system: An inquiry into the state of political science*. Knopf.
Easton, E. A. (1965). *Framework for political analysis*. Prentice-Hall.
Finer, S. E. (1997). *The history of government from the earliest times*. Oxford University Press.
Goldsmith, M. J., & Page, E. C. (2010). *Changing government relations in Europe: From localism to intergovernmentalism*. Routledge.
Kettl, D. F. (2002). *The transformation of governance: Public administration for twenty-first century America*. The Johns Hopkins University Press.
Lane, J.-E. (1996). *Constitutions and political theory*. Manchester University Press.
Lijphart, A. (1968). *The politics of accommodation: pluralism and democracy in the Netherlands*. University of California Press.
Martin, D. W. (1987). Déjà vu: French antecedents of American public administration. *Public Administration Review, 47*(3), 297–303.
Osborne, S. P. (Ed.). (2010). *The new public governance? Emerging perspectives on the theory and practice of public governance*. Routledge.
Ostrom, V., & Ostrom, E. (1977). Public goods and public choices. In E. S. Savas (Ed.), *Alternatives for public service delivery: Toward improved performance* (p. 12). Westview Press.
Page, E. C. (2012). *Policy without politicians: Bureaucratic influence in comparative perspective*. Oxford University Press.
Page, E. C., & Goldsmith, M. J. (1987). *Central and local government relations: A comparative analysis of west European unitary states*. Sage Publications.
Page, E. C., & Jenkins, B. (2005). *Policy bureaucrats: Government with a cast of thousands*. Oxford University Press.
Patapan, H., Wanna, J., & Weller, P. (Eds.). (2005). *Westminster legacies: Democracy and responsible government in Asia and the Pacific*. University of New South Wales Press.
Putnam, R. D. (1994). Social capital and public affairs. *Bulletin of the American Academy of Arts and Sciences*, 5–19. (Originally published in the *American Prospect*, Spring 1993, New Prospect, Inc.)
Putnam, R. D. (2000). *Bowling alone: The collapse and renewal of American community*. Simon and Schuster.
Raadschelders, J. C. N. (2017a). *Handbook of administrative history*. Routledge.
Raadschelders, J. C. N. (2017b). The United States of America as *Rechtsstaat*: State and administrative law as key to understanding the administrative state. *Public Administration Review, 77*(3), 458–465.
Raadschelders, J. C. N. (2019). The iron cage in the information age: Bureaucracy as tangible manifestation of a deep societal phenomenon. In E. Hanke, L. Scaff, S. Whimster (eds.), The Oxford Handbook of Max Weber. Oxford University Press, 557–574.
Raadschelders, J. C. N. (2020). *The three ages of government: From the personal to the group, to the world*. University of Michigan Press.

Raadschelders, J. C. N., Vigoda-Gadot, E. (with Mirit Kisner) (eds.). (2015). *global dimensions of public administration and governance: A comparative voyage*. Jossey Bass/John Wiley and Sons.

Raadschelders, J. C. N., Larrison, J., & Thapar, A. V. (2019). Refugee migration as a 'wicked problem': American controlling, palliative, and governance policies in the global context." World Affairs, Autumn, 228–255.

Rainey, H. G. (2003). *Understanding and managing public organizations*. Jossey-Bass.

Rhodes, R. A. W. (1997). *Understanding governance: Policy networks, governance, and accountability*. Open University Press.

Stoker, G. (1998). Governance as theory: Five propositions. *Institutional Social Science Journal, 50*(155), 17–28.

Tatham, M., Hooghe, L., & Marks, G. (2021). The territorial architecture of government. *Governance, 34*(3), 607–620.

Wamsley, G. L., & Zald, M. N. (1973). *The political economy of public organizations*. Heath.

Weimer, D. L., & Vining, A. R. (2005). *Policy analysis: Concepts and practice* (4th ed.). Prentice-Hall.

Wills, G. (1999). *A necessary evil: A history of American distrust of government*. Simon and Schuster.

Wright, D. S. (1990). Federalism, intergovernmental relations, and intergovernmental management: Historical reflections and conceptual comparisons. *Public Administration Review, 50*(2), 168–178.

CHAPTER 3

The Sovereignty of Government

Chapter 2 defined government and governance and gave examples of how they differ. More importantly, we learned about the need to understand the separation of the individual and the private sphere from the collective and the public sphere. Knowing this, we can now discuss what government, as a sovereign tasked with governance of civil society, could, should, and should not do and how this is determined. This chapter defines sovereignty and explores the imagery that represents it. You will learn that various types of sovereignty exist and how people perceive sovereignty. We present theories of sovereignty and explain their importance to the contemporary functioning of government.

What Is Sovereignty?

Sovereignty is the locus of power that officials use to govern a nation. In the current *Merriam-Webster*'s online dictionary (n.d.), *sovereignty* is defined as ""supreme power, especially over a body politic"" (n.p.). This definition has several features deserving attention. First, it is a definition that fits our times perfectly. It suggests that sovereignty defines the authority of government in a country. The ultimate power and authority of government in most countries worldwide is highly centralized. It is invested in a combination of identifiable institutions, organizations, and elected officials at the national level of government: a Parliament or Congress, a national high court, a head of state (president, monarch), or a head of government (prime minister).

When describing a country in relation to other countries around the world, we often refer to the territorial place as a state or nation. The structure of the state can feature an equal standing between national and subnational governments called a federation. Or, the state can have a unitary government where power is centralized at the national level, and subnational units are created for convenience in the implementation of national policies (OECD, 2016).

The highest level is referred to as the national government and the political and geographical subdivisions of the state as subnational governments. Common names for subnational governments include state, regional, provincial, municipal, local, prefectures, province, township, village, settlement, and autonomous or special region. Some countries have only one subnational level of government, others can have more levels as well as subnational entities such as deconcentrated districts or agencies, special-purpose entities, sub-municipal locations, and special areas (OECD, 2016, 59).

Subnational governments and their government officials have power and authority, but these are not sovereign powers. Furthermore, powers and authority at the subnational levels are either granted by the national government to a regional level (e.g., a state in Germany, a province in France, and the Netherlands), or from the country level to local government levels. Sovereignty may thus present at the subnational level of government, but only extends policymaking authority over a specific subnational geographic level (Maaka & Fleras, 2000).

Second, the definition also suggests that sovereignty defines the boundaries, or borders, of a political state. Sovereignty includes the institutions and organizations of government necessary to carry out the decisions those in power make within those borders. Sovereign powers do not extend beyond the sovereign's borders, at least not in international law. Third, it recognizes the existence of other political and territorial states that are equally sovereign.

These definitions contain two fundamental elements in the concept of sovereignty. One is the authority of a territorial state"s government over its society. This concerns its *domestic* dimension. The second is the relation of the territorial state to other states, which concerns the *international* dimension. For instance, when negotiating the Asia-Pacific Economic Cooperation, the international dimension concerned the preservation of the sovereignty of each of the 21 nations. The domestic dimension concerned the possibility that signing the agreement may result in job losses or gains in each of the three states because of the opening of international borders.

The domestic aspect of sovereignty is essential for the study of public administration. This is because it is concerned with the structure and functioning of government, plus the organizations and the services provided to people within or citizens of sovereign borders living abroad. On the other hand, comparative government and international relations scholars usually study the international aspect of states and their governments. However, these topics seem to be gaining momentum in the study of public administration as well (Stone & Moloney, 2019).

The primary element of the international state system is a sovereign and *territorial state*. Some are extremely large, including Brazil, Canada, China, and Russia. Many larger sovereign states are organized as a *federal-state* system (Watts, 1999), where the national government shares sovereignty with subnational government units. Medium and smaller states are mostly *unitary state* systems, where subnational governments are creations of and subordinate to the national level. For instance, medium-sized sovereign states include Italy, Mexico, and Sweden. Several sovereign states are small, such as Belgium and the Netherlands. There is also a category of small states that include various island states in the Atlantic, the Caribbean, the Mediterranean, the Pacific, and Indian Oceans, and various small (city) states such as the Grand Duchy of Luxembourg, Andorra, Liechtenstein, Malta, Monaco, San Marino, and Vatican City (Baker, 1992). Their existence is reminiscent of when sovereignty was dispersed between different *secular and spiritual rulers.*

Over time, around the world, we have grown accustomed to the idea of a nation-based system where governments have the authority to make binding decisions for their citizens on domestic and international policies. However, in the international arena, all states are considered sovereign. Therefore, all are entitled to equal treatment regardless of size, military might, or geographical location (Shaw, 1987).

Usually, states that border the sea hold sovereignty over a 10- to 15-mile-wide strip of territorial waters on the coastline. Oceans outside these territorial waters are international waters, under no state's control. Sometimes the distance from the coast of territorial waters is a source of conflict. For example, in 1972, Iceland unilaterally extended its territorial waters to 50 nautical miles to protect its fisheries, which are the primary source of income for Icelandic citizens. This expansion was contested by Great Britain, whose fishers frequently went north to the abundant fishing grounds around Iceland. Finally, in 1976, the countries agreed to extend Iceland"s territorial waters to 200 nautical miles.

The concentration of sovereign power and authority in about 200 sovereign and territorial states today is a process that started only 240 years ago. Less than 200 years ago, there were no more than 23 states worldwide. By 1900, this number had increased to about 40 (Wallace & Singer, 1970). At the time of this writing, the world is divided into 195 United Nations recognized sovereign states; however, the United Nations reports an additional 50+ country codes on the ISO Standard List. For example, the 195 countries do not include autonomous territories such as Greenland, the Isle of Man, or Puerto Rico. The creation of states continues today.

The Imagery of Sovereignty

One way that we can understand sovereignty is through imagery. Much symbolism is attached to things representing the authority of government and its power over its citizens, and much pageantry is associated with transferring power from one leader (or group) to the next.

Whenever authority and power are transferred from one person to the next, it happens in a highly ceremonial way with great symbolic value and according to formal rituals. For example, the inauguration of a new president of the United States represents much more than merely passing the gavel. Indeed, the head of state for any form of government can have multiple and substantial executive powers. These could include being head of state (president), head of government (like a prime minister), and commander in chief of the military with the power to declare war.

The transfer of presidential power in the United States is symbolized by swearing an oath to uphold the American Constitution. Presidents usually do not wear visible and symbolic signs of the high office and authority they are invested with during their inauguration. Instead, they are generally sworn into office in the presence of members of the three branches of government and in, or close to, a significant public building. Perhaps the most illustrative symbol of the power of the American president is the Seal of Office, often part of the floor covering in the Oval Office and always adorning the lectern wherever the president speaks. Given the enormous power of the American president, one might expect a grand ceremony with much pomp and circumstance. Instead, it is a rather dull affair designed to draw attention to the power of the people in the republic, not the power of the head of state.

Unlike presidents, monarchs are usually handed visible symbols of their power, called regalia, during their coronation. The royal or imperial crown is the cap of sovereignty. The monarch holds a mace in their left hand, signifying the ultimate power over life and death. Indeed, most have the authority to pardon criminals. While the American president holds no mace, he also can pardon criminals. The monarch"s right hand holds a globe topped by a cross to signify that their secular power is subject to spiritual authority. Often a full ermine fur mantle is hung around their body, signifying authority and dignity on the one hand and purity and honor on the other. In England, some individuals express their aristocratic rank (e.g., dukes) or judicial authority with an ermine shoulder cape but never a full robe. Indeed, while wealthy people could afford to purchase this garment, no one ever wears one in public unless their official status allows it. The degree of pomp and circumstance is unrelated to the degree of power held by the newly inaugurated.

Inaugurations and coronations are crucial moments in the political life of a country. They symbolize the transfer of authority to an individual representing the sovereignty. They remind citizens that one among them is invested with ultimate political authority. In a way, an inauguration or coronation makes this political authority transparent. However, this investment with ultimate political authority is symbolic. After all, the government of contemporary democracies is characterized by a carefully balanced fragmentation of power, called checks and balances. In that fragmentation of political power, sovereignty is not as transparent. The increasing involvement of other elected officials further challenges government transparency. This chapter discusses domestic and international dimensions of sovereignty to understand the legal-institutional context in which governments operate.

Different Labels for Sovereign Entities

Before we examine how sovereignty has changed over time, defining the concepts of the state and a nation is crucial. The primary difference is that the first describes a geographic territory. The second refers to the people in that area. This can be confusing since, in several countries, the regional government units are also called states (e.g., Brazil). When speaking of sovereignty, the term state can also be used for subnational units of government which are administrative divisions (units, entities, regions, or areas) or portions of a country given a certain degree of autonomy and manage themselves through municipal governments.

There are several types of state. An empire is a vast state like the Chinese, Mongol, Ottoman, and Roman Empires. A city-state is a tiny state like Vatican City, and a principality, like Monaco. There are very few empires, city-states or principalities left. The dominant political unit is the territorial state, from tiny to vast territories. In other words, sovereign states are the main building blocks of the international state system. It is within the boundaries of each sovereign state that government has the authority to issue laws and protect against internal and external threats.

The concept of nation, in everyday language, is synonymous with a country. Still, it also refers to people who share a sense of belonging based on language and history. When a state"s population comprises 97% indigenous peoples, it is called a nation-state. An example of a nation-state is Iceland. Nearly 70% of the 370 million people who identify as indigenous are from the Asia and Pacific region of the world. Many Western countries are no longer nation-states because of the immigration of people from other parts of the world.

Semi-Independent Territories

There are 56 small states and more than 100 small territories globally, often called *microstates*. Many have acquired status as independent states or semi-autonomous units, such as the Federated States of Micronesia in the Pacific Ocean. The more significant majority are islands or island federations. Some of these small territories are semi-sovereign since they administer their domestic affairs. However, they rely on a larger neighboring country to provide defense and foreign policy services. This is the case with Monaco"s principality on France"s south coast. In addition to security and diplomatic services, Monaco also relies upon France for postal services. Plus, they use the Euro as their official currency.

While some small territories prosper because of oil (Bahrain, Qatar, Brunei), tourism (Monaco), or from providing an offshore tax haven (the Channel Island of Jersey, the Cayman Islands), most of them have small domestic markets and cannot offer essential government services. Consequently, they have started to engage in regional and even global cooperation. In 1991, the Alliance of Small Island States (AOSIS) was founded with 40 members worldwide.

Small territories are influential because their growing numbers have resulted in a disproportionate representation of African and Asian-Pacific members in the United Nations. While membership in the United Nations has great symbolic value in showing that they are genuinely independent, the financial and resource contribution of small-state members of the United Nations for its operations is minimal. Still, their vote is equal to that of member states with large populations.

Substantial numbers of small territories are not states but are *enclaves* that are part of a country but surrounded by a foreign country. They are an oddity in the political landscape. For the country to which these enclaves belong, they are exclaves. According to one count, there are 240 enclaves and exclaves (Melamid, 1968). Bangladesh alone currently has 102. Another example is Baarle-Nassau in the south of the Netherlands, a Belgian territory and Baarle-Hertog, a Dutch territory in the north of Belgium. Enclaves and exclaves are generally the product of a settlement reached during border negotiations for a peace treaty between two bordering countries. They are typically not a focus of interest for international organizations. With this understanding of state and nation, examining the historical background of the sovereignty concept is essential. Then, we provide definitions of sovereignty.

What Is the History of State Making?

During the European Middle Ages, the power and authority of *monarchs* were contested by the secular power and authority of aristocrats and by the spiritual power and authority of religious leaders. Can you imagine a monarch, prime minister, or president today discussing policy with the Pope or a cardinal of the Catholic Church before proposing some policy to the legislative branch or a cardinal burning state secrets on the order of the head of state (cf. a painting by John Pettie 1874)?

Monarchs centralized power and created sovereign states in the twelfth and thirteenth centuries. This happened in France and the United Kingdom, later in Portugal and Spain in the fifteenth century, in the Dutch Republic in the sixteenth and seventeenth centuries, in Russia in the eighteenth century, and in Germany, Italy, and the United States in the nineteenth century. Five hundred years ago, the political map of Europe had hundreds of political and territorial government units that were independent or sovereign (Tilly, 1990). Some larger countries, such as France and England, were genuinely independent. Other larger states, such as Spain, belonged to the Holy Roman Empire with a string of smaller states. Indeed, the most common political unit throughout the world was not a country as we know it but the empire, a city-state, or a principality. There were also vast areas not controlled by a political state. Instead, they were home to various (semi-) nomadic or indigenous peoples, such as in the ""unexplored"" lands of North America, Africa, and Australia (Scott, 2009).

When Western countries ventured out into the world hoping to discover new territory and riches, they brought their traditions of political organization and public administration with them. As a result, those parts of the world that did not belong to an identified political state were colonized. It was then that the notion of the national, territorial state as the official political unit emerged.

States and their political systems have been categorized in various ways (Magstadt, 1994). In democratic *regimes* (unlike Aristotle, democracy nowadays is understood as a *good* form of government), the people have active participation through the right to vote and passive participation in the right to be elected. Vital to this type of state is trust between the governed and those who govern. Trust is a kind of social glue that results from individuals working together for a common purpose (see Chap. 2; also Walsh, 1997).

In democracies, there is variation in how the chief executive is selected. For example, in France, the president is popularly elected. In contrast, in the United Kingdom, the chief executive is selected by elected officials and called the prime minister. In the Netherlands, the chief executive is usually the leader of the party that receives the most popular votes and is then appointed by the monarch as ""formateur"" (Dutch title of the one who is to form a cabinet) to form a cabinet through selecting people for ministerial and under-ministerial positions. Once those are distributed among coalition partners, the new cabinet is sworn in by the monarch, and at that moment, the ""formateur"" becomes prime minister.

In *authoritarian regimes*, states and their political systems are controlled by a wealthy elite class closely related to the ruling class and the military. As a result, authoritarian regimes have little tolerance for the opposition, and sometimes civil rights are suppressed. Examples are President Idi Amin of Uganda; military juntas, often found in Latin America until the 1980s; and dynastic regimes or monarchies, such as Imperial China and the People's Republic of China.

The third primary type of state is the *totalitarian regime*. These lack any political liberties and human rights. Instead, an official state ideology touches every aspect of life through a single political party, state control of the media, state control of the economy, and secret police. The best examples were the Soviet Union between 1917 and 1989, Nazi Germany between 1933 and 1945, Albania between 1944 and 1989, and North Korea starting in 1948.

Sovereignty Evolving

In authoritarian or totalitarian regimes, the head of state has significant powers. The typical situation is that heads of state in democratic countries mostly have symbolic power, whether a hereditary monarch or an elected president. Executive power in most democracies is vested in the head of government, often called the prime minister and their cabinet. The prime minister and their cabinet serve as the executive branch leaders. The executive, legislative, and judicial branches share the highest authority in the country. Each branch of government has formal powers to check the others. For example, the executive can veto legislation. The legislative branch can overturn vetoes and block executive appointments. And the judiciary can overturn legislative and executive action.

Supranational Government Structures

The creation of the European Union (EU) as an economic and political union in 1993 was remarkable. With 27 member nations in 2020 after Britain left the EU, this intergovernmental body is the only example of a supranational government that operates with authority delegated to it by the member states. From a legalistic point of view, a supranational state sits between a *confederacy* and a federal state. The EU member states are entirely sovereign but have agreed to delegate specific duties to the supranational level.

Several international organizations have achieved some degree of integration. Examples are the African Union of 55 nations; the Association of Southeast Asian Nations (ASEAN), representing 10 nations; the Caribbean Community (CARICOM) with 15 member nations; the Central American Integration System (SICA), with eight national members as well as regional and extra-regional observers; the Cooperation Council for the Arab States of the Gulf (GCC), a trade bloc of six countries; and the Union of South American Nations (USAN) with 12 states.

When states agree to join supranational organizations, they forgo some of the rights and responsibilities of their sovereignty to benefit from the management of common pool resources (CPR) available in a shared *governance* system. Common pool resources were initially perceived as part of the natural and physical environment. However, the CPR concept was expanded to include social and governmental settings. Common pool resources are natural or manufactured resources (such as an alpine meadow for grazing, a lake for fisheries, or a system of irrigation canals for agriculture) that are not owned or used exclusively by one person or organization. Instead, all people living nearby may use it. However, suppose the people living nearby the resource do not work together to protect the regenerative capacity of the CPR. In that case, there is a chance that use of all individuals will soon deplete the resource and thus jeopardize everyone's livelihood when no one can use the resource. If the neighbors establish shared administration of the resource, they can assure that everyone can benefit, and everyone will pay a fair share to maintain common pool resources.

Many common pool resources are limited to one municipality or region. This makes it relatively easy for people to see that cooperation and organization are necessary to preserve the resource for the future. Indeed, residents have a sense of ownership, that is, an awareness that restrained individual use will make a difference for the whole.

The literature on common pool resource management systems has focused on municipal and regional systems. However, the concept can also be applied to global CPRs (such as the oceans and global climate) to better understand the enormous challenge that sovereign governments face. Governments facing this kind of challenge often work together formally or informally. This is necessary because no other international actor has the authority to make binding decisions on behalf of all who are impacted.

There is no sense of ownership of the world"s two largest CPRs: the oceans and the atmosphere. We can document increasing problems related to global warming and sea-level rise. We know about the garbage patches in the oceans. We also know what is scientifically possible to preserve these resources. However, the biggest challenge is getting sovereign states to cooperate and to subject their populations to restrictive measures.

Four problems must be addressed no matter which sovereign unit protects common pool resources. First is a question of scale: the global CPR involves seven billion people organized at the municipal, regional, and national levels. The coordination of all these overlapping levels of government can get in the way of finding truly global solutions. Second is a problem of cultural diversity: does everybody perceive the global environmental issue similarly? The third problem involves the management of interconnected CPRs: how do land use patterns impact the flow of water and the quality and temperature of the air, what happens to fresh and salt water when they meet and affect earth's air temperatures and the opposite is a concern what happens to the atmosphere will also affect the earth"s waters. It is challenging to deal with the interconnection and management of CPRs when current styles of administration and management are specialized by land, water, and air. The final problem is securing unanimous agreement: what can we do when powerful states refuse to join or withdraw from international agreements? Examples are Japan refusing to sign an international whaling treaty and administrations, such as the Trump administration, pulling out of the Paris Climate Agreement that dealt with climate change.

What Are the Theories of Sovereignty?

From a theoretical perspective, sovereignty can be understood in several ways. We divide them into four groups:

1. Sovereignty as the final, absolute authority in society. In this definition, sovereignty is vested in the state, such as in Argentina, China, New Zealand, South Africa, or Spain. This definition emphasizes sovereignty as a domestic characteristic of the state. This is the most common definition of sovereignty around the world. The leaders of these sovereign states have officially designated powers, authorities, and responsibilities.
2. Sovereignty as royal rank, authority, or power. Here, the concept refers to an individual invested in society"s ultimate power. Such an individual is called a sovereign or monarch, such as a king/queen or emperor/empress. Authority is generally handed down through familial relationships. Nowadays, most monarchs have only ceremonial roles and wield soft power in politics.
3. Sovereignty is the supremacy of authority to rule over a body politic. This definition concerns the sovereignty exercised by individuals like monarchs or presidents and exercised by a combination of institutions,

including the executive, the legislature, and the judiciary branches of government.
4. Sovereignty as complete independence and self-government. In this case, sovereignty is synonymous with the autonomy of one political unit with another. Under this definition, a political unit can be a state or a subnational unit within a federal state, such as Bavaria in Germany, or even a tribe, such as the various tribes in South Africa.

Regardless of how we think about these four conceptualizations, sovereignty is the product of historical and contextual circumstances. In other words, we cannot think about it outside our own experience. Jean Bodin of France and Thomas Hobbes of England were among the earliest sovereignty students in the Western world. Both firmly believed that the centralization of all power would solve societal instability. This is not surprising since the studies for which they are most famous were written after devastating civil wars in their respective countries.

Domestic Sovereignty

The concern of early political philosophers, such as Bodin and Hobbes, was domestic sovereignty, which refers to the ability of government organizations to effectively regulate the behavior of people, organizations, and institutions such as the free market (Krasner, 2001). Domestic sovereignty concerns action and control, demonstrated by generating financial resources through taxes and enacting policies to benefit the collective even when it may cause harm to specific individuals (Sørenson, 2004).

Some illustrations of domestic sovereignty may be helpful. First, in the world, generally, only government has the authority to impose and collect taxes. Second, only certain government officials have the right to convict and incarcerate law violators. Third, only the state has a legitimate monopoly over physical violence against offenders within its territory (Weber, 1946 [1919]). Fourth, remember that no matter how heinous the crime, all individuals have a right to due process. Only the government can pass judgment after the rules for due process have been observed. Only government can impose sentences and execute the death penalty. One could argue that citizens pass judgment in countries with a jury system (Australia, Canada, and the United Kingdom). Still, we must keep in mind that they do so after being sworn in as members/officers of the court (sovereign) for the trial duration. In this case, citizens act with the authority of the state.

The third illustration of domestic sovereignty is that only public servants which include elected officials, political appointees, and career civil servants, can make decisions binding to society. They design policies governing criminal trials and sentencing and prepare budgets determining how our taxes are spent. Organizations like for-profits and non-profits, special interest groups, and advocacy organizations may be the contractual providers of government goods and services and be funded by government. Still, they cannot make decisions that are binding for society.

Interdependent Sovereignty

Domestic sovereignty gives authority and powers to the state in a territory clearly defined by geographic boundaries. Through this, the government can control the movement of people across borders, creating a situation of interdependence sovereignty (Krasner, 2001; Sørenson, 2004). The most physical expression of this is the passport or identification card required for international travel.

A more abstract expression of interdependent sovereignty is that other states do not interfere with a sovereign state"s domestic policies and politics. This is the principle of non-intervention. Sometimes this principle is set aside. This usually occurs when another state has violated one state"s sovereignty or committed serious crimes against humanity. Currently, invading other countries is more justified when removing a cruel dictator from power. While the principle of non-intervention generally appears to be upheld, there have been violations, suggesting that the principle may be interpreted differently based on the situational context. The difficulty of operating under the principle of non-intervention is apparent when considering the Russia-Ukraine conflict since 2014 and the ongoing tensions between the People"s Republic of China and the areas known as Hong Kong and Taiwan.

Constitutional Independence

The ultimate expression of sovereignty is constitutional independence. In many contemporary states, a country"s ultimate or supreme authority is defined in a constitution. The constitution is the juridical core of a state"s sovereignty. The importance of a constitution can be inferred from the fact that it is very difficult to change, and changes are infrequent over time. Several continental-European countries pursued constitutional change when the political, economic, and social circumstances warranted this. The original text of the U.S. Constitution has never been changed, but it has had 27 amendments since 1791. Changing a constitution often requires a significant qualified or super-majority vote of the national legislature. A constitution is meant to be enduring, but many are written to endorse a principle of change. A principle of change is meant to describe emergent and changed social, economic, political, cultural, and geographic changes and how these are to be reflected in a new legal interpretation of the meaning of the words in a constitution.

People often think of a constitution as a document that outlines the necessary institutional arrangements of government with society. However, what constitutes society is not just a constitution but also a whole range of values and customs that are not made explicit in the constitution as a document. Over time, some of these values and traditions may become part of a law. When this occurs, one can also think of all those laws and regulations as documents that enable the government to operate in society. The constitutional school of thought in the study of public administration emphasizes the normative underpinnings of government.

One normative area explores the importance of the *rule of law* for society (Newbold & Rosenbloom, 2016; Raadschelders, 2017). It is indivisible when sovereignty is defined as absolute statehood or *de jure* sovereignty. This means it is vested in one individual, such as a monarch, one body, or a set of bodies like the legislature, executive, judiciary, or an institution, such as a constitution. But there are exceptions. For instance, the principality of Andorra was governed by France and Spain together between 1278 and 1993 of the Common Era (CE). England and Egypt ruled Sudan from 1898 to 1955 (Lapidoth, 1997). Another exception is countries with various nations or peoples living within their borders. The nationhood of each of these can be expressed in terms of a *de facto* sovereignty. This concept allows a nation, such as indigenous nations (the Inuit, Australian aboriginals, native Americans, and southern African tribes), a significant degree of autonomy on their lands even though the geographic boundaries are within a country.

We must also pay attention to different intellectual traditions when defining sovereignty. For instance, sovereignty is generally perceived as residing in the country"s constitution and the law. Both are as far away from the people as possible. Since 1688, in Britain, sovereignty has been more commonly identified as vested in the Crown-in-Parliament and, nowadays, basically in the parliamentary political parties. Finally, sovereignty resides mainly in the centralized administrative institutions on the European continent rather than political officials (Nettl, 1968).

WHY IS SOVEREIGNTY NECESSARY FOR SOCIETY?

There are two possible answers. When sovereignty is invested in government, you could argue that it assures just one ultimate center of power in society. No matter how influential other actors might be, the government holds the highest authority (Dror, 2001). Government is a more neutral arbiter in handling conflicts between citizens than any other societal actor can be. In Western countries, the government is also constrained so that neither wide-scale abuse of power nor naked oppression of the citizenry is possible. Government not only monitors citizens, but it also monitors itself to assure that behavior is following the law (Rosenbloom, 2003). The concept of government as a neutral arbiter has become indispensable to our globe"s densely populated (urban) areas. In some states, it is highly appreciated, such as in Scandinavian countries; in other countries like Argentina, the government is distrusted (cf. Edelman Research's latest Trust Barometer). Whatever the case may be, people often think of government in pejorative terms: it works slowly, has lots of red tape, many lazy civil servants, etc. In a 2018 TED talk, Raadschelders describes how we can reconceptualize government by recognizing that many of the services and policies it provides and develops benefit us.

Of course, government officials are not the only actors involved in policy-making. A wide range of interest groups also influence policies. Other governments and non-governmental organizations place pressure upon states in the international arena. However, of all organizations, only government protects society at large. No other actor can secure a certain level of societal stability and public safety. No other actor can shoulder the responsibility of looking after the concerns and needs of the entire population. Indeed, the recipients of government are the whole population in a country, not just a category of consumers.

To this point, we have looked at domestic and international actors and issues that have emerged as potential challenges to the sovereignty of a nation. On the domestic front, sovereignty is contested by phenomena such as the influence of *non-constitutional branches*, the emphasis on business-like government, and regionalization. What are the effects of these challenges on domestic sovereignty?

The Influence of Non-Constitutional Branches

The literature often references fourth, fifth, and sixth branches of government. These are not identified in a constitution, but they do have significantly influence on most countries. The number of people working in government organizations has become so large that some started referring to bureaucracy as the fourth branch of government. They did this to suggest that the government would cease functioning without civil servants. Another reason government agencies are sometimes called the fourth branch is because they serve all three branches. The legislature, executive, or judiciary cannot function without the help of civil servants.

Government activities, both by the three branches of government established in a constitution as well as the organizations that provide the programs, goods, and services of government, capture much attention from the media, which provides citizens with information about how and why government acts. Initially, media reporting covered the news in an even-handed manner based on information collected from the government and other sources. However, in recent decades, media communication has become more partisan. Some even suggest that the media distorts, spins, and selectively reports information and creates news stories (Steurley et al., 1998). The media"s influence over citizens" perceptions of how government does, can, and should operate has led to it being labeled by some as the fifth branch of government.

The growth of government also led to interest group formation to represent the specific and unique interests of sub-populations of society and influence policymaking. The perceived privileged position of interest groups has led to them being labeled the branch of government. In the early days, interest groups focused on people"s work in government. However, a wide range of interests has been organized in recent decades. Each represents their constituency"s interests, not necessarily considering the collective interest. Government officials represent the interest of society. Interest groups are generally only interested in one sub-population of citizens. The influence of non-constitutional actors is essential since they are one of the actors in a system of governing with multiple actors.

Following the Atlantic Revolutions, reformers were determined to limit political power and authority to elected officials. Therefore, they organized government into institutions separate from other societal organizations and institutions. But they also wanted a participatory democracy where the government served the people"s interests through, for example, allowing and even desiring a role for actors not defined in the constitution. Indeed, a robust government has no problem dealing with various influences.

Business-Like Government

Another development that represents a challenge to sovereignty is the call for the government to operate using business-like principles like those used in for-profit organizations. Many reforms aim to make the government more business-like. Recent examples include *contracting-out* government services and *deregulation* of rules and policies that govern the for-profit and non-profit sectors in favor of relying on market-type mechanisms to force consumer protection. The most far-reaching type of reform is *privatization*, where government services are transferred to organizations in the for-profit sector. In the case of privatization, government oversight is non-existent.

Many government reforms are efforts to reduce government regulation and free the market of unnecessary government regulation or to streamline existing regulations to make them less burdensome to individuals, organizations, and private industry. However, deregulation is not only about removing the government from market transactions. It is as much, if not more, a political effort by producers of market-based goods and services to structure the rules of the regulatory game to their benefit (Kettl, 2002).

Regionalization

When we think about government, we may consider it significant and inseparable, like a state. However, we can also think of the population as homogeneous, as a nation. However, there are times when the population is not homogeneous and subnational areas seek recognition or when a territory larger than the nation has shared interests and seeks special recognition to form a collection that takes unified actions. Demands for *regionalization* can happen in two ways. First, there is the regionalization that happens when minorities attempt to gain autonomy or complete independence from the state. Second, regionalization results from direct interactions of subnational governments with international and supranational organizations. We first look at minorities in existing states who wish to split off. Then, we consider interactions that can occur in varying combinations between subnational, national, and supranational organizations.

The population of many states is not homogeneous. Few people realize that minorities constitute about one-sixth of the world population or almost a billion people (Gurr, 1995). Most are found in sub-Saharan Africa, North Africa, the Middle East, Asia, and Eastern Europe, but Western Europe and North America are not without politically active minorities. The Basques in Spain and the Québécois in Canada come to mind, but also ethnic groups of African, Muslim, and Asian origin demand political and economic equality next to cultural self-expression. Examples are the Saami in the northern regions of Scandinavia (Finland, Norway, Sweden), the Maori in New Zealand, the Aborigines in Australia, the various Kung tribes in South Africa, and the Native American tribes in Canada and the United States in indigenous rights movements.

Countries are more multi-ethnic and multi-cultural than ever before. This multi-ethnicity poses significant challenges to the government. One can think, for example, of the civil tensions related to immigrants from Mexico, Central America, and various Asian countries. Tensions are also rising between the native communities in Western Europe and the immigrant workers from northern Africa, the Middle East, and Eastern Europe. The same situation is occurring with political refugees worldwide (Raadschelders et al., 2019). While the nature of these ethnic and cultural challenges does not undermine government"s sovereignty; it can put the government"s ability to maintain peace and order to the test.

The category of people that genuinely challenges the government"s sovereignty is that of *minority nations*, which can be a self-identified ethnic group (Inuit, Aboriginal, Tribal), or a historically defined territorial grouping (Kurds, Basques, Québécois) that strives for some degree of autonomy or even independence while residing within the boundaries of a territorial state. Many ethnic groups pursue these objectives through peaceful negotiations, treaties, and covenants. However, domestic strife can occur as seen in the dissolution of Czechoslovakia into Slovakia and the Czech Republic in 1992.

The second type of regionalization that results from the increased activity of subnational governments in the national and international arenas is very different. In the European Union, subnational levels of government have increasingly dealt directly with it rather than going through their national government representatives. Several American state governments have their trade-representative or foreign policy monitor located in countries they trade with frequently.

Both types of regionalization constitute a challenge to sovereignty. The first one, minority groups striving for independence, can lead to the break-up of political unity. The second one increases subnational government autonomy and creates potential tensions between decisions made at each level of government. However, the second type of regionalization also suggests the flexibility and resilience of sovereignty and the structure and functioning of governments. Indeed, sovereignty is a weak rather than robust mechanism of a political organization since it manages to co-exist with other societal organizations. The emergence of three pseudo-branches of government, the role of business-like practices in government, and regionalization are examples of domestic challenges to sovereignty. There are also changes at the international level that can challenge the sovereignty of a nation. We turn to these next.

International Challenges to Sovereignty

In the international arena, globalization challenges the government"s sovereignty. Also, in various parts of the world, populations are governed as a territory of another country. This, too, challenges the existing states since their sovereignty rests upon the right of self-determination. Just as special interest groups have emerged in many countries, *non-state actors* in the international arena, such as supranational governments, international forum organizations, and alliances, have increasing societal influence. This section explores the presence and meaning of these challenges in the international arena.

Globalization

One influence that nibbles away at the state"s sovereignty is globalization, a concept denoting a world in which people are ever more connected and interdependent, especially in financial transactions, communications, and the sustainability of the world"s environment. Globalization is often thought of as a characteristic of our age. Even in prehistory people migrated, but globalization has been accelerating since the 1500s when Western European explorers (or, if you will: conquerors) roamed over the oceans and established trading posts and colonies on other continents.

Globalization, that started with colonization in the early modern period, gained momentum in the twentieth century. Technological changes were a significant factor in this, especially communication developments, which have connected the various parts of the world more. Two centuries ago, a letter from an immigrant in Philadelphia sent to his family back home in Bergen, Norway, would take about 40 days to arrive. Then, it would take another 40 days to receive a reply (Fraser, 1987). Imagine a communication speed of 2.5 months! The invention of the telegraph and the telephone sped up the time needed for international communications. Still, nothing compares to the speed of computer networks and telephones today. Communication and information flows have radically altered how governments, organizations, and people work. Communication technology enables almost everyone to acquire information and participate in the global community in real time.

Globalization is not only a result of economic interdependency or technological revolution. All over the world, authoritarian regimes have been replaced between the 1960s and 2000s by democracies (Baker, 2002). Since then, democracy has come under siege in various countries (Bauer et al., 2021). Your parents may remember that evening in 1989 when broadcasts worldwide showed how people from East and West Germany brought down the Berlin Wall. It is one of the most dramatic illustrations of the worldwide movement toward democracy. It has become clear that the democratic political system of government cannot be taken for granted. It is disturbing to see how easily autocratically inclined leaders can subvert it. The most dramatic illustration of that is the January 6, 2021 insurrection, where supporters of President Trump tried to alter the outcome of the national election.

One could say that democracy is globalizing. In developing countries, reform efforts modeled after Western countries aim at strengthening fledgling democracies (Adamolekun, 1999). Globalization is evident in creating supranational organizations, such as the Organization of African States or the European Union. The European Union is an example of a supranational organization voluntarily created by a group of 27 states (2022) that gave up some degree of sovereignty in the creation and further development of a European identity. After more than 60 years of European integration, more than 90% of national legislation in the member states must conform to the rules and directives of the European Union. As a result, European Union member countries" domestic sovereignty is at stake. However, recent developments such as the departure of the United Kingdom from the European Union may be a harbinger of a kind of fluidity of membership in supranational organizations. Globalization for the economic strengthening of nations is a common theme worldwide. The New Silk Road, that is, China"s Belt and Road initiative, is a modern-day example. The impact of supranational organizations on sovereignty is ever-changing and must be carefully examined by nations before actions are taken.

International Territories

Very few territories in the world do not belong to one state. In other words, almost the entire landmass of the world is incorporated (Scott, 2009). The one major exception is Antarctica, a continent not discovered until 1820. By the late 1950s, seven countries had announced territorial claims over Antarctica (Argentina, Australia, Chile, France, New Zealand, Norway, and Great Britain). In 1959, 12 countries signed the Antarctic Treaty to resolve the incorporation issue, which established a joint government of the landmass. According to NTI (n.d.), the Treaty stated that ""Antarctica shall continue forever to be used exclusively for peaceful purposes and shall not become the scene or object of international discord"" (n.p.). Another 30 states have signed the Treaty since 1959, but the 42 signatories do not have equal status. According to the Scientific Committee on Antarctic Research, 26 consultative members agreed to conduct substantial research in Antarctica and maintain a permanent scientific station. Together, they constitute the Consultative Meeting, the continent"s legislative body. The 16 other signatories are contracting parties who have agreed to the terms of the Treaty but do not conduct substantial research (Dosman, 1989; Jorgensen-Dahl & Ostreng, 1991).

International Forum Organizations and Alliances

Though small independent and semi-independent states and territories are an object of interest precisely because they have few resources to advance their shared interests, in 1990, in response to the rapid growth of small independent states in the 1970s and 1980s, a unit for relations with small member states and their policy concerns was established within UNESCO, the United Nations-affiliated organization for educational, scientific, and cultural affairs. It has 28 member states in the Caribbean, Africa, and the Pacific and three associate members (Aruba, the British Virgin Islands, and the Netherlands Antilles). This is just one example of how states and territories relate to one another through international forum organizations and alliances.

While various international forum organizations exist, we will only focus on those created by sovereign states. Of these, there are two main types. First, international organizations are voluntarily established by countries that maintain their independence. They can be created for political, economic, or military reasons. Truly universal or global international organizations have no membership limitations. That is, any independent state can become a member. The largest intergovernmental organization is the United Nations, which serves as a world political forum. It is also an umbrella for many subsidiaries and specialized organizations (such as the International Monetary Fund, the World Bank, the World Health Organization, and the United Nations Development Program). The European Union is an example of a multinational economic organization that has expanded its activities beyond mere economic to social collaboration in recent decades. The North Atlantic Treaty Organization (NATO) is a military alliance of Western democracies to prevent war on the European continent.

International forum organizations provide opportunities for discussions between states and non-governmental organizations to more effectively advance minority rights, human rights (Ishay, 2004), and reform agendas. They often have open membership (at least in principle) and are concerned with a specific functional area of interest. An example is the World Trade Organization (WTO), which succeeded the General Agreement on Tariffs and Trade or GATT in 1993. There are also regional intergovernmental organizations. However, membership is only open to states in a geographic region, such as the North American Free Trade Association of Canada, Mexico, and the United States in 1993.

The United Nations and the European Union are examples of generic alliances because they serve a wide range of functions and develop a wide array of policies. On the other hand, functional organizations serve a specific objective. For example, the North-Atlantic Treaty Organization is a military alliance; the

Organization for Economic Cooperation and Development (OECD) is an economic alliance.

Few governments are not involved in or influenced by the existence of international forum organizations. To varying degrees, the functioning and policies of sovereign states and their governments are subject to scrutiny by international organizations. Whatever policies governments develop and the decisions they take are influenced by third-party interest or lobbying organizations. Most attention in the public administration literature is devoted to domestic interest groups rather than international organizations. Still, the international forum organizations and alliances sometimes exercise as much, if not more, influence. Indeed, sovereign states are increasingly forced to consider the international arena before finalizing a domestic policy decision or reform, especially in developing countries (Dimitrakiopoulos & Passas, 2003).

In addition to serving as a forum for member states and providing services to member states, international organizations are also best equipped to deal with global problems that can only be solved through the cooperation of states. We already mentioned global warming, but environmental pollution, international drug and human trafficking, and international crimes and terrorism are issues that call for some degree of involvement through international organizations. The success of international cooperation depends on the degree to which member states are willing to live by the stipulations of an agreement or a treaty, such as for Antarctica.

In this section, we discussed various domestic and international challenges to sovereignty. These challenges make government less transparent because power and authority appear to be more dispersed than ever among domestic and international actors. Some authors argue that sovereignty is under siege, while others (including us) believe sovereignty is here to stay. Why? The answer is quite simple: the only actor with authority to make legally binding decisions is the government for all people living in a country. Whether we like it or not, we need government for various collective services that would not be offered if left to the private sphere. Very few citizens would argue that government is unnecessary, but it faces challenges.

The fight against international terrorism illustrates how sovereignty is both a strength and a weakness. On the one hand, international terrorists elude traditional police and military tactics and seek safe harbor in countries with few, if any, extradition agreements. However, the government is not the only actor attempting to eradicate or constrain international terrorism.

In contemporary society, many actors share power, but only one is truly sovereign. On the other hand, you could argue that sovereignty is too divided among various actors to be meaningful. Some scholars refer to this as pluralistic sovereignty, a situation where a country"s government is dominated by various political, economic, social, and religious groups (Laski, 1917). The notion of a pluralistic system suggests a difference between what government does and how societal policy is established. The difference can be best understood using two similar but conceptually different terms: governance and government.

Chapter Summary

This chapter opened with a recap of the difference between government and governance and then posed a question about whether sovereignty is achieved through government or governance. Various authors use governance as a synonym for government. However, it is not synonymous. To some, the concept of governance encompasses all those organizations and institutions that play a role in structuring, steering, and organizing society. In addition to governmental actors, governance can be provided by non-governmental actors such as for-profit and non-profit organizations, and public interest groups. We find this definition of governance too expansive because it creates the impression that all these societal organizations have the same authority and responsibilities as the government. But they do not. Instead, we define governance as a shared process between public, non-profit, and for-profit actors where only government has the authority to make decisions on behalf of the people. With that definition, the term government refers to the structural arrangements of the state.

Using these distinctions, you can argue that governance, with the fragmentation of power across many actors, is compatible with the classical notion of sovereignty as the ultimate center of political authority. Indeed, in contemporary states, governments are increasingly relying upon non-governmental actors to help provide public or collective services for the benefit of society. Knowing the differences in the definition and use of these two concepts will be important in Chap. 4, where we explore the role of culture and climate on the form of governance regime and the government"s institutional structure. Some surprising patterns help to understand why nations ""run"" their governments so differently!

Practical Applications for Students

1. Illustrate the various theories of sovereignty through analysis of governance and government in your country.
2. Consider why sovereignty is necessary for any large-scale society and why it was not needed in the hunter-gathered bands of old.
3. Read a journal article about how government strives to make sovereignty applicable in changing political, environmental, and social contexts. How well does this essay describe what is currently happening in your country? What can explain the differences between theory and reality?
4. How are power and authority in your country transferred from one head of government to the next and from one head of state to the next? By what ceremonies and symbols is that transfer of power signaled?

In-Class Instructional Suggestions

1. Ask students to identify any enclaves and exclaves in their country. What differences do they have in terms of the government of the country overall?
2. Characterize your country"s type of political system: federal or unitary; presidential or monarchical; one-party, two-party, or multi-party system. Use this to engage students in understanding the ways in which these translated into governmental actions may differ in another type of political system.
3. Do subnational levels of government in your country have some degree of autonomy? Use this information to help students recognize how that expression autonomy is expressed and how that impacts sub-populations in the nation.
4. Provide examples of supranational and international organizations in which your country has a membership. Assist the students in understanding how these have changed the way how the government services operated before and after joining or working with these organizations.

References

Adamolekun, L. (Ed.). (1999). *Public administration in Africa: Main issues and selected country studies.* Westview Press.

Baker, R. (Ed.). (1992). *Public administration in small and island states.* Kumarian Press.

Baker, R. (Ed.). (2002). *Transitions from authoritarianism: The role of bureaucracy.* Praeger.

Bauer, M. W., Peters, B. G., Pierre, J., Yesilkagit, K., & Becker, S. (Eds.). (2021). *Democratic backsliding and public administration: How populists in government transform state bureaucracies.* Cambridge University Press.

Dimitrakiopoulos, D. G., & Passas, A. G. (2003). International organization and domestic administrative reform. In B. G. Peters & J. Pierre (Eds.), *Handbook of public administration* (pp. 443–449). Sage.

Dosman, E. (Ed.). (1989). *Sovereignty and security in the Arctic.* Routledge.

Dror, Y. (2001). *The capacity to govern: A report to the Club of Rome.* Frank Cass.

Fraser, J. T. (1987). *Time: The familiar stranger.* The University of Massachusetts Press.

Gurr, T. R. (1995). *Minorities at risk: A global view of ethnopolitical conflicts.* United States Institute of Peace Press.

Ishay, M. R. (2004). *The history of human rights: From ancient times to the globalization era.* University of California Press.

Jorgensen-Dahl, A., & Ostreng, W. (1991). *The Antarctic Treaty system in world politics.* Macmillan.

Kettl, D. F. (2002). *The transformation of governance: Public administration for twenty-first-century America.* Johns Hopkins University Press.

Krasner, S. D. (2001). Abiding sovereignty. *International Political Science Review, 22*(3), 231–232.

Lapidoth, R. (1997). *Autonomy: Flexible solution to ethnic conflicts*. United States Institute of Peace Press.

Laski, H. (1917). The sovereignty of the state. In H. Laski (Ed.), *Studies in the problem of sovereignty* (pp. 1–24). Yale University Press.

Maaka, R., & Fleras, A. (2000). Engaging with indigeneity: Tino Rangatiratanga in Aotearoa. In D. Ivison, P. Patton, & W. Sanders (Eds.), *Political theory and the rights of Indigenous peoples* (pp. 93–94). Cambridge University Press.

Magstadt, T. M. (1994). *Nations and governments: Comparative politics in a regional perspective*. St. Martin's Press.

Melamid, A. (1968). Enclaves and Exclaves. In D. Sills (Ed.), *International Encyclopedia of the Social Sciences*. The Macmillan Company and Free Press.

Nettl, P. (1968). The state as a conceptual variable. *World Politics, 20*(4), 573–574.

Newbold, S. P., & Rosenbloom, D. H. (2016). *The constitutional school of American public administration*. Routledge.

Organization for Economic Cooperation and Development (OECD). (2016). *OECD/UCLG (2016), Subnational Governments around the world*. Structure and finance.

Raadschelders, J. C. N. (2017). The United States of America as Rechtsstaat: State and administrative law as key to understanding the administrative state. *Public Administration Review, 77*(3), 458–465.

Raadschelders, J. C. N., Larrison, J., & Thapar, A. V. (2019). Refugee migration as a 'wicked problem': American controlling, palliative, and governance policies in the global context." World Affairs, Autumn, 228–255.

Rosenbloom, D. H. (2003). *Administrative law for public managers*. Westview Press.

Scott, J. C. (2009). *The art of not being governed: An anarchist history of Upland Southeast Asia*. Yale University Press.

Shaw, M. N. (1987). *International law*. Grotius Publications.

Sørenson, G. (2004). *The transformation of sovereignty? The transformation of the state. Beyond the myth of retreat*. Palgrave Macmillan.

Steurley, C. E., Gramlich, E. N., Heclo, H., & Smith Nightingale, D. (1998). *The government we deserve: Responsive democracy and changing expectations*. Urban Institute Press.

Stone, D., & Moloney, K. (Eds.). (2019). *Oxford handbook on global policy and transnational administration*. Oxford University Press.

Tilly, C. (Ed.). (1990). *Coercion, capital, and European states, AD 990-1990*. Basil Blackwell.

Wallace, M., & Singer, D. (1970). Intergovernmental organization in the global system, 1815-1964: A quantitative description. *International Organization, 24*(2), 239–297.

Walsh, M. L. (1997). *Building citizen involvement: Strategies for local government*. International City/County Management Association.

Watts, R. L. (1999). *Comparing Federal Systems*. Queens University Press.

Weber, M. (1946 [1919]). Politics as a vocation. In H. H. Gerth and C. W. Mills (Eds.) *Max Weber: Essays in Sociology* (pp. 77-128). Oxford University Press.

CHAPTER 4

Government Culture and Climate

Chapter 3 reviewed theories of sovereignty, noting differences in conceptions of authority and rank, power over and independence from, and the opportunities for self-governance as well as differences in domestic and international sovereignty. These factors are often an outgrowth of the form of governance for that specific nation. Not surprisingly, the form of government and people's perceptions of sovereignty and government organizations will vary tremendously from nation to nation. In this chapter, we examine the concepts of culture and climate to see how they contribute to popular perceptions of government and governance processes.

It is trendy for politicians running for office to appeal to the public's poor perceptions of government by claiming that government is an enormous *bureaucracy*. This means they perceive it as an organization with many procedures that make it difficult to do what you want it to do. The procedures are often described as red tape because it is hard to unravel when it gets stuck to something, and red symbolizes stopping. In addition, some scholars depict a bureaucratic organization as the problem that prohibits the government from "working better while costing less." Slogans like this strike a chord with people who share negative perceptions of government as being filled with bureaucrats who like red tape, are lazy and wasteful, and are looking for ways to abuse the system and commit fraud. Also, remember that all organizations, even public organizations, larger than a mom-and-pop store are structured and function as a bureaucracy.

Perceptions such as these thrive in a climate of deep distrust of government (Wills, 1999). No matter how much government does for people and how well it does it, it cannot escape from this stereotypical image of being a massive bureaucracy that is impermeable, big, costly, inefficient, and wasteful. The passage of the Freedom of Information Act in 1966 in the United States and similar acts in other democracies in the 1960s and 1970s paradoxically reinforce

© The Author(s), under exclusive license to Springer Nature Switzerland AG 2023
A. L. Franklin, J. C.N. Raadschelders, *Introduction to Governance, Government and Public Administration*,
https://doi.org/10.1007/978-3-031-32689-9_4

57

the idea that what goes on in bureaucracy cannot always be seen in the light of day. Is government this secretive? Is it virtually impossible for the average citizen to penetrate its boundaries? Do the people and processes in a bureaucracy dehumanize citizens by treating them as cases and not individuals?

This chapter examines how organizational culture and climate influence government operations, and contribute to people's perceptions. This topic is vital because negative perceptions about government and its officials are quite persistent. Yet, at the same time, we might wonder why so many people seek to become a public servant.

Why Do We Refer to The Government as a Bureaucracy?

Bureaucracy is a concept with a wide variety of meanings. However, these can be grouped into two categories (Albrow, 1970). First, bureaucracy is a specific organization suited to serving many people. It operates based on following formal rules and standardized procedures, precise and specialized positions, observing a clear hierarchy for action, and complying with written documents. A civil service job is not owned, so it cannot be inherited or passed on from a parent to a child, nor can it be sold to the highest bidder.

A second meaning is that of bureaucracy as a personnel system. In the public sector, those who work in an appointed position are known as civil servants. In government organizations, formal rules and standardized procedures apply equally to all employees. For example, civil servants are selected based on merit, educational background, and relevant experience. They are paid according to rank, with all persons at the same rank having similar salaries established in a publicly available salary table. Finally, civil servants do not work at the pleasure of elected officials. Any decisions regarding their employment must be made by administration officials within the organization that employs them.

Albrow's distinction is based on Max Weber's observations of bureaucracy in late nineteenth and early twentieth-century Germany. Weber was the first to distinguish between bureaucracy as an organization and bureaucracy as a personnel system. The organizational features of bureaucracy today are pretty much the same as in Weber's time. However, some features of bureaucracy as a personnel system have changed. This is especially true for employee security, promotion, and compensation. There was a time when one of the best incentives for seeking a public sector position was the job security it offered. This is no longer the case. The turnover of civil servants has increased significantly, especially at the top organizational levels. Today, individuals do not seek job security as much as they do a challenge found in a position elsewhere (Light, 2000).

Keep in mind, though, that there is significant variation between and within countries. In some countries, a public sector job is still very attractive, while in others it is not. For instance, employee turnover rates can be 20% or higher for certain government positions, such as correctional officers or social workers, compared to 10% in the entire personnel system. We discuss developments in personnel management in greater detail in Chap. 10. This chapter focuses on bureaucracy as an expression of government culture.

Why has bureaucracy become so identified with government culture and climate instead of being characterized as an organizational structure typical for almost all organizations? In the early twentieth century, Weber predicted that bureaucratization would continue and be almost impossible to stop. That is indeed what happened to organizations in all sectors. Concerning the public sector, given the expansion of programs and services government offers, could the welfare state have been created without bureaucracy?

The growth of government programs and services has given rise to the idea that bureaucracy is the fourth branch of government that is very difficult to control by the three main branches of government. Political cultures featuring fragmented powers and adversarial politics limit the chance of bureaucracy becoming too influential. Does this mean that bureaucracies in other political cultures are more influential? Not always, because in some political structures, like democracies, civil servants are subordinate to elected officials. Finally, bureaucratic culture is regarded as rigid, inert, and too massive to change. Is that true? Is bureaucracy unable to improve its ways and thus serve the citizenry better?

Government is a product of society. As members of society, citizens get the government they want or need. While people may perceive the government as acting opposite to their interests, governance as an institution is structured to serve us and our collective preferences. To better understand the tension between a government that serves us but seems to be acting opposite to our interests, we must explore what characterizes bureaucratic culture and climate. Thus, we need to define societal culture and organizational climate.

If government reflects society at large, we can only assume that its organizational structure and functioning reflect these cultural foundations and climate features. We will present governmental development into an organization that is bureaucratic, like other large organizations. In terms of organizational structure, bureaucracy in one country is comparable to bureaucracies elsewhere. Each provides the same essential functions: aid to vulnerable persons, protection of the environment, public safety and military defense, and public infrastructure. However, how the ways these government functions are carried out in each country can be very different. We consider the development of American government as an example by first looking back at its founding period, then considering the enormous influence that business-like practices have had on government development since the late nineteenth century.

How Do Culture and Climate Differ?

Before considering government culture and climate characteristics, we need to define them. That is not as simple as it may seem; many definitions exist (Martin, 2002). In this section, we define culture and climate in society and government. Then we define organizational culture and climate to illustrate that all definitions of culture and climate have some standard features.

As a general definition, *social culture* is the entirety of values, norms, goals, and expectations in each society. Social culture is learned, not inherited. Values are shared opinions about what is right and what is wrong. Norms are more specific and concrete guidelines for behavior. Whether in written or unwritten form, norms guide social interaction and communication. Law is an example of formalized, written norms. Privacy is an example of an unwritten norm protected by law. Norms are embedded in values. For instance, the use of the secret ballot (a norm) for voting and the structure of institutional checks and balances gives expression to freedom of speech (a value) and freedom from tyranny. Values and norms also encourage goals such as smaller but better government and expectations such as accessible government. Values and norms are less visible and more implicit than laws (including law-like things such as an agency's rules and standard operating procedures).

On the other hand, expectations and goals and expectations are more explicit or tangible. They indicate the social climate, defined as people's perceptions of events, procedures, and behaviors and how they are expected to accomplish shared goals. Societal and organizational climate includes shared attitudes on issues like trust, openness, risk-taking, warmth, support, and conflict (Isaac & Pitt, 2001). Thus, the social climate is the visible, or more tangible, manifestation of culture. Furthermore, culture changes less quickly than climate because underlying values do not change with the day's trends. These definitions of social culture and climate can be further refined by understanding the difference between organizational culture and organizational climate.

Perhaps the most widespread definition of organizational culture is the one that distinguishes between three levels: basic underlying assumptions, fundamental values, and the artifacts and creations of the organization (Schein, 1985). The underlying assumptions concern ideas about how the world operates, including understanding human nature, the universe, and relationships in the political system. We unconsciously act upon these; they determine how we perceive, think, and feel. This is the least tangible or observable level of culture. Our fundamental values create clear ideas about how the world is and ought to operate, which makes these values more observable. We defined these as social norms above, but that definition also applies to organizational norms.

The most tangible and observable manifestations of culture are artifacts and behavior patterns. Artifacts are visible expressions of culture. They can include ceremonial dress like the robes of judges, buildings such as that of the legislature (Parliament, Congress), technology as found in toll roads and computers, as well as symbols like war memorials, songs such as the national anthem, national heroes such as Prince William of Orange in the Netherlands, Nelson Mandela in South Africa, and George Washington and Abraham Lincoln in the United States, as well as the nation's foundational texts such as constitutions. Behavior patterns include formal and informal (or unspoken) rules that define or constrain our choices and habits. They also include rituals, such as an annual Address to Parliament or the State of the Union; rites, such as the coronation of a monarch and the inauguration of a president; and celebrations, such as national holidays (Labor Day, Liberation Day, Memorial Day, etc.). Artifacts and behaviors help us visualize organizations, such as government, what they stand for, and how they are connected to us.

Organizational climate is an integral part of organizational culture. Organizational climate is represented by how people directly or indirectly perceive what they are supposed to do as part of their work, how they are supposed to relate to others and how this influences their motivations and behaviors (Litwin & Stringer, 1968). These perceptions may initially not be shared at the individual, group, or organizational levels. However, the norms become more robust when there is considerable overlap in perceptions of the organization's climate from the individual up to the organizational level. Shared perceptions of workplace responsibilities and relationships eventually can become part of the organization's culture.

Climate refers to situations subject to manipulation designed to present some image of the organization (or about society). For example, you can think about what an office's appearance tells you about its occupant. When someone is important, you might see that reflected in the size of the office, the size and covering of chairs, the quality of the carpet, the presence of windows, a conference table, or a comfortable sitting area, and whether there is an outer office with an assistant who allows you to enter the office of their boss. You can also infer meaning about an individual's position and status by finding out where they are located on the official organizational chart. However, the organizational chart does not necessarily reflect the power relations between organizational members.

You can intuitively assess the organizational climate of an office area by the absence or presence of artwork, the quality of the office furniture (metal or wood), the lighting (natural or neon), and the space between the desks (larger or smaller). The smaller the office space, the fewer the visual images, the cheaper the furniture, the lack of windows, and cramped space for workers, suggests that people working in that area are not very important. As a result, the organization may be signaling that it values them less than others and is willing to spend less on these employees' comfort as they work.

However, organizational climate encompasses more than material features. The patterns of behavior or actions that occur within the organization are as important. For instance, organizational climate can easily change when a new colleague does not fit in as is expected and disrupts existing relations between colleagues. Or, when a new manager does things very differently from a predecessor. In this case, long-time employees may resist changes because they create uncertainty, and requirements to change may alter the organization's climate.

Public organizations have particular cultures. For instance, a department of defense is much more hierarchical than the departments of education or social welfare. Teachers and social workers approach their clients differently than military service members. Differences in organizational culture can be found in for-profit organizations as well. When Microsoft started in the early 1980s in a garage, the leaders wore jeans, emphasized that the job had to be fun, and focused on individual people. Microsoft still embraces a relatively informal organizational culture, believing it fosters creativity. The organizational culture of IBM stands in stark contrast to that of Microsoft. When Microsoft started, IBM had a black suit and tie, corporate, business-oriented culture. The leaders were not concerned with making personal computers for individuals but with making mainframe computers that would be used in organizations. We all know who captured the personal computer market!

What Are the Different Layers of Culture and Climate?

Culture is usually defined as a multi-level phenomenon. This section discusses the differences between the societal and governmental levels.

The Societal Level: Individualism, Authority, and Trust

The society with the highest emphasis on individualism in the Western world is undoubtedly the United States. This individualism may be overstated in retrospect (Coontz, 1992), but it fuels a distrust of government and authority. This section considers the nature of the American emphasis on freedom and individualism and how it may contribute to distrust of government, loss of respect for authority, and a growing sense of entitlement.

Freedom and Individualism

Despite the safeguards the American Founding Fathers put in place to avoid the concentration of political power, individual Americans have always been suspicious of public authority, especially a strong central government. Simultaneously, government was expected to protect its citizens, help develop the country, and serve those in need (Croly, 1914). For most of the nineteenth century, settlers endured the hardships of everyday living through unlimited optimism and an unshaken belief in the promise of American life. This belief was tested toward the end of that century as for-profit organizations industrialized, people moved to the cities in high numbers, and government regulations diminished individualism. These changes strengthened long-standing concerns about the future of American culture and the role government could and ought to play in it.

The first to express concerns about the effect of these changes was Alexis de Tocqueville. He wrote in the mid-1830s: "It is a strange thing to see with what sort of feverish ardor Americans pursue well-being and how they show themselves constantly tormented by a vague fear of not having chosen the shortest route that can lead to [their] success" (de Tocqueville, 2000, p. 511). He further argued that Americans came to place their personal fortune before others, isolating themselves from their neighbors and disregarding the prosperity of society. Americans, he wrote, "...owe nothing to anyone, they expect so to seek nothing from anyone; they are in the habit of always considering themselves in isolation, and they willingly fancy that their whole destiny is in their hands" (de Tocqueville, 2000, p. 514).

This sense of isolation was further compounded by the relatively rapid transition from an agrarian and craft-based society to an industrialized and urbanized one in the late nineteenth century. As a result, people moved from rural areas where they knew their neighbors to cities where they did not; de Tocqueville had warned that this kind of individualism could lead to selfishness. This prediction was repeated 80 years later when, in 1909, Herbert Croly observed that the traditional American confidence in individual freedom had created a morally and socially undesirable distribution of wealth (Nisbet, 1969).

To Croly (1909), this undesirable distribution of wealth came from political and economic pressures favoring individualism over serving the collective members of society. He advocated constructive individualism, where individuals serve their fellow citizens. Five years later, he urged that the prevailing live-and-let-live ideology of Jeffersonian individualism ought to be abandoned in favor of a live-and-help-live ideology called progressive democracy (Croly, 1914). Some argue that this live-and-let-live ideology has only become more pronounced so that Americans now live in a time where freedom is defined as the right to be left alone (Howard, 2001).

Shifts caused by an undesirable distribution of wealth were not limited to the United States. On both sides of the Atlantic, industrialization and urbanization alienated people from their work and social environments to the point that it was believed that people were adrift (Lippman, 1961 [1914]). What could the government do in this situation? In Europe, citizens could turn to a state whose administrative capabilities had been in the making for centuries and tested before the introduction of democracy. European governments and bureaucracies quickly responded to social and economic change by building a welfare state based on minimal equality of conditions. This meant that the government took responsibility for providing extensive welfare services so that everyone had a social safety net (Flora & Heidenheimer, 1984; Esping-Andersen, 1990).

In the United States, democracy was shaped by the demand for individualism and a distrust of government well before creating the administrative state (Nelson, 1982). American government initially took steps comparable to those in European countries, especially in support of Civil War veterans. In the early twentieth century, though, it moved away from this and favored a limited state advancing minimal equality of opportunity. This meant that the government created the conditions under which citizens could get ahead if they tried (Skocpol, 1992).

In countries with a single leader or a few elite leaders, the notions of freedom and individualism are constrained. But this does not mean that citizens are not supportive of their government. On the contrary, for many, it is viewed as a trade-off between the security of service delivery for everyone versus the freedom of political expression. In this situation, trust in government is based on the efficiency, quality, and continuity of service delivery and not on the potential impact of changes in political leadership.

Loss of Authority

The concern with a loss of authority is not vital for citizens who are governed by a single or a few elite leaders. This can be because the value to the collective of government service provision outweighs concerns about the reach of the government's authority. By comparison, Western democracies operate in societies that have experienced a loss of respect for authority juxtaposed with a strong sense of individual entitlement where individuals rely less on themselves and more on government. What can explain this apparent contradiction that people want both more and less government?

During the twentieth century, various American and European authors expressed the feeling of losing government authority in general (Lasch, 1978). This feeling has been forcefully and frequently expressed, so it is helpful to summarize the main elements because it tells us something about American culture and perceptions of government's economic role.

The feeling that authority had been lost was related to the massive consequences industrialization and urbanization had on diminishing the social ties between people. In the early twentieth century, one social commentator called industrialization and urbanization the "acids of modernity" dissolving the old social order (Lippman, 1957 [1929). As a result, people became less connected in the cities than before the industrial revolution.

As the "acids of modernity" ate away at social ties and connections, it was argued that citizens became alienated from their original communities and traditions. Fewer social ties between people undermined the ancient idea that law reflected reality. This meant that people increasingly felt that law was a means for creating, not reflecting, reality (Nisbet, 1975).

In other words, you could no longer rely on tradition to guide people's actions. Loss of authority was not only visible in the political arena, where citizens appeared to have less confidence and less respect for government. It was also seen in social relations between parents and children, teachers and students, and supervisors and subordinates (Arendt, 1958). Consequently, people could no longer rely upon a shared understanding of governmental authority and social values.

Authors who argue that there is a crisis of authority in the Western world see it as a decline in societal values (Friedman, 1990). Alternatively, how people define authority may have changed over time. Nowadays, the authority may not rest solely with the government but can also be created by people, as individuals, or in groups or organizations. In this light, the idea that authority is a human-made "thing" is not bad. On the contrary, it is an excellent example of what democracy can be: citizens making the law instead of being mere subjects to the law.

One final comment must be made regarding the government's loss of authority. It has been argued that little data testify to such a loss of authority (Bok, 1996; see also Shoen, 2013; and Gurri, 2018 who pays attention to the role of social media). However, one could argue that the declining trust in public institutions is indirectly a sign of loss of authority. Indeed, when people suffer because of natural disasters, are attacked on the street by a stranger, or have a dispute with each other, they may not be able to seek mediation or get compensation by themselves. Instead, they turn to the government for help in today's rural and urban communities. This is because government has sufficient authority for people to rely on its intervention to make things right. Therefore, citizens expect quite a lot from the government.

Despite an alleged reduction in authority, citizens still expect their governments to provide a wide range of services. Many argue they are entitled to public services. With the growth in public services available to disadvantaged persons, such as food stamps and unemployment benefits, social security, and public health care, democracies have become redistributive governments. How that redistributive government is appreciated varies. In continental-European democracies, social services are regarded as fundamentally social and human rights for those who cannot care for themselves (children; the elderly, physically or mentally challenged; the unhoused). Social services are generally perceived as a hand-up in hard times, not a hand-out that is necessary because individuals have failed to provide for themselves. However, as the sense of individual responsibility declined, the United States entered the Age of Entitlement. During the 1980s and 1990s, people came to think that the government should do more for everyone, not just for those who had fallen on hard times (Samuelson, 1995).

The Governmental Level: Origins and Appearance

There are various ways in which government culture can be characterized. To illustrate this, we examine British origins and American originality contributed to a culture emphasizing the separation of powers, checks and balances, a mix of a weak and strong state in a confederal system, and the appearance of government in buildings and what this visually communicates about the relationship between government and the people it serves.

A Mix of British Origins and American Originality

Perhaps more than in any other country, the American people struggle with a fundamental distrust of government, born from the way the people in the colonies were treated by the English king, his government, and Parliament. Efforts to increase control over the colonies to extract more revenue without consultation turned British colonists into American nationalists. The Boston Tea Party, with its cry of "No taxation without representation" was, at first, viewed as nothing but a skirmish of some rebels. But it was just one event in a series of British actions and American responses that reset the power and authority balance between the British and the Americans.

Its British origins define the nature of the American government system as much as the Founding Fathers' originality defines it. The continuity of British traditions is visible in the fragmented political structure, already described by Locke's political theory that the individual must be protected from the state. British heritage is also evident in the manner of representation, decided by the competition of different societal, territory-based interests through the voting process (Diamond, 1997). Like Britain, the United States emphasizes societal initiative, self-regulation, and the market. And, as described below, in both countries, the rapid growth of capitalism and the market produced a weak state.

Another example of the continuity of British origins is the legal system. In both countries, the law is referred to as common law, meaning that laws come from the lowest courts and are procedural. Common law was the means of conflict resolution between people (Knill, 2001). During the twentieth century, however, primary and secondary laws have become comparable to common law and generally supersede common law in sheer volume (Hurst, 1977; Raadschelders, 2017). At the same time, the common law origins remain essential as the volume of judicial rulings and the use of judgment by a jury of one's peers persist.

A final example of continuity is that both British and American governments initially tended to rely on amateurs, that is, government by gentlemen born to rule rather than educated to administer. By contrast, France and Germany have used trained professional administrators in government since the early eighteenth century (Mosher, 1982). Toward the end of the nineteenth century, the American government shifted to a government by specialists rather than personal relationships or prior experience as the basis for government employment. In Britain, this change was made after World War II (Rhodes, 1996).

As pervasive as these British origins have proven, there are also quite a few new features Americans introduced to government practice. These include a written Constitution developed by a Convention instead of imposed from above, a Bill of Rights, the separation of powers because of a distrust of centralized government power, a system of judicial review, and a federal system balancing national and subnational governments.

Separation of Powers and Checks-and-Balances

The United States would establish a *novus ordo seclorum* or a *new order for the ages*. Citizens expected and wanted something different from governments than what they had experienced in their homelands or countries of origin. During the years between the Confederate-Continental Congress and Washington's presidency, the debate focused on how to fragment political power to overcome the absolutism, corruption, and centralization common in European governments at the time. The language in the Constitution and the Bill of Rights characterizes the American political system in a nutshell. It is a society-led state, or a government by civil society, where political influence fundamentally rests in and comes from the values held by people in society (Badie & Birnbaum, 1983). Through government, society rules, and it rules to protect the individual's inalienable rights.

The United States is a Western country claiming a "stateless" origin. Stateless society refers to a situation where a country is governed without the conventional political and administrative institutions and organizations (Nettl, 1968; Stillman, 1999). The twentieth-century shift to increased and decisive government intervention created the phenomenon of the administrative state. However, the change from a stateless society to an administrative state has been more difficult for Americans than for continental European citizens due to individualism as a fundamental societal value (Waldo, 1984; Evans et al., 1989[1985]).

What the Founding Fathers did in America in 1787 in Philadelphia was nothing short of revolutionary. They created a foundation of government theorized about but never put into practice: separation of powers balanced by a system of checks and balances. The separation of powers avoids the potential for a concentration of power in the hands of one institution or individual. The system of checks and balance insures that each government branch can monitor the other branches. However, citizens cannot take democracy for granted. For democracy to work, citizens must be active participants. They also must understand the position and role of government in society, especially when they know government's position and role in democratic political systems differs from its role and position in authoritarian political systems. Ask anyone growing up and living in a democratic political system whether they would prefer to live in, for instance, Nazi Germany or contemporary North Korea. That the survival of democracy depends on the active engagement of informed citizens becomes clear when we consider that in many democratic systems of government, extreme right-wing parties are on the rise. How fragile it is became clear when witnessing the January 6, 2021, events at the U.S. Capitol building. At the same time, it seemed strong enough as the insurrection failed.

American Political Culture

Political culture is often described as being a strong or a weak state. Strong states have centuries of experience with a centralized, interventionist government. Governments are powerful, and civil servants are generally trusted and highly involved in policy and decision-making.

In weak states, the perceived role of government is to improve the conditions wherein individuals can take free action in a society with multiple semi-independent groups (Vincent, 1987). More than two centuries ago, Benjamin Franklin observed that when everyone takes care of themselves, all boats will rise. This phrase meant that individual responsibility automatically leads to improved conditions for everyone. In a weak state, the government is suspect, and civil servants are kept at arm's length in policymaking (Bok, 2001). However, considering how much national and subnational levels of government have improved people's way of life in the past 200 years and to what extent people expect government support, like many other countries, the United States can no longer be characterized as a weak state.

Even though the United States is characterized as a strong state, there are differences in the role of government in its society. These differences are evident in the subnational government types caused by immigration patterns (Woodard, 2011) and westward expansion (Hackett Fischer, 1989). In the commonwealth tradition of the northeast, the settlers, who mainly came from northwest Europe, adopted municipal self-government based on a constitution where state government does not play a significant role. Spaniards and Frenchmen initially settled in the southern part of the United States, and just as in Spain or France, a tradition of centralized state government was adopted. Over time, the state level of government in the northeast became as important as the municipal level of government. In contrast, the county and city governments became as important as the state level in the south. The north and the west were not settled until the middle of the nineteenth century and appear to have more in common with the northeast (Elazar, 1966). As people became more mobile, these differences became muted.

Elazar (1972) hypothesized that two contrasting views characterize American political culture. On the one hand, the political system is a marketplace where individuals interact, and bargain based on self-interest. On the other hand, it is a commonwealth where individuals create and uphold the best government possible. These two contrasting views are influenced by three political subcultures Elazar distinguished. We discuss each using the sale of liquor as an example to illustrate how different political subcultures affect what government does.

In the *individualist culture*, government is a marketplace where bureaucracy is undesirable, politics is a dirty business, and parties compete for power. Government action is mainly concerned with regulating the economy and less concerned with morality policies that regulate individual behaviors. In an individualist culture, liquor can be sold anywhere, at any time (Meier, 1994).

The *moralist political culture* perceives government as a commonwealth, bureaucracy as the positive means to enhance welfare, politics as a healthy business, and political competition dominated by societal issues. Therefore, in the moralist political culture, the government is much more interventionist. For example, it may require that liquor be sold in locations separate from vulnerable populations such as minors. However, liquor policy will be established based on extensive consultation with citizens.

Finally, the *traditionalist political culture* is one where government exists to maintain order, bureaucracy is negatively regarded, and politics is a privilege. Party competition is mainly conducted between elites. This type of government political culture strictly applies existing regulations for liquor sales and does not seek citizen input.

Generally, one can say that traditionalism was influential in the south. Moralism was intense in the northeast, far north, and northwest. Individualism was strong in the northern states of the Midwest and the western states (Elazar, 1966). In later years, individualism rose in various states (Bowman & Kearney, 1993). So, while Americans, as a nation, have high levels of agreement, there are different political cultures and climates at the subnational level. The same is the case in many other countries; at a 30,000-foot level, most countries will appear homogeneous, but closer inspection will reveal different political cultures at a country's subnational and regional level.

What Are the Dimensions for Comparing Culture and Climate?

We distinguished between the societal and organizational levels to structure the discussion of culture and climate. The dimensions of culture and climate have become more nuanced in the scholarly literature since the early 1980s. Most attention has focused on an organization's technical and managerial levels because it is assumed that these are the ones most easily reformed. However, this is too limited. Take, for example, the prevalent metaphor that suggests that bureaucracy is a machine since it seeks to provide services in the most efficient manner (the societal level), is the most suitable to offer a wide range and number of services (the governmental level), and can be fine-tuned (the organizational level). The individual level is also important in bureaucracies where employees are viewed as replaceable cogs in the machine.

Systematic research into culture and how it cuts across analytical levels has grown in the past 50 years. As a result, a set of five dimensions of organizational culture and how these translate into specific school and family relations and state/government cultures in various countries has become very popular (Hofstede et al., 2010). These five dimensions are power distance (large or small), individualism or collectivism, masculinity or femininity, uncertainty avoidance (large or small), and time orientation (short or long term). Each of the dimensions identified by Hofstede and his colleagues (2010) is discussed below; however, pure cases of the dimensions in societies do not exist. More recent work, found on the Hofstede Culture Compass (see: Hofstede Insights), will give you further detail about different countries' cultures.

Large or Small Power Distance

Countries with small power distances tend to emphasize decentralization. Regarding the government, small power distance countries tend to change their political system in an evolutionary rather than a revolutionary way. As a result, there is more discussion, much less violence in politics, and a tendency to have pluralist governments based on majority voting. Finally, countries with small power distances are wealthier globally, with a strong and sizeable middle class.

In large power distance countries, the situation is quite different. Officials show their status. The political system is much less easy to change unless through revolutionary force. Politics, in general, tends to be more violent, and political party competition is more limited. This is a situation more characteristic of developing countries.

Individualist or Collectivist Cultures

In individualist societies, the government treats everybody as equal under the law. At the same time, individual freedom is regarded as higher than the ideology of equality of condition. Organizations pay more attention to the task at hand than the relationships between employees and supervisors. The nature of the subordinate-manager relationship is based on a labor contract and not one perceived as an extended family as in more collectivist countries. In individualist countries, government plays a restricted role in the economy.

In collectivist countries, the individual is less important than the community and society. Government is also less inhibited, adopting an interventionist role for the good of the whole. The United States policy and service reforms following the Great Depression regarding social security and the 1960s changes concerning civil rights are illustrative. States in Western Europe have collectivist values that are like those in the United States, yet they protect individual freedoms to a considerable extent. The protection of individual freedom is lower in the less democratic developing countries even though collectivism is also high.

Masculine or Feminine Cultures

This dimension relates to the degree to which countries and organizations value masculine or feminine characteristics. In a masculine culture, gender roles are clearly defined, mom takes care of the home, dad goes to work. Regarding the government, masculine societies support the strong competitor, are more focused on correcting behavior, and embrace an adversarial political-administrative system. Indeed, public sector organizational culture in the United States has features of a marketplace where only the strong survive.

In feminine cultures, gender lines are blurred or non-existent as males and females perform the same functions. For example, the Scandinavian countries and the Netherlands are highly feminine. This means men also change diapers and do the laundry, while women change tires and paint the house. The differences reflect valuing the quality of life and caring for others, which is more frequently found in a feminine culture rather than in a masculine one.

High or Low Uncertainty Avoidance

The fourth dimension of societal culture is the degree of uncertainty avoidance. High uncertainty avoidance countries generally have a negative attitude toward political and administrative officials and the legal system. Regarding the government, high uncertainty avoidance countries such as Germany, Greece, and Portugal have a bias in favor of precision and punctuality and, thus, emphasize detailed laws. Many civil servants have a law degree.

In low uncertainty avoidance governmental culture, civil servants have wide-ranging educational backgrounds. Low uncertainty avoidance cultures accept and feel comfortable in unstructured settings. People in these cultures tend to be more pragmatic and tolerant of change. They understand that situations change and try to have as few rules as possible. Examples include Denmark, the United Kingdom, and the United States.

Short- or Long-Term Orientations

The final dimension of culture is a short-term or long-term orientation. Short-term cultures seek immediate gratification of needs, demand measurable value for money, and subject the organizations that implement policies to extensive performance accountability. The electoral cycle forces public officials to focus on the short term, and elected officials will not be inclined to think beyond surviving the next election. For-profit organizations in short-term orientation countries tend to focus on the bottom line and this year's profits. Canada, the United Kingdom, and the United States tend to have short-term orientations.

Long-term orientations focus on the future, even if it means giving up short-term gratification. In countries like China, Japan, and South Korea, there is an emphasis on the long-term and society values perseverance, adapting, and saving for the future.

Cross-National and Cross-Time Variations

It is crucial to remember that these value dimensions will not change, but the nature of these dimensions in a country can change as societal values evolve. A group of scholars replicated the work done by Hofstede 25 years later in the late 1960s and found that the United States had simultaneously become more feminine and much stronger on uncertainty avoidance. In contrast, power distance and individualism rankings had not changed by much (Fernandez et al., 1997).

It is equally important to emphasize that the value dimensions, and thus cultures, vary from country to country. Here is an example. American Professor Stevens taught at a renowned business school in France and provided his French, German, and English students with a problem-solving exercise concerning conflict management. The French students were inclined to solve the problem with their immediate superior. To them, the organization was, first and foremost, a pyramid of people. Germans opted to consider first the proper procedures for conflict resolution. Professor Stevens concluded that they viewed organizations more as well-oiled machines that merely needed to be correctly calibrated through more detailed rules. Finally, the English students were guided by the characteristics of the situation. To them, the organization was a village market where neither hierarchy nor rules determined what should happen. Expanding on these metaphors, in discussions with Asian colleagues, Hofstede identified an organizational type where the organization is like an extended family, where the manager or owner is like a father or grandfather who is the ultimate authority. In addition, the employees are often highly loyal to the organization and stay for a long time (Hofstede et al., 2010).

How Is Culture Reflected in Expectations for Public Servants?

During birth of the American state, the organization of its government was structured to be different from the European centralized and monarchical governments. However, the Founding Fathers and their successors adopted the time-honored practice of appointing people to public service based on nepotism. This is where jobs are accessible based on kinship or friendship rather than merit and expertise. Initially, political appointments were limited to 12% of federal employees (Van Riper, 1983). However, nearly 40% of President John Adams's high-level appointees were relatives of other high-level appointees in his or President George Washington's administration. Of President Jefferson's appointees, 34% were related to other appointees in his or earlier administrations. Thus, elite relations more than legal expectations strongly influenced the development of a fledgling democracy.

Consider a second example: many years ago, government workers had a different understanding of what was necessary to get a public job and what was acceptable to do once they had the position. During the nineteenth century, many civil servants obtained their jobs through an inheritance and then assumed a right to their office like owning property! They claimed that one could not be fired for inadequate work or behavior when the job is a property right. If the job is part of your estate, you can pass it on to your son, cousin, nephew, or another family member. Many claim that because of nepotism, patronage, and assumed property rights, American public service was plagued by fraud and corruption from the start. For example, President Jackson's customs collector in New York City left for Europe taking $1,250,000 in public funds (Nelson, 1982). President Jackson was in office between 1829 and 1837. Imaging how much $1.25M is in your currency today! But government workers were not the only ones who abused their positions. Between 1820–1850, Senate leaders such as Thomas Benton (MS), Henry Clay (KY), John Calhoun (SC), and Daniel Webster (MA), as well as various cabinet members and at least three vice presidents, accepted bribes (Douglas, 1952).

By the late 1800s, trust in government had deteriorated rapidly. Government reformers were concerned that these abuses eroded the public's trust in government. What could be done to improve it? In the 1880s, the civil service system was reformed, explicitly creating a non-partisan administrative class hoping it would eliminate the nepotism, favoritism, and corruption rampant in the nineteenth century. Creating the federal merit-based civil service was touted to accomplish this goal.

The civil service reform movement that occurred after the Civil War was much more concerned with improving the morality and righteousness of government than with efficiency. Several practitioners whose reform efforts would make a lasting impact on the American government presented their ideas on the moral high grounds of merit, service, public interest, mission, and nonpartisanship (Walker, 1990). Among them, Woodrow Wilson's early writings expressed concern about restoring the moral qualities of the government to ensure its trustworthiness, honesty, and responsibility (Stillman, 1973).

For several decades, attention was mainly directed at the ethics of individual behavior. In this climate, the International City Managers Association (ICMA; nowadays, the International City and County Managers Association) created one of the earliest codes of ethics in 1924. This was the conclusion of four decades of reform toward a more professional, responsive, and less corrupt civil service. The ICMA ethics code has 12 elements related to the integrity of the public office, the obligation to serve the public interest, the impartial support of elected officials, and corruption.

In 1972, the ICMA adopted guidelines to clarify the codes through additional guidance. Code 12 on corruption had the most changes adding seven guidelines. Each of the ICMA codes is considered by some to be the most elaborate and operational of all public sector codes (Cooper, 1998). However, others point out that the ICMA codes are not as applicable because they must be understood and interpreted in the context of political theory and the administrative state (Pugh, 1991) which makes them difficult to apply uniformly in different situations. Furthermore, few would argue that these codes instill such character traits as integrity, love, respect, and personal courage, which are, at the least, implied in codes two and three of the ICMA Code of Ethics (Chandler, 1994).

At the end of World War II in 1945, reformers' attention shifted to organizational ethics. Advancing an ethically responsible work culture and climate increasingly became an organization's responsibility. The concern was no longer about individual civil servants' ethical behavior but about securing accountability through organizational engineering (Gortner, 1995). Public sector ethics would now depend upon institutional arrangements as much as on mental attitudes and moral qualities (Appleby, 1952).

Since the 1970s, the understanding of public sector ethics has moved away from prescriptions about the inner state of mind to preventative laws and regulations that assume that outside circumstances or actions may lead to "impaired mental states" (Stark, 2000). So, in a way, you can say that ethics in the twentieth century has become codified or written down in ethics codes. Several Presidential Executive Orders deal with accepting gifts, using government information for personal gain, conflict of interest, lobbying, and so on (Roberts & Doss Jr., 1997). If a kind of behavior is not described somewhere as unethical, then it must be OK!

Ethics and Integrity for Today's Civil Servants

Many professional and governmental organizations, including the federal Department of the Interior's Ethics Office, have created principles of ethical behavior and developed codes of ethics for their members. These organizations have also identified typical situations where unethical behavior may occur. These are described below.

Financial impropriety is usually called corruption, defined as the acceptance of financial or other advantages from third parties in exchange for services, or as maladministration which concerns behaviors that demonstrate lack of judgment. The definition of corruption is generally limited to violations that involve money. In Table 4.1 you see examples of maladministration and corruption.

Few disagree that laziness, tardiness, drunkenness, dishonesty, unwanted sexual advances, and disloyalty are examples of unacceptable behavior. Pursuing

Table 4.1 Types of maladministration and corruption

Source of guidance	Maladministration	Corruption
Subjective integrity: internal moral compass	Laziness, drunkenness on the job, tardiness, disloyalty, dishonesty, predisposition, the pursuit of power, nepotism, partiality, blind obedience	Undue influence, accepting gifts
Objective ethics: external moral codes	Revolving door Personal use of office supplies	Personals payments for public acts, fraud, bribery, self-dealing, abuse of office, personal gain from public office

power is not wrong, but consider what you find preferable: an executive who pursues power for selfish reasons such as acquiring possible financial advantages, one who desires power for vanity, or one who seeks power as a means of defining what is suitable for the public? Partiality and predisposition are not acceptable behavior in civil servants. We expect them to be impartial in their dealings with clients (whether citizens or not). On the other hand, some degree of bias is expected from elected officials. Therefore, civil servants should reflect upon the degree to which their values may predispose them when developing or implementing policy. Nepotism, the appointment of relatives or friends in critical positions, is generally unacceptable except for jobs requiring legislative approval. In various countries, political appointments at the highest administration level are allowed so that the policy agendas of elected officials are prioritized. This practice, to some, may seem like patronage. However, they are a very small proportion of all appointments to the civil service.

When blind obedience occurs, individual moral judgment is suspended. Under normal circumstances, individuals, including civil servants, can resist specific actions if they seriously violate their sense of morality. In a totalitarian government, this might not be so easy. Even in a democracy, it is not easy to stand up for what you believe is right or publicly report on company violations or violations of public trust. Ask any whistleblower whether it was worth it (Bovens, 1998)! While many will say it was, they may also acknowledge that they might have thought twice had they known about the pain and suffering whistleblowing would cause them and their families (Taylor, 2002). Who would acknowledge that it was not worth it?

Blind obedience deserves a little more attention because this involves a case where civil servants can be confronted with a significant dilemma. The primacy of politics doctrine requires civil servants to serve the objectives of the directly elected representatives to the best of their abilities. And the sovereignty of the people doctrine demands that public servants serve the common good. Yet, they must suspend their moral convictions in obeying these two doctrines. Does this mean that they must obey, regardless of what they value? Or is there a point where individual morality supersedes organizational command?

To find this out, in the mid-1960s, Yale University social psychologist Stanley Milgram designed an experiment to test the following hypothesis: when an authority figure gives regular people instructions to do something that might hurt another person, at least some of them will obey, under carefully designed circumstances. Participants believed the experiment measured the effect of punishment on recall memory. A teacher had to administer an electric shock to a learner when they made a mistake recalling a pair of words. With every mistake, the voltage of the shock would go up. In front of every teacher, the shock generator went from 15 volts (slight shock) to 450 volts (dangerously severe shock).

The learner in the experiment was an actor strapped in an "electric chair," whose loud crying of pain or extent of body-jerking varied with voltage levels. If the teachers asked who would take responsibility if anything went wrong, the experimenter replied that he would. The teacher could see what the shocks did to the learner. At 150 volts, the learner begged to be released; at 180 volts, he cried that the pain was too much; at 300 volts, the yelling and screaming were enormous; and after 330 volts, the learner could no longer respond. Of 40 teachers, 25 (or 63%) went up to 450 volts. When asked why they said because they were told to do so. These teachers came from all walks of life. In other words, we may all be susceptible to the power of command.

Milgram concluded that obedience increases when responsibility is divided—that is when someone else can be held accountable for your actions. Changing the experiment to emphasize personal responsibility where the teacher thought they were responsible significantly decreased obedience. Also, the teacher's resistance to specific actions was slowly broken down because the experiment started with a minor punishment that was increased in steps (Milgram, 1974).

Will others in the same circumstances respond the same? Replications of the Milgram experiment have confirmed that participants will respond the same. For example, more than 85% of the teachers administered a lethal electric shock in Germany. At the University of Utrecht, second-year students, who had learned about the Milgram experiment in Psychology 101 the previous year, behaved no differently than "teachers" who had no way of knowing about this famous experiment.

When in a situation of peer pressure and superiority, good people will be hard-pressed to behave inhumanely (Zimbardo et al., 1973). This was the case with the Abu Ghraib prison scandal in Iraq, where Iraqi prisoners were humiliated and psychologically tortured by young American soldiers (Adams & Balfour, 2004). When is a system evil? A lack of supervision, lack of enforced accountability, and heightened secrecy about what goes on inside an organization can dehumanize human beings. Also, people usually are induced into certain behaviors gradually, and it only takes one or two leaders to make the rest follow their example (Zimbardo et al., 1973). Some scholars argue that bureaucracy, as a type of organization, dehumanizes people and leads normal human beings into behaviors they would not condone under normal circumstances (Hummel, 1977).

In Table 4.1, the revolving door is placed in the middle because it includes behaviors that can occur in any of the four cells. The revolving door is a conflict of interest that refers to a job or financial opportunity after public service. The individual can take advantage of knowledge gained while holding public office. The Ethics Reform Act of 1989 included revolving door restrictions for Members of Congress (Roberts, 2001).

Dealing with corruption and maladministration has been a focus throughout the twentieth century in the United States and elsewhere. In the United States, Executive Order 12834 on January 20, 1993, specifically imposed a five-year lobbying ban on former executive branch employees, a five-year ban against representing a foreign government or a for-profit organization after participation in trade negotiations on behalf of the U.S. government, and it wholly prohibited activity on behalf of a foreign government after leaving federal service.

Other Executive Orders forbid monetary gain from public office. Executive Order 10939, adopted on May 5, 1961, prohibits heads and assistant heads of federal departments and agencies and full-time members of federal boards and commissions appointed by the president and White House staff from accepting fees. It also advises these public officials to avoid behavior such as using public office for personal gain, preferential treatment of individuals, or partiality that might negatively affect public confidence in government. In addition, Executive Order 11222 (May 10, 1965, and clarified by Executive Order 12674 on April 12, 1989) forbids the acceptance of gifts, self-dealing, and outside employment (see examples in Table 4.2).

Examples to Test Your Understanding

Scenario 1: Arm's Length Transaction

Margot is a civil engineer, three years out of college, married with one child and another on the way. She and her wife want to move to a larger home, but they cannot afford it. Margot works at a public transportation agency; her primary responsibility is obtaining federal highway and bridge maintenance grants and judging bids from contractors. Margot's brother-in-law, Joe, happens to own a construction company. Last week, at a family cook-out, he told Margot he submitted a bid to the transportation agency for highway and bridge

Table 4.2 Definitions and examples of corrupt actions

Abuse of office	When one official accepts something of value from a private party whose interest he or she can affect in office, but who must pay full market value for services delivered so that the official can claim not to be beholden; for instance, a political appointee who can influence in his or her official capacity the interests of a private company, and whose law firm provides full-value legal services to that private company
Bribery	When an official has the ability to influence the interests of a private party who gives him or her something of value, and to whom the civil servant then becomes beholden to perform an official act by way of compensation
Private gain from public office	A high-level official accepting a lucrative contract from a publisher to write memoirs as soon as leaving office
Private payment for public acts	An official accepting payment from a private party but without having the official capacity to influence private interests; for instance, when private companies underwrite the public salary
Self-dealing	When an official can affect his interests
Undue influence	Involves two officials: one can change interest in the official role, the other is directly associated with the private interest but not able to influence it in the official role

Source: Stark (2000). *Conflict of interest in American public life*. Harvard University Press, pp. 7–8, 36–37, 40

maintenance. He hoped that Margot would help him since business had been slow lately. Joe mentions that there could be something in it for her. When Margot considers the various bids, she notices that Joe's is slightly higher than most. In earlier contracts with the transportation agency, Joe developed a reputation for meeting deadlines and delivering quality work. A bid from another company is significantly lower. Still, there is much less known about the quality of that company's work. Which is a better use of taxpayer funds: to pick the lowest bid or to select a slightly higher bid that can be depended upon to be the best value. By the way, no one knows that Margot is John's sister-in-law. What should Margot do?

Scenario 2: Conflict of Interest

Antonio graduated 20 years ago with a Master's in Environmental Science degree from the Department of Chemistry. He has worked on and off in government positions for ten years. During this time, he also worked for consulting firms when not in government employment. After his last job in the energy agency, he started his consulting firm, lobbying on proposed industrial waste legislation. Because of his expertise and professionalism, he is asked to accept a political appointment at the energy agency's executive level. He is responsible for developing legislation to relax industrial waste standards and contracting and outsourcing clean-up operations. Government organizations frequently contract with for-profit companies to clean up dumpsites. Antonio had several of these firms as clients of his consulting business. Would accepting the job at the energy agency raise a conflict-of-interest concern?

Each of these scenarios describes a type of inappropriate public employee behavior. Margot's decision is influenced by the possibility of helping her brother-in-law and perhaps getting some extra income. Antonio's political appointment may well create conflict between his interests as a business owner and his responsibility as a civil servant. These scenes do not have the same level of seriousness, but all have to do with accountability. In each case, the public employee in question is confronted with the possibility of overstepping the boundaries of acceptable conduct. The line between acceptable and unacceptable behavior varies with time and place. Bottom line: Ensuring public confidence in government requires ethical behavior from all persons who work on behalf of the government. It is commonly said that "Public Service is a Public Trust."

Chapter Summary

We started this chapter with definitions of culture and climate to help you understand the differences and how this impacts government operations. There are two different layers for studying culture and climate: societal and governmental. One could also examine five dimensions, including power distance and other things, such as uncertainty avoidance, to understand the culture and climate of a sovereign nation. Next, we described the development of ethics codes and how they can focus on creating shared administrative values as well as provide guidance for what to do in specific situations. Culture, climate, and ethical codes (implicit or explicit) are powerful forces for setting expectations for appropriate bureaucratic behavior and the level of maladministration and corruption that society considers "acceptable."

Practical Applications for Students

1. Why do we refer to government as bureaucracy? Could you say that for-profit organizations are also bureaucracies? Elaborate your answer.
2. Provide examples of what makes most non-governmental organizations operate like bureaucracies. Does this suggest that societal culture can impact all organizations similarly? Justify your conclusion.
3. Could administrative evil be considered part of the culture or the climate of an organization? How might your answer change based on the situational context and time.
4. How does social culture influence the expectations we, as a society, have for ethical behavior? How can organizational climate change expectations of what is ethical behavior for civil servants?

In-Class Instructional Suggestions

1. Discuss examples of bureaucratic organizations in your country's for-profit and non-profit sectors. Illustrate how these are the same and how they are different from expected activities in governmental organizations.
2. Discuss whether there are political subcultures in your country and how these are visible. You can consider the literature on social cleavages based on religion (protestant or catholic in the Netherlands in the past; French and English speakers in Canada; aboriginals and descendants from imprisoned colonists in Australia, etc.). Engage the students in discovering the ways cleavages make the political system of your country unique.
3. How important are political appointees in the political-administrative system of your country? There are multiple layers of political appointees in the United States between the career civil service and the political executive. In other countries, this is far more limited or even non-existent.
4. How prevalent are ethics codes in public sector organizations in your country? Use recent examples to show how ethics codes do not work as they were intended and how people can purposefully decide to ignore ethics codes and guidance for appropriate behavior. Invite students to reflect on how characteristics of the situation and the person may have contributed to purposeful disregard of the ethics codes.

References

Adams, G. B., & Balfour, D. B. (2004). *Unmasking administrative evil*. M.E. Sharpe.
Albrow, M. (1970). *Bureaucracy*. Macmillan.
Appleby, P. H. (1952). *Morality and administration in democratic government*. Louisiana State University Press.
Arendt, H. (1958). What was authority? In C. J. Friedrich (Ed.), *Authority* (pp. 81–112). Harvard University Press.
Badie, B., & Birnbaum, P. (1983). *The sociology of the state*. The University of Chicago Press.
Bok, D. C. (1996). *The state of the nation: Government and the quest for a better society*. Harvard University Press.
Bok, D. C. (2001). *The trouble with the government*. Harvard University Press.
Bovens, M. A. P. (1998). *The quest for responsibility: Accountability and citizenship in complex organisations*. Cambridge University Press.
Bowman, A. O.'. M., & Kearney, R. C. (1993). *State and local government*. Houghton Mifflin Company.
Chandler, R. C. (1994). Deontological dimensions of administrative ethics. In T. L. Cooper (Ed.), *Handbook of administrative ethics* (pp. 147–156). Marcel Dekker.
Coontz, S. (1992). *The way we never were: American families and the nostalgia trap*. Basic Books.
Cooper, T. L. (1998). *The responsible administrator: An approach to ethics for the administrative role?* (4th ed.). Jossey-Bass Publishers.
Croly, H. (1909). *The promise of American life*. Routledge.
Croly, H. (1914). *Progressive democracy*. The Macmillan Company.
de Tocqueville, A. (2000). *Democracy in America*. The University of Chicago Press.
Diamond, J. (1997). *Guns, germs, and steel: The fates of human societies*. W.W. Norton & Company.
Douglas, P. H. (1952). *Ethics in government*. Harvard University Press.
Elazar, D. J. (1966). *American federalism: A view from the States*. Thomas Y. Crowell Company.
Elazar, D. J. (1972). *The American partnership*. University of Chicago Press.
Esping-Andersen, G. (1990). *The three worlds of welfare capitalism*. Princeton University Press.
Evans, P. R., Rueschemeyer, D., & Skocpol, T. (Eds.) (1989 [1985]). *Bringing the state back*. Cambridge University Press.
Fernandez, D. R., Carlson, D. S., Stepina, L. P., & Nicholson, J. D. (1997). Hofstede's country classification: 25 years later. *Journal of Social Psychology, 137*(1), 43–55.
Flora, P., & Heidenheimer, A. J. (Eds.). (1984). *The development of welfare states in Europe and America*. Transaction Publishers.
Friedman, R. B. (1990). On the concept of authority in political philosophy. In J. Raz (Ed.), *Authority* (pp. 56–91). New York University Press.
Gortner, H. F. (1995). Ethics and public personnel administration. In S. W. Hays & R. C. Kearney (Eds.), *Public personnel administration. Problems and prospects* (3rd ed., pp. 273–288). Prentice-Hall.
Gurri, M. (2018). *The revolt of the public and the crisis of authority in the new millennium*. Stripe Press.
Hackett Fischer, D. (1989). *Albion's seed: Four British folkways in America*. Oxford University Press.

Hofstede, G., Hofstede, G.-J., & Minkov, H. (2010). *Cultures and organizations: Software of the mind. Intercultural cooperation and its importance for survival.* McGraw Hill.
Howard, P. K. (2001). *The lost art of drawing the line: How fairness went too far.* Random House.
Hummel, R. P. (1977). *The bureaucratic experience.* St. Martin's Press.
Hurst, J. W. (1977). *Law and social order in the United States.* Cornell University Press.
Isaac, R. G., & Pitt, D. C. (2001). Organization culture: It's alive! It's alive! But there's no fixed address! In R. T. Golembiewski (Ed.), *Handbook of organizational behavior* (2nd ed., pp. 113–144). Marcel Dekker.
Knill, C. (2001). *The Europeanisation of national administrations: Patterns of institutional change and persistence.* Cambridge University Press.
Lasch, C. (1978). *The culture of narcissism: American life is in an age of diminishing expectations.* W.W. Norton and Company.
Light, P. C. (2000, January 1). The new public service. *Government Executive.*
Lippman, W. (1957 [1929]). *A preface to morals.* Time-Life Books.
Lippman, W. (1961 [1914]). *Drift and mastery: An attempt to diagnose the current unrest.* Prentice-Hall.
Litwin, G., & Stringer, R. (1968). *Motivation and organizational climate.* Harvard University Press.
Martin, J. (2002). *Organizational culture: Mapping the terrain.* Sage.
Meier, K. J. (1994). *The Politics of Sin: Drugs, Alcohol and Public Policy.* Routledge.
Milgram, S. (1974). *Obedience to authority.* Harper and Row.
Mosher, F. C. (1982). *Democracy and the public service* (2nd ed.). Oxford University Press.
Nelson, M. (1982). A short, ironic history of American national bureaucracy. *Journal of Politics, 44*(3), 747–778.
Nettl, P. (1968). The state as a conceptual variable. *World Politics, 20*(4), 573–574.
Nisbet, R. A. (1969). *Social change and history: Aspects of the Western theory of development.* Oxford University Press.
Nisbet, R. A. (1975). *Twilight of authority.* Oxford University Press.
Pugh, D. L. (1991). The origins of ethical frameworks in public administration. In J. S. Bowman (Ed.), *Ethical frontiers in public management* (pp. 9–32). Jossey-Bass.
Raadschelders, J. C. N. (2017). The United States of America as Rechtsstaat: State and administrative law as key to understanding the administrative state. *Public Administration Review, 77*(3), 458–465.
Rhodes, R. A. W. (1996). From institutions to dogma: Tradition, eclecticism, and ideology in the study of British public administration. *Public Administration Review, 56*(6), 507–516.
Roberts, R. N., & Doss, M. T., Jr. (1997). *From Watergate to Whitewater: The public integrity war.* Praeger.
Roberts, R. N. (2001). *Ethics in U.S. government: An encyclopedia of investigations, scandals, reforms, and legislation.* Praeger.
Samuelson, R. J. (1995). *The good life and its discontents: The American dream in the age of entitlement 1945–1995.* Random House.
Schein, E. (1985). *Organizational culture and leadership.* Jossey-Bass.
Shoen, D. E. (2013). *The end of authority: How a loss of legitimacy and broken trust are endangering our future.* Rowman & Littlefield.
Skocpol, T. (1992). *Protecting soldiers and mothers: The political origins of social policy in the United States.* The Belknap Press of Harvard University Press.

Stark, A. (2000). *Conflict of interest in American public life*. Harvard University Press.

Stillman, R. J. (1973). Woodrow Wilson and the study of administration: A new look at an old essay. *American Political Science Review, 67*, 582–588.

Stillman, R. J. (1999). *Preface to public administration: A search for themes and direction*. Chatelaine Press.

Taylor, T. S. (2002, August 18). Whistleblowers say exposing an employer can deal a career-crushing blow. *Chicago Tribune*, p. 5.

Van Riper, P. (1983). The American administrative state: Wilson and the Founders – An unorthodox view. *Public Administration Review, 43*(4), 477–490.

Vincent, A. (1987). *Theories of the state*. Basil Blackwell.

Waldo, D. (1984 [1948]). *The administrative state: A study of the political theory of American public administration*. Holmes and Meier.

Walker, L. S. (1990). Woodrow Wilson, progressive reform and public administration. In P. P. Van Riper (Ed.), *The Wilson influence on public administration: From theory to practice* (pp. 83–98). American Society for Public Administration.

Wills, G. (1999). *A necessary evil: A history of American distrust of government*. Simon and Schuster.

Woodard, C. (2011). *American nations: A history of the eleven rival regional cultures of North America*. Penguin.

Zimbardo, P. G., Haney, C., Banks, W. C., & Jaffe, D. (1973, April 8). The mind is a formidable jailer: A Pirandellian prison. *New York Times Magazine*, pp. 38–60.

CHAPTER 5

Government: Institutions, People, Interactions

The topic of the previous chapter was the role of culture and climate in determining acceptable behavior for the activities of government and people in society. What is acceptable is a question that is applied to governance and government on a nearly constant basis. This can be attributed, in part, to the fact that many of the interactions we have with government are involuntary—meaning we do not ask for government assistance. Still, we are impacted by the government through its programs and policies numerous times in our daily lives. Many perceive this as unnecessary and intrusive, not to mention costly, since we not only pay taxes but also often pay fees and charges for specific services. The culture and climate of our nation often determine how and what we, acting as a collective, want from government. The comparison of desired to actual performance occurs as people interact with the institutions and officials of government, which is the topic of this chapter.

How Does Government Appear to the Public?

Government can be characterized by discussing some of the fundamental ideas upon which it is based which guide how it operates. However, the government is also visually present in our lives, which tells us something about the political and administrative culture. One of the ways governments are visible is in their architecture and the layout of public buildings. Charles Goodsell (1997) studied this in the United States; we know of no similar type of study in other countries. His study of statehouses, city council chambers, and bureaucratic buildings provides excellent descriptions and illustrations of how Americans visualize government. Let's start with the state capitol, known as the statehouse.

The statehouse is typically set on park-like grounds to emphasize the American state government's relatively open, accessible nature. At the same time, a State Capitol building is meant to articulate authority. The most visible feature of many statehouses is the dome. Goodsell (2001) describes three levels of meaning a dome has:

(a) low or instrumental meaning: in the ability to draw attention from afar,
(b) medium or status meaning: in the identification as the State Capitol, or
(c) high or cosmological meaning: in the resemblance to a giant head of authority.

The front of the statehouse is often raised above the ground and reached by steps. It is a natural space from which to look at the world below. The steps are often surrounded by podium arms, reminiscent of the arms of a sphinx and suggesting energy. In the rotunda, visitors often see a chandelier hanging from the ceiling. This reflects the ancient idea about sacred space: the egg of creation floating in the world. Statehouses are generally built from stone. That may not seem very remarkable, but many buildings are constructed from less durable materials like wood. In other words, stone means the government is here to stay. The statehouse's interior further testifies that it is a building where decisions are made that influence us all. Often the state seal is displayed. Sometimes the state's founding document is on display. In some legislative chambers, we can see mace or fasces, an ancient and traditional symbol of authority of Etruscan origin and adopted by the Romans.

Goodsell (1988) observed that the statehouse is intended to exude authority, power, and prestige and to emphasize and define the heritage and culture of a state. Many statehouses contain evidence of important moments and people in the state's history through murals, paintings, and sculptures of famous citizens and politicians.

The inside and outside architecture and ornamentation within the statehouse are a visual representations of government culture. They also reveal things about organizational culture and how it is related to political ideology. You can find several floor plans in Goodsell's, 2001 book showing how both houses are situated on the same floor in bicameral legislatures and occupy about the same amount of space. Within these areas, people who sit on the same level are equal. However, in the judicial system, a raised dais suggests an authoritarian separation.

Similarly, different ideas about the role of local government can be discerned by studying the buildings where city government officials work. In a study of American city council chambers, Goodsell (1988) distinguishes three types and describes how each is representative of a conception of political authority.

The first type is the traditional council chamber, where the council members face the presiding officer, usually the mayor, who is seated on an elevated bench. Seating capacity for the public is limited, and the room exudes authority through elaborate entrances, large windows, and private doors for the officials. Chambers like this convey imposed authority and emphasize the power of elected officials.

The second type of council chamber exhibits confronted authority where the power of superiors is balanced with that of inferiors. There is much more space for the public to sit, and all council members face the public as a corporate body. This chamber is just another room, nothing special, suggesting that the city leaders are like the citizens.

Finally, the contemporary council chamber represents joined authority where power is shared and subtle symbols of power. Also, seating space for the public is more significant than in the other two types of chambers. This council chamber stands out as a separate room to be entered via a foyer, vestibule, or plaza or in a separate building.

The organizational culture of government as a bureaucracy also has physical expressions. These were explored in a study of the buildings of state agencies (Goodsell, 1997). As we describe below, three types of bureaucratic houses have been labeled as not very appropriate, and three types as very suitable for the government. Determining which type of building is appropriate depends on whether it comes across as inviting or restricting access. Remember that parts of government buildings are open to the public, called civic spaces, which "…refers to governmental interiors dedicated to ceremonial use before the observing public" (Goodsell, 1997, p. 133). Civic space must be inviting because that underlines the accessibility of democracy.

Among the inappropriate but often used designs is the bureaucratic space that comes across as a corporate building. It is a block-like mass made of concrete or steel with a glass facade. This design radiates efficiency as well as impersonal transactions. It does not appear inviting to the citizen. The second inappropriate type is that of the government fortress. This is a public building, often near a state capitol building that is often so large that accessibility is unclear because entrances are not distinct. The last inappropriate type is the consumer city, which seems more like a hotel lobby. In this type of building, the government is part of the broader environment. Public access is easy, but where one needs to go is not as clear, such consumer cities frequently provide space or connect to shops, arts events, and conventions. The presence of government in this type of building is unclear. An excellent example is the City Hall building in The Hague, the Netherlands.

Three types of attractive or inviting local government buildings are identified: the traditional temple, the local curiosity, and the postmodern delight. Many public office buildings look like traditional temples with Greek-style columns, a tympanum, and stairs leading up to the building. The local curiosity is a building with unusual shapes, often built in the early years of statehood. Finally, the postmodern delight includes buildings with very playful, distinctive designs. But each of these three is a government building. The following section describes the government workers in these buildings and how they are perceived by the people interacting with them.

Who Provides Government Services?

As noted in Chap. 1, most of the globe's landmasses are part of a government except Antarctica. These governments provide many services, some very visible, others less visible to the public. Both institutional and individual actors provide these services. Institutional actors include government departments and agencies at all levels of government. The most visible to citizens are the services provided by local agencies such as the police department, fire department, parks and recreation, water utilities, health, human services, public schools, sanitation department, etc. Individuals provide these services: police officers, schoolteachers, firefighters, garbage collectors, and so on.

How these services are provided varies from country to country, but it often involves some mix of public, non-profit, and private institutional actors. Collaboration in the delivery of collective services is labeled variously: *co-production*, public-private partnership, or collaborative management. There are countries where certain collective services are partially *privatized*, meaning they are executed by non-governmental organizations. This is, for instance, the case in the United Kingdom with the creation of for-profit prisons next to government-managed incarceration facilities. Governments can also use *contracting* for the delivery of certain services. In that case, governments have supervisory authority over the proper execution of contracted work. As you can imagine, many people are involved in governance and public service management and delivery. The personnel size of governments varies from country to country. By way of illustration, we will use the American government size. We think this will be a good basis for comparison to the size of public sector personnel in your country.

From 2001 to 2022, between 18–20% of the population of the United States has been directly employed by the U.S. government. We know them as public servants, a generic term that refers to all individuals who work in government in some capacity and are paid for their services. Under that generic term both elected officials and garbage collectors are public servants. There are differences in the types of public servants, however. The first distinction is between *elected officeholders, political appointees,* and *citizen functionaries* on the one hand and *civil servants* on the other. The significant difference between these two groups is that the latter are ideally appointed based on merit. In contrast, elected officeholders serve at the voters' pleasure, while political appointees and citizen functionaries serve at the pleasure of the elected officeholders. Politicians do not hire civil servants. Instead, the latter are employed in a career personnel system where hiring and promotion are based on merit and an individual's expertise, experience, and performance.

Division of Labor Between Elected Officials and Civil Servants

It is hard to imagine a case where elected officeholders comprised nearly 50% of the public workforce. Yet, this was the case in the early seventeenth-century local government in the Dutch Republic (Raadschelders, 1994) and, we suspect, in most Western countries between the sixteenth and eighteenth centuries (Goodnow, 1900). This is likely the case in most countries. In the early seventeenth century, there were very few civil servants. Some local government officials were elected, including the mayor and council members. However, there is very little knowledge about the size of civil service except that it was small. For instance, on New Year's Eve of 1789, there were 39 employees listed for the Treasury Department. It is unclear how many were political appointees and civil servants (Goodnow, 1900). Most were substantially engaged in mundane, routine tasks that nowadays would be left to clerical personnel, who would be civil servants rather than politicians (White, 1956). This would be common for any government in its early stages of development, regardless of when the government originated.

As the demand for public services increased in the late nineteenth century, so did the demand for professionally trained civil servants. After all, we could not expect elected officials to keep up with all the tasks of public service provision. There was also a reform movement calling for removing civil service positions from direct political influence, arguing that this situation had been responsible for much of the corruption within government in the nineteenth century. Reformers regarded politicians as responsible for policymaking, while administrators were expected to faithfully implement policy and act following the letter and intent of the law.

Today, the government maintains a separation between those with the authority to write laws and those tasked with implementing the laws. Still, the separation is not as distinct. Those implementing the laws may not be direct government employees due to contracting and co-production with organizations and people in non-governmental organizations. However, civil servants must still set the administrative rules for implementing laws and assure, through monitoring and oversight, that the laws of the land are upheld. Reforms that led to the current division of labor are considered next.

By Way of Illustration: The American Civil Service

Following the American and French Revolutions, the public service was significantly restructured. In most Western European countries, politics and administration were separated from the early nineteenth century. This meant those in political office were elected, and those working in the career civil service were appointed based on educational or experiential background. In other words, the career civil service professionalized.

This process of professionalization took a little longer in the United States. The history of the American civil service can be divided into two significant periods. Until the 1880s, a *spoils system* existed, and many civil service appointments were under elected officials' influence. After the Civil War, public officials argued for reforms to make employment in government less subject to political patronage and more based on merit, professional background, and employment experience.

It was common for public servants, such as leaders of government organizations and citizen functionaries, to be replaced by the friends of a new president since the late eighteenth century. However, by the mid-nineteenth century, civil service workers inside government organizations were replaced with supporters after a new president's swearing-in. This practice was embraced after President George Washington and greatly expanded by President Andrew Jackson. He firmly believed that the ideals of democracy were best served through widespread participation in government. In his view, government by the commoners was best.

Participation was achieved at the state and local level through direct elections of most officeholders; this was done through a spoils system at the federal level. Based on this saying "to the victor goes the spoils of war," a spoils system allows elected officials to put anyone they want in civil service positions, even if they have no qualifications.

Higher-level positions in the civil service, such as the chief clerk, and the highest-ranking civil servant in a department, were usually exempted from the spoils system, meaning they had to be hired based on merit, but lower-level positions were fair game for replacing government workers. Federal jobs in Washington and the various field offices were increasingly brought under the control of Members of Congress, acting upon the pressure of local parties. Consequently, people were appointed without relevant administrative skills. Even illiterate people could become civil servants (White, 1956). By 1901, the number of patronage positions filled by the spoils system increased to 150,000 (White, 2000). Imagine that the president had to fill about 150,000 positions.

Proposals for ensuring that civil servants have the knowledge, skills, and abilities (KSAs) for the job surfaced in the mid-nineteenth century. Still, they were limited to oral competency examinations (White, 1956). The matter of partisan influence over appointments was not yet a public concern. It became so after President Garfield was assassinated in 1881 by Charles Guitot, a former campaign worker who pursued but was denied appointment as U.S. Consul in Paris. Congress acted quickly, passed the Civil Service Reform Act, and created the Civil Service Commission (CSC) in 1883 (Ingraham, 1995). The CSC was given the authority to supervise the civil service exams required for anyone aspiring to a federal civil service career. In effect, this created the merit system that exists today. The CSC consisted of three commissioners, one of whom was Theodore Roosevelt. During his two terms as president of the United States, he significantly expanded the control of the CSC over civil service appointments.

Why was the Civil Service Reform Act so important? First, it reduced the number of positions subject to the spoils system. Initially, only 10% of all civil service positions fell under the authority of the Civil Service Commission. By the early 1950s, civil service positions subject to the Civil Service Reform Act grew to 92% of all federal positions (Van Riper, 1958). Today, the number of patronage positions has fallen to around 3000, for which recent presidents must find suitable candidates.

Second, and more importantly, this Act underlined the need to somehow separate administration from politics. How could a responsive, professional, and efficient administration be developed if incumbents of civil service positions could be removed so easily by partisan concerns? One of the earliest calls for a separation of politics and administration (called the *politics-administration dichotomy*) came from a young scholar who would rise to become the president of the United States. In his 1885 Ph.D. dissertation, Woodrow Wilson (1900 [1885]) wrote: "One of the conditions precedent to any real and lasting reform of the civil service [...] is the drawing of a sharp line of distinction between those offices that are political and those that are non-political" (p. 290).

The origins of this powerful idea go back to early nineteenth-century French public administration scholars, whom Woodrow Wilson and his contemporaries were very familiar with (Martin, 1987). Frank Goodnow, a law professor, shared Wilson's ideas. He observed that "... administration has been subjected too much to the control of politics in the United States. This has had the effect of decreasing administrative efficiency" (1900, Note 23, p. 74). It would be far better when "[p]olitics has to do with policies or expressions of the state will. Administration has to do with the execution of these policies" (Goodnow, 1900, Note 23, p. 74). While the ideas of Wilson and Goodnow concerned government at all levels, their interest—and that of their contemporaries—was in strengthening municipal government. The need for new public services and professionalism was felt most acutely at the local level. After all, that is where many public services were, and still are, provided and where most government workers are employed. The subject of the next section is how those who provide government services are perceived.

What Are the Stereotypes of Interactions with the Government?

Stereotyping is a human condition testifying to how people simplify complex phenomena (Simon, 1958). What characteristics do stereotypes include? First, they describe an entire group, or subgroups, of people. Second, stereotypes are based on deviant or abnormal behaviors rather than conforming or normal behaviors (Latz et al., 1975). Is it not true that news about adulterous, unethical, or outright corrupt public servants tends to dominate many citizens' perceptions of politicians and civil servants? In a way, this is understandable since the "normal" behavior of most elected officials and civil servants is simply not newsworthy. Let's face it. It is not juicy or sensational enough.

Elected Officials

Politicians are often stereotyped by their promissory nature with phrases like George H. W. Bush's 1988 "Read my lips, no new taxes." Or, more recently, "A Green New Deal for America" by Jill Stein and "Making America Great Again" by Donald Trump. Elected officials focus on short-term solutions because of the electoral cycle. Due to this, they tend to operate in sound bites rather than substantive messages. As individuals, elected officials are characterized as lusting for power and easily being corrupted. But politicians must also commit to serving the common good. That elected officials are torn between serving the common good and providing sweeping visions on the one hand, and serving a constituency, on the other hand, does little to balance the negative stereotypes (Ashworth, 2001).

We also stereotype elected officials as if they had certain familiar occupations. For example, some are described as lawyers (e.g., Abraham Lincoln), others as the corporate chief (e.g., the president), or the Beltway insider (someone with a Washington-based political career), such as President George H.W. Bush. We could also consider their style of conducting politics, such as the populist who focuses on simple messages like President Ronald Reagan, the academic who focuses on complexity like John Kerry, the philosopher-king who knows best such as Jimmy Carter or Franklin Roosevelt, or the elitist who is aloof, with Woodrow Wilson as an example. In Table 5.1, we summarize stereotypes about politics and elected officials. Elected officials of all public servants are generally regarded with the most suspicion by citizens.

Civil Servants

According to Raadschelders (2020), no matter how much elected officials are criticized and stereotyped, more attention has been devoted to critiquing and stereotyping civil servants. Table 5.2 organizes stereotypes and reality about government organizations and civil servants by distinguishing between government as a type of organization and as a group of individuals within an organization.

Discussions about government and public servants frequently turn to a discussion of the worst stereotypes. Stereotypical characterizations of the

Table 5.1 Stereotypes about politics and elected officials

	Abstract: Politics as an actor	*Concrete: Elected officials as individuals*
Stereotypes	Short-term vision, "promissory politics," soundbites with no substance	Lust for power, corruptible
Reality	Represents the common interest	Representatives of specific electoral interests, visionaries for change

Source: Tables 5.1, 5.2, and 5.3: Jos C.N. Raadschelders (2020). *The Three Ages of Government. From the Individual, to the Group, to the World*. University of Michigan Press

Table 5.2 Perceptions about and reality of government and civil servants

	Abstract: Government as a whole	Concrete: Government as subunits (including individuals)
Perception	Big bureaucracy, inaccessible, inefficient, red tape, corrupt	Bureaucrats are self-seeking, formalistic, distant, corruptible, and power-hungry and follow the lead of elected officeholders
Reality	Balancing myriad and conflicting demands, largest single employer, most substantial possible clientele, a considerable degree of organizational differentiation	Pro-active; citizen-oriented, concerned, professional, indispensable to politics

organization present images of government as too big, inaccessible, inefficient, and having too much red tape. Stereotypes of civil servants often emphasize their hunger for power (Downs (1994 [1967]); Niskanen (1975).

Citizens

Politicians often view citizens as voters and seek ways to convince them they are worthy of their trust at the ballot box. However, not all citizens are treated equally by politicians—after the election, campaign donors often have greater access to the politician they supported. Civil servants view citizens as cases, meaning they attempt to treat each person equally and according to laws and rules (cf. Weber). They do not provide any special treatment based on an individual's circumstances. There are also perceptions that citizens only become involved in government when unhappy. And civil servants can feel threatened by citizens who are active in government and have high political efficacy since they challenge the subject matter expertise of the civil servant and can complain to the elected officials who oversee government organizations.

In some cases, the stereotypes seem to hold. The reality, though, is more complicated. There are numerous other cases where citizens are actively involved, such as on school boards, planning boards, park boards, citizen police review commissions, and many more. Table 5.3 summarizes the difference between stereotypes and reality based on abstract and concrete circumstances.

We have described how public servants and citizens perceive each other and categorize them. The stereotypes of elected officials, civil servants, and citizens provide images of widely held perceptions about government and its clients. They also explain how government operates in a societal environment that stereotypes its work and how these stereotypes influence trust in government. The reality of how and why elected officials, civil servants, and citizens interact can help us assess these stereotypes' validity.

Table 5.3 Stereotypes about and reality of citizens

	Abstract: The citizenry	*Concrete: The citizen*
Stereotypes	Voting cattle, public policy too challenging to understand for people	Uninformed, entitlement mentality, uninterested, lack of civic duty, and emphasis on rights
Reality	Limited knowledge about government	Active in interest groups, involved in public affairs relevant to personal life, emphasis on rights and duties

How Do Elected Officials and Civil Servants Interact?

Policymaking can be conducted in a command-and-control style, where legislators make little effort to negotiate with stakeholders and seldom leave the drafting of legislation to civil servants (Bok, 2001). Elected officials may informally consult with civil servants but are under no obligation to do so. One way to keep civil servants at arm's length is to increase the number of political appointee positions, as happened during the Eisenhower and Reagan administrations (Light, 2017, 2019). A more direct way of holding civil servants at bay is to explicitly exclude them from attending meetings where policy changes are considered (Golden, 2000). Finally, top-level civil servants feel the heat of politics when called to testify before Congressional committees. Legislators may raise questions to gather facts, embarrass the civil servant, and irritate other committee members. If the civil servant provides too much detail, they lose the committee's attention. Or, if their answers are too general, they risk being accused of holding back information. In other words, civil servants must walk a fine line between protecting the general interest and catering to elected officials' goals (Ashworth, 2001).

The relationship of civil servants to political officials in the United States is starkly different from the best practices in other advanced democracies where central policymaking involves civil servants and societal stakeholders such as labor unions, employer associations, and interest groups. This type of collaboration is known as corporatism. Civil servants in these countries draft the policy and legal texts because they are the experts who can judge the text's content to guarantee its optimal implementation and results (Page & Wright, 1999). As a result, pluralist systems are perhaps less efficient than some of the more corporatist systems.

Civil servants hold some significant advantages over the political appointees who have shorter government involvement, often leaving when there is a new president despite a command-and-control environment. The benefit for civil servants is organizational memory, developed by working in a government organization for more years than their political superiors. In their employment, civil servants build expertise in a particular area. No generalist political executive can master the same level of detail as a specialist civil servant. Civil servants also have tenure, which means that, unlike political appointees, they do not serve at the pleasure of the top executive. However, disagreeing vocally with the direction of political leaders might jeopardize a civil servant's employment and career prospects. Various studies have investigated the nature and development of political-civil servant relations. We discuss these in the next section.

Types of Political-Civil Servant Relationships

The relationships between elected officials and civil servants can be understood using a formal, legal, or more informal sociological perspective. The formal-legal perspective generally refers to the relationship as a politics-administration dichotomy since the core idea is the primacy of politics. This means that in government affairs, politics is superior to administration. Elected officials are the authority under which civil servants serve. In this view, politics and administration are separate. Political officials are elected, while civil servants are appointed on merit. Elected officials establish policies by enacting laws, while civil servants implement these laws according to legislative intent.

The idea of a politics-administration dichotomy originated in early nineteenth-century France. It became attractive to reformers in the United States in the 1880s (Martin, 1987). More than anything, reformers wanted to improve government performance by removing the extensive influence elected officials had over administration. This situation was characteristic of the spoils system and was counteracted by developing professional training for civil servants. If politics could be removed from the administration, it was expected that administrators would be able to function more efficiently, more like a business (Wilson, 2004 [1887]).

The politics-administration dichotomy has been described in at least two different ways. The first way considers the degree to which elected officials and civil servants are separate. The list below presents citizens' perceptions of the relationships between elected officials and civil servants. Perceptions 1 and 2 are considered to apply more to lower-level civil servants. In contrast, perceptions 3 and 4 are more appropriate for the higher levels in the governmental hierarchy. Using the continuum of roles from rigorous separation to complete fusion, we can see that all perceptions clarify the relationship between elected officials and civil servants.

Perceptions of Elected Officials and Civil Servants Relationships

- Perception 1: rigorous separation of politics and administration—elected officials lead and decide while civil servants execute dutifully
- Perception 2: elected officials articulate interests and values, while civil servants provide facts and neutral expertise
- Perception 3: elected officials give the energy and the passion, while civil servants serve with pragmatism and caution
- Perception 4: the two roles of elected officials and civil servants are not distinct

Another typology of political-administrative relations includes a formal-legal perspective and a more informal sociological model (Peters, 1985). In the village life model, civil servants and elected officials share similar values and goals and bargain for mutually acceptable agreements so that elected officials and civil servants are winners. Policymakers are related according to community ties in the functional village life model. They include elected officials, civil servants active in the policy area, and interest groups. The adversarial model is based on conflict and a winner-takes-all approach. Finally, there are no elected officials in the administrative state model since the government is run by civil servants (Peters, 1985). Examples of administrative states are few and far between, but nineteenth-century Norway resembled this model the closest since civil servants governed the country. The head of state was the Swedish king.

The formal-legal model stresses separation; the more informal sociological model focuses on intertwinement. Initially, it was suggested that the traditional separation of elected officials and civil servants would erode. Further research seemed to confirm that conclusion (Campbell, 1988). However, data from the 1980s and 1990s indicate that politics and administration have separated again (Aberbach et al. 1981; Aberbach & Rockman, 1997).

It has been argued that relationships between politics and administration are related to changes in the balance of power between the president and Congress. Toward the end of the nineteenth century, the U.S. Congress was the dominant actor, and civil servants were appointed for partisan loyalty rather than administrative expertise. Each election provided new opportunities for patronage appointments, and the tenure of those selected was short. After the turn of the century, the powers of Congress and the president were more balanced. The civil servant was politically neutral and appointed based on professional competence. From the 1930s on, the president became the dominant actor in American government and politics. Following this, civil servants are selected for their professional expertise. Still, political affiliation is considered for middle and upper-level positions (Arnold, 1998).

Political-administrative relations have increasingly become politicized in democracies because of an increase in the number of political appointee positions and increased *agency-ification*. From a theoretical point of view, agency-ification assumes that the governance, provision, production, and provision, of public goods and services can be separated (Arnold, 1998). The governance function concerns the policymaking process and decision-making about production and provision. The provision function mainly concerns decisions about what goods and services can and should be available to citizens through collective means. An example of a provision function is taxes to pay for road maintenance. Finally, the production function refers to the activities involved in making goods and services available. Advocates of the New Public Management (NPM) approach think various functions can easily be privatized or contracted out.

In the United Kingdom, the idea that policy and implementation can successfully be separated gained popularity when Margaret Thatcher was prime minister. What has been forgotten in the enthusiastic pursuit of NPM-type reforms and the introduction of more market-type mechanisms is that a new policy-operations dichotomy has emerged, suggesting that government has responsibility for policy and may or may not have responsibility for service delivery through program operations. Ironically, this makes the entrepreneurial civil servant more accessible to outside influence and pressure. In contrast, it makes the elected official less accessible (Du Gay, 2000).

So, what are the relationships between politicians and civil servants? In the formal-legal model, you now know that elected officials hold the upper hand, and civil servants implement the policy. From a more sociological perspective, civil servants and citizens are vital information suppliers, with the former as a crucial part of the entire policy and decision-making process. To see how citizens have influence, we will first discuss why participation is essential and then turn to a discussion of civil servant-citizen relations.

Why Do We Want Participation?

One of the most compelling explanations for citizen participation is ensuring that government serves society's needs, interests, and preferences. Often, we complain that the government, especially elected officials, are out of touch with what the people want. One of the most critical participation goals is to determine what is in the public interest or what people want. There are other goals as well. These can include educating citizens about government operations, gathering input for decisions, gauging support for proposed courses of action, changing resource allocation or current government actions, enhancing trust in government, and building a sense of community (Ebdon & Franklin, 2004).

Organizations in all sectors have been concerned about stakeholders, such as citizens, stockholders, and clients for a long time (Barnard, 1968 [1938]; Follett, 1918). Early for-profit sector organization research described stockholders, or shareholders, as the leading group to whom corporate management needed to be responsive. They later modified this definition to include people or groups and competitors whose interests were directly opposed to the corporation, such as residents in a community where the business's operations created harmful environmental air quality effects.

The necessity of interacting with stakeholders is also apparent in the non-profit sector. Representatives of key groups, such as clients and funders for non-profit organizations, are often asked to serve on advisory boards because of their expertise. This was the case when exhibits were developed for the University of Oklahoma's Sam Noble Oklahoma Museum of Natural History in 2000. An advisory board with 26 of the 39 state-recognized Native American tribes helped plan the People of Oklahoma exhibit. The advisory board's participation created a wall of 136 handprints and one baby footprint, symbolizing the tribal members and the importance of preserving their 30,000+ year histories by telling their origin stories. The board members wanted the gallery to describe the native peoples' history and convey the cultural importance of orally passing indigenous traditions from one generation to another. Without input from the advisory board, the staff at the museum believe they may have missed critical ethnological perspectives.

Public officials often considered stakeholder preferences at the time the government was formed. As a result, it is not unusual for government founding documents to include language affirming that the governance structure should encourage people to participate in the electoral system. This is important since elections determine who represents the people and who can make decisions on behalf of society.

Stakeholders also become involved in specific issues that interest them or affect them. An example is when someone goes to a land use zoning hearing for a new business that wants to locate in a neighborhood. Residents participate because they want their preferences heard regarding this proposed action. This form of participation is intended to solve a problem or address dissatisfaction with how one has been treated (Orbell & Uno, 1972).

Requiring government agencies to be open to those they serve is viewed as a way to make government, at all levels, more responsive. Officials in government often enact legislation to foster stakeholder access, requiring agencies to solicit and consider public comment before new administrative policies can be adopted. The European principles of good administration recognize this process of codifying procedural rights in administrative relations (Kovač, 2016). While administrative rulemaking can be a significant undertaking for public officials, having access to public meetings and commenting on proposed government regulations and activities reflects a desire for the government's business to be conducted in the "sunshine," meaning that everything happens in public, making it transparent and ensuring accountability to the people.

In the 1960s, government officials struggled to find a way to address more than a decade of social protests that sought to enhance the power of minorities and provide access to government activities (Ståhlberg, 1997). Stakeholder involvement was encouraged based on a concept of maximum feasible participation (Moynihan, 1970). This concept argues that the best way to spend government funds in a community is to get as many people to participate in the allocation process as feasible. Asking those most likely to be impacted by government-funded programs to participate in the allocation of funds earmarked for their community is quite different from politicians or civil servants in the nation's capital determining whether a city should build a senior center or a skate park with national funds.

From the 1970s to the 1990s, calls for participation were reduced. A renewed concern replaced them with calls for efficiency and the demands to reduce the cost of government (Ståhlberg, 1997). During this time, active citizen involvement declined, with fewer citizens serving on neighborhood associations and government boards (Putnam, 2000; Walsh, 1997).

Gathering citizen viewpoints on how government should operate had a resurgence in the 1990s. In the United States, the passage of the Government Performance and Results Act of 1993 (GPRA) required federal agencies to "consult with stakeholders" when developing their strategic plans. The goals of participation in this Act vary slightly from those in previous periods. Instead of being valued to gather input on community preferences (Morone, 1990), participation was desired to improve the quality of government operations (Ståhlberg, 1997). When the quality of service is emphasized, citizens seek a share in governing rather than relying on experts to establish policies that may not be relevant (Lappe & DuBois, 1997). In this case, participation is a way for stakeholders to recognize and assert their duties as citizens and as vital members of society (King & Stivers, 1998).

Extensive stakeholder input can bring forth fresh perspectives, alert government officials to changes in the public interest, and identify future needs. In Denmark, there is an emphasis on patient-centered care to provide quality public health care. Through a process known as shared decision-making, national and private funding and stakeholder input are included in the national plan for cancer treatment (dahl Steffensen et al., 2017).

To summarize this section, many different types of stakeholders for government can be identified, including people, plants, animals, the environment, and future generations. All of them may experience short- and/or long-term effects from the decisions government makes today (Franklin, 2020). Stakeholder participation is an activity valued by organizations in all sectors since it can fulfill many goals, such as making government responsive and giving community members a say in organizational activities. For government organizations, participation helps to ensure that government serves its citizens. The nature of this participation is considered next.

What Are the Interactions Between Citizens and Civil Servants?

This section distinguishes two types of civil servant-citizen relations: those between civil servants and groups of organized citizens, more commonly known as interest groups, and those between civil servants and individual citizens. In these interactions, the citizen is the government's client (Gordon, 1999). As part of an organized group or as individuals, citizens interact with two types of civil servants: street-level bureaucrats and policy bureaucrats. Interactions with each are described next.

Street-level bureaucrat is a term that refers to all those civil servants who come into direct contact with individual citizens while performing their daily duties (Cohen, 2021; Lipsky, 1980). They include police and correctional officers, judges, garbage can collectors, public school teachers, and social welfare workers. They are among the most important civil servants for several reasons. First, they significantly impact our lives: teachers educate our children, police officers keep neighborhoods safe, social workers help people become self-sufficient, and so forth. Second, they are the group of civil servants that has grown fastest since the 1960s; perhaps as many as 70% of the public sector workforce can be labeled street-level bureaucrats. Public school teachers comprise half of the public workforce at the local level. Third, they have substantial discretion in determining what to do because their supervisors are generally not around when a decision must be made. For example, a police officer deciding to let a speeder go with a warning instead of a ticket is exercising discretion. The law says that speeding is illegal and requires a ticket, but, at times, a warning is given instead.

In the case of speeding, using discretion has a limited impact on your life. If you get a ticket, it will cost you. Still, it does not otherwise limit your life unless you lose your license because of prior violations. However, the use of discretion can have profound impacts, such as when a social welfare worker determines whether an individual is eligible for a particular program.

There are very detailed laws and regulations to guide a civil servant, but, at times, the rules seem not to fit the circumstances and may be circumvented. Should civil servants rigidly apply the rules so that the doctrine of administrative impartiality is maintained, or should they use discretion and show compassion and flexibility? This is a tough decision to make. On the one hand, a civil servant is expected to treat everybody equally and ignore the specific circumstances of the situation. On the other hand, civil servants are human beings with a natural inclination to consider an individual's circumstances (Lavee, 2021).

Street-level bureaucrats have the most contact with citizens and shape people's impressions of government employees. Citizens' judgments about their experiences with civil servants are mainly satisfactory to very good at the local, state, and federal levels. This is so because most street-level bureaucrats advocate for their clients rather than acting like the stereotypical pencil-pushing, red-tape-supporting bureaucrats portrayed in literature and movies.

Few people realize how difficult the street-level bureaucrats' job is. For instance, most social workers have large caseloads that do not allow them to spend too much time with each client and require quick decision-making. Second, there are limitations to the number of people working at an agency, the amount of program funding available, and the quality of the facilities in which they work. We know of one social welfare agency housed in the basement of a government building with old furniture, no carpet, and, worst of all, the ceiling dripping water that had to be collected in buckets so visitors would not slip. Third, they have significant responsibilities but little influence on organizational or public policy. Fourth, they often deal with disadvantaged populations whose situations might seem like the client's own making (Romzek & Johnston, 2000). Finally, the pay for many street-level bureaucrats is meager. It is said that some types of civil servants, especially low-level employees in the human service and defense organizations are one paycheck away from being on the client's side of the desk.

Policy bureaucrats are a smaller category of civil servants whose job is to help write policy and monitor and analyze implementation (Page & Jenkins, 2005). While street-level bureaucrats often work at lower levels, policy bureaucrats work at middle and upper-middle levels. Both groups, though, are highly trained professionals.

The difficulties in the policy bureaucrats' jobs are quite different. Policy bureaucrats do not generally interact with individual citizens. Still, they work with elected officials, people representing a specific interest, and groups of individuals. Policy bureaucrats maintain regular contact with their policy clientele. For instance, civil servants from a department of agriculture have close connections with farmers' and ranchers' organizations. Through these contacts, policymaking considers the needs of stakeholders. In some countries, this type of interaction is not as institutionalized as in several corporatist European countries. Still, the interaction between policy bureaucrats and policy clientele is frequent and essential.

Civil Servant and Citizen Interactions

The interactions between street-level or policy bureaucrats and citizens can be analyzed in various ways. How can citizens quickly get in touch with the proper civil servant? Can city government organizations influence policy and decision-making? Is bureaucracy accessible? We approach the discussion from the citizen's perspective because theories from the bureaucratic perspective have been discussed above; it is the perspective most familiar to you.

The most general way of examining citizens' interactions with civil servants is by distinguishing between high and low citizenship (Cooper, 1984). This distinction is based on the degree to which authority is dispersed throughout society. In the case of high citizenship, authority is widely distributed and shared. All citizens are regarded as peers in government. This view is most closely associated with the ideas of Aristotle and John Locke about participative government. Low citizenship is when authority is available to some but not all citizens. In other words, citizen participation in this sense is minimal. This view is best represented by the ideas of Thomas Hobbes, who believed in the concentration of authority in the hands of one person.

The notions of high and low citizenship have also been paired with high and low administration (Frederickson & Chandler, 1997). The four possible combinations are shown in Table 5.4. In the case of high administration, civil servants are regarded as representatives of the people or trustees of the public good. In the case of low administration, civil servants are first and foremost citizens and perceive themselves as servants of the citizenry.

The combination of low citizenship and low administration is characteristic of the United States decades after independence. The Founding Fathers preferred a government by gentlemen rather than popular rule and a low profile of civil servants. Perhaps it is still characteristic of American's desired situation since it is a compromise between the Federalist's desire for low citizenship and the anti-Federalist's advocacy for low administration.

The situation of high citizenship paired with high administration is characteristic of many Northwestern European countries: a high degree of citizen

Table 5.4 Citizen and administrative participation in government

Engagement as governance ideal type??	Citizenship or as stakeholders (Sidebar: in for-profit organizations, it was stockholders 1st)	
	High—citizens as peers with authority	Low—some citizens have authority
Administration Pol D.M. To Consultation Collaboration Partnership — High	Corporatist arrangements: Ancient Rome, Scandinavian countries	Representatives of people: Ancient Egypt, the former Soviet Union
Low	High citizen visibility: Ancient Athens, Switzerland	Government by gentlemen: United States

Source: Frederickson, H. G. and Chandler, R. C. (1997). The public administrator is a representative citizen. In H. G. Frederickson (Ed.) *The spirit of public administration* (p. 213). Jossey-Bass

participation through corporatist arrangements and high visibility of civil servants because of significant government intervention in society. Civil servants working in a high-high situation regard their position as a public trust, that is, something entrusted to them. Such officials are susceptible to and mindful of societal needs. Ancient Athens provides an example of high citizenship for adult free males (but not women nor enslaved people) and low administration, which is very little administration. Totalitarian regimes such as the former Soviet Union are characterized by low citizenship and high administration.

By contrast, civil servants guided by a low citizenship and low administration outlook regard their position mainly as one of entrepreneurship. This type of official has less regard for promoting the public good that is to be provided by the government for the benefit of society and is more interested in pursuing their self-interest.

In which cell would you place your country today? After all, opportunities for citizen participation and active citizen involvement have increased significantly in the past two centuries. Civil servants indeed regard themselves nowadays as public trustees and hence represent a situation of high citizenship combined with a continued desire for a smaller or larger government (low or high administration).

How is the notion of high and low citizenship related to high and low administration relevant to the civil servant-citizen relationship? The answer is quite simple. The citizen is best served by a civil servant whose actions are grounded in notions of high citizenship and high administration because that group cares most about society and their clients and can deal with their concerns and needs professionally. Their professionalism includes respect for and obedience to the law as much as possible, respect for the individual applicant, and discretion to apply the laws and rules in a fair and just manner.

So far, the discussion of civil servant-citizen relations concerns the individual citizen and the street-level bureaucrats who most directly affect our personal lives. Other theories about citizen participation consider the interactions between civil servants, interest groups, and citizens' representatives. In this section, we discuss theories about the perceived legitimacy of these interactions.

The most concise discussion of perceptions about the legitimacy of relations and interactions between citizens and civil servants has been offered by Guy Peters (2020). Under high citizenship and high administration, the most likely type of interaction is legitimate interaction. This is comparable to the situation under corporatism described above: interest groups and civil servants are mandated to have frequent interactions about a wide range of topics. Since legal requirements mandate interactions, they are perceived as legitimate. Representatives from government and interest groups have equal influence. The outcomes of this type of interaction are highly influential in policymaking. It is almost inconceivable that government, either civil servants or elected officials, would ignore interest groups and try to get around them when developing policy. These interest groups typically focus on redistributive policies that use taxes to assist those in society who are the most vulnerable.

More characteristic for the United States are *clientela* relations, which is the situation where an interest group or a group with comparable interests seeks government access to advance their preferences. The range of topics is limited and their influence on policymaking is not guaranteed. Influence varies with the perceived economic importance of the issue, the membership size, and the financial capacity of the interest group. It is suggested that corporate interests are well organized, act through interest groups, and quickly get the attention desired from civil servants.

Interest groups with large and active memberships, such as professional associations of engineers, doctors, lawyers, etc., have clout because they are frequent voters, and their members are generally affluent. But it is also possible that relatively small but well-financed interest groups get attention and wield influence. A well-known example is the U.S. National Rifle Association, whose 5.5 million members have successfully blocked national and state gun control measures. This category of interest groups mainly focuses on personal rather than societal interests and is driven more to influence distributive policies. Increasingly, and in recent years, the NRA's objectives are challenged by "Moms Demand Action: for gun sense in America," a grassroots informal network with chapters in every state and nearly 10 million supporters.

Parantela relations do not differ much from *clientela* relations, except it is not so much a policy issue determining who interacts with whom but kinship or friendship relations. This type of civil servant-citizen interaction was common throughout the U.S. government in the nineteenth century and usually is referred to as the spoils system. Nowadays, whenever there is a case of corruption, fraud, or bribery, it probably involves *parantela*-type relations.

The final type of interaction between administrators and citizens is illegitimate interaction. These are not necessarily illegal but are perceived as outside the realm of acceptable political action. An example is violent attacks on government officials, buildings, or meetings by extremist groups. If these groups have a particular policy objective, it is usually redistributive, aiming to reform the existing political, economic, and social situation.

Another way to look at the group level of civil servant-citizen relations is co-production, or governments and citizens working together to provide public services. In the past, co-production often had a compulsory nature, especially for people in the lower classes. Citizens performing the night-watch or the fire-watch are examples. These were civic duties few adult males could avoid. For the higher income classes, their civic duty was like the government by gentlemen envisioned by the Founding Fathers. Because of your familial associations, you were expected to do your duty by serving in public office. Nowadays, co-production is voluntary and includes citizens serving on city commissions, school boards, and neighborhood associations.

Chapter Summary

In our everyday lives, we probably do not realize how much the government influences or controls our actions. In these situations, we are highly influenced by our and society's stereotypes of government officials. These perceptions can be different when considering elected officials versus civil servants (government workers) since the culture and climate of societies differ dramatically based on history as well as the characteristics of the population. However, when we have interactions with government officials they are influenced by our perception of government, and the influence can be perceived differently if it is a *parentela* or *clientela* relationship. In Chap. 6, we provide data about the size and structure of government. Both influence our as well as societal stereotypes about governance, government, and those who represent the government.

PRACTICAL APPLICATIONS

1. How does government appear to the public? The answer to that question may differ based on the person's age and may vary with whether the individual lives in a rural or an urban setting. And the answer will vary from country to country.
2. Who provides government services is a question that may have different answers at different times? Who is the main service provided where you live: the municipality, the country, province or state, or national government?
3. What about interactions between citizens and civil service? Transparency is a valued characteristic. However, not all citizens and public servants see it as a positive. Why can this be the case?
4. Are public servants and citizens in your country stereotyped? How are these similar or different from what was described in this chapter?

IN-CLASS INSTRUCTIONAL SUGGESTIONS

1. How do public buildings near your students appear? Describe some of the public buildings in the city or place you live. Encourage students to identify the difference in the appearance of government agency buildings and buildings inhabited by elected officeholders?
2. How many people work in the public sector in your country? You may find overall figures, but it would be interesting to break them down into personnel size at the local, regional (province or state), and national or federal levels. Which is the most significant level of government? Ask the students to determine if the number of employees matches the significance of that level of government.
3. How are citizens, elected officials, and career civil servants stereotyped in your country? Discuss why these stereotypes developed and how they have changed over time.

REFERENCES

Aberbach, J. D., Putnam, R., & Rockman, B. A. (1981). *Bureaucrats and politicians in western democracies*. Harvard University Press.

Aberbach, J. D., & Rockman, B. A. (1997). Back to the future? Senior federal executives in the United States. *Governance: An International Journal of Policy, Administration, and Institutions, 10*(4), 323–349.

Arnold, P. (1998). *Making the managerial presidency: Comprehensive reorganization planning, 1905–1996* (2nd ed.). University Press of Kansas.

Ashworth, K. (2001). *Caught between the dog and the fireplug, or how to survive the public service*. Georgetown University Press.

Barnard, C. (1968 [1938]). *The functions of the executive*. Harvard University Press.

Bok, D. C. (2001). *The trouble with the government*. Harvard University Press.

Campbell, C. (1988). The political roles of senior government officials in advanced democracies. *British Journal of Political Science, 18*(2), 243–272.

Cohen. (2021). *Policy entrepreneurship at the street level*. Cambridge University Press.

Cooper, T. L. (1984). Citizenship and professionalism in public administration. *Public Administration Review*, Special issue, March, pp. 143–149.

dahl Steffensen, K. D., Baker, V. H., & Vinter, M. M. (2017). Implementing shared decision making in Denmark: First steps and future focus areas. *Zeitschrift für Evidenz, Fortbildung und Qualität im Gesundheitswesen, 123*, 36–40.

Downs, A. (1994 [1967]). *Inside bureaucracy*. Waveland Press.

Du Gay, P. D. (2000). *In praise of bureaucracy: Weber, organization, ethics*. Sage.

Ebdon, C., & Franklin, A. L. (2004). Searching for a role for citizens in the budget process. *Public Budgeting and Finance, 24*(1), 32–49.

Follett, M. P. (1918). *The new state: Group organization, The solution of popular government*. Longmans, Green and Company.

Franklin, A. L. (2020). *Stakeholder Engagement*. Springer Nature.

Frederickson, H. G., & Chandler, R. C. (1997). The public administrator as representative citizen. In H. G. Frederickson (Ed.), *The spirit of public administration* (pp. 209–223). Jossey-Bass.

Golden, M. M. (2000). *What motivates bureaucrats? Politics and administration during the Reagan years*. Columbia University Press.

Goodnow, F. (1900). *Politics and administration: A study in government*. The Macmillan Company.

Goodsell, C. T. (1988). *The social meaning of civic space: Studying political authority through architecture*. University Press of Kansas.

Goodsell, C. T. (1997). Bureaucracy's house in the polis: Seeking an appropriate presence. *Journal of Public Administration Research and Theory, 7*(3), 393–418.

Goodsell, C. T. (2001). *The American Statehouse: Interpreting democracy's temples*. University Press of Kansas.

Gordon, S. (1999). *Controlling the state: Constitutionalism from Ancient Athens to today*. Harvard University Press.

Ingraham, P. W. (1995). *The foundation of merit: Public service in American democracy*. The Johns Hopkins University Press.

King, C. S., & Stivers, C. (1998). *Government is us: Public administration in an anti-government era*. Sage.

Kovač, P. (2016). Openness and Transparency in (Slovene): Administrative procedures as fundamental European principles. *NISPAcee Journal of Public Administration and Policy*, December.

Lappe, F. M., & DuBois, P. (1997). Building social capital without looking backward. *National Civic Review, 86*(2), 119–128.

Latz, D., Gutek, B. A., Kahn, R. L., & Barton, E. (1975). *Bureaucratic encounters: A pilot study in the evaluation of government services*. Institute for Social Research.

Lavee, E. (2021). *The hidden tier of social services: Frontline workers' provision of informal resources in the public, nonprofit and private sectors*. Cambridge University Press.

Light, P. (2017). *The true size of government: Tracking Washington's blended workforce, 1984–2015*. Volcker Alliance.

Light, P. (2019). *The government-industrial complex: The true size of the federal government, 1984–2018*. Oxford University Press.

Lipsky, M. (1980). *Street-level bureaucracy: Dilemmas of the individual in public services*. Russell Sage Foundation.

Martin, D. W. (1987). Déjà vu: French antecedents of American public administration. *Public Administration Review, 47*(3), 297–303.

Morone, J. (1990). *The democratic wish: Popular participation and the limits of American government*. Yale University Press.

Moynihan, D. P. (1970). *Maximum feasible misunderstanding: Community action in the war on poverty*. Macmillan Publishing.

Niskanen, W. (1975). Bureaucrats and politicians. *Journal of Law and Economics, 18*, 617–643.

Orbell, J. M., & Uno, T. (1972). A theory of neighborhood problem solving: Political action vs. residential mobility. *American Political Science Review, 66*(2), 471–489.

Page, E. C., & Jenkins, B. (2005). *Policy bureaucracy: Governing with a cast of thousands*. Oxford University Press.

Page, E. C., & Wright, V. (Eds.). (1999). *Bureaucratic elites in Western European states*. Oxford University Press.

Peters, B. G. (1985). Politicians and bureaucrats in the politics of policy making. In J.-E. Lane (Ed.), *Bureaucracy and public choice* (pp. 256–282). Sage.

Peters, B. G. (2020). *The politics of bureaucracy. An introduction to Comparative Public Administration* (10th ed.). Routledge.

Putnam, R. D. (2000). *Bowling alone: The collapse and revival of American community*. Simon and Schuster.

Raadschelders, J. C. N. (1994). Understanding the development of local government: Theory and evidence from the Dutch case. *Administration and Society*, 25(4), 410–442.

Raadschelders, J. C. N. (2020). *The three ages of government. From the individual, to the group, To the world*. University of Michigan Press.

Romzek, B. S., & Johnston, J. M. (2000). Reforming state social services through contracting: Linking implementation and organizational culture. In J. L. Brudney, L. J. O'Toole Jr., & H. G. Rainey (Eds.), *Advancing public management. New Developments in theory, methods and practice* (pp. 173–196). Georgetown University Press.

Simon, H. (1958). The decision-making schema: A reply. *Public Administration Review*, 18(1), 60–63.

Ståhlberg, K. (1997). Hæmeenlinna: Enhancing citizen and community participation. *International strategies and techniques for future local government: Practical Aspects towards innovation and reform*. Bertelsmann Foundation Publishers.

Van Riper, P. (1958). *History of the U.S. civil service*. Peterson and Company.

Walsh, M. L. (1997). *Building citizen involvement: Strategies for local government*. International City/County Management Association.

White, L. D. (1956). *The Jacksonians: A study in administrative history 1829–1861*. The Macmillan Company.

White, R. D. (2000). Theodore Roosevelt as civil service commissioner: Linking the influence and development of a modern administrative President. *Administrative Theory and Praxis*, 22(4), 696–713.

Wilson, W. (1900 [1885]). *Congressional government: A study in American politics*. Houghton Mifflin.

Wilson, W. (2004 [1887]). The study of administration. In J. M. Shafritz, A. C. Hyde, & S. J. Parkes (Eds.), *Classics of public administration* (5th ed., pp. 22–34). Thomson, Wadsworth Learning.

CHAPTER 6

The Services and Size of Government

As central as the government has become to modern society, it is no wonder that its organizations and workers are subject to stereotyping and criticism based on the accumulation of scholarly writings and bad civil servant behaviors. For example, Max Weber (1946 [1922]) believed bureaucracy to be the most efficient organization. Still, as we concluded in Chap. 5, the government is often stereotyped as too big and complex. Is it too big or too complicated? In comparison to what standard?

ELEPHANTITIS IN GOVERNMENT?

German scholars in the nineteenth century wrote about the stereotypical images of bureaucracy and bureaucrats. They argue that bureaucracy suffers from *elephantitis*, a disease where certain parts of the face grow disproportionately. They also said that numbers of civil servants multiply and tend to suffer from a personal lack of manners. Yet, they also have integrity and willingly make sacrifices to hold their jobs. On the other hand, they are formalistic pencil-pushers, engage in improper behavior, and lack an understanding of intimate relations beyond technical performance (Raadschelders, 2003).

However, despite these images, when asked about actual experiences with public services and individual civil servants, people representing the public report being very satisfied with the direct services they receive (Goodsell, 2014). Today, the government and its officials are very different from a century ago. The transformation of government from providing the essential functions of policing, defense, justice, and taxation to one that offers an incredible range of services to its citizens has occurred quickly. Government was small for most of history. In the past 150 years, it has enlarged to a point where government organizations occupy a central place in society.

Since the 1970s, politicians have criticized government size, claiming that civil servants have gained too much influence. Prime Minister Margaret Thatcher of the United Kingdom firmly believed that the civil service had to adopt a more managerial and less political focus. Efforts to reform government have been quite prominent in various countries, such as the United States (Light, 1997; Moe, 2003) with the emergence of New Public Management (OECD, 2005). President Carter reorganized the civil service again with the Civil Service Reform Act in 1978. His successor, President Reagan, observed: "Bureaucracy is not the solution; it is a problem!" Presidents G.H.W. Bush and W.J. Clinton continued with reform efforts. Finally, President G.W. Bush promised to cut the federal civil service by 800,000 jobs in his first inaugural address. However, more government workers keep being added, and the size of the government keeps growing. One of the most significant expansions after 9/11 was the creation of a Department of Homeland Security in 2003 and additional of some 100,000 officers in the Transportation Safety Administration.

Government is big, but how big? Look around when you leave the classroom and go home to the dorm, the apartment, or wherever you live. Write down all that you see. Next, list how much of what you see is regulated by the government (as far as you know). Finally, note how much is paid for by the government. Virtually anything you see or sense: trees, asphalt, streetlights, shops, cars, bicycles, clothes, baby strollers, the air you breathe, cosmetics, houses, dogs, car exhaust, all sorts of materials (textiles, rubbers, plastics), cigarette filters, and so on are influenced by government policy and regulation. The chances are that there is very little that you will see that is not somehow regulated, paid for, or directly provided by the government.

Government is very much present and visible in our everyday lives through regulations, police presence on the street, government buildings, the taxes we pay, the various services citizens receive, etc. For instance, some citizens see more government, especially those who need social welfare workers, or rely upon law enforcement or emergency services. However, the omnipresence of government also has a less visible side, like when governments install surveillance cameras in public buildings and on the streets. Since the 1960s, governments have increasingly used cameras for monitoring, such as at intersections, to catch red-light runners. We are entering a new age of surveillance (Raadschelders, 2019).

This approach of 24/7 monitoring was first developed in London in the early 1990s to upgrade the response to the Irish Republic Army (IRA) terrorism. Law enforcement relies upon CCTV (closed-circuit television) to solve crimes in British mystery and detective shows. The system includes hundreds of "smart" cameras that are remotely operated. These cameras can rotate 360 degrees, point up and down, and zoom in to detect whether an object is a cell phone or a gun. In addition, the cameras are programmed to register unusual behavior, such as walking in circles or lingering in front of a public building and to go into alert mode when registering a gunshot. These cameras enable police officers to engage in the virtual chase by tracking a suspect's activities with cameras along potential escape routes.

Since the evidence of government is all around us, it is understandable to expect people to believe its size is too large. You can get a good idea of the size of government by counting the number of territorial units (i.e., jurisdictions) at all levels. Let us compare a small country with a large one. The Netherlands has a national government (one), 12 provincial governments, 352 municipalities that provide a wide range of different services (2022), and 21 water boards (2018) that provide one type of service. So that is a total of 385 jurisdictions. Compare that to the United States, with more than 87,000 territorial government units at the federal, state, and local levels. Of these, about 35,000 are general-purpose governments, while another 40,000 are specific-purpose governments (e.g., school boards). While government size at all levels is significant, its size varies depending on the variable used to measure it.

In this chapter, we discuss the full range of services government provides. We describe this impact by examining the number of personnel, organizational structure, revenues and expenditures, and regulations. Is government too big? In what ways? These are questions you can consider while reading, and answer when you finish this chapter.

As citizens, we are expected to know the law and to be able to find our way through the maze of organizations that provide government services. This is not an easy task. How can we possibly know all the laws and regulations? How can we find the right program for assistance? Knowing the laws or finding the proper government office in a small town may not be difficult. However, this task can be much more difficult in Amsterdam, Beijing, Buenos Aires, Cape Town, Melbourne, and Toronto. Budgets and programs offered in these cities are more extensive than regional governments and even many nations.

WHAT SERVICES DOES THE GOVERNMENT PROVIDE?

The government provides a wide range of services to its citizens. We can categorize these in several ways. One way is to distinguish them according to the impact of a service. The government provides individual services to fit the needs of individuals, and only one recipient consumes services. Examples are unemployment benefits, health care benefits, licenses, and permits for businesses and homeowners. Although it is an individual service, it is not provided, nor custom-tailored to an individual since it is supposed to provide equal treatment to all who are eligible. Some services, such as unemployment insurance, require you to meet specific criteria to be eligible. However, the government offers the same access to unemployment benefits to everyone in the government's jurisdiction. Similarly, the interstate highway system benefits everyone in the nation, just as defense and environmental protection services do.

We can also distinguish government services according to their function. When the government was relatively small, most services were provided locally and were limited to a small range of repressive services. These services mainly secure order and safety in public areas and are provided by what is known as the *night watch state* (Flora & Heidenheimer, 1984). Local governments also provided preventative and caring services that mainly involved those in need (especially the elderly and the sick). Social policies expanded from the late nineteenth century at all levels of government. Especially after World War II, these social services became the core of the *welfare state*.

In the welfare state, there is a distinction between repressive services on the one hand and preventative and care services on the other; this is the most significant difference between government today and government more than a century ago. For most of history, governments provided repressive services, and care for those in need was left to charitable organizations and organized religion via the churches, mosques, synagogues, and temples. The spirit of government was captured by Hubert Humphrey in 1977,

> It was once said that the moral test of government is how that government treats those who are in the dawn of life, the children; those who are in the twilight of life, the elderly; and those who are in the shadows of life, the sick, the needy and the handicapped. (Wikipedia n.d., n.p.)

We now consider repressive and preventative and care services in more detail.

Repressive Services

Repressive services include public safety services such as police, fire, emergency services, and the judicial system to maintain order and stability. In many European countries and the United States, a few full-time or part-time officials provided night-watch service. Examples are the sheriff, who was helped by a night-watch like today's citizens' block or neighborhood watch. On both sides of the Atlantic, professionally trained and full-time police officers generally did not appear until the 1880s (Szymanski, 1999), except for the French *garde champêtre* (rural police, like the sheriff) who appeared in the late eighteenth century and the English bobby who appeared in the 1820s. There was also a judicial system to prosecute and punish law violators. Before the late eighteenth century, it was common for one person to perform the duties of the sheriff, prosecutor, and judge. Also, punishment differed from today: people received corporal punishment, were banished, or put to death, but were seldom placed in prison for a long time.

While police and justice services provide some degree of local order and stability, the armed forces protect a country. Indeed, most governments had armed forces that government employees did not staff. Instead, they could include volunteers doing their civic duty, people drafted (for instance: by conscription for the night-watch or in the military), or mercenaries for hire. It was not until about 300–400 years ago that some governments created a standing army, which is an army of professional military paid by the government.

Since ancient times, taxation has been the final repressive service governments have been engaged in. Of course, you might argue that this is not much of a service, but keep in mind that government, then and now, can only provide services through the taxes it levies. You might even consider what former

U.S. Chief Justice Oliver Wendell Holmes said: "When I pay taxes, I buy civilization."

Of course, the repressive services of the night-watch, judiciary, defense, and taxation have changed considerably in the past century. Each still fulfills its historical function of protecting the territory. In addition to these traditional repressive elements, though, each has adopted new tasks befitting a preventative and care providing government. Thus, community policing has been introduced in the past six decades to establish a bond of trust between a neighborhood and police officers. Prisons are not only used for punishment in the form of hard labor or corporal punishment but are also seen as rehabilitative institutions. The judiciary imposes incarceration as a punishment but also sentences people to community service, house arrest, and uses ankle monitors, which are less constraining. Each of these changes is more considerate of the rights of the criminal than complete incarceration. Finally, armed forces personnel learn how to fight and be a soldier and have also been trained in peace-keeping activities since the 1980s. As to purpose, taxation has not changed, but how it is collected and what is collected have changed.

Preventative Services

It was not until the early seventeenth century that some political economists and philosophers, specifically Antonio Serra in the early seventeenth, Veit Ludvig von Seckendorf in the mid-seventeenth, Christian von Wolff in the mid-eighteenth, and Adam Smith in the late eighteenth century, suggested that governments accept responsibility for providing preventative and care services for the population. However, their ideas about what we would come to call the welfare state did not become a reality until the twentieth century (Rutgers, 2001). Welfare services started to emerge at the local level centuries after scholars theorized about the need for a welfare state (Raadschelders, 1995, 2022).

This is not to say that governments before the late eighteenth century provided no care services. Most of us have heard the story of Joseph advising the Egyptian pharaoh to store grain for the lean years. In effect, this was a welfare or care service since the government acted to protect the citizenry against hardship by storing grain to overcome a series of bad harvests. The Romans also had grain storage facilities. In addition, they provided other services, such as supplying water through aqueducts, constructing highways, and offering some health care services. For example, the Appian Way is the oldest highway built by the Roman government between 312–264 BCE. However, after the fall of the Roman Empire, many public services, such as the maintenance of the highway system, disappeared.

The early Catholic Church took over the maintenance of Rome's aqueducts, city walls, hospitals, and charity organizations throughout the empire (Gladden, 1972). In fact, between the fifth and fifteenth centuries, most welfare services in Europe were provided through the church, including health care, care for the elderly and orphans, and education. So, in a way, you can say that when it came to the provision of public welfare services, the Catholic Church was a competitor to government. This came about, in part, because before the early sixteenth century, most people in the Western world belonged to the Catholic Church.

This situation changed with the reformation movement led by Martin Luther, who demanded reforms in the Catholic Church. Once it was clear that the church was not inclined to change, Luther and other reformers such as Calvin, Zwingli, and Wesley established churches collectively known as the Protestant denominations (e.g., Lutherans, Calvinists, Presbyterians, Baptists, Methodists, etc.) (Hofstede et al., 2010; Raadschelders, 2002). From that time on, church-related collective services in countries that had turned Protestant were moved to the purview of the municipal government. Churches held onto welfare services much longer in the parts of Europe dominated by the Catholic and Russian or Greek Orthodox religions. In some countries, like France, the state took those services from the church (Archer, 1979; Immergut, 1992). Currently, governments in most Western countries, and an increasing number of developing countries, provide preventative and care services for health care, welfare assistance, education, unemployment support, social security and retirement, and child and family services. A state that offers a wide range of repressive, protective, preventive, and care services is generally known as a *welfare state*.

From a historical point of view, the most recent public services to develop on a large scale are public utilities such as electricity and gas and infrastructures such as streetlights, water systems, and sewer systems. In Europe, public organizations are expected to provide these services. In other parts of the world, it is often a mix of public, semi-public, and private organizations (Raadschelders, 2005).

What Are the Types of Government Policies?

In this section we shift from looking at the kinds of services that are provided, and who they are provided to, to an examination of who pays for the service and who benefits from the service. The best-known categorization of policies is the one provided by Theodore Lowi in 1969. He made a distinction between distributive, redistributive, and regulatory policies. To Lowi (2009 [1969]), the term policy does not refer to a policy area but a type of service.

Distributive

A distributive policy involves a decision focused on the collective or a group of individuals with similar interests. Many government programs are funded by the income tax revenues that are paid by every taxpayer and there are no eligibility criteria to receive the public benefits from these programs. These programs are examples of distributive policy since everyone pays and everyone benefits. Examples of a distributive policy or service include the federal government's support of national parks, crop insurance, health research, social security, and urban grants (Meier, 2000). Distributive services are among the most common types of federal government programs. Lowi and Ginsberg (2000) further refined distributive services to describe promotional techniques that changed government from a service provider that directly funded programs to a service enabler tasked with helping others. These included organizations in the for-profit and non-profit sectors and individuals who offered the services provided by the government. Promotional techniques include subsidies, grants, contracting, licensing, franchises, and permits. The nineteenth-century land-grant colleges in the United States are an excellent historical example of such grants. The military's extensive weapons systems contracts exemplify government contracting with for-profit organizations. Finally, anyone who desires to practice medicine needs a license to do so, and those are an example of the distributive services of modern government.

Redistributive

The second category of policies includes services that aim at improving the quality of life for the less fortunate. Redistributive services include social security, health care, education, elderly care, housing, and income support. They are mainly financed by income, social security, and unemployment taxes and include economic instruments such as tax deductions or credits. Redistribute government programs are paid for by the majority of taxpayers. However, there are eligibility criteria to receive benefits from the program. Like the story of Robin Hood, these programs often take money from the rich and give it to the poor and less fortunate people in society.

Regulatory

The final group of services is regulatory policies. These services, like distributive policies, have an individual and specific impact but mainly concern government efforts to control the conduct of individuals, as well as organizations in all sectors. When we violate regulations, there are penalties.

Writing and enforcing these regulations are usually the responsibility of administrative agencies. A good example is regulations enforced by the government agency tasked with environmental protection concerning the output of hazardous materials or emissions from industrial production plants. In addition, the government regulates the degree to which we can enjoy common pool resources, such as land, water, and air, so we preserve them for long-term collective use. Administrative regulation can include control of organizational behavior, such as price regulation for businesses. Other examples are workplace regulations or health inspections to assess the adequacy of sprinklers and the cleanliness of restaurants.

Regulatory taxation imposes fees on certain products to nudge people into lesser and lesser use. The best examples are the "sin' taxes on alcohol, tobacco, and marijuana purchases. The success of these taxes is subject to dispute. Some people reduce or quit smoking or drinking because of tax increases. However, others are willing to pay almost any price (Meier, 2000).

Developmental

While Lowi's policy types focus mainly on the relationship between government and the individual, Peterson et al. (1986) suggested a fourth type, developmental policies. These policies deal more with intergovernmental transfers aimed at a community's economic and infrastructural development. Government funds are used for large, long-term projects such as building airports, constructing community centers, developing water transport systems such as canals and renovating and updating water and sewer lines and plants.

Substantive, Procedural, Material, and Symbolic Policies or Services

In addition to distinguishing policies and services according to their distributive, redistributive, regulatory, and developmental nature, we can also distinguish between substantive versus procedural, and between material or symbolic policies and services. Substantive policies or services provide goods to individuals, organizations, or governments. Procedural policies or services are more concerned with developing and providing rules determining whether a recipient is eligible for service. Material policies or services concern programs that do something. Symbolic policies or services pay lip service to an issue but do not provide, for instance, actual funding.

Combining the four types of services with the two dichotomies allows us to analyze a policy or service using a matrix (Table 6.1). For example, a municipality is considering a school bond issue to update the existing school facilities and expand the number of classrooms in school districts with fast-growing populations. If the money generated by the bond issue is distributed according to the state school funding formula, what type of policy would this be? First, it is redistributive because it focuses on schools with infrastructure needs. Second, it is substantive because the objective is tangible and funded. Third, it is material. The desire for better schools is met by efforts to generate financial support from the taxpayers.

What if the bond issue made money available to all schools for all school-related needs if they applied providing data such as daily student attendance? Then, this policy or service would be more distributive and procedural by nature since all schools would be eligible to receive money based on daily student attendance. Finally, if policymakers want to improve education but do not

Table 6.1 Matrix of Government Policies or Service

	Substantive	*Procedural*	*Material*	*Symbolic*
Distributive				
Regulatory				
Redistributive				
Developmental				

NOTE: Analysts often organize data in a table, which allows them to consider the entire range. Let us take a concrete example. A 2 x 2 table has four cells since they are two mutually exclusive and exhaustive options for the column variable and two mutually exclusive and exhaustive options for the rows. In Table 6.1, the table is a 4 x 4 since there are 16 possible combinations. For example, a distributive policy could be substantive, procedural, material, or symbolic.

provide legislative and executive support, that would be a substantive and symbolic policy.

The matrix in Table 6.1 serves as an aid in characterizing policies and services. The boxes can overlap since policies and services display various features. No matter the type of services the government provides, or the instruments used in service provision, all have grown over time. We explore explanations for this growth in the next section.

WHAT THEORIES EXPLAIN GOVERNMENT GROWTH?

We can measure government size in various ways (Larkey et al., 1981). But, as we suggested in the introduction to this chapter, the size of government must be compared to something. In this section, we limit ourselves mainly to comparisons of size at different levels of government in the United States. However, comparative data from other countries are included to show how a country's culture and norms influence perceptions of size.

We can divide tentative answers to why government services have grown into three main groups. First, demand-side theories explain government growth as a function of increased demands by citizens for more and better public services. Second, supply-side theories emphasize changes in the political system and resource availability to demonstrate growth in government. Finally, bureaucracy-internal theories stress that government organizations grow as more and more people use government services. We discuss each of these below and provide data to illustrate government size.

WHAT ARE DEMAND-SIDE THEORIES?

Demand-side theories focus on environmental influences at large and, more specifically, on the influence of economic development upon government. For example, climate and latitude, population size and density, the emancipation of the masses, and globalization explain the increased demand for government services.

Climate and Latitude

Where people live can help us understand differences in the size and services of government. Some people live near the equator's warmer tropical zone that offers fewer government services. Others in the northern and southern regions of the planet live in more temperate or even colder climates where the size and services of government are larger. It has been suggested that, in the tropics, nature provides abundant food and water, requiring only limited agricultural intervention from human beings, and housing is not much of an issue since most people spend much of their time outdoors. However, in the higher and colder latitudes, the lack of nature's abundance may cause people to seek employment in industry rather than agricultural jobs (Hofstede et al., 2010).

Also, providing care services, such as shelter against the hazards of colder weather, is more important in the northern latitudes. In the history of humankind, we have evolved from a nomadic to an agrarian and, eventually, an industrial-based urban existence. Nomadic societies were primarily self-sufficient, consuming what they produced and having few, if any, public servants. Agricultural communities may require some government, but it is informal by nature. However, once people settled down in one place and started to farm the land and produced a surplus of food for trading, a division of labor emerged between rulers, priests, soldiers, artisans, and laborers. Likewise, the concentration of people living collectively in a smaller geographic area increased. Today, in many parts of the world, a vast majority of people live in urban areas.

Government services are much more varied and substantial in the industrialized Western world than in the developing world, including nations with limited industrialization and where many people live at or below subsistence levels. In this respect, climate and income level are correlated. After all, more than 90% of the poor are found between the Tropic of Cancer and the Tropic of Capricorn (Woo, 2004). Also, various innovations in agriculture and construction are not easily transferred from one climate region to another (Diamond, 1997). Finally, there is a strong correlation between current wealth and whether a country has been a colonizer or a colony in the past two centuries (Hofstede et al., 2010). The effects of all this on the size of government services are not entirely clear, but differences in climate and latitude are related to differences in government size and services.

Population Size and Density

Population size and density provide a second explanation for the demand for government services. Smaller populations can easily be governed with limited government. Conversely, larger populations generally need more extensive government, especially when the state occupies a sizeable territory. The commonly accepted explanation for the demand for public services in the Western world is that population density was the combined effect of industrialization, urbanization, population growth, and human migration patterns. This resulted in higher public service demands and enhanced citizens' political rights.

Imagine what it must have been like to move from rural Germany to burgeoning cities like Hamburg, Düsseldorf, and Essen in the late 1880s. People left behind not only their agricultural-based livelihood but also their lifestyle. They left a community where everyone knew everyone else and could count on neighborly help in times of hardship. They went to the cities searching for work since agricultural workers experienced significant job losses and looked elsewhere for employment. The industries and factories emerging around the big cities provided ample job opportunities.

Once in the city, these workers did not know anyone. So, people increasingly turned to the local government for help. When this happened, the government took on the responsibility for alleviating the dire living circumstances by constructing water and sewage systems, developing minimum housing standards, creating garbage collection services, etc. Services were essential when many people lived in a relatively small area without proper sanitation leading to the threat of health epidemics, so, the nature of the services provided by the government changed as population density increased. And, as populations grew, so, too, did the demand for government services. Initially, local demand drove the growth of public services. But, once newspapers informed citizens of public services available in other cities, it was only natural that people wanted the same level of services.

Emancipation of the Masses

The growth of demand for public services in the nineteenth century occurred alongside growth in professional associations, labor unions, interest groups, and new political parties. Once union membership increased, the union's demands were taken more seriously. Unions, interest groups, and political parties called for government program expansions to ensure safe working conditions, which attracted new members. Over time, they gave all males and females the right to vote. This led to increased party membership and political participation, such as individuals among their ranks pursuing political office. Unionization and political participation brought attention to services citizens wanted and pressured the government to expand services to fill a broader range of needs. They had, so to speak, mobilized their bias, meaning that through opportunities for political participation, they were making their preferences about government services known (Schattschneider, 1990 [1959]).

Globalization

Globalization also influenced the growth of government services. In a way, colonization was a form of globalization, especially since it encouraged Western-style government administrations in the structure and functioning of the colonies. International aid organizations such as the World Bank and the International Monetary Fund insist upon reforms like deregulating the market and privatization (Woo, 2004). Today, residents in developing countries see what level of government services is possible when comparing their economic, political, and social situation to developed countries. So, as people travel to other countries and learn more about what other governments provide, one can expect demands for the same kinds of services.

Demand-side explanations for government services' growth argue that citizens demand government intervention to relieve social tensions caused by conditions like poverty, poor housing, and unequal treatment when individuals see that they cannot make a difference through their efforts (Wilensky, 1975). We now discuss supply-side theories as explanations for government growth.

WHAT ARE SUPPLY-SIDE THEORIES?

From the 1960s to today, *supply-side theories* have emerged. Supply-side theories suggest that government grows because people are willing to pay for services; that is, the availability of resources causes an increase in government taxing and spending. Closely related is a theory that government size will plateau then rise in crisis (Peacock & Wiseman, 1961). Finally, some supply-side theories suggest that more democracy must be supported by more government. So, when political officeholders and political parties want to gain support, they authorize more government programs and take credit for serving those constituents eligible for the new services.

Are these reasonable explanations? Let's look at some facts and trends to help us decide. First, from a historical perspective, tax revenues as a percentage of the Gross Domestic Product (GDP) in the United States increased from 6% in 1865 (Peters, 1991) to 25.5% in 20 (OECD, 2021).

In 1902, local governments collected 51% of public revenues, the federal government collected 38%, and state governments collected the remaining 11% (Mosher & Poland, 1969). Of the $5.3 trillion collected by U.S. governments in 2016, 65% was from the federal government, 20% from state governments, and 15% from local governments. So, federal government revenues rose in the first half of the twentieth century. In the second half, state and local governments regained their importance regarding revenues. The revenue increase reflects the government's need to charge more taxes to fund increased public services.

The pattern of government spending has changed dramatically over time as well. In 1792, the total government spending in the United States was $5.1 million. However, revenues in that same period were $1.4 million lower. So, even at the dawn of American democracy, government spending exceeded revenues. By 1900, spending was $1.6 trillion, and the deficit was $41 million for that year. In 2020, the estimated spending will be $8.14 trillion. Still, the revenue estimate is $7.17 trillion, which is $1.1 trillion lower than the estimated spending amount.

Revenue will generally increase during times of hardship, such as war, economic depression, or a global pandemic. Yet, paradoxically, people are more willing to pay through tax increases during hard times than during economically prosperous times. Indeed, historical data demonstrate that during World War I, the Depression, and World War II, revenues in Western countries increased to cover additional spending, then dropped significantly following these periods. Others argued that the availability of tax revenues better explains the growth in expenditures rather than market failure or crisis, a situation where a social problem cannot be resolved. Therefore, we call upon the government to intervene.

The third set of supply-side theories of government growth concerns the political climate and dominant party. From the 1930s to the late 1970s and inspired by the theories of the British economist John Maynard Keynes, it was proclaimed that government spending was good for the economy because more spending created more jobs. Government spending was also good because it supported the needy through social welfare programs, which, in turn, legitimized the existing political system. It has been said that liberal political parties tend to spend more than conservative parties. Focusing on the party's political orientation only, it appears they have some influence. Liberal political parties are credited with a stronger emphasis on government services and, thus, with support for government growth (Aikin & Bacharach, 1978). However, when the influence of the political system is regarded in connection to other influences on government growth, it is not as crucial as economic influences are (Webber & Wildavsky, 1986).

WHAT ARE BUREAUCRACY-INTERNAL THEORIES?

Another set of theories seeks to explain the size and services of government, called *bureaucracy-internal theories*. These theorists argue that more demands for government services create the need for more organizations that provide government (Stillman, 2004). When considering bureaucracy-internal theories, three main factors explain the growth in government services: personnel size, territorial and organizational structure, and regulation.

Personnel Size

How does American government employment compare with that of other countries? Is it bigger, or is it smaller? As it turns out, American government employment as a percentage of the total workforce ranks low compared with other Western countries. As these data suggest, there is a lot of variation in the percentage of government workers in the total workforce. In 1995, the government workforce was 6% in Japan and went up to a high of 32% in Sweden. With a public workforce around 15% of the total workforce, the United States sits in the middle. The differences can be explained by cultural values related to the role of government and the programs that will be provided by the public or the private sectors in society.

Since the late 1980s, the general trend in government personnel size in the Western world has been downsizing. This can be done using a cookie-cutter approach, meaning that all departments and agencies give up a certain percentage of their total positions. Or it can be done by targeting specific positions and eliminating or privatizing these. Either way, the effect is a smaller government personnel size. However, no matter the approach used, downsizing hits the middle and lower-level employees hardest.

The larger the state becomes in terms of population size and density, the more it must be ruled by *bureaucracy*. No other organizational type is as efficient as a bureaucracy for developing and delivering society-encompassing services. Weber (1946 [1922]) not only defined bureaucracy as a type of organization, but he also defined bureaucracy as a personnel system where individuals were appointed civil servants based on expertise and promoted according to merit and seniority.

Bureaucracy-internal explanations mainly focus on the theory that the expansion of bureaucracy varies with the personal desires of civil servants who seek to maximize their power. For instance, public managers strive to increase the number of people they supervise. The more people subordinate to them, the more important they believe they are. Also, they assume that bureaucrats always try to increase the budget, whether they need more or not (Downs, 1994 [1967]). These theories seem to build upon the negative image of civil servants, which has been with Americans since independence (Brutus, 1986).

It is important to note that empirical research has not supported the theories about greedy and power-hungry bureaucrats. Also, important to note is that the stereotype of the lazy and status-hungry civil bureaucrat is not just American; we can find similar stereotypes in nineteenth- and twentieth-century Europe. Indeed, an investigation into downsizing in the 1980s falsified theories showing that civil servants were more than willing and able to cut both budget and personnel size (Dunleavy, 1991).

Territorial and Organizational Structure

Another group of theories used to explain government growth uses geography as an explanatory factor. They have also suggested that technological changes rather than crises cause growth (Kaur & Rubin, 1981). Technological changes in government include changes in organizational specialization, division of labor, and degree of urbanization of society. We label these factors as territorial and organizational structure factors.

While it is easy to determine how many territorial units of government there are, getting a handle on the degree of organizational differentiation is much more difficult. The reason is simple: public organizations have multiple units inside the organization. The larger an organization, the more units it will have. An investigation into the development of organizational units in national government departments in the Netherlands between 1862–1992 showed 75 identifiable units in seven departments in 1862. By 1992, the number of organizational units had risen to 2744 in the 15 existing government departments (Raadschelders, 1997).

The number of organizational units in a jurisdiction can grow horizontally and vertically. One response to growing personnel size is to grow the number of organizational units horizontally by dividing one unit into various subunits, each with its own supervisor. An example is distinguishing in a police department between the patrol, the special victim's unit, the crime scene investigation, and the general detectives' units.

When an organization grows to a specific size, it often must add supervisory layers. The addition of an organizational layer is an example of vertical organizational differentiation. In other words, civil servants professionalize and specialize, but so do organizational units. Organizational units will increasingly reflect the specialization achieved in the workforce.

With regard to the U.S. federal government, organizational layers at the top of the organization have been called a thickening of government (Light, 2004, 2019). One explanation for organizational differentiation is that increasing personnel size requires that, at each level, subdivisions are created and that managerial/supervisory levels are added. In other words: personnel size influences the degree of organizational differentiation.

The idea that (personnel) size precedes (organizational) structure dominates the literature in organizational theory and is known as the size precedes structure hypothesis (Blau, 1970). Another body of theory argues that changes in personnel size and organizational differentiation run parallel, noting that structure precedes size. This is also known as the bureaucratic structure hypothesis. A study of the organizational development of Chicago, Detroit, and Philadelphia finance departments during the 1890–1975 period concluded that the number of units or divisions increased with personnel size. But, with the addition of each new unit, personnel size also increased by about 10% above the average growth rate. While their findings suggest that organizational differentiation and personnel size increase almost simultaneously, the authors found that the bureaucratic structure hypothesis better explained developments in organizational structure (Marshall et al., 1989).

The relationship between organizational units and personnel size over time in The Netherlands was investigated to refine both hypotheses (Raadschelders, 1997). The growth rate in the number of organizational units increased until the 1940s and has declined significantly since then. Personnel size fluctuated much more but was much lower after the 1950s.

Regulation

This is the final predictor of government size we discuss. We distinguish between two main types of regulations. First, there are the laws passed by the legislature. These laws are also known as *primary legislation* and generally concern issues of high politics. They often concern contentious issues over which the citizenry is divided, and elected officials must find a solution. Since the 93rd American Congress, the legislation passed has ranged from 7991 to 26,222. In comparison, the British Parliament passed about 60 pieces of primary legislation a year during the 1990s (Page, 2001; Raadschelders, 2017).

Does that mean that the government is issuing less regulation? No, it is not quite that simple. These numbers hide the enormous increase in omnibus legislation, which is the practice of combining measures from a variety of policy areas into one massive bill (Krutz, 2001). What does this mean? For the answer, we must look at *secondary legislation* that concerns issues of low politics (West, 1985). It includes all those government regulations issued by government organizations upon delegated authority from the legislature (Raadschelders, 2017).

We do not often think about all the things that government regulates. It ranges from grading beef products to house construction requirements and workplace safety standards, price regulations, and social regulations. We may immediately agree that an elected official should not be forced to consider standards governing the grading of beef. This is best left to experts employed by a department of agriculture. This leaves elected officials time to concentrate on society's genuinely contentious issues and policies.

To do this, public administrators enact secondary legislation. How many pieces of secondary legislation are there? We do not know; there is no data. But we know that the number of pages of the Federal Register, the daily publication that provides information about the number of proposed and adopted regulations in the United States, started at 2619 pages in 1936. Until the late 1960s, the number of pages seldom rose above 20,000. After this time, the regulation's text and explanation have significantly increased.

As expected, the number of regulations in other countries has also increased. For example, research into primary and secondary legislation in the United Kingdom showed that in the ten years between 1987 and 1997, 28,000 statutory instruments (known as secondary legislation in Britain) were issued. This is an average of almost 3000 per year. In other words, in terms of quantity, secondary legislation has become very important in many countries (Page, 2001). The main explanation for government regulation's growth may be population size and density. When the population grows and concentrates in geographical areas, tensions that might arise from that density may be addressed through government controls such as those provided by laws and regulations (Morris, 1996 [1969]).

Chapter Summary

This chapter describes the size and services of government and examines them using typologies of government that organize the intent of government organizations and programs. These basic categories illustrate the growth of government over time and the expansion of repressive and preventative services. Government programs perform different societal functions (distributive, promotional, redistributive, regulatory, and developmental) and provide different services (substantive, procedural, material, and symbolic). These functions and services may not exist at all levels of government, but often they do, as we can see in theories of intergovernmental relations. Combinations of these contribute to the overall size of government. Different explanations related to how government meets demand or supplies services to pursue economic and social goals through primary and secondary legislation and monetary and fiscal policy are found in demand and supply-side theories of government growth. In the next chapter, we move from a description of the size and structure of government to an understanding of the policymaking, implementation, and regulatory processes and how these impact the size of organizations and the programs government offers.

Practical Applications

1. What services does the government provide? Look for examples of enhanced services provided in some geographic regions.
2. This chapter looked at what are the types of government policies. Find an example of tax and redevelopment policy. How are the goals similar, how are they different?
3. We described two groups of theories to explain government growth. To what extent is demand (versus escalating costs) an explanation in the growth of health care provided by government?
4. The government offers to increase services based on providing one resource to save another. Often this is seen in environmental protection efforts. An example is the tradeoff between congestion and pollution and public transit for a cleaner environment. Can you provide another example?
5. Government programs have grown dramatically in contracting. How can program procurement policies be improved to keep the administrative costs of government contracting to a minimum?

In-Class Instructional Suggestions

1. Table 6.1 provides a matrix that helps characterize the variety of government public services. Students and the instructor can fill this out for their own country.
2. The size of government is frequently complained about in most countries. This happens because people are not informed about how the public sector size in their country compares to that of other countries, nor have they been informed about the size of the public sector at the time of their (great-) grandparents. So, what is the size of the public sector in your country at the local, regional, and national levels? At least four indicators can assess this:

    a. Personnel size at each of these levels of government
    b. Revenue and expenditure
    c. Horizontal and vertical organizational differentiation, and
    d. The ratio between primary and secondary legislation.

    Of these four, the first two will be the easiest to get. The third one requires counting organizational units in government address books, almanacs, etc. The fourth may be the most difficult, especially concerning secondary legislation.

3. Provide examples of distributive, redistributive, and regulatory policies in your country. Use these to assess how they constrain certain types of behavior or encourage other types of individual behavior.

References

Aikin, M., & Bacharach, S. B. (1978). The urban system, politics, and bureaucratic structure: A comparative analysis of 44 local governments in Belgium. In L. Karpiak (Ed.), *Organization and environment. Theory, issues, and reality* (pp. 199–250). Sage.

Archer, M. S. (1979). *The social origins of educational systems*. Sage.

Blau, P. M. (1970). A formal theory of differentiation in organizations. *American Sociological Review, 35*(2), 201–218.

Brutus (a pseudonym). (1986 [1787]). Essays I, VI, X-XII, and XV. In R. Ketchum (Ed.), *The Anti-Federalist Papers and the constitutional convention debates* (pp. 269-308) Penguin Books.

Diamond, J. (1997). *Guns, germs, and steel: The fates of human societies*. W.W. Norton and Company.

Downs, A. (1994 [1967]). . Waveland Press.

Dunleavy, P. (1991). *Democracy, bureaucracy, and public choice: Economic explanations in political science*. Harvester Wheatsheaf.

Flora, P., & Heidenheimer, A. J. (Eds.). (1984). *The development of welfare states in Europe and America*. Transaction Publishers.

Gladden, E. N. (1972). *A history of public administration*. Frank Cass.

Goodsell, C. T. (2014). *The new case for bureaucracy: A public administration polemic*. C.Q. Press.

Hofstede, G., Hofstede, G.-J., & Minkov, M. (2010). *Cultures and organizations: Software of the mind. Intercultural cooperation and its importance for survival.* McGraw Hill.
Immergut, E. M. (1992). *Health politics: Interests and institutions in Western Europe.* Cambridge University Press.
Kaur, J. B., & Rubin, P. H. (1981). The size of government. *Public Choice, 37*(2), 261–274.
Krutz, G. S. (2001). *Hitching a ride: Omnibus legislating in the U.S. Congress.* Ohio State University Press.
Larkey, P. D., Stolp, C., & Winer, M. (1981). Theorizing about the growth of government. *Journal of Public Policy, 1*(2), 161–163.
Light, P. C. (1997). *The tides of reform: Making government work.* 1945-1995 Yale University Press.
Light, P. C. (2004). *Fact sheet on the continued thickening of government.* The Brookings Institution.
Light, P. (2019). *The Government-Industrial complex: The true size of the federal government, 1984-2018.* Oxford University Press.
Lowi, T. J. (2009 [1969]). *The end of liberalism: The second republic of the United States.* W.W. Norton and Company.
Lowi, T. J., & Ginsberg, B. (2000). *American government: Freedom and power.* W.W. Norton and Company.
Marshall, C., Mitchell, D., & Wirt, F. (1989). *Culture and education policy in the American States.* Falmer Press.
Meier, K. J. (2000). *Politics and the bureaucracy: Policymaking in the fourth branch of government.* Harcourt College Publishers.
Moe, R. C. (2003). *Administrative renewal: Reorganization commissions in the 20th century.* University Press of America.
Morris, D. (1996 [1969]). *The human zoo: A zoologist's classic study of the urban animal.* Kodansha International.
Mosher, F. C., & Poland, O. F. (1969). *The costs of American governments: Facts, trends, myths.* Dodd, Mead and Company.
OECD. (2005). *Modernizing Government: The Way Forward.* OECD.
OECD. (2021). *Revenue Statistics 2021.* OECD.
Page, E. C. (2001). *Government by numbers: Delegated legislation and everyday policymaking.* Hart Publishing.
Peacock, A. T., & Wiseman, J. (1961). *The growth of public expenditure in the United Kingdom.* Princeton University Press.
Peters, G. B. (1991). *The politics of taxation: A comparative perspective.* Blackwell.
Peterson, P. E., Rabe, B. G., & Wong, K. K. (1986). *When federalism works.* The Brookings Institution.
Raadschelders, J. C. N. (1995). Rediscovering citizenship: Historical and contemporary reflections. *Public Administration, 73*(4), 611–625.
Raadschelders, J. C. N. (1997). Size and organizational differentiation in historical perspective. *Journal of Public Administration Research and Theory, 7*(3), 419–441.
Raadschelders, J. C. N. (2002). Woodrow Wilson on the history of government: Passing fad or constitutive framework for his philosophy of governance? *Administration and Society, 34*(5), 579–598.
Raadschelders, J. C. N. (2003). *Government. A public administration perspective.* M.E. Sharpe.

Raadschelders, J. C. N. (Ed.) (2005). *The institutional arrangements for water management (19th and 20th Centuries)*. Cahier d'Histoire de l'Administration no.8, IIAS. IOS Press.

Raadschelders, J. C. N. (2017). The United States of America as Rechtsstaat: State and administrative law as key to understanding the administrative state. *Public Administration Review, 77*(3), 458–465.

Raadschelders, J. C. N. (2019). The iron cage in the information age: Bureaucracy as tangible manifestation of a deep societal phenomenon. In E. Hanke, L. Scaff, & S. Whimster (Eds.), *The Oxford Handbook of Max Weber* (pp. 557–574). Oxford University Press.

Raadschelders, J. C. N. (2022). Antonio Serra, Early Modern Political Economist: From Good Government as Idealized Behavior to Good Government as Practical Policy. *Administory, Journal for the History of Public Administration, 6*. (Yearbook, based in Austria), 240–251.

Rutgers, M. R. (2001). The prince, His welfare state, and its administration: Christiaan Von Wolff's administrative philosophy. *Public Voices, 4*(3), 29–45.

Schattschneider, E. E. (1990 [1959]). The scope and bias of the pressure system. In P. Nivola and D. H. Rosenbloom (Eds.), *Classic readings in American politics* (pp. 20-46). St. Martin's Press.

Stillman, R. J. (2004). *The American bureaucracy: The core of modern government*. Wadsworth/Thomson.

Szymanski, A.-M. (1999). Dry compulsions: Prohibition and the creation of state-level enforcement agencies. *Journal of Policy History, 11*(2), 115–146.

Webber, C., & Wildavsky, A. (1986). *A history of taxation and expenditure in the western world*. Simon and Schuster.

Weber, M. (1946 [1922]). *Bureaucracy*. In H. H. Gerth and C. W. Mills (Eds.), *Max Weber: Essays in sociology* (pp. 196-235). Oxford University Press.

West, W. F. (1985). *Administrative rulemaking. Politics and processes*. Greenwood Press.

Wilensky, H. (1975). *The welfare state and equality*. University of California Press.

Woo, W. T. (2004). Some fundamental inadequacies of the Washington consensus: Misunderstanding the poor by the brightest. In J.-J. Teunissen & A. Akkerman (Eds.), *Diversity in development. Reconsidering the Washington consensus* (pp. 9–43). Fondad.

CHAPTER 7

Setting the Course of Government

In Chap. 6, we described the size and services of government. Acknowledging that many people complain that government is too big, we explored how government pursues economic and social goals. This is done through various programs that provide either repressive or preventative services. When designing or refining government programs, we estimate the demand and associated costs of these demands. Then we can determine the way the service will be provided to achieve the intended results and improve the condition of the intended service recipient and society.

Beginning with this chapter and continuing through the remaining chapters, we transition from describing governance and government through an institutional lens, that laid the foundation for the remainder of this book, which is using an administrative lens to examine how the government carries out the collective policy preferences of the people. Setting the course of government requires collaborative interactions between elected officials as policymakers and the government administrators tasked with implementing policy.

In this chapter, we introduce the intergovernmental relations system and describe how it impacts policy analysis, policymaking, program implementation, and regulatory processes. These activities set the course for government action by establishing what level of government is responsible for funding programs and what level is responsible for providing the goods and services of these programs. When combined, these activities foster transparency by letting people know what government intends to do. They also suggest the direction in which the government is moving. The future course of government can be established by looking at what the government has done or is accomplishing. Then, by measuring what is accomplishing we can hold government accountable for results and understand the societal impacts of government.

© The Author(s), under exclusive license to Springer Nature Switzerland AG 2023
A. L. Franklin, J. C.N. Raadschelders, *Introduction to Governance, Government and Public Administration*,
https://doi.org/10.1007/978-3-031-32689-9_7

Who Sets the Course of Government?

In Chap. 4, we described how everyone can influence the course of government through the relationships they have with public servants. In this chapter, we describe four kinds of government officials who are given the authority to make decisions that set the course of government: elected officials, political appointees, citizen functionaries, and public administrators or civil servants.

As the name suggests, *elected officials* are selected by the public's vote. They serve in the legislative, executive, or judicial branches of government. Many elected officials are not full-time politicians and receive very little payment for their services when you consider the amount of time they devote to governing. There was a time when elected officeholders constituted a large percentage of total public sector personnel, given that the civil service was tiny. Nowadays, elected officials do not constitute a large proportion of government workers.

The next two categories of public servants are neither elected by the people nor appointed to a career position. They are political appointees and citizen functionaries. *Political appointees* are selected by and serve at the pleasure of elected officials. In most countries, the elected executive leader can appoint individuals to high-level positions in government departments and agencies. For some of these executive appointments, legislative approval and confirmation are necessary. For others, there is no external confirmation.

The citizen functionary works in government in a non-elected office, voluntarily and without salary. These are people who serve on all sorts of boards, councils, and advisory committees. Examples at the local level include local planning and zoning committee members and the library board. Also, elected officials can create ad hoc advisory committees for specific issues and designate citizen functionaries as members of these advisory committees. The number of citizen functionaries compared to the number of government workers is quite small. However, the service they provide to government is crucial since they provide expert advice and increase access into government actions, especially locally.

Public administrators, also referred to as *civil servants*, have perhaps the most robust access for providing input in the policy process. Many are street-level bureaucrats and thus have day-to-day interactions with residents where they learn about their wants, needs, and preferences. This input can inform the provision of government goods and services. It can help to improve the programs government offers. And it can inform policymaking when preferences are communicated through political-administrative relationships. Goodsell (2004, 2014) studied government workers and found that they are excellent proxy representatives of the people in a country in terms of socio-demographic and ideological positions. Further, he documented that people have a high degree of confidence in public workers based on the direct interactions, making them critical to the functioning of democracy (nota bene: Just as Georg Hegel already argued in his *Philosophy of Right* in 1820).

While not having official status in terms of determining government actions, the largest group of people who can set the course of government is all the people, whether they act on behalf of themselves as individuals or as a member or representative of a group. The people's will is being served by elected officials, citizen functionaries, and civil servants (Raadschelders, 2003). The ability for people to provide input into government decisions and actions and the responsibility for government officials to uphold a duty to consider this input is well established. It is a crucial form of civic engagement.

Civic engagement is defined as "...individual and collective actions designed to identify and address issues of public concern. Civic engagement takes many forms, from individual to organizational involvement to electoral participation. It can include efforts to address an issue directly, work with others in a community to solve a problem or interact with the institutions of representative democracy."

How Does the Intergovernmental System Set the Course of Government?

Designing the structure of governance for a nation is a daunting task. In 1887, Woodrow Wilson characterized the American government system as interdependent, with government systems at the federal, state, and local levels interacting. Establishing the powers and functions of the government and the hierarchical arrangements between different government units is necessary (as discussed in Chap. 5). But so are the details of operating government to provide goods and services which require collaboration and coordination. Aligning the structure and operations of government has grown more complex as the number of governmental units, and relations between civil servants have increased.

This section explores the specific powers and functions granted to those in government, how they can be distributed between the levels of government, and how relationships between two or more governments are characterized using metaphors to describe these interactions. We define federalism and explain the differences between the terms federalism, intergovernmental relations, and intergovernmental management.

Federalism generally refers to two levels of government, the national level (also called the federal level since it represents the entire nation) and the regional level. Scholars have identified historical shifts in relations between levels of government (Diamond, 1974). The first was *dual federalism*, when there were shared responsibilities between national and state governments (Elazar, 1966). The second was *cooperative federalism*, reflecting increases in the federal government's role in fostering programs that could benefit the nation. When comparing intergovernmental relations in Sweden, Norway, and Denmark and comparing the Scandinavian systems with France and Germany, Blom-Hansen

(1999) found that cooperation wanes when one government can threaten intergovernmental actors with exit.

Concentrated (or centralized) federalism occurred next, where professionalism in government relationships was enhanced (Elazar, 1966). Creative federalism placed a stronger emphasis on the role of local government (Anders & Shook, 2003). Competitive federalism was notable in its efforts to devolve programs and funds to lower levels of government. At the same time, contractive (or fend-for-yourself) federalism featured budget reductions at higher levels of government and devolution of program responsibility without funding guarantees (also known as unfunded mandates) (Shannon, 1983). Collaborative federalism, featuring networks of national and regional organizations providing services, often partners with non-profit and private actors to deliver government programs and services (McGuire, 2006; Durant, 2020). The phases of federalism underemphasize the increasing role of other levels of government. Two new terms have emerged to capture better the complex web of interactions: intergovernmental relations and multi-level governance.

WHAT IS INTERGOVERNMENTAL RELATIONS AND MULTI-LEVEL GOVERNANCE?

The term *intergovernmental relations* (IGR) describes the relationships between any two governmental units and analyzes interactions between units of governments and government officials. Several factors including demographic and geographical, social, and cultural, historical, constitutional and institutional, political, and circumstantial influence the nature and extent of relationships between governmental units (Cameron, 2001). In a comparative study of the dynamics between the national and state levels of government in Canada, the United States, and Switzerland. Bolleyer (2006) found that a region's internal dynamics, such as power-sharing between the executive and the legislature, can strengthen and stabilize intergovernmental arrangements and make them more productive.

The term intergovernmental relations is particularly important for nations that share a border, like Canada and Greenland. It can also refer to nations operating within overlapping geographic space, such as Canada and the indigenous nations located within its boundaries. Finally, the term can also describe relations governed by a supranational authority such as the African Union and its activities on behalf of multiple African nations.

And, of course, intergovernmental relations can be used to describe relations between organizations at the same level of government, such as two regions in Armenia or municipalities in Ireland or councils in Scotland. In Australia, the term is commonly used to describe the increased engagement between actors at different levels of government (Phillimore, 2010). This includes different combinations of federal, state/provincial, and local governments (known as general-purpose governments) and special-purpose governments (independent school districts, water districts, and toll or port authorities). IGR is a dynamic concept since relationships constantly change based on social and economic forces, political factors, and preferences of residents (Burke, 2014; Krane & Wright, 2018).

Multi-Level Governance

Over time, it has become more common to speak of *multi-level governance* (MLG) when describing relationships between governmental units (Bache et al., 2016). Described as the crossroads of the vertical (intergovernmental) and horizontal (state-society) dimensions for an organization that functions as a "polity in the making" with different levels and arenas for decision-making. It also useful for describing, interpreting, implementing, and evaluating policy decisions (Ongaro et al., 2010, p. 3). MLG is nearly universal in the international arena, where climate action must be accomplished in a polycentric, multi-sector, multi-actor setting. However, just like the challenges described for some of the types of federalism, in China, it was found that multi-level governance interactions can be hampered when power, political-economic coalitions, and technology practices at the local level cannot be overcome and deliberative interactions between partners are restricted (Westman et al., 2019).

Over time, the number of local general-purpose and special-purpose governments delivering government programs and services has increased significantly. Despite local governments' essential role, their authority can be limited in the federal government system. For example, in the United States, cities cannot exist without the state's authorization since an 1868 ruling, called Dillon's rule, upholds total state sovereignty in placing limitations and constraints on cities.

However, cities have more power in states that allow a *home-rule charter*. Under a home-rule charter, the city can "frame, adopt, and amend a charter for their governments and [...] exercise all powers of local self-government, subject to the constitution and general laws of the state" (Levy et al., 1974, p. 220). These powers allow each city to have the independence to determine its form of government and how and from what geographical areas their officials will be elected. Home-rule cities can also make a policy that differs from the state without seeking state government approval. Degrees of autonomy are not just possible with local governments but can also be relevant to territories that are part of a sovereign nation yet are allowed a degree of independence. Thus, the island of Aruba in the Caribbean has a "*status aparte*" in the Dutch monarchy. It has the right to govern and regulate local matters while remaining under the auspices and international legal protection of the Netherlands. Aruba can adopt its own constitution as long as it does not contradict the Dutch constitution. Another example is the Faroe Islands which are part of the Danish realm but enjoy self-governing capacity.

The relationship between state (i.e., regional) and local governments is often described as a love-hate relationship (Morgan & England, 1999). States provide financial support, but cities must take a defensive position to avoid: (1) mandates to provide certain services their citizens do not desire, (2) cost-shifting, (3) reductions in revenue sharing formulas, and (4) restrictions of local revenue sources (Anders & Shook, 2003). For example, in Louisiana, there are ongoing debates about the ability of local governments to control fracking and if the lack of control signals a retreat from home rule (Ritchie, 2018). Partisan politics and interest group lobbying often explain why the pre-emption of local law is becoming more prevalent (Hicks et al., 2018, p. 28). The principle of home rule is subject to continuous adjustment (Briffault et al., 2020).

What Are Metaphors for Intergovernmental Relationships?

Intergovernmental relations are often described by using metaphors. The earliest metaphor was a *layer cake* because two distinct layers of government, federal and state, bonded together. Later, this metaphor was amended to a *marble cake*, with a swirling effect of duties and responsibilities between the layers instead of separate layers (Grodzins, 1960).

The *picket fence* metaphor recognized the increasingly complex relationships where more than two levels of government had policy and program delivery responsibilities (Wright, 1988). The pickets represent the policy areas, and the support beams represent the levels of government. The differences symbolized by the support beams are the type of work done at each level.

Let's consider the picket fence metaphor. Each picket is a policy area (education, environment, public safety) and the pickets are connected by the levels of government (municipal, regional, national). We can apply this to, for instance, education policy. The federal government provides funds for specific education programs, particularly for students with special needs. Some regional governments can establish the number of classroom hours required each year and devise a funding formula to be paid to the schools to consider individual needs. The local level of government (in the United States) is responsible for establishing school conduct policy and the local level of school funding through the school board and administrators.

The metaphor of the picket fence has been replaced by a *bamboo fence* (Milakovich & Gordon, 2004). Unlike pickets, bamboo shoots grow randomly and have greater flexibility, mimicking the flexibility between government levels. Song and Meier (2018) recently described federalism using the image of a *kaleidoscope*, reflecting the shifting nature of intergovernmental relationships during the COVID-19 pandemic. He argues that the standard expectations are that national and regional levels of government work together. Yet, at the same time, they also may function as separate, autonomous entities to promote and provide for the general welfare through the establishment of public health policies for their jurisdiction. During the pandemic and across the globe, the various levels of government experienced fault lines where ideological differences led to disconnects in implementing public policy.

Intergovernmental management refers to the activities of the civil servants charged with carrying out programs involving multiple governments (Agranoff, 1986). Over time, as expertise develops and administrators at different levels establish ongoing relationships, associations begin to form in the policy areas represented by the pickets in the picket fence metaphor. Combined, each actor has varying levels of influence in the intergovernmental policy process (Duff & Wohlstetter, 2019). Common issues experts discuss are funding requirements for government programs (Radin, 2007), the ability to cross boundaries in program implementation (Agranoff, 2017), and the potential for bargaining and negotiation (Agranoff & McGuire, 2004).

What Is the Judiciary's Role in Intergovernmental Relations?

In any set of institutional arrangements for governing, the judiciary provides important guardrails for the structuring and functioning of intergovernmental relations. It is impossible to address the variety of these arrangements across the globe. Thus, we will focus on the role that the courts have played in shaping the American intergovernmental system. Within 15 years after the nation was created, during the 1800s, the U.S. Supreme Court heard cases involving challenges to the division of power and authority that was vested in the national or state levels of government.

In studies of the judiciary's role in intergovernmental relations, it has been suggested that there are specific periods of judicial activism where the highest national court actively favors one level of government over the others (Conlan & De Chantal, 2001; Pickerell & Clayton, 2004). In the early 1800s, the U.S. Supreme Court led by Marshall saw its role as an instrument of national cohesion and, as a result, favored the national level of government. During the 1950s and 1960s, the Warren Court defended the rights of "discrete and insular minorities" and shifted back to a more dualist approach supporting intergovernmental relations. Like a pendulum effect, the Rehnquist Court extended the protections of the power and authority of state governments by overturning Congressional statutes that intrude into state sovereignty or exceed Congress's delegated powers under the Constitution. As the American example shows, the judiciary's role in resolving intergovernmental disputes will always be necessary and will be influenced by shifts in the ideological position of the courts as judges leave and are replaced.

What Is Policy Analysis?

The judiciary performs legal analysis to establish if laws are being properly carried out through the cases it hears. Likewise, analysis is completed by elected officials, and government works to decide what and how government should provide goods and services and if these should be codified into laws or other legal instruments such as rules and policies of government organizations. Althaus et al. (2020) define *policy* as an authoritative statement by a government about its objectives and public values. *Policy analysis* is the systematic investigation of alternative courses of public action using evidence for and against each option and introducing these into the discussion before deciding (Anderson, 2000).

The Australian government has policymaking routines and structures that feature bureaucratic coordination while retaining the control of elected officials. Governments achieve these objectives through *policy instruments* such as advocacy, networks, funding, government laws, policies, and narratives that encourage collective behaviors. Institutions, regulators, think tanks, public experts, and peer organizations or governments can be included in the policy instrument list (Rose, 2004). What these policy instruments have in common is the recognition that public policy is a purposive course of action the government undertakes to deal with a social condition or challenge that no other actor can resolve or improve.

A key component of policy analysis is identifying the cause-and-effect relationships between the problem to be addressed and the results that can be expected from different alternatives based on prior experiences and social science research (Mohr, 1988). Unfortunately, this analysis can never be wholly objective or rational since we can never have complete information, and we seldom, if ever, can confidently identify causal relationships.

Even when we have good information and agree on *causal models*, policy analysis is never free from subjective valuations. People often prefer an alternative based on their own interests rather than objective evidence. While analysis is highly concerned with information and evidence, politics and personal preferences can trump analysis (Lindblom & Woodhouse, 1993). Why does this occur? Often it is because how you view a situation depends on your goals and self-interests, plus how well you can strategically portray them to persuade a government official to accept your preferred policy solution (Stone, 1997).

As we all try to persuade each other, we often use different information, reasoning, or strategies to defend our preferred alternative (Lindblom, 1959). Since no one can be wholly rational and overcome their self-interests, all debate between decision-makers is rhetoric. That is, we may spend more time presenting information that supports our preferences and minimizes, or even ignores, information about other alternatives. Policy analysis attempts to reduce the influence of rhetoric by systematically gathering information about different options and self-consciously limiting the presentation to objective details.

What Are the Limits of Policy Analysis?

All people gather facts, interpret them, and debate public issues. Therefore, we need to understand the limits of policy analysis. We can do this by acknowledging the role of politics, uncertainty, and value conflicts, and encouraging a competition of ideas (Lindblom & Woodhouse, 1993). This competition will combine both objective and subjective information. Because of this, policy analysis has been characterized as both an art and a science (Wildavsky, 1979). As an art, it requires insight, creativity, and imagination. As a science, it requires knowledge of analytical techniques and skills for policy analysis (Weimer & Vining, 2005; Vining & Weimer, 2017). These skills include communicating information within the deadlines and in an appropriate format. We must also understand the issue's political, social, and ethical context and the values in tension.

There is no one right way to do policy analysis. Instead, an approach suitable for entry-level analysts called the Eightfold Path has been offered by Bardach and Patashnik (2019). As the name suggests, these eight steps foster practical problem-solving, which can be used whenever policy analysis is needed. These eight steps are: define the problem, assemble evidence, construct alternatives, select criteria, project outcomes, confront trade-offs, decide, and tell your story. The primary objective of policy analysis is to look at the net effect of alternative courses of action for government that are flexible and evidence-based (Weimer, 2012; Meltzer & Schwartz, 2018). The net effect is what is left after all the costs and benefits have been considered. Hopefully, the value of the benefits will exceed the costs of the alternative being considered (a positive net effect).

To determine the net effect, you may start by considering who pays and who benefits under each different policy alternative and whether the winners will benefit enough to compensate the losers (called *Kaldor-Hicks criterion* analysis). Determining the net effect of who benefits and who pays for government actions often relies heavily on quantitative data and features mathematical computations.

One popular form of policy analysis is *cost-benefit analysis* (CBA). This analytical technique identifies the costs and benefits of a policy alternative. A dollar value is assigned to each cost and each benefit. Then all the costs are subtracted from all the benefits to determine the net effect. This value shows the proposal's net gain or loss. The policy alternative with the highest net gain (or lowest loss) is recommended.

From this description, you might conclude that cost-benefit analysis is straightforward. In theory, it is, in practice, it is not. There are many types of costs and benefits. Most policy analysis considers costs and benefits in the first two rows of Table 7.1. Direct effects are those experienced by the intended policy recipient(s). Indirect effects are felt by people or groups who are not the intended policy recipients but could be impacted by the recommended action.

Table 7.1 Costs and benefits for a community park

	Benefits	Costs
Direct Indirect	Teams play ball Siblings play on the playground	Maintenance of fields Police patrols
Intended	Kids play sports games	Staff for officiating and concession
Unintended	Parents and kids interact	Staff for garbage collection after the game
Tangible Intangible	Kids exercise	Staff for database management Less funding for library
Spillovers Externalities	Regional tournament entry fees Area merchants get tourism revenue	Lack of parking for soccer matches during the tournament Traffic congestion on game days
Transaction Opportunity		Need to manage league and tourney play Cannot build a walking path

Consider a community park; can you identify other costs and benefits to add to Table 7.1? Once you do, the challenge is deciding how comprehensive the analysis should be. The more costs and benefits you identify, the more complicated and time consuming the analysis becomes. You may have also noticed that assigning values to some costs and benefits would be easier than others. But the values you assign may not be the same ones I would assign. These are some of the challenges in cost-benefit analysis.

The last three rows in Table 7.1 portray additional categories that should be considered but for which it is hard to assign a value. These include tangible and intangible costs and benefits. It is much easier to assign a value to tangible costs and benefits or things seen and measured.

Costs and benefits can be established for *spillover effects* and *externalities*, also called second-order consequences (Sylvia et al., 1997). These refer to effects on a population other than the one intended. *Transaction costs* represent the participants' time, materials, and information-gathering efforts needed to determine the costs and benefits of different alternative actions. Finally, *opportunity costs* reflect a loss caused by choosing one alternative since funds devoted to one alternative cannot be used for another, perhaps more profitable or less risky, alternative.

Another challenge for cost-benefit analysis arises when you consider alternatives that span multiple years. When this happens, the cost estimates need to consider time: what is the value of money to be expended or benefits received in future years using today's currency? (Posavec & Carey, 1997). There are mathematical techniques to account for the differences in the timing of the costs and benefits so that projects with costs and benefits occurring in different periods can be compared.

The subjectiveness of the analysis can cause the results to be challenged. For example, we seldom have a pre-established list of all the costs and benefits of a proposed alternative. Even less frequently are agreed-upon values to use for different types of costs and benefits. One way to avoid this is for the analyst to prepare a list of costs and benefits without assigning monetary value. Also, the analyst can make a list of assumptions as part of the cost-benefit analysis. This information is presented to decision-makers for review and approval before the analysis. Doing so reduces the challenges to the cost-benefit analysis.

WHAT OTHER POLICY ANALYSIS TOOLS?

Cost-effectiveness analysis (CEA) relates the cost of an alternative to how well it meets pre-specified goals (Kee, 1994). Cost-effectiveness analysis (or means-ends analysis) does not itemize and assign values to all benefits; the results are presented in terms of cost per unit of service. This technique is inexpensive for providing comparative data on different alternatives to decision-makers. These characteristics of CEA are essential because, in some situations, it is difficult to assign dollar values to benefits, but we still want the ability to compare alternatives.

Another technique often used is *sensitivity analysis*. In sensitivity analysis, you rerun the cost-benefit or cost-effectiveness analysis using different assumptions about the monetary value of various costs or benefits. Sensitivity analysis suggests the point at which an alternative has no net benefit. It also allows comparisons between options to see which better meets outcome or financial goals. This method is often preferred since we do not know the future. Using sensitivity analysis, one can assign reasonable values to costs and benefits and identify the threshold at which an alternative no longer makes sense.

Despite our best attempts to make the information in our analyses as reliable as possible and resistant to challenge, there is evidence that the results from policy analysis suffer from low usage by decision-makers (Weimer & Vining, 2005). To avoid this, the decision criteria should be established before the analysis is started. Another strategy is to identify the alternatives to consider or identify what assumptions are to be used. This can make it more likely that the results will be used. The policy analysis results should clearly describe the sources of information and where subjective values have been utilized so that the decision-maker can independently judge the credibility of the results. Analysis that uses credible sources of information, which is candid about assumptions made, and notes how the analysis would change if different assumptions were used is more likely to get used.

HOW ARE DECISIONS MADE IN GOVERNMENT?

Decision-making can be as easy as choosing between alternative courses of action in response to changing conditions. Decisions can range from taking no action, even though the situation has changed, to modifying the current response or adopting a new alternative (Bachrach & Baratz, 1963).

Decision-making becomes complicated when more than one goal must be achieved. Often satisfying one goal may reduce the chances of achieving another goal. For example, you may decide to go to a movie that meets your entertainment goal; however, by going to the movie and not studying, you may reduce the likelihood of getting a good grade in this class. Or you may pick an alternative that maximizes cost-efficiency, like renting a video, but that still does not maximize long-term effectiveness since you still are not studying.

A variety of approaches can be used to make decisions (for an overview, see: Landsbergen & Raadschelders, 2018). As the name suggests, the *comprehensive rational model* assumes that all decision-makers act rationally. This means that they make decisions to maximize the achievement of some pre-established goals. Comprehensive means that all possible alternatives are considered objectively, based on how well each satisfies the pre-established goal (Simon, 1957). To do this assumes that information is available on every possible alternative. Once all the alternatives are identified and analyzed, each is ranked based on how well it satisfies the goal. The alternative with the highest ranking is the one selected.

The model assumes that decision-makers have the resources to identify and analyze all alternatives. The strength of this approach is that decisions are made rationally based on pre-established criteria rather than decision-makers' preferences. The weaknesses are that it is unclear who identifies the alternatives or how they are ranked. Further, preferences do not remain constant for one decision-maker or across decision-makers, and one goal seldom is pursued when public decisions are made (March & Simon, 1993).

A variation of the comprehensive rational model is called *satisficing*. This model collects information on known alternatives one at a time. Decision-makers accept the best possible of all the known alternatives that meet or exceed their expectations without considering others (March & Simon, 1993). The decision rule is to optimize, not maximize, goal achievement. The satisficing concept assumes that people are boundedly rational since their information processing and storage capabilities are limited. This concept of *bounded rationality* was coined by Herbert Simon and is considered a significant challenge to classical economic theory that assumes a decision-maker is omniscient, or all-knowing. Many argue that satisficing is a better reflection of governmental decision-making than the rational-comprehensive model. This is because limited resources and the tendency to favor the status quo rather than consider a comprehensive range of alternatives are evident in decision-making.

Another model, the *incremental model*, is commonly used when allocating resources. This model starts with determining the amount of change in resources government has gained or lost since the previous decision. That amount of change is called the increment. Instead of deciding on the total allocation of resources, decision-makers start with the current allocation and then decide how the incremental change should be allocated. In this model, there is no need to establish a goal beforehand. Instead, decisions about how to allocate the increment are made based on the preferences of the current decision-makers. Incremental decisions result in limited changes to existing policy and create a bias toward gradual adjustment that supports the status quo rather than radical changes (Lindblom, 1959). They provide a fast and pragmatic solution that everyone benefits from, creating a higher likelihood of agreeing on what should be done. However, this strength is also a weakness since this model assumes that allocating resources from previous decisions is appropriate, meaning nothing has changed in the operating environment. This assumption limits the discussion of alternatives.

Etzioni suggested that a better approach is *mixed scanning*. This method uses elements of both the rational-comprehensive and incremental models. The rational model is used for macro-level policy decisions, and the day-to-day operational decisions are made using the incremental approach (Etzioni, 1967).

Yet another decision-making model is *political bargaining*. This model recognizes that there are multiple decision-makers with different preferences. This results in bargaining, negotiation, and exchange instead of finding one alternative that satisfies everyone's preferences. Different alternatives are discussed, and slight variations are traded until a solution is found that ensures a minimum winning coalition or a situation where just enough decision-makers are willing to vote for an alternative to approve it. There are three conditions for bargaining to be successful: all parties must be willing to negotiate, each party must have something to trade, and each party must want something different. When these conditions are met, the likelihood that a minimum winning coalition can be formed increases.

Bargaining activities can be implicit or explicit; mostly, they are implicit—occurring outside of the public eye. Explicit bargaining is evidenced when military bases, senior citizens centers, or museums in one city or region are included in the appropriations bill to benefit a specific legislative member to gain their vote. This is often referred to as bringing home the bacon or pork-barrel projects.

The *advocacy coalition framework* is a variant of political bargaining (Sabatier, 1988). An advocacy coalition occurs when additional actors, such as interest groups, provide information about their members' preferences to influence decision-makers' preferences. Advocacy coalition frameworks focus on the competition between opposing viewpoints and how information is given to decision-makers supporting these multiple viewpoints. This model assumes that the best solutions are created through an open competition of ideas when many groups representing different views become involved in discussions about possible alternatives (Lindblom & Woodhouse, 1993).

One strength of the political bargaining and coalition advocacy models is that they acknowledge that self-interests affect decisions; the models seek to limit actions based purely on self-interest by purposefully including the interests of a broader range of actors. When we speak of self-interest for public officials, we aren't so much talking about what they want personally, although they may think of that too, but rather what they want to satisfy their constituents (Golden, 2000) and their organization (for sources of information upon which decision-makers draw, see Raadschelders & Whetsell, 2018). The weaknesses of these models are that they do not recognize some goals that decision-makers work toward despite their self-interests. Additionally, advocacy groups may misrepresent their members' interest(s) or become involved in the political bargaining model's bargaining, negotiation, and exchange tactics.

As the name suggests, the expert model of decision-making relies on the advice of a group of experts gathered explicitly for decision-making. It is also called the nominal group technique or the *Delphi method* (Delbecq et al., 1975). This model starts with individuals brainstorming various alternatives with no discussion or critique of the ideas between these experts during multiple rounds of review. The experts indicate their preferred course of action from the proposed alternatives in each review round. Then, they learn the decisions made by all the other experts. The process is repeated until consensus, or some pre-established level of agreement, has been achieved (Gortner et al., 1997).

The strength of this model is the use of experts to generate and evaluate a wide range of alternatives. The voting process results in an aggregation of individual preferences without the negotiation process of the incremental or political bargaining models. By bringing together a group of experts, the overall quality of the decisions is enhanced even further. The weakness of this model is that the expert decision-makers may not account for the varying value preferences of everyone who is impacted by the decision.

After decisions are made, there are always critics. This is not surprising because there is seldom agreement about what goals are to be served before deciding what to do. The acceptance of decisions can be improved by establishing criteria before gathering any information. Another way to improve decision-making is to have pre-agreement on the process and decision rule(s). Decision-making does not always have to be consensual, where everyone must agree or where the majority rules. Pre-established criteria for analysis, ranking criteria, and making decisions can overcome a winner-take-all mentality.

What Are the Purposes of Strategic Planning?

Deciding which policy option is preferred does not mean the course of government action has been set. Moving from a policy decision to policy action often starts with *strategic planning* or disciplined decision-making that guides an organization to what it wants to do. Strategic planning asks where we are now and where we want to be to determine what activities are needed to reach future desired end states.

Strategic planning is both a process and a product. It is a process because it forces the members of an organization to think, decide, and act proactively and systematically. It is a product because you have a strategic plan document at the end of the planning process. Yet the document is not the final step. Instead, it is a guide for action that must be flexible enough to respond to changing circumstances. Strategic planning is valuable because it encourages strategic thinking rather than rigid conformance to a planning document. It is also essential for establishing internal and external communication processes that help set and manage common expectations for improving government performance.

Learning about strategic planning can be confusing because there are many different strategic plans. Strategic plans can be for different entities in government. Some are for an entire level of government, such as a municipality; others are for specific policy areas, like providing services for the city's homeless persons; some are for organizational units, like a community services program; others are for services provided by operating units in an organization, like a homeless shelter. And finally, some are for the processes and internal operations in an organizational unit, like food vouchers for homeless shelter residents.

The longest-term strategic plans include capital and infrastructure development, such as highways. Long-term strategic plans can also be developed in policy areas such as national health care and for the future solvency of a social security system. Looking 15 to 20 or even 30 years into the future is not unusual for these kinds of plans.

When you design a strategic plan for a longer term, you must deal with higher levels of uncertainty and are forced to make more assumptions about how the future will look. It is easier for us to predict what might happen in the next three years than five or ten years, let alone 30 years into the future. However, when you plan for ten or more years into the future, you often look at accomplishing something that will take significant resources. To ensure that these resources are available, you need to plan now.

Longer-term strategic plans are more abstract, and the goals more ambitious since they deal with outcomes and impacts or changes in social conditions. These reflect the societal level reasons for why we created government programs. Shorter-term and more detailed plans are necessary to operate these programs. Called tactical plans, these documents describe what resources will be used, what units and persons are responsible for performing program activities, and the deadlines by which results must be accomplished. Chapter 8 provides a more in-depth review of strategic planning, who is involved in plan creation, and what is included in the plan.

Who Makes Government Rules and Regulations?

When taken together, policy decisions, strategic plans, and government rules and regulations prescribe acceptable behaviors for individuals and organizations and government organizations and workers (Thompson & Jones, 1982). Rules and regulations are almost universally described as too complex (Crowley & Stewart, 2020) and intruding into private affairs. However, they are also a necessary evil since we ask the government to protect the public interest (Gerston et al., 1988).

Vedung (1998) describes rules and regulations as carrots, sticks, or sermons. Carrots refers to the regulatory instruments that gives or allows material resources in money or kind. In 2011, the UK Public Bodies Act, which affected some 900 regulatory public bodies, was designed to re-orient regulators to consider creating advantages for the regulated in ways that would reduce costs, enhance efficiency, and stimulate innovation (Browne, 2020). When we refer to regulations using sticks, we are describing the power of government mandates for people to act in a certain way and punish them if they do not. An example is issuing tickets for exceeding the maximum speed on the roadways. Finally, informational regulatory instruments represent the sermons since these are government efforts to influence people to act in the interest of society. Informing the public about the benefits of recycling or recommended times for watering your lawn to reduce water consumption are examples of this instrument.

Rulemaking by government agencies is described as the *administrative state*. We need the administrative state because the legislative branch cannot keep up with the need for laws that regulate policy action (Rosenbloom, 2003; Newbold & Rosenbloom, 2017). Just like laws, administrative rules can influence the behaviors of individuals, groups, organizations, governments, and governance regimes at the collective and societal or constitutional levels.

Administrative rulemaking must follow specific steps purposefully designed to encourage transparency and accountability of government administrators who interpret legislative intent through their rules. Any rules created under legally authorized administrative procedures carry the force of law. Generally, proposed rules must be announced and posted, and a period for gathering comments from the public follows. Next, government officials describe how they considered and responded to the comments. Following that, a final rule is published in a document and manner accessible to everyone.

Administrative rules are categorized in two ways. The first categorization is *legislative, procedural, and interpretative rules* (Rosenbloom, 2003). Legislative, or substantive rules, are primary legislation and have the force of law. Procedural rules mainly concern and govern a government organization's internal operations. They also involve how requests from citizens for information or benefits are processed. Finally, interpretative rules are policy statements that reflect a program's approach to explaining how it understands the rules it must implement.

The second categorization is into *economic and social regulation* to regulate society's behavior for the collective's benefit. Government regulation was originally introduced to control marketplace activities (Neiman, 2000). This type of regulation, called economic regulation, impacts an entire industry and may control factors such as entry, exit, price, output, and profit. Market regulations serve to avoid the emergence of a single or small number of firms that controls the market, called conditions of monopoly or oligopoly (Arrow, 1977[1970]). Firms are also regulated to control destructive competition, oversee natural monopolies, ensure that the costs of externalities and spillovers are considered in market prices, and increase information transparency (Lemak, 1985).

Social regulation protects consumers from harm when using a product or receiving a service. Social regulation is not targeting one specific industry. Instead, what is regulated is a good or service people consume. Unlike economic regulations, social regulation can also protect scarce collective resources such as air, water, and land.

Regulation activities are provided by one of two different types of organizations. The first, the independent regulatory board or commission, was typical in the early days of market regulation. Organizations such as a country's central bank are institutionally independent of political interference. Still, limited control by the executive and legislative bodies exists. Its members are usually practitioners or experts in the industry for which the market is regulated. The enabling act of the independent regulatory board specifies the composition of the board/commission and the selection and term of the members. Typically, the members' term is staggered so that not all members are replaced simultaneously, and organizational memory is preserved. These boards or commissions may not have a single director. Instead, all members make decisions for the organization.

The second type of regulatory organization operates within the government's administrative structure and is under the executive's authority. These agencies are headed by individuals who may or may not be practitioners or experts in regulated areas. An example of a supranational regulatory organization is the European Medicines Agency, which centralizes the approval process for medical drugs and devices. However, an EU member nation could also have procedures for approving drugs beyond those required by the centralized process (Van Norman, 2016). The dispensing of approved drugs and devices could be further regulated locally by ordinances or laws describing the types of businesses and employee credentials needed for those who could dispense these medicines.

Why Do We Want Regulatory Reform?

There have been nearly constant attempts to reform regulation. Reform efforts can be substantive, where an entire industry or class of goods or services is no longer under government regulation or brought under regulatory control. They can also be procedural, where existing regulations and activities are modified for more effective and cost-efficient regulation.

Deregulation is a popular reform that occurs when the government reduces its intervention in society, often due to changes in the economy, changes in technology, an ideological shift to or away from free market ideas, or compelling evidence that reform is in the public interest (Thompson & Jones, 1982). Over time, there has been little demand for reductions in social regulation. Calls for reregulation, or the reintroduction of regulation in areas that have been deregulated, often occur in policy areas where perfect markets may no longer exist. The need for additional consumer protection and safety as spillover effects and externalities emerge as other explanations for reregulation (Gerston et al., 1988). A current example is unfolding related to the harmful effects of vaping (electronic cigarettes), with demand for increased regulation.

Once the rules are in place, the program officials who wrote the rules are responsible for monitoring behavior to enforce the rules and taking action when there is non-compliance. Non-compliance, or not following regulations, can occur because people do not support the rules. If objections to a rule are strong enough, selective disobedience can occur, meaning that people refuse to follow what they believe to be a bad law. Anyone who has run a red light or exceeded posted speed limits is guilty of non-compliance. However, non-compliance may also be unintentional and caused by ignorance or a lack of understanding of the rules. Anyone who has filed tax returns can probably empathize with this non-compliance given the complexity and unfamiliar language of the tax system.

What solutions are available to government when confronted with non-compliance? What tools do governments have to coerce or nudge their citizens into compliant behavior (Hood & Margetts, 2007)? First, a strategy of information and education campaigns can make people aware of and understand regulations. Second, technological advances and the adoption of plain language standards have dramatically reduced unintentional non-compliance. Third, Sparrow (2000) suggests that deliberate or repeated non-compliance can be addressed through a system that establishes and communicates the monitoring systems that are used to detect non-compliance. This is combined with progressively increasing consequences and enhanced monitoring for those exhibiting characteristics suggesting they are non-compliant. Finally, artificial intelligence is used by tax preparers and tax organizations. For example, if you use an automated computer program to prepare your tax filings, the likelihood you might have a tax audit is reported at the end of a filing process. This information is drawn from data analysis comparing your tax filing to others and the type of violations commonly levied by the taxing authority. When seeing these red flags, many people will go back and change their tax filing to avoid the risk of a tax audit.

Once a regulatory organization detects and charges an individual or organization with non-compliance, the organization is responsible for *adjudication*. They apply existing laws or rules to individual cases to determine if the correct action and if the action was taken by the person or organization that was not complying with the rules. Adjudication is handled by a court system within the regulatory organization or conducted by designated parties who act on behalf of the regulatory organization (Gerston et al., 1988). An administrative law judge can hear testimony and review evidence provided by all parties, then will render a decision that can be appealed, just like a court decision. Since the judges in the courts generally do not have scientific training, they do not evaluate the substantive nature of standards. Instead, they try to ensure that standard rulemaking and adjudication processes were used, and that administrative action was not arbitrary and capricious (Greenwood, 1984).

Not all disputes are handled through adjudication. Other mechanisms for regulatory non-compliance are advisory opinions and consent orders. In an *advisory opinion*, the regulator reviews an organization's or industry's practices and issues guidance to encourage voluntary compliance before violations occur or are discovered. A *consent order* is a formal agreement created when a violation has occurred. The violator agrees to cease the non-compliant activity in exchange for a promise of no punitive action by the government regulators (Milakovich & Gordon, 2004; Shover et al., 1986).

One way to avoid adjudication is to ensure that the regulators have the right expertise and strong stakeholder interaction skills. This is especially challenging for complex industries when expertise on economic impacts and public safety regulation is required. For example, in a study of the Australian gas supply industry (Hayes et al., 2022), the government decided to use external consultants with technical expertise. This was necessary to find ways to reduce expected expenditures and increase the industry's profit potential (the economic aspect) while also evaluating and recommending safety-related items for the final regulation (the public safety aspect). As the authors describe, this required determining effective regulations and regulators while promoting interactions with a broad range of stakeholders (p. 8).

The regulatory process is often characterized as adversarial because of the enforcement and adjudication responsibilities. However, as the example above suggests, a shift has been made to promote more cooperative relationships, such as negotiated rulemaking. When using *negotiated rulemaking*, the regulators work with the regulated and the public to devise rules that do not place significant burdens on those being regulated yet maintain the public protection expectations embedded in the original purpose of the regulation. Negotiated rulemaking features co-developed and flexible laws and regulations that encourage the industry to adopt better consumer and environmental protection technologies. This encourages regulators to tell the industry what needs to be done, not how to do it (Benforado & Koenigsberger, 1985).

When looking for opportunities to negotiate regulation, there is a need to balance the amount of control necessary for the regulators with the most up-to-date knowledge about the regulated industry. Heclo used *iron triangles* to describe cozy relationships between elected officials, industry representatives, and government workers in the public policy literature. This term recognized the advantages of information sharing between the three stakeholders to create evidence-based public policy. However, the word "iron" recognized the risk that other stakeholders could not break through to provide input. A similar situation in the regulatory arena has been labeled indirect governance triangles. This refers to EU regulation and the need to balance competence and control (Biermann et al., 2020).

There are other cooperative tools that differ from traditional regulatory approaches, where the government sets standards, and the industry must comply. For example, market-based tools are intended to foster cooperation by offering incentives for companies to voluntarily reduce product or collective hazards (Bryner, 2003). However, cooperative regulation through voluntary protection programs and corrective action plans may not always be successful.

When this occurs, government regulators are authorized to assess a fee to the violators.

Another tool, called *cooperative enforcement* allows regulators to make those regulated aware of the standards and help them understand what is necessary for compliance. It also minimizes opposition, reduces compliance burdens through customer-tailored solutions, reduces conflict, and reduces resources needed for enforcement (Sparrow, 2000). On the other hand, critics claim there is a danger of capture or cozy relationships between those being regulated and the regulators (Posner, 1974).

What Is the Value of Risk Assessment and Scientific Standards?

There are circumstances where regulation is necessary because of the potential for severe negative outcomes to occur if harmful products are sold (such as flammable children's pajamas, autonomous vehicles, or jeans dyed with cobalt blue) or inaccurate information about the likelihood and severity of a risk is communicated (like the side effects of prescribed drugs). When these situations arise, the public may not have sufficient information or expertise to judge individual risks. To protect the public, government experts in regulatory agencies establish scientific standards. After studying what exposure to a harmful product or service will do to the average person, a minimum or maximum level of exposure is set in regulations.

Determining scientific standards often involves quantitative risk assessment and cost-benefit analysis to understand the value of benefits compared to the cost of compliance. To accomplish this requires employees with scientific and engineering knowledge. Scientific expertise helps assess the risk level associated with different products and activities in their regulated industries. They use this knowledge and discretion to write the rules for regulated activities (Greenwood, 1984; Wagenaar, 2020). Discretion is required because risk assessments lack complete quantitative detail or may use information that is inaccurate and biased due to the self-interests of the information provider. Further, not all the costs and benefits of proposed activities are identified and monetized, and standards do not exist for costing certain costs and benefits (Greenwood, 1984). Combined these factors make the process of determining scientific facts complicated as well as subject to challenge by those offering other "facts" intended to support their preferred standards.

The use of facts when making decisions, especially about regulations, is valued. However, the facts are always subject to interpretation and multiple facts may need to be considered and balanced. When faced with unclear or conflicting potential courses of action based on the "facts," the administrator(s) have a certain amount of discretion. Four types of *administrative discretion* are: interpreting statutory language, balancing conflicting values, determining priorities, and answering scientific and engineering questions (Greenwood, 1984).

The challenge for public administrators is determining which types of discretion should be allowed when scientific standards must be established. From this list, we might agree that the first and the fourth, interpreting statutory language and answering scientific and engineering questions, are reasonable. But what about balancing conflicting values and determining priorities? Should the scientist decide these matters? What is the proper role of civil servants? Of elected officials? Of those at-risk? Of the public?

In the past, elected officials have given specific and general guidance about establishing scientific standards by a sub-class of the risk being studied. However, in recent years, there has been a trend to create one standard for categories and treat all risks equally. One example of this is cancer. Instead of establishing a uniform safe standard for environmental toxins in each of the four mediums—air, water, land, and waste, the environmental protection organization may establish scientific standards that vary based on toxicity levels at certain concentrations and within certain time periods. The most significant advantage of this approach is that it fosters precision in the amount of acceptable exposure. The most significant disadvantage is that the cost to remove some carcinogens or reduce the ambient level of the carcinogen can be substantially higher for one type than for others. An example is the amount of radiation exposure from different activities arranged along the electromagnetic spectrum. Computers and power lines have very low levels of non-ionizing radiation. Most of us experience this form of radiation on a regular basis. However, therapeutic radiation for the treatment of certain kinds of cancer has high levels of ionizing radiation and there are strict guidelines about radiation exposure time and frequency based on the health status of the individual.

Another alternative is to regulate transparency to provide information to the consumer. With this information, consumers can be aware of the risk and make independent decisions about their actions. An example of this is food labeling requirements. Even though the costs of obesity to society is known, government scientists do not have the discretion to control what foods are sold. Instead, they try to use the information to guide us in our food choices and make us better aware of the potential health-related risks of our actions.

Risk assessment to establish standards is particularly challenging when technology changes and our knowledge and regulations cannot keep pace. Two examples are: (1) technological breakthroughs of artificial intelligence decision algorithms and (2) autonomous machines. Artificial intelligence based on machine learning is promising in health care, where machine learning can dramatically improve diagnosis, treatment efficacy, and patient outcomes (Beaulieu-Jones et al., 2021). However, until the ability of artificial intelligence to capture the nuances of physician behaviors and the connection to patient treatment decisions is fully understood, the establishment of standards of care and the basis for an appeal of machine-based decisions are difficult. Without these, regulations will be less precise, and a more significant administrative burden related to legal challenges to care decisions is possible.

It is also possible that the same technological advance can be framed differently, leading to regulation in contiguous governmental units that is not the same which creates an enforcement challenge. Hansson (2020) presents this issue for autonomous vehicles in a study in Sweden and Norway. Some countries see autonomous vehicles as prohibited unless otherwise stated in the regulations. Others take the opposite view, that is, anything not explicitly prohibited is allowed. Seeking to find out what can explain this difference, it was determined that external pressures and international conventions alongside internal preferences shape regulations.

Chapter Summary

In this chapter, we reviewed the everyday activities that occur when setting the course of government. Much of this is accomplished during the policymaking process through intergovernmental relations and multi-level governance. Making policy that sets the course of government requires collaboration between elected officials and the government executives tasked with implementing the decisions. Setting the course of government requires analysis of alternative strategies that provide input for decisions, planning, then the development of laws, rules, and regulations that set the framework for government implementation can be established and implemented. Chapter 8 introduces what happens after the course of government has been set. At this point servants lead the process for deciding how to carry out the decisions to ensure the course of government is followed and the desired results achieved.

Practical Applications for Students

1. Find another example of how revenues are shared between levels of government. Why is it advantageous for one level of government to collect and then distribute money to other governments?
2. Conduct a sample policy analysis for a proposal for a new student service. What makes policy analysis practical and impractical?
3. Analyze why there are different processes for laws, regulations, and rules and compare the roles of street-level workers and clients (or their representatives) in the different processes.
4. Explore the different unintended consequences (positive and negative) of deregulation versus delegated regulation.
5. Is the concept of diffusion relevant only to policy implementation between levels of government. Identify other ways diffusion may occur and provide an example in the public works arena.

In-Class Instructional Suggestions

1. Discuss an example of asset forfeiture in law enforcement during class.
2. Discuss how policy analysis, particularly the assumptions that guide the analysis, differs for organizations across the sectors.

3. Locate a media article or professional organization publication about rule updates processes.
4. Present a case of deregulation that led to unintended consequences and encourages examination of the different policy actors.
5. Discuss the difference between vertical and horizontal policy diffusion in the health care policy arena.

REFERENCES

Agranoff, R. (1986). *Intergovernmental management: Human services problem-solving in six metropolitan areas.* State University of New York Press.

Agranoff, R. (2017). *Crossing boundaries for intergovernmental management.* University Press.

Agranoff, R., & McGuire, M. (2004). Another look at bargaining and negotiating in intergovernmental management. *Journal of Public Administration Research and Theory, 14*(4), 495–512.

Althaus, C., Bridgman, P., & Davis, G. (2020). *The Australian policy handbook: A practical guide to the policy-making process.* Routledge.

Anders, K. K., & Shook, C. A. (2003). New federalism: Impact on state and local governments. *Journal of Public Budgeting, Accounting and Financial Management, 15*(3), 466–486.

Anderson, J. E. (2000). *Public policymaking: An introduction* (4th ed.). Houghton Mifflin Company.

Arrow, K. (1977 [1970]). The organization of economic activity: Issues pertinent to the choice of the market versus market allocation. In R. A. Haveman & J. Margolis (Eds.). *Public expenditure and policy analysis* (pp. 59–73). Rand McNally.

Bache, I., Bartle, I., & Flinders, M. (2016). Multi-level governance. In *Handbook on theories of governance.* Edward Elgar Publishing.

Bachrach, P. S., & Baratz, M. S. (1963). Decisions and non-decisions: An analytical framework. *American Political Science Review, 57*(2), 641–651.

Bardach, E., & Patashnik, E. M. (2019). *A practical guide for policy analysis: The eightfold path to more effective problem solving.* CQ Press.

Beaulieu-Jones, B. K., Yuan, W., Brat, G. A., Beam, A. L., Weber, G., Ruffin, M., & Kohane, I. S. (2021). Machine learning for patient risk stratification: standing on, or looking over, the shoulders of clinicians? *NPJ Digital Medicine, 4*(1), 1–6.

Benforado, D. M., & Koenigsberger, M. (1985). Pollution prevention pays. In G. A. Daneke & D. J. Lemak (Eds.), *Regulatory reform reconsidered* (pp. 124–133). Westview Press.

Biermann, F., Rittberger, B., Abbott, K. W., Genschel, P., Snidal, D., & Zangl, B. (2020). Balancing competence and control: Indirect governance 'triangles' in EU regulation. In K. W. Abbott, B. Zangl, D. Snidal, P. Genschel (eds.) *The governor's dilemma: Indirect governance beyond principals and agents.* Oxford University Press, ch.9.

Blom-Hansen, J. (1999). Avoiding the 'joint-decision trap': Lessons from intergovernmental relations in Scandinavia. *European Journal of Political Research, 35*(1), 35–67. (download).

Bolleyer, N. (2006). Federal dynamics in Canada, the United States, and Switzerland: How substates' internal organization affects intergovernmental relations. *Publius: The Journal of Federalism, 36*(4), 471–502.

Briffault, R., Davidson, N. M., Diller, P. A., Fox, S., Reynolds, L., Scharff, E. A., Schragger, R., & Su, R. (2020). Principles of home rule for the twenty-first century. *Virginia Public Law and Legal Theory Research Paper No. 2020-16*, National League of Cities. February 12, 2020, *Fordham Law Legal Studies Research Paper No. 3539617*.

Browne, J. (2020). The regulatory gift: Politics, regulation and governance. *Regulation and Governance, 14*(2), 203–218.

Bryner, G. C. (2003). New tools for improving government regulation: An assessment of emissions trading and other market-based regulatory tools. In M. A. Abramson & A. M. Kieffaber (Eds.), *New ways of doing business* (pp. 319–348). Rowman and Littlefield.

Burke, B. F. (2014). Understanding intergovernmental relations, twenty-five years hence. *State and Local Government Review, 46*(1), 63–76.

Cameron, D. (2001). The structures of intergovernmental relations. *International Social Science Journal, 53*(167), 121–127.

Conlan, T. J., & De Chantal, F. V. (2001). The Rehnquist court and contemporary American federalism. *Political Science Quarterly, 116*(2), 253–275.

Crowley, K., & Stewart, J. (2020). *Reconsidering policy: Complexity, governance and the state*. Policy Press.

Delbecq, A., Van de Ven, A., & Gustavson, D. (1975). *Group techniques for program planning: A guide to nominal group and Delphi processes*. Scott, Foresman.

Diamond, M. (1974). What the framers meant by federalism. In R. A. Goldwin (Ed.), *A nation of states* (pp. 25–41). Rand McNally.

Duff, M., & Wohlstetter, P. (2019). Negotiating intergovernmental relations under ESSA. *Educational Researcher, 48*(5), 296–308.

Durant, R. F. (2020). *Building the compensatory state: An intellectual history and theory of American administrative reform*. Routledge.

Elazar, D. J. (1966). *American federalism: A view from the States*. Thomas Y. Crowell Company.

Etzioni, A. (1967). Mixed scanning: A third approach to decision making. *Public Administration Review, 27*, 385–398.

Gerston, L. N., Fraleigh, C., & Schwab, R. (1988). *The deregulated society*. Brooks Cole.

Golden, M. M. (2000). *What motivates bureaucrats? Politics and administration during the Reagan years*. Columbia University Press.

Goodsell, C. T. (2004). *The case for bureaucracy: A public administration polemic*. C.Q. Press.

Goodsell, C. T. (2014). *The new case for bureaucracy: A public administration polemic*. C.Q. Press.

Gortner, H. F., Mahler, J. B., & Nicholson, J. B. (1997). *Organization theory: A public perspective*. Wadsworth.

Greenwood, T. (1984). *Knowledge and discretion in government regulation*. Praeger.

Grodzins, M. (1960). The federal system. The report of the President's Commission on National Goals. *Goals for Americans: An Overview of The Report of the President's Commission on National Goals*. Prentice-Hall.

Hansson, L. (2020). Regulatory governance in emerging technologies: The case of autonomous vehicles in Sweden and Norway. *Research in Transportation Economics, 83*, 100967.

Hayes, J., Chester, L., & King, D. K. (2022). Outsourcing risk governance: Using consultants to deliver regulatory functions. In J. Hayes & S. Tillement (Eds.), *Contracting and safety* (pp. 79–87). Springer.

Hicks, W., Weissert, C., Swanson, J., Bulman-Pozen, J., Kogan, V., Riverstone-Newell, L., et al. (2018). Home rule be damned: Exploring policy conflicts between the statehouse and city hall. *PS: Political Science and Politics, 51*(1), 26–38. https://doi.org/10.1017/S1049096517001421

Hood, Chr. C., & Margetts, H. Z. (2007). *The Tools of Government in the Digital Age.* Palgrave.

Kee, J. E. (1994). Benefit-cost analysis in program evaluation. In J. S. Wholey, H. P. Hatry, & K. E. Newcomer (Eds.), *Handbook of practical program evaluation* (pp. 456–488). Jossey-Bass.

Krane, D., & Wright, D. S. (2018). Intergovernmental relations. In *Defining public administration* (pp. 83–101). Routledge.

Landsbergen, D., & Raadschelders J. C. N. (2018). Decision making. In A. Farazmand (ed.), *Global encyclopedia of public administration, public policy and governance.* Springer (May 25, online first), 1–9.

Lemak, D. J. (1985). Social regulation: A swing of the pendulum. In G. A. Daneke & D. J. Lemak (Eds.), *Regulatory reform reconsidered* (pp. 39–54). Westview Press.

Levy, F., Meltsner, A., & Wildavsky, A. (1974). *Urban outcomes: Schools, streets, and libraries.* University of California Press.

Lindblom, C. E. (1959). The science of muddling through. *Public Administration Review, 19*(2), 79–88.

Lindblom, C., & Woodhouse, E. (1993). *The policymaking process* (3rd ed.). Prentice-Hall.

March, J., & Simon, H. (1993). *Organizations* (2nd ed.). Blackwell.

McGuire, M. (2006). Collaborative public management: Assessing what we can know and how we know it. *Public Administration Review, 66*(1), 33–43.

Meltzer, R., & Schwartz, A. (2018). *Policy analysis as problem solving: A flexible and evidence-based framework.* Routledge.

Milakovich, M. E., & Gordon, G. J. (2004). *Public administration in America.* Thomson/Wadsworth.

Mohr, L. (1988). *Impact analysis for program evaluation.* Dorsey Press.

Morgan, D. R., & England, R. E. (1999). *Managing urban America* (5th ed.). Chatham House.

Neiman, M. (2000). *Defending government. Why big government works.* Prentice-Hall.

Newbold, S., & Rosenbloom, D. H. (Eds.). (2017). *The constitutional school of American public administration.* Routledge.

Ongaro, E., Massey, A., Wayenberg, E., & Holzer, M. (Eds.). (2010). *Governance and intergovernmental relations in the European Union and the United States: Theoretical perspectives.* Edward Elgar Publishing.

Phillimore, J. (2010). Intergovernmental relations in Australia: increasing engagement. In *Dialogues on intergovernmental relations in federal systems—A global dialogue on federalism volume 8* (pp. 12–15). Forum of Federations and IACFS.

Pickerell, J. M., & Clayton, C. W. (2004). The Rehnquist Court and the political dynamics of federalism. *Perspectives on Politics, 2*(2), 233–248.

Posavec, E. J., & Carey, R. D. (1997). *Program evaluation: Methods and case studies* (5th ed.). Prentice-Hall.

Posner, R. A. (1974). Theories of economic regulation. *The Bell Journal of Economics and Management Science, 5*(2), 335–335.

Raadschelders, J. C. N. (2003). *Government: A public administration perspective*. M.E. Sharpe.

Raadschelders, J. C. N., & Whetsell, T. A. (2018). Conceptualizing the landscape of complex public problem solving. *International Journal of Public Administration, 41*(14), 1132–1144.

Radin, B. A. (2007). The instruments of intergovernmental management. In *The handbook of public administration* (pp. 365–376). Sage Publications.

Ritchie, A. (2018). Local control of fracking in the bayou and the retreat from home rule. *62 Annual Institute on Mineral Law, 62*, 263–319.

Rose, R. (2004). *Learning from comparative public policy: A practical guide*. Routledge.

Rosenbloom, D. H. (2003). *Administrative law for public managers*. Westview Press.

Sabatier, P. A. (1988). An Advocacy Coalition Framework of Policy Change and the Role of Policy-Oriented Learning Therein. *Policy Sciences, 21*(2/3), 129–168.

Shannon, J. (1983). Federal and state-local spenders go their separate ways. *Intergovernmental Perspectives, 8*(4), 23–29.

Shover, N., Clelland, D. A., & Lynxwiler, J. (1986). *Enforcement or negotiation? Constructing a regulatory bureaucracy*. State University of New York Press.

Simon, H. (1957). *Administrative behavior* (2nd ed.). Macmillan.

Song, M., & Meier, K. J. (2018). Citizen satisfaction and the kaleidoscope of government performance: How multiple stakeholders see government performance. *Journal of Public Administration Research and Theory, 28*(4), 489–505.

Sparrow, M. K. (2000). *The regulatory craft: Controlling risks, solving problems, and managing compliance*. The Brookings Institution Press.

Stone, D. (1997). *Policy paradox: The art of political decision making* (2nd ed.). W.W.

Sylvia, R. D., Sylvia, K. M., & Gunn, P. E. M. (1997). *Planning and evaluation for the public manager* (2nd ed.). Waveland Press.

Thompson, F. L., & Jones, L. R. (1982). *Regulatory policy and practices: Regulating better and regulating less*. Praeger.

Van Norman, G. A. (2016). Drugs and devices: Comparison of European and US approval processes. *JACC: Basic to Translational Science, 1*(5), 399–412.

Vedung, E. (1998). Policy instruments: Typologies and theories. In M.-L. Bemelmans-Videc, R. C. Rist, & E. Vedung (Eds.), *Carrots, sticks and sermons: Policy instruments and their evaluation* (pp. 21–58). Transaction.

Vining, A. R., & Weimer, D. L. (2017). Policy analysis: A valuable skill for public administrators. In J. C. N. Raadschelders & R. J. Stillman (Eds.), *Foundations of public administration*. Melvin and Leigh Publishers.

Wagenaar, H. (2020). Discretion and street-level practice. In *Discretion and the quest for controlled freedom* (pp. 259–277). Palgrave Macmillan.

Weimer, D. L. (2012). The universal and the particular in policy analysis and training. *Journal of Comparative Policy Analysis: Research and Practice, 14*(1), 1–8. https://www-tandfonline-com.ezproxy.lib.ou.edu/doi/full/10.1080/13876988.2011.646819

Weimer, D. L., & Vining, A. R. (2005). *Policy analysis: Concepts and practice* (4th ed.). Prentice-Hall.

Westman, L. K., Broto, V. C., & Huang, P. (2019). Revisiting multi-level governance theory: Politics and innovation in the urban climate transition in Rizhao, China. *Political Geography, 70,* 14–23.

Wildavsky, A. (1979). *Speaking truth to tower: The art and craft of policy analysis.* Little and Brown.

Wright, D. S. (1988). *Understanding intergovernmental relations.* Brooks/Cole.

CHAPTER 8

Administering Government Programs

In Chap. 7, we described the activities of elected officials and government administrators use to determine the course of government for dealing with social issues. We also suggested other actors who are involved in setting the course of government. These can include officials from other governments, organizational partners, and even government's clients. These collaborations result in the laws, rules, regulations, policies, procedures, and practices guiding how government services are provided and to whom, or another way to put it is administering government.

The administration of government programs occurs through many different management processes, such as policymaking, strategic management, program implementation. This chapter introduces these administrative processes inside government organizations as components of a strategic management cycle that includes stakeholder and service delivery partner engagement. The focus of this chapter is planning and implementation. More in-depth discussions of the other four components are provided in the four following chapters.

What Is Included in the Strategic Management Cycle?

Strategic management is creating and carrying out an integrated strategy for internal organizational operations. As seen in Fig. 8.1, a strategic management cycle begins with strategy formulation based on the laws passed by the legislature, policy guidance provided by the executive, and legal boundaries established through judicial actions.

sIn Chap. 7, we explained how strategic planning was necessary to set the course of government. Strategic planning is carried out when government leaders decide how government programs will be administered. However, the focus shifts from planning by elected officials and government executives to a broader collection of stakeholders and now emphasizes the actions that will

© The Author(s), under exclusive license to Springer Nature Switzerland AG 2023
A. L. Franklin, J. C.N. Raadschelders, *Introduction to Governance, Government and Public Administration*,
https://doi.org/10.1007/978-3-031-32689-9_8

Fig. 8.1 Strategic Management Cycle

take place inside government organizations to achieve the social impacts desired when decisions are made about the course of government (Bryson & George, 2020). For strategic management to be successful, dialogue and collaboration are necessary to assure that government programs and services encourage and monitor the achievement of the outcomes and impacts expected from government activities. The next section introduces the concept of stakeholder engagement as a dialogue and collaboration process.

Why Is Stakeholder Engagement Important?

We define a *stakeholder* as "… any group or individual who can affect or is affected by the achievement of the activities of an organization" (Freeman, 1984, p. 46). Stakeholders interact with organization officials to make their preferences known. Note that stakeholders do not need to be citizens, residents, or even taxpayers; they simply must have a stake in government actions. Stakeholders can be individuals and people who, or things that are represented by an organized group (Franklin, 2020). This definition of a stakeholder is very inclusive because, as public administrators, we value the right of every individual to have a say in government. We can say that any government program has an infinite number of stakeholders. When it comes to planning government actions and considering their impact on the future, the definition of a stakeholder can include people from other countries and their governments, plants, animals, and the unborn future generations who will experience the futurity of today's decisions.

Ideally, stakeholder engagement involves internal and external stakeholders. The *internal stakeholders*, or those who have official status with an organization, should include personnel from all levels and units inside the organization. *External stakeholders*, or those who have an interest but not an official position in the organization, should represent organizations, groups, and individuals who can influence or are influenced by the organization's current and expected future activities. Learning stakeholder perspectives is necessary to understand how well it has performed in the past, how well it is performing today, and to know what future expectations for performance are held by stakeholders.

Stakeholder engagement is a purposeful process for the ongoing facilitation of stakeholder interactions. Stakeholder participation refers to the ways and times when stakeholders communicate their preferences to those considering or responsible for taking action. Stakeholder engagement and stakeholder participation are vital for all kinds of organizations, public, for-profit, non-profit, and social and voluntary groups.

Think about a family as a voluntary group, using the idea of stakeholder, is it easier to understand why kids want their parents to listen to them? They will be impacted by the decisions of their parents. But sometimes just being heard can be enough. Just like a family, it is important for stakeholders to respectfully listen to the perspectives of others and to learn their preferences. However, like some "family" decisions, government listens but do not always give stakeholders what they want. Sometimes difficult choices must be made to ensure that sustainable decisions, which are good for the many rather than the few, are taken.

One of the most compelling explanations for stakeholder participation in government is that it ensures that government serves society's needs, interests, and preferences now and in the future. Often, we complain that the government, especially elected officials, are out of touch with what the people want. One goal of stakeholder engagement is to determine what people want and what is in the public interest. There are other goals, as well. These can include educating stakeholders about government operations, gathering input for decisions, gauging support for proposed courses of action, changing resource allocation or the current implementation of government programs, enhancing trust in government, and building a sense of community (Ebdon & Franklin, 2004).

Extensive stakeholder input can bring forth fresh perspectives, alert government officials to changes in the public interest, and identify future needs. For example, in Denmark, there is an emphasis on patient-centered care to provide quality public health care. Through a process known as shared decision-making, private funding and stakeholder input are included in the national plan for cancer treatment (Dahl Steffensen et al., 2017).

WHEN DO WE WANT PARTICIPATION?

There are three stages in the policy cycle when stakeholders can give input. First, when a new program is being considered and adopted. Second, when implementing a new program or modifying an existing program. Third, when existing programs are being implemented and evaluated. Table 8.1 suggest participation activities that can occur during each stage and different governmental actors are involved.

Reviewing Table 8.1, we conclude that stakeholders have many options for accessing government operations. Scholars have suggested that stakeholders prefer participating in a policy venue with the most convenient access and the highest perceived level of influence to achieve their preferred actors (Berry, 2015). So, if you think you have proper access to the legislative branch, you will favor the policy adoption stage as a good place for participation. Or, if you like the current executive's policies and think they will support the outcome you favor, you may choose to contact them. Finally, if they believe success will come from working with public administrators, you will likely participate during the policy implementation and evaluation stage. Participation at any stage

Table 8.1 Participation in the policy process stages

Policy/Program stage	Participation activities	Primary actors/Branch (who is being contacted)
Proposal consideration and adoption	Direct contact with officials	Legislature and executive
	Committee hearings	Courts
Program design and modification (new or change)	Request for proposal	Agencies
	Rulemaking	Agencies
	Special meetings	Agencies
	Direct invitation	Agencies
	Councils, committees, boards	Agencies and/or political
Program implementation and evaluation (ongoing operations)	Public meetings, Surveys, focus groups	Legislative and executive Agencies
	Legal challenges	Judicial
	Direct contact with officials	Legislature and executive

is done to influence the future actions of government. The next section describes the strategic plan as the mechanisms that established what activities government will undertake in the future and why these activities are important in terms of achieving desired collective outcomes.

What Are Important Components of Strategic Plans?

Over time, many different components have been included in a strategic or tactical operations plan. Often different labels are used to describe the same component. We use the labels vision, mission, internal/external assessment, goals, and action plans to describe common components of strategic plans. The ordering of these terms suggests movement from a long-term to a short-term time perspective and from abstract intentions to concrete actions designed to achieve the abstract intentions. Except for the internal/external assessment, the primary differences between the different components are the specificity of the results they describe and the time-period in which results can be achieved.

The *vision* statement represents a shared idea about the organization's desired future and suggesting the reason why this organization was created or what the desired level of performance is that drives the organization. Urban legend suggests that at one time Pepsi's vision was "Beat Coke." A vision statement is aspirational. For government organizations, the vision is the amelioration of a societal problem. That is a very big task since the people could not solve the problem on their own. Even though government organizations may never achieve the level of performance suggested by the vision statement, it is helpful to create a shared vision because it reminds employees of the difference the organization makes in society. The vision statement must be brief, memorable, and present a compelling and shared image of the desired future. High-quality vision statements should suggest to each employee how their efforts contribute to the organization's success.

A critical component found in most every strategic plan is the *mission* statement. We define an organization's mission as what its employees do, for whom they do it, what accomplishments they seek, and how well these align with what was intended when the organization was created. The mission statement cannot be accomplished in three, five, or even ten years. Achieving the mission also takes a very long time, but progress can be measured. As a collective, we want to reduce the amount of crime. That will not happen overnight or even with a few years. However, as a society we need measures of the rates of crime to know if we are making positive progress.

One reason it is difficult to achieve the mission is that it often depends on the cooperation of actors in the external environment. Success may depend on client co-production, getting more or reallocating resources, establishing partnerships with other organizations, or having the correct operating conditions. Things outside the organization's control could cause it not to achieve its mission; however, organizations need to measure progress. Even though that progress may come very slowly, and changes may be minimal, organizations need to report what they are doing and whether they are making a difference.

A third component of the strategic planning process is the *internal/external assessment* (also called a SWOT analysis. SWOT is an acronym for Strengths, Weaknesses, Opportunities, and Threats). The internal/external assessment looks at all three dimensions of time: past, present, and future. During strategic planning, organizations must imagine opportunities and threats in the future to exploit, or to combat, by strategic decision-making in the present. To do this, they must identify the strengths and weaknesses of the organization in the past and the present to judge how well the organization is equipped to respond to opportunities and threats in the future.

The internal/external assessment usually includes multiple stakeholders rather than one specific person to gather a wide range of perspectives. It is best when people gather purposefully from inside and outside the organization. Having both kinds of stakeholders assures that many people with diverse experiences and expertise offer their insights and expectations about the future. This will, hopefully, also improve the accuracy and quality of the assessment. As shown in Table 8.2, when doing the internal assessment, current levels of performance (inputs, processes and outputs) are considered since they could strengthen or weaken the organization's future activities.

The second part, the external assessment, identifies opportunities and threats in the organization's operating environment and how they can impact future operations and the organization's performance on the measures considered as part of the internal assessment. Potential changes in politics, policies, the economy, socio-demographic characteristics, technology and information acquisition, management and security strategies and legal issues could be explored. These are compared with strengths and weaknesses to see how the organization could respond to positive, negative, or threatening environmental changes.

Table 8.2 Things to consider in Internal/External Assessments

STRENGTHS	WEAKNESSES
Internal assessment of:	
Inputs—resources that come in.	
Processes—efficiency and effectiveness of current activities	
Outputs—the value of goods created, or services provided	
External assessment of:	
Politics—look at the enacting legislation and key actors	
Economy—how unexpected economic shifts will impact	
socio-demographic shifts	
Technology—the impact of changes	
Information acquisition strategies: public policy issues—legal issues	
OPPORTUNITIES	**THREATS**

In the external assessment, documenting how the organization has responded to uncertainty, complexity, and changes in the external environment helps envision responses to similar changes in the future. The black box, logic and theory of change models are well-known and often-used examples for assessing the operating environment and its relation to the organization's inputs, processes, outputs, outcomes, and impacts. Often carrying out the strategic plan requires creating or modifying laws, rules, or regulations that specify how the policy decision will be carried out through the goods and services provided through the organization's programs.

How Do We Transform Strategic into Tactical Plans?

Strategic plans often include goal statements. *Goals* are the desired results at the end of the planning period. When you establish the organization's goals, it is essential to consider two different types of goals. The first type represents the primary activities, or the expected results from the organization, to which a substantial portion of the budget is allocated. The second type represents strategic directions or special initiatives. The organization can use strategic direction goals to address opportunities and threats identified during the internal/external assessment. Because strategic direction goals are new initiatives, the organization may allocate resources to emphasize accomplishment of these goals within the planning period. Once a strategic initiative is accomplished, the activities might become a part of the organization's everyday activities and will then be represented in the primary activity goals.

Whether primary activities or strategic directions, *goals* describe the results we desire from the organization. The combination of goals should cover all the organization's activities. However, avoiding writing goal statements for each organizational activity is essential. Instead, goals should focus on results. Management experts claim that what gets measured gets done.

Organizations should limit the number of goals because the more goals you create, means there are more results you are accountable for, and more effort is necessary to monitor, measure, and report performance. Having too many goals can reduce the amount of actual work done because of the administrative burdens of performance tracking. To avoid having too many goals, a good rule of thumb is three to five goals, of which one or two are strategic directions and the remainder are primary activities (Franklin, 1999).

We defined the *mission statement* as a broad, comprehensive statement of the organization's purpose. On the other hand, goals are the desired result at the end of the planning period. A strategic plan's elements should have performance measures to track what is accomplished. To measure the mission, we look at the long-term outcomes or impacts that suggest changes in some social conditions. It may take multiple years to measure any changes; even then, these changes can be small.

Goals are further broken down into action plans describing the specific strategies that will be taken to produce the results desired. Action plans identify who will be responsible for these actions, the resources that will be devoted to these efforts, and the time frame for completion, usually measured in weeks or months but less than a year.

Though the different strategic plan components are presented separately, in practice, they must be integrated as part of the planning process. Think of it like the child's game called "Barrel of Monkeys." It is a plastic barrel containing around 20 tiny monkeys with their arms outstretched on each side of their body. The game's object is to take one monkey out of the barrel and get it to link arms with a monkey still in the barrel. This process is repeated until all the monkeys are holding hands in a chain. Like the barrel of monkeys' game, the strategic plan components need to link arms—or be connected—so that accomplishment of one level contributes to achievement at a higher planning level and so on.

What Makes Planning Processes Successful?

For organizations that have never done it, strategic planning can be challenging. One reason is that there are a lot of new words for participants to learn. Another reason strategic planning does not work well the first time is that the process challenges the status quo (Franklin, 2002). It can set up a competition of ideas about the desired future course of the organization.

What is needed is an attitude of collaboration. The collaboration required in the strategic planning process may be complex if the organization operates as a strict hierarchy that enforces the chain of command. When planning, people should participate as equals; however, the front-line workers may be reluctant to say what they think. This might happen because in the organization's operations, "this isn't the way things are done" by people at lower organizational levels.

For this reason, an outside facilitator can be helpful so that all those involved participate as equals (Franklin & Long, 2003). The importance of equal status participation was apparent in a Belgrade waterfront project that suffered from misuse of legal procedures and spatial planning instruments, neglect of private property rights, and a lack of public debate (Perić, 2020). Returning to the norms of public engagement overcame these problems and reduced perceptions of corruption.

Other ways to increase the likelihood so that the planning process is successful include: 1) making it adaptive and flexible, 2) encouraging many stakeholders representing many perspectives to participate, 3) presenting strategic plans as working documents and not "final" products, noting that they will change as environmental conditions change, 4) revisiting the plan periodically to check performance against expectations and fine-tuning as necessary (Haynes, 2003), and 5) developing action or *tactical plans*, which are accountability documents that identify who or what organizational unit is tasked with goal achievement and provide specific, measurable results that will be achieved by a particular time. In addition, some tactical plans provide additional details, such as the specific action steps that will be taken. Using these suggestions to overcome planning challenges can make the process easier; they can also improve the likelihood of using the plan rather than becoming a document that gathers dust on a shelf.

What Are Benchmarking and Best Practices?

Part of planning is knowing how you compare to similar organizations and planning future performance targets based on this information. *Benchmarking*, or best-practice research, involves finding out what other organizations do and determining if your organization can import and adapt these practices to make it operate more successfully. Best-practice research helps us break loose from standard operating procedures and assumptions about what is best. Best practices are finding out what solutions others have used when faced with similar problems and evaluating how they worked in those organizations. The best practice is how the best in the field do it. Typically, it is better than how you do it. In a benchmarking project for information technology Nuncio (2020) identified four elements useful for organizing initiatives to improve performance: contextual, technical, pedagogical, and organizational elements.

Even if your search does not reveal the "best practice," or you cannot implement the best practice due to resource constraints, you can often uncover innovative practices or clever, tangible, and visible behaviors used by other organizations to lead to innovation through creative problem-solving (Bardach, 2004). There is even merit in benchmarking when you are already the best. In these situations, you simply compare organization processes to those of organizations out of your industry but performing the same generic processes. An example is a hospital looking at a full-service hotel. Both organizations serve many customers, each with a different need. Both profit from filling their beds and not having empty beds. Hotels have systems to clean rooms quickly so that the room can be rented out again. Through benchmarking, hospitals can find out how to and the benefits of doing this too.

The benchmarking process can be broken down into steps. Many authors offer models ranging from four to six and even fourteen steps (Keehley et al., 1997). We like a model emphasizing four activities that mirror the *Plan, Do Check, Act* model used in Total Quality Management. First, a project is selected, and the benchmarking study is planned. The second activity is done by researching best practices from various sources and getting information about potential partners occurs. Comparison and analysis to check comparability and feasibility are the main activities in the third stage. Next, we act by adapting the practices of others and implementing the modified practices, then measuring processes and results to see if improvement has occurred and where fine-tuning may be necessary. Adaptation and fine-tuning are essential because we do not want to do as well as our competitors; after the benchmarking study, we want to leapfrog the competition and do better.

Even though we have suggested just four easy steps in a benchmarking study, pitfalls can be encountered while studying and implementing best practices. To avoid these, it is essential to develop realistic expectations. It is also necessary to analyze innovative practices, not just how an organization does something, but also how the employees think these actions solve a problem or achieve a goal. Benchmarking studies are also more successful when you determine what factors in your organization will positively or negatively impact the success of importation and adapt the process to fit your operating situation (Bardach, 2004).

How Does Implementation Turn Decisions into Actions?

Policy implementation happens after a bill, or citizen referendum, becomes law. Once this happens, civil servants determine the specifics of how the law will be carried out and by whom. Developing programs and the policies under which they operate are necessary before government goods and services can be delivered. Policy implementation has three main activities: 1) interpreting statutory language to determine feasible actions and guidelines, 2) designing or reorganizing the program's structure to provide goods and services, and 3) providing goods or services or overseeing and compensating those who provide these goods or services. There is no one model of effective policy implementation. Models often vary by policy area (Ripley & Franklin, 1982). There are, however, six conditions that make implementation more successful (Parsons, 1995, 486): clear and consistent objectives, adequate causal theory, legal structures for implementation, committed and skillful implementers, support of interest groups and politicians, and favorable socio-economic conditions.

An essential part of the implementation process is determining the best way to make policy decisions a reality. This is difficult because the laws that create programs or direct government actions are ambiguous, suggesting what the elected officials intended and sometimes results they desired, but not what should be done to achieve these results. The language is often abstract such as ordering a regulatory organization to ensure that the best available technology that is economically achievable is required to reduce water pollution (Anderson, 2000). Using non-specific language is often necessary to get enough votes to pass a bill. It also has the advantage of giving flexibility to subject matter experts, rather than elected officials, to decide the best way to accomplish what the public desires, as understood by the political intent when passing the law.

Non-governmental organizations (NGOs) can play a role in policy implementation that fosters sustainability in situations where pluralist politics are gridlocked. For example, in a study of forest policymaking in Ethiopia, these NGOs were influential even though they were not officially invited to be part of the policy design process. Labeled the policy arrangement approach (Ayana et al., 2018), NGOs used indirect strategies to achieve success by implementing pilot projects, documenting, and communicating field evidence and best practices, forming solid networks with like-minded actors, forging alliances with key decision-makers, and investing sufficient human and financial resources to push the adoption of a new policy.

Scholars have offered suggestions about different approaches that administrators can take during implementation. First, decisions must be made about whether implementation activities will be centralized or decentralized (O'Toole Jr., 1986). The degree of control desired by those inside and outside the program is essential. A centralized approach uses top-down policy direction to give organization leaders greater control of the implementation process (Sabatier, 1986). A decentralized approach relies on input from front-line workers, who have the ultimate responsibility for program delivery, to assure the right amount of flexibility and discretion (Hjern & Porter, 1981; Lipsky, 1980). Finally, a mixed implementation approach features top-level policy guidance combined with front-line workers' input (Goggin et al., 1990). The choice of approach often depends on whether policy represents a new direction or a modification of, or enhancement to, a current program.

Who Are Street-Level Bureaucrats and What Is Implementation Discretion?

The people who implement government programs are administrators at all levels of the organization who may or may not have been involved in policymaking deliberations. These employees play an essential role in designing programs since they interpret legislation and write rules (Peters, 1996). They also make public policy when they apply laws and rules to individual cases. *Street-level bureaucrats* (Lipsky, 1980) can shape how public policy occurs. For example, police officers use their administrative discretion when deciding how far over the speed limit a person can drive without being pulled over and whether the speeder gets a warning or a ticket. Since the desired outcome is public safety, they will take into consideration how risky the driver's behavior was to themselves and to others on the roadway.

Called, *administrative discretion*, many situations have special circumstances not anticipated by the laws of the rules governing program implementation. When this happens, the street-level bureaucrat is tasked with determining what course of action is best. If they comply with the "spirit" or intent of the law, the use of judgment is seldom questioned. However, when the intent of the law is disregarded and the intended outcomes are no longer achieved, there is a concern that policy intent is being subverted through policy implementation actions.

Making sure that policy intent is being upheld can be more complicated when people outside government are implementing government programs. It is not just government employees involved in program implementation; other public, for-profit, and non-profit organizations are often involved in service delivery through contracting, intergovernmental transfers, or collaboration. When other people get involved, they are called policy functionaries (Lindblom & Woodhouse, 1993). Their presence improves policy implementation because exposure to competing values makes the program more likely to do what policymakers intended and serve its clients well. However, it can dilute policy intent when their preferences outweigh concerns for the intended recipient.

What Are Common Implementation Problems?

As we suggested above, involving more people and people outside government in the implementation of government programs can be challenging. The difficulties caused by numerous policy functionaries were documented in a book analyzing economic development activities in Oakland, California (Pressman & Wildavsky, 1984). Significant conflicts or dramatic breakdowns were not uncovered in searching for explanations for why implementation failed. Instead, what was found were problems that public employees face every day, such as the difficulty of complying with hiring requirements that favored hiring hard-core unemployed minority workers. The company for which they were building the project wanted to hire people with higher qualifications to improve the cost and time efficiency of the project. Pressman and Wildavsky (1984) suggest that, in this instance, the designers of program implementation did not fail but that the reciprocal relationships necessary to complete the project created complexity that was not easily managed because the government's values for economic development activities did not match the employer's values.

Program implementation problems are common. People frequently assume that implementation happens without realizing that ambiguity exists, and discretion is necessary to make program design successful. Another potential area for implementation problems is that the government often does something new, and program theory describing cause-and-effect relationships seldom exists. This uncertainty often affects policy outcomes (Nakamura & Smallwood, 1980).

Problems can also result from the structure of government operations, the processes used during implementation, and the actors involved in the implementation process (Franklin, 2001; Franklin & Long, 2003). Structural implementation problems can be caused by a mismatch between the organization chart and exacting requirements describing how implementation must be carried out or how participants must interact. Another structural problem may be determining whether the program should be located inside a government organization or whether a non-governmental organization should provide the goods or services. Or the organization, irrespective of the sector that is charged with implementation, may be required to work with other governmental and non-governmental organizations in a network of intervention activities. Crossing organizational boundaries can be challenging.

Process implementation problems relate to the steps used to plan and carry out service delivery. Processes may be mandated outside the program, using a one-size-fits-all approach (Franklin, 2000). Rigidity in implementation created by this approach often leads to unsatisfactory outcomes since the emphasis is on compliance with mandates more than getting results (Long & Franklin, 2004).

Process problems also occur inside the organization and can include difficulties securing resources and personnel, gathering input, and maintaining the interest of key personnel, and integrating processes with those currently in existence, especially integration with existing staff functions. Another contributing problem is that large organizations have developed routines (Spence, 1999), and reliance on routines may overlook how the policy differs from previous policies and may not encourage custom tailoring of an appropriate program implementation design (Allison, 1971).

Difficulty in carrying out a policy can be encountered when many actors are involved in program implementation. Why is it hard for these actors to work together? Problems can arise because of the incompatibility of concurrent and multiple program commitments, an actor's preference for other programs, dependence on others for authorizations or resources, differences of opinion about what is the best approach to take, or legal and procedural differences in how to carry out or fund operations (Starling, 2002).

Many implementation problems can be attributed to communication problems between multiple actors. It is helpful if all participants speak the same language or use the same terms, share information widely among collaborators, utilize multiple communication channels, and distribute information in various formats (Stewart, 1997). In some organizations, such as public utility companies, communication can be problematic when the workforce consists of technical experts on the one hand (electricians, engineers, and so forth) and administrators who are not trained in those technical areas on the other hand.

A lack of understanding of the program and the relationships between inputs, processes, and outcomes is often identified as a problem in implementation (Peters, 2019). Two standard techniques to understand the program model are forward and backward mapping (Weimer & Vining, 2005). As the name suggests, we identify what actions are necessary in *forward mapping* and the order to reach some pre-specified outcome (Elmore, 1979). *Backward mapping* starts by determining the end goal, the intermediate goals, and the starting objectives. Like forward mapping, it also considers the steps necessary from start to finish in the implementation process. But it focuses on what client behaviors are to be changed (the end result) and what alternative implementation actions could facilitate this change (Elmore, 1979).

Both forward and backward mapping requires imagining what could go wrong during implementation. Then, taking action to reduce the potential for these problems to occur. Or if problems occur, strategies are identified to resolve them quickly (Weimer & Vining, 2005). One of the main barriers to successful forward and backward mapping is making predictions. There is always a great deal of uncertainty about the future. To overcome this, an internal/external assessment could also be beneficial.

For all implementation problems, seeking ways to encourage *mutual adaptation* is important (Sabatier & Mazmanian, 1978). Efficient and effective service delivery is more likely if programs processes are flexible and program personnel willing to make changes as they encounter the unexpected. Policy implementation never looks like what was planned. Reviewing practices in Uganda, Ledger and Meny-Gibert (2018) emphasize that implementation must allow adaptation as circumstances change over time. Anticipating flexibility is necessary since it ensures policy survival when we encounter problems and improves policy implementation to assure better the desired program results (Majone & Wildavsky, 1984).

Over time, higher education institutions have created branches of their organizations worldwide. Many residents of the international communities welcome the opportunity to study at a prestigious university with a name recognized worldwide. Leaders of authoritarian states also welcome these partnerships since they foster their knowledge economy. Over time, a discourse has been engaged about the degree to which these higher education initiatives in the Arabian Peninsula, China, Singapore, and Central Asia juxtapose ideas of liberalism within the illiberal, authoritarian contexts (Koch & Vora, 2019). Studying Qatar and the UAE, these authors found that the concept of authoritarianism is discursively produced in and through these university projects, which mitigates existing and emerging inequalities. In this example, we can see the importance of mutual adaptation during policy implementation.

What Can Organizations Do to Leverage Advances in Information Technology?

Knowledge management, which is the process of systematically capturing the knowledge of the employees of the organization, has benefited tremendously from information technology innovations over the past 40 years. Starting with a network of networks in the 1980s, the introduction of the world wide web (www) in the 1990s was a quantum leap in rapid knowledge management and dissemination synchronously worldwide.

The explosion of knowledge and its availability through technology has created a need for knowledge management systems that can accurately record, classify, and make information accessible. Organizations often use technology to deliver their services, such as obtaining information about whom to contact, renewing driver's licenses, applying for building permits, filing taxes, and paying traffic tickets. These technology-driven data sources can make the delivery of services faster and cheaper and increase customer satisfaction (Haynes, 2003). The relationship between using information technology to deliver government services and overall levels of customer satisfaction strengthens as the public becomes more and more comfortable with technology and demands more and more virtual services. In addition, technology advancements led to consumer co-production, such as apps that crowdsource traffic data.

Webpages are the primary area of technology innovation for government organizations. There are four ways webpages improve the government's interactions with its clients: providing information, making it possible to query for simple information, allowing customers to track and pay bills or get or change services, and completing service integration (Agranoff & McGuire, 2003). While there have been advances, local governments have struggled to achieve these interactions and provide websites that meet best-practice guidelines. Most government websites provide information and facilitate communication (Fountain, 2001).

eGovernment is the exchange of value through an electronic medium, including services, programs, and information. eGovernment includes interactions and relationships between government and clients, citizens, other organizations, and employees. eGovernment is enabled by various electronic, multimedia, and digital solutions.

With the popularization of the internet, developed countries have utilized e-Government and Information and Communications Technology (ICTs) to create a cooperative environment for innovation with internal and external stakeholders (Seo & Myeong, 2021). Tim O'Reilly, who contributed to popularizing the open-source concept and Web 2.0, initially suggested Government as a Platform (GaaP) that goes beyond the e-Government in his research. In a report on Estonia by Margetts and Naumann (2017) mentioned that GaaP originated in earlier public management reform initiatives based on Osborne and Gaebler's (1992) publication *Reinventing Government*, where the mantra was steering rather than rowing. Government should be an enabler rather than a first mover or governor. This notion can promote public-private partnerships and voluntary participation.

Information and technology systems must be aligned and information on the different strategic management functions must be accessible to integrate into customer service delivery. Flexibility and getting user feedback during the implementation process are crucial to creating a system that meets users' needs and expectations. It is also essential to include managers, users inside and outside the organization, and information technology professionals in systems development. Yet these people are often left out of the planning process (Perlman, 2002).

As you might expect during an innovative activity such as this, problems encountered when developing information systems are not limited to leaving people out of the planning process. Many transactions involve more than one organization, making information technology innovations challenging to implement (Gurwitt, 2002) and challenging knowledge management systems. Other problems include trying to adopt off-the-shelf models that are standardized but inflexible (Haynes, 2003); obsolescence of existing technology and systems; rapid development without adequate contingency planning; hidden costs leading to unproductive behaviors; requirement creep where new systems become outdated before implementation is complete (Starling, 2002); and an administrative culture that cannot adapt to meaningful change in the organization (Ehrenhalt, 2002). The rate of technological change is rapid and only shows signs of accelerating in a knowledge economy. Finding ways to overcome these challenges will be as important as developing new technology application that can improve the individual and collective lives of all people around the world.

Chapter Summary

This chapter examined strategic management functions commonly used in all organizations. Organizations should design internal processes for stakeholder engagement to identify novel ways to improve the delivery of government goods and services. Strategic planning must understand an organization's operating environment and how it has or could change. Benchmarking is a way to identify best practices to improve organizational processes and outcome. To succeed, the organization must understand its processes and adapt what has been learned to fit the organizational context. Then, these changes can be accomplished by encouraging administrative practices such as innovation, knowledge management, and cutting-edge information technology and management. Chapter 9 describes how the strategic plan created for managing these administrative processes is carried out or, in the words of Captain Pickard of Star Trek, how organizations "Make It So" through organizational activities.

Practical Applications

1. Imagine you were tasked with benchmarking online permitting systems to enhance positive benefits for constituent services in local government. Outline a process for doing this.
2. Identify more ways smartphone applications can help cities.
3. In the last section, we ask: What can organizations do to leverage advances in information technology? Answer this question in terms of avoiding cyber threats and providing cybersecurity.

In-Class Instructional Suggestions

1. Describe the building permit system for new home construction.
2. Review the use of Smart Technology partnership in your geographic area.
3. Describe the safe technology practices employees must follow in your organization.

References

Agranoff, R., & McGuire, M. (2003). *Collaborative public management: New strategies for local governments*. Georgetown University Press.

Allison, G. (1971). *The essence of decision: Explaining the Cuban missile crisis*. Longman.

Anderson, J. E. (2000). *Public policymaking: An introduction* (4th ed.). Houghton Mifflin Company.

Ayana, A. N., Arts, B., & Wiersum, K. F. (2018). How environmental NGOs have influenced decision making in a 'semi-authoritarian' state: The case of forest policy in Ethiopia. *World Development, 109*, 313–322.

Bardach, E. (2004). The extrapolation problem: How can we learn from the experience of others? *Journal of Policy Analysis and Management, 23*, 205–220.

Berry, J. M. (2015). *Lobbying for the people: The political behavior of public interest groups*. Princeton University Press.

Bryson, J., & George, B. (2020). *Strategic management in public administration*. Oxford Research Encyclopedia of Politics.

Dahl Steffensen, K., Hjelholt Baker, V., & Vinter, M. M. (2017). Implementing shared decision making in Denmark: First steps and future focus areas. *Zeitschrift fur Evidenz, Fortbildung und Qualitat im Gesundheitswesen, 123-124*, 36–40.

Ebdon, C., & Franklin, A. L. (2004). Searching for a Role for Citizens in the Budget Process. *Public Budgeting and Finance, 24*(1), 32–49.

Ehrenhalt, A. (2002). *Governing: Issues and applications from the front lines of government*. CQ Press.

Elmore, R. F. (1979-1980). Backward mapping: Implementation research and policy design. *Political Science Quarterly, 94*(4), 601-616.

Fountain, J. (2001). *Building the virtual state*. Brookings Institution Press.

Franklin, A. L. (1999). Managing for results in Arizona: A 5th-year report card. *Public Productivity and Management Review, 23*(2), 194–209.

Franklin, A. L. (2000). An examination of bureaucratic reactions to institutional controls. *Public Productivity and Management Review, 24*(1), 8–21.

Franklin, A. L. (2001). Serving the public interest: Federal agency experiences with participation in strategic planning. *American Review of Public Administration, 31*(2), 126–138.

Franklin, A. L. (2002). An examination of the impact of budget reform on Arizona and Texas. *Public Budgeting and Finance, 22*(3), 26–45.

Franklin, A. L. (2020). *Stakeholder Engagement*. Springer Nature.

Franklin, A. L., & Long, E. (2003). The challenges of changing federal management processes: Implementation barriers relating to strategic planning and the Government Performance and Results Act. *International Journal of Organization Theory and Behavior, 6*(4), 534–552.

Freeman, R. E. (1984). *Stakeholder management: A strategic approach*. Pittman.
Goggin, M., Bowman, O., Lester, J., & O'Toole, L. J., Jr. (1990). *Implementation theory and practice: Toward a third generation*. Harper Collins.
Gurwitt, R. (2002). Behind the portal. In A. Ehrenhalt (Ed.), *Governing: Issues and applications from the front lines of government* (pp. 64–68). CQ Press.
Haynes, P. (2003). *Managing complexity in the public services*. Open University Press.
Hjern, B., & Porter, B. (1981). Implementation structure: A new unit of administrative analysis. *Organization Studies, 2*(1), 211–227.
Keehley, P., Medlin, S., MacBride, S., & Longmire, L. (1997). *Benchmarking for best practices in the public sector: Achieving performance breakthroughs in federal, state, and local agencies*. Jossey-Bass Publishers.
Koch, N., & Vora, N. (2019). Laboratories of liberalism: American higher education in the Arabian Peninsula and the discursive production of authoritarianism. *Minerva, 57*(4), 549–564.
Ledger, T., & Meny-Gibert, S. (2018). The challenge of prioritisation and alignment in public sector planning and implementation-literature review. Uganda
Lindblom, C., & Woodhouse, E. (1993). *The policymaking process* (3rd ed.). Prentice-Hall.
Lipsky, M. (1980). *Street-level bureaucracy. Dilemmas of the individual in public services*. Russell Sage Foundation.
Long, E., & Franklin, A. L. (2004). The paradox of GPRA implementation: Top-down direction for bottom-up implementation. *Public Administration Review, 64*(3), 298–308.
Majone, G., & Wildavsky, A. (1984). Implementation as evolution. In J. L. Pressman & A. Wildavsky (Eds.), *Implementation* (3rd ed., pp. 163–180). University of California Press.
Margetts, H., & Naumann, A. (2017). *Government as a Platform. What can Estonia show the World*. European Union/European Social Fund, and Estonian government.
Nakamura, R. T., & Smallwood, F. (1980). *The politics of implementation*. University Press of America.
Nuncio, R. V. (2020). Benchmarking ICT for education in Japan: Best practices, trends, challenges and lessons learned for Philippine ICT-based education and development. *Asia-Pacific Social Science Review, 20*(2), 136–148.
O'Toole, L. J., Jr. (1986). Policy recommendations for multi-actor implementation: An assessment of the field. *Journal of Public Policy, 6*(2), 181–210.
Osborne, D., & Gaebler, T. (1992). *Reinventing government: How the entrepreneurial spirit is transforming the public sector*. Westview Press.
Parsons, W. (1995). *Public policy: An introduction to the theory and practice of policy analysis*. Edward Elgar.
Perić, A. (2020). Public engagement under authoritarian entrepreneurialism: the Belgrade Waterfront project. *Urban Research and Practice, 13*(2), 213–227.
Perlman, E. (2002). Our dying data. In A. Ehrenhalt (Ed.), *Governing: Issues and applications from the front lines of government* (pp. 69–75). CQ Press.
Peters, B. G. (1996). Political institutions, old and new. *A new handbook of political science, 1*, 205–220.
Peters, G. B. (2019). *American public policy: Promise and performance* (10th ed.). Sage Publications.
Pressman, J. L., & Wildavsky, A. (1984). *Implementation* (3rd ed.). University of California Press.

Ripley, R. B., & Franklin, G. A. (1982). *Bureaucracy and implementation*. Dorsey Press.
Sabatier, P. A. (1986). Top-down and bottom-up approaches to implementation research. *Journal of Public Policy, 6*(1), 21–48.
Sabatier, P. A., & Mazmanian, D. (1978). The conditions of the effective implementation process - particularly regarding regulatory policy. *NSF Sponsored Research Paper*. University of California - Davis and Pomona College.
Seo, H., & Myeong, S. (2021). Determinant factors for government adoption as a platform in South Korea: Mediating effects on the perception of intelligent information technology. *Sustainability, 13*(18), 10464.
Spence, D. B. (1999). Agency discretion and the dynamics of procedural reform. *Public Administration Review, 59*(5), 425–442.
Starling, G. (2002). *Managing the public sector* (6th ed.). Harcourt College Publishers.
Stewart, T. A. (1997). *Intellectual capital: The new wealth of organizations*. Currency/Doubleday.
Weimer, D. L., & Vining, A. R. (2005). *Policy analysis: Concepts and practice* (4th ed.). Prentice-Hall.

CHAPTER 9

Designing Government Organizations

In the spring of 2020, the world was gripped by a virus that had started to spread in late 2019. The COVID-19 virus spread fast. Governments and health care organizations had to figure out an adequate and swift response. First, lockdowns were announced in many countries. People could no longer gather, even in small groups. Then, people were urged to wear masks to stop the spread of this airborne virus. Next, governments financed research efforts to rapidly develop a vaccine that would protect the population. COVID-19, and its several variants (Delta, Omicron), jeopardized the functioning of societies and economies all around the globe. It was a true pandemic.

How do people respond to something so unbelievably disruptive to the normal dynamics of the day? How do governments respond to something for which experiential knowledge was two decades old (i.e., the swine flu: Cohen et al., 2002) or at least a century old (the flu pandemic of 1918–1919)? Who was responsible for initiating and doing the necessary things to respond to unexpected societal traumas such as COVID?

Rapid response to mitigate the impacts of the pandemic and to return to normal activities required coordinating the responses of multiple organizations: national, regional, and local government agencies, as well as for-profit and not-for-profit organizations. Many public health and safety activities (research for medical treatment development, vaccine and drug approval, public health services, supply chain distribution, monitoring of vaccinations, regulation of public activities, etc.) were needed. There was not one but many organizations involved in these efforts. This was the case with the response to 9/11 (Glendening, 2002), as well as with the response to COVID-19. Even under these unprecedented and extremely trying conditions, the skill and intensity of the government's responses were commendable (on COVID-19 response, see special issue of Public Administration Review, 2021a, 2021b).

© The Author(s), under exclusive license to Springer Nature Switzerland AG 2023
A. L. Franklin, J. C.N. Raadschelders, *Introduction to Governance, Government and Public Administration*,
https://doi.org/10.1007/978-3-031-32689-9_9

Would this coordination and integration have been possible without prior preparation? Most experts would say no. They would instead say that the effectiveness of these efforts was due, in large part, to planning and training exercises done beforehand (Newman, 2002). In addition, ideas for therapeutic medical interventions and vaccines were drawn from prior experiences with different strains of influenza, AIDS, and other viral infections. As a result, coordination internationally by pharmaceutical companies and public health authorities was almost automatic since it was based on prior coordination efforts.

In Chap. 8, we described different administrative processes used to implement government programs and provide services that improve the lives of individuals and impact the functioning of society. As we noted, much of program administration involves collaborations with organizations, groups, and even the government's clients who co-produce the societal outcomes. We compare what was accomplished to what was expected, to discover where service delivery could be approved through internal processes, and what could be accomplished another way by benchmarking with external organizations.

This chapter considers how to best structure the delivery of government programs using organizational design principles. For nearly every government activity you can imagine whether it is setting policy, delivering services, funding programs, or assuring quality and compliance, there is seldom one public organization with complete and sole responsibility. Instead, there is often a complicated web or network of government and non-governmental organizations contributing valued public outcomes. The design of a network of actors involved in the production of public goods becomes especially clear when we visualize any policy area as a *policy field*, an approach developed by public administration scholar Jodi Sandfort (2010). She mapped the policy field of early childhood education in Wisconsin and documented the interconnections between levels of government and non-governmental organizations. Policy field maps are well suited to show the extent to which local, regional, national, and even international levels of government, together with non-governmental organizations at each of these levels, are involved in the development of policy and services (see the field map of Raadschelders et al., 2019 on refugee migration). This chapter examines the processes and systems established within and between organizations to provide government goods and services.

What Are Theories of Organizational Structure?

An important starting place for structuring the organizations that provide public goods and services is the context when the public organization was created. We create public organizations through laws called *enabling acts*. These acts reflect agreement by the legislative and executive branches that we need some type of public organization to address a specific social condition. In the enabling act, the government organization is named. The government branch, which will have control of operations (executive, legislative, or judicial), or whether the organization will operate independently, is clarified. The enabling act spells out the membership composition and member selection process for independent agencies. For all agencies, the enabling act generally describes the activities the organization will engage in but does not specify what kinds of people will be hired, how the activities will be carried out, or how the organization should be structured.

Structuring an organization so people and systems work well together is a question that receives much consideration for all organizational types. Decisions about organization structure are about how to group employees' activities to promote efficiency and effectiveness. These decisions often involve dividing work into individual responsibilities and grouping work into units where individual's work activities are coordinated (Gortner et al., 1997).

When you make choices concerning organization structure, you can select from several different formats or bases of departmentalization used to group work units with similar activities. Following Gulick (1992 [1937]), we describe four primary rationales or bases underlying organization structure: product, function or process, geography, and client.

Historically, organizations have been arranged either by product or by function. If the organization is organized by product, each unit produces a different product or provides a different service. For example, an education agency creates many products to assure high-quality education for students of all ages. If arranged by product, you may see units for early childhood education, common education, and higher (or post-secondary) education. If an organization is arranged by function or process, the organizational units are structured around the things people do. For example, for an education agency, the functions could be teaching, athletics, extracurricular activities, student services, and administration.

The third type of organizational structure is where the units are arranged by geography or location. An example is the United Nations, with four headquarters duty stations: New York City, Geneva, Vienna, and Nairobi. Another is the African Union which organizes the 55 member nations into 5 areas (North, Central, South, East, and West). Organizations are typically organized by geography when what the organization does requires proximity to citizens, or services need to be custom-tailored to the circumstances of a geographic area.

Another way to structure an organization is by client type. When an organization is arranged to serve a particular clientele, specialists in each unit have different products or process knowledge and work for individual clients. For example, in Peru, the *Superintendencia Nacional de Administración Tributaria* (SUNAT) arranges its expertise by the type of tax: Corporate, Personal, Value-Added, Import, Excise, and Double Taxation Treaties. This is valuable because each category has different tax laws, treatments, and forms. In recent years, client type has been one of the most popular structures organizations in all sectors have adopted, primarily because it is the most responsive to a client's needs.

The bases of departmentalization are not permanent and do not describe the structure of every organization. Instead, they are just categories used to characterize the nature of an organization. No organization is characterized by only one; all organizations have features described within the four bases. Thus, an agriculture agency serves farmers through its regulatory authority and consumers by, for instance, supervising the quality of food products.

When Are Hybrid Organizational Structures Valuable?

While all organizations can be characterized by mixes of these four bases of departmentalization, hybrid organization structures have also evolved. A hybrid organization uses a combination of two or more different types of organizational structures. One level of the organization might be arranged by product, and another level might be organized by function.

Many organizations use a combination approach that starts with geographic location. Then, within the geographic location, they are arranged by client type. For example, the environmental protection agency in Iceland is organized this way. Country-level policy is set by the Ministry for the Environment and Natural Resources and carried out by the Environment Agency of Iceland in collaboration with ten municipal control districts across the country. These Environmental and Public Health offices often have units for three functional areas: food safety, environmental protection, and general hygiene.

One common type of hybrid organization structure is the matrix, which features temporary work units arranged by function and special projects that may have to do with one or more of the organization's products or services. In the *matrix organization*, members are selected from a pool of specialists in different functional areas, such as information technology, finance, and direct client service, based on the combination of skills needed to provide all the services needed by the client. The participants in the matrix organization answer to the supervisor in their functional area as well as to the supervisor of the project.

Another type of hybrid organization structure is the team-based or *project organization*. In this structure, front-line experts from different areas are brought together to improve integration between specialized work units and to increase effectiveness. An example is the child welfare system. The child in an abusive home can be served by a team that includes child protective services, foster care or adoption services, family reunification, and permanency planning. This type of structure breaks down the silos, or stovepipes, that develop when an organization is arranged hierarchically by product, process, or function (Wall, 2004). This hybrid organization is a cross between the client and the matrix basis of organizing since the team is temporary, formed for each client based on the client's specific needs. The team or project workgroup members provide services to improve a particular integration problem.

Hybrid organizations are effective structures because they draw from the expertise of different units based on what is needed to accomplish the task at hand. Also, they provide considerable attention to serving the unique needs of different customers based on a group of available experts. Plus, all members work toward a common goal and plan to return to their home unit after the project. In addition, they are short-lived, so concerns about the long-term integration of people with various specializations are minimized.

One disadvantage of a hybrid organization structure is that workers often report to two supervisors. This violates the principle of *unity of command*, where a worker should have only one supervisor to avoid undermining authority, discipline, and order (Fayol, 1992 [1949]). The first supervisor is in the functional specialist's home unit in many hybrid organizations. This supervisor is responsible for permanent supervision. The second supervisor is the project supervisor, who has temporary oversight of the project members. Having two supervisors can create challenges because employees try to meet the needs and expectations of both supervisors since both supervisors will evaluate them.

Other barriers that workers in hybrid structures face that can reduce effectiveness are conflicting goals between home units and the team or project goals, lack of clear direction or priorities, competition for resources, and overlapping responsibilities. There can also be a leadership issue for a team consisting of employees who are not used to working together. In this situation, the potential for conflict is high, and leaders must be skilled in managing interpersonal relationships to be effective (Robey, 1986).

What Do Organization Charts Tell Us?

The bases of departmentalization that are being used can be determined by looking at an organizational chart. Organization charts have two main features: boxes and lines. The boxes represent different operating units and can be divided into two main types of units: line and staff. *Line units* are directly responsible for producing a good or service. *Staff units*, on the other hand, provide support functions used by all the line units, such as personnel, training, budgeting, planning, auditing, evaluating, as well as information technology, fleet services, and facility maintenance.

Organization charts are arranged in different horizontal levels that signify reporting relationships within the hierarchy. Lines connecting these different levels depict horizontal and vertical relationships between operating units, whether line or staff. Usually, there are multiple units (boxes) at the bottom or lowest level of the organization chart. Each of these units reports to a higher level in the organization, denoted by the lines. The next level of the organization will have fewer units since these are the supervisory and management levels responsible for overseeing the operations of multiple units. This pattern continues until you reach the organization's top, or apex, where the executive level is found. Generally, the line units are noted at the bottom of the organization chart, and the staff functions are toward the middle of the organization chart.

Organization charts vary in how much detail they provide. A general rule of thumb is that the organization's structure should be as simple as possible. However, there can be situations where multiple functions are in one line or staff operating unit to achieve the organization's key objectives. When this happens, you will find a listing of other subunits inside the box representing a distinct operating unit; at an even more detailed level, you may see the names or numbers of people who hold different positions within the work unit.

An organization chart shows how tall or flat the organization structure is. A tall organization has many hierarchical levels, while a flat organization has fewer levels. Early organization theorists favored tall structures since they were highly centralized to assure rationality and control through stability and predictability (Tompkins, 2005). There have been attempts to shrink the height of large organizations, primarily by removing the middle management levels. The desired result of this type of downsizing is to reduce the number of levels that information and decisions must travel. This is thought to be a way to increase the speed of the decision-making and implementation processes. However, research suggests these positions are later re-created (Pollitt, 2003).

Determining and changing an organization's structure over time can be driven by factors relating to the organization's operating environment. The next section reviews principles for designing organizations based on the needs of internal operations and the demands of the external environment.

What Are Organizational Design Principles?

In the nineteenth century, Max Weber considered the problem of how organizations should be structured (Weber, 1946 [1922]). The elements of bureaucratic administration are grouped into two areas, the first describing the characteristics of bureaucracy and the second elaborating on the position of the official. Weber developed his theory of bureaucracy as an ideal type, a methodological instrument that enabled him to discern the extent to which real-life bureaucracies mirrored the ideal type. He believed bureaucracy would be a better way of organizing efficiently than any other organization. However, he never claimed that bureaucracy was the best type of organization. Instead, it was just better than any other in being efficient.

At the turn of the twentieth century, other scholars were also interested in finding the one best way to organize. They argued that certain principles about organizing operations could be discovered through scientific study and, with these results, recommendations for all organizations could be made (Fayol, 1992 [1949]). Taylor (1998 [1911]) identified principles of scientific management and introduced a body of organization theory, later called administrative or design science (Simon et al., 1981). The primary purposes of design science were to increase efficiency by accomplishing established objectives and reducing structural flaws through analysis (Gortner et al., 1997).

Establishing an organizational hierarchy was one way to increase efficiency and reduce structural flaws. A hierarchical organization is shaped like a pyramid, with a small point representing the executive level at the top. As you move to the middle of the pyramid, you have the managerial level of the organization. Finally, the organization's working units or front lines are at the bottom of the pyramid.

The principle of hierarchy reinforces a transparent chain of command, referring to the reporting relationships between employees at different levels in the organization. A strict chain of command means that as you move between the vertical levels of the organization, subordinates are found in the units below a specific organizational unit, and superiors exist at the levels above it. Both Fayol (1992 [1949]) and Weber (1946 [1922]) argued that the chain of command should be as short as possible to minimize the likelihood that instructions are misunderstood as well as to reduce the time necessary for orders to be communicated and carried out. Consultants for all organizational sectors continue to support this conclusion.

Weber (1946 [1922]) also argued that authority in a bureaucracy flows from the top to the bottom of the organization. Authority is often described as being centralized or decentralized. For *centralization* to be effective, responsibility and authority should be retained at the highest levels of the organization to ensure consistency, multi-channel communication, enhanced control, and monitoring accountability. *Decentralization* advocates claim that authority and responsibility are appropriately located at the lowest levels of the organization. This allows the experts to make decisions regarding producing goods and services. Decentralization advocates also note that front-line supervisors have the information and competence necessary to determine the best way to operate. Decentralization also permits greater autonomy and flexibility, mainly since it includes employees in decision-making and is more client responsive.

Centralization advocates have very different views of the roles of executives and supervisors in organizations, especially about where authority and decision-making responsibility should be located. Which is correct? The answer will often depend on the degree of discretion necessary for smooth operations at every organizational level. Most would say that neither is 100% appropriate. Instead, a combination approach with information flowing in both directions is necessary (Gulick & Urwick, 1937).

Regarding the centralization or decentralization of authority, a distinction between policy and administrative matters can be made. One can argue that we should centralize policy guidance, and policy decisions should flow from the top to the bottom of the organization. On the other hand, details about administrative matters should be left to subject matter experts at the lowest levels of the organization, with this information flowing from the bottom upward to the executive levels (McClusky, 2002; Osborne & Gaebler, 1992). However, it is possible to say that policy substance and guidance may also come from the experts toward the bottom of the organization to the executive level to form a feedback loop that facilitates goal-based organizational learning. There is empirical evidence for that (Moynihan, 2005; Page, 2012; Page & Jenkins, 2005).

The flows of information and communication patterns are other vital considerations in organizational design since they can decrease productivity when they are poor. In a strict hierarchy, all workers communicate vertically through the different levels of the organization. For example, front-line workers in a lower-level unit of the organization would never communicate directly with the executive level. And any communication from the executive directed to front-line employees would have to move downward from the executive to the managerial and then to the immediate supervisor level. Then, the supervisor would give that information to the front-line employees in the organization. So, vertical communications need to follow the chain of command for most organizational forms.

If you want to communicate horizontally, that is, work with another employee at the same level in the organization under the principle of hierarchy, you must communicate through the organization's structure until you find a common supervisor. This supervisor would convey the information to a subordinate in another work unit, and the message would then get handed back down through the organizational levels. To be sure, this is how the hierarchical, Weberian type of organization is supposed to operate.

A more efficient way to communicate, called *gang planking*, is to speak to the desired co-worker directly. Instead of having many people involved and risking errors in message exchange, you directly transmit information. Gang planking is a form of mutual adjustment since workers consult about what needs to be accomplished and how this can be done. It can enhance communication efficiency because employees at the same level may be more familiar with each other's work and use the same technical language for communication. The drawback is that supervisors in each unit aren't aware of what's happening. This means they may be out of the communication loop. So, gang planking is often resisted under all organization forms.

Another principle of bureaucratic organization is *specialization*, where related activities are grouped together and then assigned to a unit within the larger organization to improve productivity. An example is a call center that serves different kinds of clients and calls are routed to the worker with the specialization needed by the client. Work tasks can also be specialized by dividing them into components, each done by a different worker, like an assembly line. This can enhance performance because the worker develops expertise through repetition, reducing the need for re-working products. However, the repetitiveness of actions quickly becomes mind-numbing for the worker.

Adam Smith (1937) provided an early example of the benefits of specialization in making a pin. Initially, a pin was made by subject matter experts, called craftspeople, who were responsible for every step in the pin-making process. This is called cradle-to-grave processing, meaning that one person is responsible for doing everything from the beginning of the task (the cradle) to the end (the grave). Smith identified 18 narrowly defined steps which took an entire day to make a single pin. He suggested that instead of having workers learn all 18 steps, they should learn only one or two of these and perform these functions all day. Doing this would mean that hundreds of pins could be created each day instead of 18 independent workers creating just 18 pins in one day.

Scientific management studies, also called time and motion studies, offer an excellent way to determine who should perform different tasks, such as those associated with making a pin discussed above. In a time and motion study, scientific management experts break a process down into the various steps performed by multiple workers rather than just one individual. Doing this is more efficient since people differ in what they want to do as well as their skills, abilities, and productive capacities. Workers trained in one function gain dexterity through specialization that requires only a limited range of knowledge and expertise (Gulick & Urwick, 1937). Besides determining the appropriate division of labor into specialized tasks, scientific management experts also prescribe the tools and motions the workers should use to be the most efficient.

A well-known time and motion study was Frederick Taylor's (1998 [1911]) study of shoveling. He documented all the motions employees had to make to lift a shovel. This analysis was repeated for each type of material that would be shoveled. First, he looked at what a worker was shoveling, whether it was 3 3/4 pounds of rice coal per shovel or ore, which was 38 pounds of lump coal per shovel. He reasoned that these different commodities needed a special shovel designed to work the best for that material. Additionally, he prescribed various shoveling movements based on each material so that the worker did not tire too quickly, and the highest poundage was shoveled in a day. In today's terms, this kind of study is known as ergonomics.

This information about shovels, motions, and surfaces was used to estimate the minimum number of pounds each worker could be expected to shovel in a day. If workers exceeded these standards, they were eligible for increased or incentive pay. In 1911, Taylor was among the first to advocate using pay-for-performance incentives to motivate workers.

The worker was not the only person whose efficiency was improved through time and motion studies. At the beginning of the day, the supervisor's task was to determine what needed to be done, how many workers it would take, and what types of shovels were required based on different materials. These instructions would change based on what was to be shoveled each day. Then, when the workers came in, they could quickly find out what tasks they had been assigned for the day, gather the correct tools, and produce the most work based on the proper sequence of movements.

The advantage of scientific management studies was finding ways to re-engineer tasks to make production more time- and cost-efficient. Individuals doing one task became very good and were fast at doing each job because they did it repetitively. Interestingly, these studies helped usher in the industrial era since machines, rather than men, could now be developed to perform the specialized, but routine, tasks documented through time and motion studies.

After a time and motion study, the next step was to train employees in each motion so that the next worker could use the work they did in the assembly line without re-work. Finding ways to have a smooth hand-off between workers relates to the principle of integration or ensuring coordination between the different workers in a unit and a smooth hand-off of the work transferred between units. Integrating people and work units can maximize coordination and promote processing efficiency. Integration studies find ways to ensure that the transition is smooth and that each person in the production chain gets a product they can use without handing it back for re-work or taking time to modify it to perform their tasks.

From this concern about re-work arose suggestions about the appropriate level of differentiation. Differentiation describes how much specialization there is in the work units of an organization. Highly complex organizations have a high degree of differentiation, making it challenging to create a smooth flow of work products from one unit to another. Improved communication systems, cross-unit work meetings, and the joint development of procedures for inter-unit cooperation are common ways to strengthen the integration between work units (Gortner et al., 1997).

Another organizational design principle is the *span of control*. When we talk about the span of control, we talk about the number of subordinates assigned to a supervisor. There is no generally accepted rule of thumb for the span of control. Most scholars would say supervisors should have no more than they can reasonably oversee (Fayol, 1992 [1949]). Typically, the number is 6–12 subordinates per supervisor. This number could increase if the workforce comprises professionals who work independently or for supervisors of low-skilled workers who regularly perform routine tasks. The span of control might decrease if the supervisor has employees who require high supervision levels, need a lot of direction in non-routine tasks, or perform highly specialized tasks. Recall the movie *Modern Times* (1936) with Charlie Chaplin sitting on a platform overlooking a pool of about 100 secretaries typing letters at some point in the movie. That would be a very high span of control. The span of control at the European Space Agency is very different, as most people working there have advanced degrees in aerospace engineering, propulsion, theoretical physics, etc. The span of control there is much, much smaller.

Generally, the optimal span of control will depend on the degree to which the rules and regulations are clear and available to employees and the degree to which jobs are routine and low-skilled or highly specialized and high-skilled. If rules and regulations are accessible, clear, and understood, and if there has been adequate training, then the role of the supervisor can be minimized (Pagan & Franklin, 2003).

Is There One Best Way to Organize?

Weber and the scientific management experts identified many different principles designed to find the best way to organize. The one best way worked well for industrial organizations, where workers were trained in one specific skill. When a worker finished his/her task, the work was given to other craftspeople until the product was finished. This form of organization was appropriate in the industrial age, where production was accomplished by machines operating on assembly lines (Simon, 1946; Waldo, 1984 [1948]). However, this machine-type view of production has a severe downside. Employees found that they were reduced to being cogs in a machine, their connection to the entire production process was severed, and they were simply doing one part of a more complex task. Just imagine that you work in an assembly line and are doing the same thing, the same movement, and attaching the same part, the whole day between 8 and 5. Boring, right? And not just that, it is also killing creativity. Remember that when people made things for most of history, they did so by starting with the raw product (wood, wool fibers, metals, etc.) and shaping it into a unique finished product. Artisans derived great satisfaction from controlling the entire production process.

The industrial revolution disconnected craft and production, and as a result, people felt increasingly alienated from their work. They no longer identified with the job and certainly did not experience the satisfaction of doing it. Adam Smith was among the first in the industrial era to write about specialization; Frederick Winslow Taylor (1998 [1911]) wrote his ideas on scientific management in the heyday of beliefs to enhance the efficiency of production and work activities without regard for the human factor (boredom with, alienation from work). It is no wonder that in the 1920s and 1930s, this scientific management movement found its adversary in the human relations movement. We discuss this more in Chap. 10.

Today, early in the twentieth century, we still have industrial organizations. We also have seen a rise in service and technology-based organizations, where it is much more difficult to specify the one best way of organizing because the organizational structure is designed to meet individual client's needs rather than have a production line that assumes one size fits all. As we have seen from our organizational structure discussion, there could be almost as many ways of organizing as there are clients.

Another aspect influencing the design of organizations is the goals you are pursuing. The goals of public organizations can vary as the desires of the political and administrative leaders change. Further, goals can often conflict. For example, if you have goals of efficiency or cost-effectiveness, you might want to arrange an organization by function. As we learned from scientific management studies, this is an efficient way of organizing since people perform specialized work and produce more.

What if your goal was equity and you worked in a service-providing organization? A better way might be to organize by functional specialty so that clients could be handed off from one specialist to another based on their individual needs. Unfortunately, when this happens, the client feels like they should keep providing the same information over and over and over as they are passed from one specialist to another. So instead, and quite popular since the 1980s, is the so-called one-stop-shop service, where a client is helped by one civil servant who is knowledgeable about and can take care of all the steps required for the service you need.

The one-stop-shop service is also an example where technology can change the "best" way to organize. With the advent of technology, client information that had to be repeated with each new specialist is now available immediately to all organization employees through networked computers. Technology supports a system of one-stop shopping where all the specialists are co-located and work as a team based on each client's specific needs. Instead of giving their personal information to each specialist, each specialist can pull up the client's file and gather any additional information to perform their job duties.

The structure of organizations can be established based on the organizational design principles introduced in this chapter. However, finding the "one best way" to organize has been elusive. For example, one challenge has been shifting from a single organization that offers government goods or services to a network of organizations that provide a menu of goods and services that are needed to serve the client. An example is juvenile offenders. Not only do they interact with law enforcement and the courts, but they may also need supportive services such as education, physical, and mental health services, as well as foster care depending on the circumstances the contributed to their arrest.

What Organizational Designs Foster Collaboration?

In today's interdependent environment, the boundaries between organization sectors continuously blur, and collaboration between organizations is essential (Moe, 2003). Collaboration is purposefully facilitating interactions and operations with multiple organizations to solve problems that one organization, working independently, cannot solve. "Collaboration does not just happen … it has to be managed" (Agranoff & McGuire, 2003, p. 3). To do this, the public manager must consciously coordinate actors, resources, and services provided to carry out established collective purposes (O'Toole Jr., 2001). Next, we examine why collaboration is necessary, and describe the organizational structures used for cooperative activities between organizations and how to overcome the challenges of cooperation and coordination.

An emphasis on collaboration grew in response to criticisms that public value was not maximized. There was often duplication and redundancy in programs providing services to the same clientele (Bardach, 1998). Public value is created by establishing and operating a public organization that meets citizens' desires—that is, individuals who use social welfare programs progress in addressing the social condition that required them to seek government services (Moore, 1995). Public value can be created by giving more benefits, consuming fewer resources, or minimizing the time government services are needed when a public organization cooperates in joint service delivery.

As the number of collaborative efforts has increased, so has our understanding of principles to consider when structuring interorganizational collaboration. For example, interagency collaborative capacity, or the ability of public agencies to work with other organizations to jointly produce public value, can be increased when the means-end relationship is clear, political and financial incentives to collaborate exist, organizations encourage flexibility and joint problem-solving, and high-quality leadership is present (Bardach, 1998). In addition, maintaining the interest of key elected leaders and senior executives, developing budgets that have incentives and rewards, joint skills training and staff development activities, and standard information systems are other ways to improve the efforts of virtual organizations (Pollitt, 2003). Lastly, linking mechanisms for sharing information and resources between organizations as well as the presence of boundary spanners are also critical to successful collaboration across sectors (Hage & Aiken, 1970). With these attributes for successful collaboration, we now look at organizing structures for cooperative activities.

What Organizing Structures Encourage Interorganizational Collaboration?

Three forms of organizations—entrepreneurial, co-production, and virtual—have emerged as the goods and services expected from government expanded. These new forms of organization have fostered the continuous improvement of how goods and services are provided. These organizing structures exist outside the boundaries of any one formal organization and involve representatives from multiple organizations across the government, not-for-profit, volunteer, and for-profit sectors (O'Toole Jr., 2001).

One outgrowth of the government reform efforts of the 1990s was the creation of *entrepreneurial organizations* that envisioned a government unit as an enterprise function that could "sell" its services for a profit. Entrepreneurial organizations typically provide administrative or staff services within an organization, such as procurement or fleet services. Entrepreneurial government can be based on a cross-service model, where agencies not operating at full capacity can perform reimbursable work for other agencies or as franchises that are fee-for-service centers that serve the administrative needs of different organizations based on a contractual fee schedule (Laurent, 2003).

Entrepreneurial organizations within the public sector were initially found in the public utilities (gas, water, electricity) and transport (public transport) services. They have also been successful using entrepreneurial organization to reduce the transaction costs of public procurement (Sama et al., 2014). The notion of entrepreneurial government emerged when the reinventing government movement started (Osborne & Gaebler, 1992). In recent years, the notion of an entrepreneurial government has also come to include the idea of entrepreneurial street-level and policy bureaucrats (Cohen, 2021).

Entrepreneurial organizations encourage employees to be more cost-conscious since they are now forced to consider a bottom line. There is evidence that innovation is enhanced as the workers consciously examine the practices of other organizations in all sectors to find ways to reduce costs and increase productivity (Walters, 2002). Since the focus is on customer satisfaction and profits, partnerships often develop, leading to cooperation between units inside and outside the organization's boundaries.

Indeed, we want government officials and government organizations to be enterprising, creative, and proactive in developing and implementing policy.

The question, however, is how much we, as citizens, want the government to be entrepreneurial. In business, risk-taking behavior sometimes pays off in developing a new product, but it sometimes fails. The government, however, produces a few services on a fee-for-service basis but also provides a large variety of services that are simply paid through taxation. In many of these activities, risk-taking is not encouraged.

How prevalent are entrepreneurial government activities? Government or public parks are an example of where the goods and services of government are offered on a competitive fee-for-service basis. This business model starts as a way to generate revenue that would be retained by the organization to enhance operations to attract more visitors and to avoid layoffs. These businesses range from trail planning to billing the state for firefighters' time and handling workers' compensation claims for other public organizations (Laurent, 2003).

Canada and the United States are countries where entrepreneurialism is highly valued (e.g., Klein et al., 2020; Weiser, 2011). How widespread it is outside the Anglo-American world is unclear. However, it is vital to remember that challenges posed by rapid industrialization, urbanization, and rapid population growth around the 1900s were, at first and for quite a while, mainly addressed by upper-level career civil servants in Europe and North America. For instance, those local officials, municipal secretaries in the Netherlands, and city managers in the United States designed new ways of dealing with people's demands. Perhaps entrepreneurial or innovative government is still found locally, where one finds the most direct service delivery. In contrast, it is less critical at the regional and federal levels. More particularly, evidence from Sweden suggests that entrepreneurial governance is more effective in larger, urban municipalities than in smaller, rural areas (Klein et al., 2020; see also Krane et al., 2019 on Switzerland).

Another form of cooperation we increasingly see is *co-production*. When you have co-production, an organization works with other organizations as well as the service recipients to produce public value (Krane et al., 2019). Public organizations often depend on clients to achieve results. Co-production means increasing the client's contributions toward a mutually shared goal (Moore, 1995). Often this requires decentralizing operations, so decision-making can occur on the front lines since it must be done in consultation with the customer.

Many public organizations are created to improve the self-sufficiency of the client. To do this generally requires the cooperation of the client through co-production. For example, when the non-profit organization Habitat for Humanity builds houses, they use co-production. They partner with governmental and non-governmental organizations. They also require that the new homeowner devote a certain number of hours, called sweat equity, toward completing the project. The homeowner uses this sweat equity as partial payment for the house.

Another example would be community policing. Typically, police departments are arranged hierarchically by function. This means that traffic cops are in one unit and homicide investigators in another, police record-keeping services are yet another function, and so on. Under this form of organization, when you call the police department, the switchboard operator directs your call based on the service you are calling about or for.

In the 1990s in various countries, there was a trend toward community policing where traditional organizational structures based on function were replaced by ones based on geography. In this model, officers are placed in community substations that respond to all types of calls, whether traffic incidents or violent crimes. Many of these officers have grown up in the neighborhood where they serve. The advantage of this organizational structure was that you had police officer's familiar with the community. They knew the residents and could work with them to solve crimes and proactively reduce the possibility of future crimes. A typical feature of these community policing substations was the creation of neighborhood block watches, which encouraged citizens to work with the police and their neighbors to make the area where they lived safer.

Through these cooperative activities, ongoing relationships are built. More frequent communications and interactions create a certain level of trust. This can lead to reports about suspicious activity before they escalate into crimes and give the local police an enhanced ability to target potential criminals and take preventative measures. Overall, the community policing concept is successful since it serves the specific needs of a defined geographic area and puts a face on the local police force.

Another emerging type of extra-organizational structure is the *virtual organization*. Often referred to as partnerships, networks, or collaboratives (Rosneau, 2000; Sørensen & Torfing, 2007), virtual organizations involve multiple, interdependent organizations, often from different sectors, where one unit is not superior or subordinate to the others (O'Toole Jr., 2001). An example from business organizations is a self-organizing network called the spider's web that brings people together to solve a particular problem and leverage knowledge capabilities, then disbands once the job is done (Franklin et al., 2013; Quinn et al., 1998).

When representatives from different organizations get together, they bring expertise, resources, and authority from their specific organization. Everyone's contribution is shared. Further, all members agree on using resources for the group's good. Groups of this type might also be called ad hoc working groups or task forces. An example of a self-organizing network was introduced in Germany as early as 1957, when many government and non-governmental organizations cooperated to protect habitats for endangered species (Fisch, 2005). Governments in South Asia are attempting to reduce declining tiger populations through the Asia Ministerial Conference on Tiger Conservation, the establishment of National Tiger Committees, and the creation of Conversation Assured Tiger Standards in 100+ sites globally that cover more than 70% of the global tiger population. The distinguishing feature of this virtual organization is that organizations from different sectors and nations are working together. In these collaborations, the partners voluntarily share scarce resources and expertise to try and improve tiger habitats and best practices for endangered species conservation.

A different set of skills is required to successfully organize structures that extend beyond the boundaries of an organization. Virtual organizations need the public manager to perform linking, mediating, and coordinating functions since the boundaries of relationships are beyond traditional and formal jurisdictions. This structural arrangement is helpful but also tricky because it is hard for one individual to impact people from different organizations (O'Toole Jr., 2001). Interorganization management requires establishing and facilitating productive relationships between participants with conflicting goals, altered perceptions, and different values (Agranoff & McGuire, 2003). Successful managers must also be comfortable operating in a learning organization (Senge, 2006 [1990]) where the characteristics of negotiation, innovation, problem-solving, and power-sharing within a group setting are necessary. Cooperation across organization boundaries implies purposiveness and creativity combined with action among a group of committed professionals (Bardach, 1998).

What Is Important for Interorganizational Collaboration?

When we think about all the different organizational structures, whether intra- or extra-organizational, the common concern is how to produce the best goods or services an organization is tasked with providing. Many times, this is the responsibility of one organization. Still, at other times, many organizations share a piece of production responsibility, and they must work together to coordinate their services. In all sectors, the "unnatural acts" of alliances and collaborations have been responses to calls for enhanced outcomes and accountability for results (Renz, 1999).

But cooperation is not automatic. Studies have identified challenges that can arise, such as resistance to pooling intangible resources like authority, autonomy, money, people, political standing, and information necessary in and for joint efforts. Organizations seldom are willing to give up control over these items when there is no guarantee that results will be attributed directly to their efforts (Bardach, 1998). Also, collaborative activities do not fit easily within traditional bureaucratic structures emphasizing hierarchy, a strict chain of command, and internally focused unit management (Mandell, 1988). Another explanation for why collaboration may not occur is that the political and institutional structures reward differentiation rather than integration. In virtual organizations, a specific challenge to collaboration is that there is no central authority, and a single objective has not been established (Agranoff & McGuire, 2003). This can create a problem for efficient as well as effective decision-making since many more people are involved, each consulting with their home organization. The last challenge is lacking a leader who can foster creativity or innovation and leverage the group's problem-solving processes. Each of these challenges can weaken efforts to collaborate between organizations.

The story that opened this chapter describing the need for coordinated activities during an extreme natural event such as the COVID-19 pandemic is an example of how the structures of partner organizations influence responsiveness. It also suggests the need to consider coordinating mechanisms, not just across levels of government but also across sectors of organizations, to ensure that these cooperative activities are productive.

In the aftermath of natural and human-caused disasters, emergency response services can be provided by the governmental and non-governmental organizations. In addition, we have all heard and seen stories of individuals spontaneously and voluntarily providing direct aid as a form of co-production. Government organizations need to be flexible to coordinate their efforts from all levels inside the organization as well as with partners outside their organizations.

How can we sort out who should do what in collaborations and virtual organizations? One lesson learned after natural and human-caused disasters is that, in emergency conditions, we must assume communication breakdowns will occur and thus establish expectations for decentralized decision-making (Cohen et al., 2002). To ensure cooperation and coordination, high-reliability organizations must be created with features such as very high levels of technical competence and sustained performance; regular training; structure redundancy; collegial, decentralized authority patterns; processes that reward error discovery and correction; adequate and reliable funding; high mission valence; reliable and timely information; and protection from external interference in operations (Frederickson & LaPorte, 2002, p. 33).

Can government do this? Are there alternate ways to structure government to meet this challenge? Using the different policy areas of government, Rivlin (1992) argued for a better distinction between responsibilities assigned to each level of government. She proposed that the national government be responsible for health care. The subnational governments would be accountable for developing and implementing a strategic agenda for education, workforce skills, and public infrastructure focusing on productivity, with shared taxes funding the new arrangement. Using this framework, the national government's responsibilities would change to primarily supporting subnational governments in the operational, financial, and legal dimensions.

Other analytical frameworks for the division of duties have been proposed. For example, we could also consider who provides a service, supervises and controls the provision of the services, and pays for the service (Hovey, 1989). Analyzing the funding and provision of public programs and services using this framework could help identify the national government's role in assuring nationwide policy progress. It could also determine which matters are important to the multiple subnational governments that serve communities. This could also be helpful when considering the involvement of organizations in other sectors.

Chapter Summary

The optimal way to design an organization to accomplish its purpose is a question that has been asked since the first organization was created. Early scholars developed theories that emphasized things like organization by product or organization by process. Later, scholars expanded the list to consider when it was appropriate to organize by geography or client. Unsurprisingly, hybrid forms that combine some of the four basic organizational structures emerge. Fast forward to today, and we find ever more complex structures representing hybrids that leverage technology through multi-level and multi-organizational arrangements within an increasingly globalized network of organizations and program service delivery. While we have not entirely abandoned the quest for the "one best way," we increasingly rely on organizational analysis and the use of design principles to accommodate collaborative action and network functioning, as well as to develop a resilience attitude to promote flexibility and innovation for continuous improvement. In the next chapter, we can see how design principles assist in managing government's human assets.

Practical Applications

1. How the tables have turned. For most of history, only the public sector had to be organized. Businesses were small and few and far between. However, with the industrial revolution, corporations have grown enormously, and they have been so successful that a variety of people believe that government should start operating like a business. Develop arguments pro and contra this idea of organizing government like a business.
2. Provide examples of very hierarchical and very "flat" organizations. For instance, the military branches of any national defense organization are highly hierarchical; an example of a very flat organization is the Roman Catholic Church. Can you provide other examples of hierarchical and flat organizations?
3. Compare the organizational structure of a public, a non-profit, and a for-profit organization that all operate in the same line of work (e.g., health care, education, community development, social work). What similarities and differences do you see in how they are structured?

In-Class Instructional Suggestions

1. Identify educational organizations at the different age groups (kindergarten, elementary school, secondary school, and higher education) and analyze the organizational design principles for each.
2. Invite to class a middle to upper-level civil servant to discuss how in practice they collaborate actions in a policy field.

3. Encourage students to identify public services that are provided through collaboration with non-governmental organizations. Work with them to determine how these partnerships or collaborations are superior to government as the sole service provider.

References

Agranoff, R., & McGuire, M. (2003). *Collaborative public management: New strategies for local Governments*. Georgetown University Press.

Bardach, E. H. (1998). *Getting agencies to work together: The practice and theory of managerial craftsmanship*. Brookings Institution Press.

Cohen, N. (2021). *Policy entrepreneurship at the street level*. Cambridge University Press.

Cohen, S., Eimicke, W., & Horan, J. (2002). Catastrophe and the public service: A case study of the government response to the destruction of the World Trade Center. *Public Administration Review, 62*(Special Issue), 24–32.

Fayol, H. (1992 [1949]). General and industrial management. In J. M. Shafritz, & J. S. Ott (Eds.), *Classics of organization theory* (3rd ed., pp. 56–68). Brooks/Cole.

Fisch, S. (2005). German administration and water issues in history. In J. C. N. Raadschelders (Ed.), *The institutional arrangements for water management in the 19th and 20th centuries* (pp. 23–43). IOS Press.

Franklin, A. L., Krane, D., & Ebdon, C. (2013). Multi-level governance processes – Citizen and local budgeting: Comparing Brazil, China, and the United States. *International Review of Public Administration, 18*(1), 1–24.

Frederickson, H. G., & LaPorte, T. R. (2002). Airport security, high reliability, and the problem of rationality. *Public Administration Review, 62*(Special Issue), 33–43.

Glendening, P. N. (2002). Governing after September 11th: A new normalcy. *Public Administration Review, 62*, 21–23.

Gortner, H. F., Mahler, J., and Nicholson, J. B. (1997). *Organization theory: A public perspective.* .

Gulick, L. (1992, 3rd ed. [1937]). Notes on the theory of organization. In J. M. Shafritz & J. S. Ott (Eds.), *Classics of organization theory* (pp. 87–95). Brooks.

Gulick, L., & Urwick, L. (1937). POSDCORB. Institute of Professional Administration.

Hage, J., & Aiken, M. (1970). *Social change in complex organizations* (Vol. 41). Random House.

Hovey, H. A. (1989). Analytic approaches to state-local relations. In E. D. Liner (Ed.), *A decade of devolution: Perspectives on state-local relations* (pp. 163–182). The Urban Institute Press.

Klein, P. G., Mahoney, J. T., McGrahan, A. M., & Pitelis, Chr.N. (2020). Toward a theory of public entrepreneurship. *European Management Review, 7*(1), 1–15.

Krane, D., Ebdon, C., & Franklin, A. L. (2019). Collaborative governance of civic festivals: Brazil, Korea, and the USA. In M. N. Iftikhar, J. Justice, & D. B. Audretsch (Eds.), *Urban studies and entrepreneurship: How can cities foster entrepreneurship?* Springer Nature.

Laurent, A. (2003). Entrepreneurial government: Bureaucrats as business people. *IBM Center for the Business of Government*. http://www.businessofgovernment.org/report/entrepreneurial-government-bureaucrats-businesspeople

Mandell, M. P. (1988). Intergovernmental management in inter-organizational networks. *International Journal of Public Administration, 11*(4), 393–416.

McClusky, J. E. (2002). Re-thinking nonprofit organizations governance: Implications for management and leadership. *International Journal of Public Administration, 25*(4), 539–559.

Moe, R. C. (2003). *Administrative renewal: Reorganization commissions in the 20th century.* University Press of America.

Moore, M. H. (1995). *Creating public value: Strategic management in government.* Harvard University Press.

Moynihan, D. P. (2005). Goal-based learning and the future of performance management. *Public Administration Review, 65*(2), 203–215.

Newman, W. W. (2002). Reorganizing for national security and homeland security. *Public Administration Review, 62*(Special Issue), 126–133.

O'Toole, L. J., Jr. (2001). Different public managements? Implications of structural context in hierarchies and networks. In J. L. Brudney, L. J. O'Toole Jr., & H. G. Rainey (Eds.), *Advancing public management: New developments in theory, methods, and practice* (pp. 19–32). Georgetown University Press.

Osborne, D., & Gaebler, T. (1992). *Reinventing government: How the entrepreneurial spirit is transforming the public sector.* Westview Press.

Pagan, J., & Franklin, A. L. (2003). Understanding variation in the practice of employee discipline: The perspective of the first-line supervisor. *Review of Public Personnel Administration, 23*(1), 61–77.

Page, E. C. (2012). *Policy without politicians. Bureaucratic influence in comparative perspective.* Oxford University Press.

Page, E. C., & Jenkins, B. (2005). *Policy bureaucracy: Government with a cast of thousands.* Oxford University Press.

Pollitt, C. (2003). *The essential public manager.* Open University Press.

Public Administration Review. (2021a). COVID-19 viewpoint symposium part I. *Public Administration Review, 80*(4), 590–705.

Public Administration Review. (2021b). COVID-19 viewpoint symposium part II. *Public Administration Review, 80*(5), 755–908.

Quinn, J. B., Anderson, P., & Finkelstein, S. (1998). Managing professional intellect: Making the most of the best. *Harvard Business Review, 74*(2), 71–80.

Raadschelders, J. C. N., Larrison, J., & Thapar, J. A. (2019). Refugee migration as wicked problem: American controlling, palliative and governing policies in a global context. *World Affairs Journal, 182*(3), 228–255.

Renz, D. (1999). Adding a few pieces to the puzzle: Some practical implications of recent governance research. *New England Nonprofit Quarterly, 6*(2), 7–15.

Rivlin, A. M. (1992). *Reviving the American dream: The economy, the states and the federal government.* The Brookings Institution.

Robey, D. (1986). *Designing organizations* (2nd ed.). Irwin.

Rosneau, J. N. (2000). The challenges and tensions of a globalized world. *American Studies International, 38*(2), 8–22.

Sama, H. K., Ndunguru, P. C., & Baisi, M. D. (2014). Entrepreneurial government: Causal relationship between transaction costs and value for money. *International Journal of Managerial Studies and Research, 2*(9), 63–74.

Sandfort, J. (2010). Nonprofits within policy fields. *Journal of Policy Analysis and Management, 29*(3), 637–644.

Senge, P. (2006 [1990]). *The fifth discipline. The art and practice of the learning organization.* Doubleday.

Simon, H. A. (1946). The proverbs of administration. *Public Administration Review*, *6*(Winter), 52–67.

Simon, H. A., Langley, P. W., & Bradshaw, G. L. (1981). Scientific discovery as problem-solving. *Synthese*, *47*, 1–27.

Smith, A. (1937 [1776]). *The wealth of nations*. Random House.

Sørensen, E., & Torfing, J. (2007). Theoretical approaches to meta-governance. In E. Sørensen & J. Torfing (Eds.), *Theories of democratic network governance* (pp. 169–182). Palgrave Macmillan.

Taylor, F. W. (1998 [1911]). *The principles of scientific management*. Harper and Brothers.

Tompkins, J. R. (2005). *Organization theory and public management*. Thomson Wadsworth.

Waldo, D. (1984 [1948]). *The administrative state. A study of the political theory of American public administration*. Holmes and Meier Publishers.

Wall, S. J. (2004). *On the fly: Executing strategy in a changing world*. Wiley.

Walters, J. (2002). Understanding innovation. In M. A. Abramson & I. D. Littman (Eds.), *Innovation* (pp. 13–58). Rowman and Littlefield.

Weber, M. (1946 [1922]). Bureaucracy. In H. H. Gerth and C. W. Mills (Eds.), *Max Weber: Essays in sociology* (pp. 196-235). Oxford University Press.

Weiser, P. J. (2011). Innovation, entrepreneurship, and the information age. *Journal on Telecommunications and High Technology Law*, *9*, 1.

CHAPTER 10

Managing the Human Assets of Government

The focus of Chap. 9 was on government organizations and how they were structured. In this chapter, we switch our focus to the people in those organizations and how they are selected and managed. As described in Chap. 9, early organizational theorists sought the "one best way" to organize for the most efficient structure through normative organizational design principles. These principles worked well in their time, especially in for-profit organizations and in organizations that government would run like a business.

However, government programs and services diversified and increased to include non-governmental organizations leading traditional governmental programs to find design principles to address other values such as representativeness, equity, justice, and effectiveness of outcomes beyond cost or speed. Combined with this, the collaborations and service delivery networks meant that program management was more complex. This chapter describes a similar pattern of diversification, growth, collaboration, and alternative service delivery in managing government's human assets.

What can you expect from interactions with the government as a human asset? You may have already had an experience that impacts your expectations. Most people have filled out job applications. Several of you likely have a job to help finance your studies. What did you do when you were invited for a job interview? You probably thought about your appearance at the interview, made sure you had clean, nice clothes, styled your hair, and shaved or put on your makeup. You may have also researched the organization and prepared answers to questions you thought might be asked during the interview. Immediately before the meeting, you may have wiped your hands on your pants or skirt to ensure they were not sweaty. After all, you did not want to appear nervous.

You entered the interview room and saw a group of people serving on the interview panel. These interviewers developed an impression of you based on your appearance and responses to the questions they posed. After the interview

© The Author(s), under exclusive license to Springer Nature
Switzerland AG 2023
A. L. Franklin, J. C.N. Raadschelders, *Introduction to Governance, Government and Public Administration*,
https://doi.org/10.1007/978-3-031-32689-9_10

was finished, the interviewers discussed their impressions of you. They ranked your performance and qualifications as compared to the other job applicants. You might have even been asked for a second interview if you did well. After completing the interview, your ranking among all candidates and "fit" for the job and the organization was assessed.

Initially called personnel management, the organizational function tasked with finding and managing the workers who provide goods and services is now called *human resources management* (HRM). Human resource management is a core function for any employer for organizations in all sectors since, without proper personnel, no organization can accomplish its objectives. For government organizations, the challenge of hiring the right people is magnified. They not only need employees who are a good fit in terms of skills, knowledge, and abilities, but they also want people with a clear interest in working in the public sector for the good of society. To serve the public interest, civil servants must produce publicly value outcomes while, at the same time, prudently use public resources. This requires attention to the administrative values of efficiency, effectiveness, and economy while also considering democratic values such as fairness, impartiality, equity, and due process.

What Is Involved in Human Resource Management?

Human resource management is a core staff function in any organization. Human asset management involves hiring, managing, and retaining a workforce that can balance administrative demands with democratic values. These core functions of human asset management are comparable to what is done in the other sectors. However, the service to society and the need to uphold democratic values make government organizations unique.

Public personnel management is essential since a significant portion of the government's annual expenditures are for payroll and benefits. Civil servants seldom work in government because of high salaries or profit-sharing. Government salaries for jobs are consistently lower than in the for-profit sector since working for government is not as profitable, government employees are often found to work there due to a *public service motivation* (PSM) (Perry & Wise, 1990; Perry, 1996; Bozeman & Su, 2015; Wang et al., 2020), meaning that they think what they do serves the public good and has other benefits besides the level of compensation they receive. Indeed, PSM is about who public servants are and how they relate to the larger society. This idea of public service has been a topic of interest since Antiquity (Raadschelders, 2020). However, it has only become an object of active research in our study since the 1990s (Vandenabeele & Schott, 2020). PSM studies suggest that those in the public sector have unique behavioral and psychological characteristics such as serving something more significant than personal interests. Does it interest you to work in government? If so: why? If not: why not?

This link between psychology and public administration started in the 1950s and has developed into behavioral public administration (BPA) in the past several years. Scholars of BPA argue that this will improve how civil servants tackle public problems, increase diversity in the workplace, and reduce burnout (Tummers, 2020). Others are more critical about the potential of BPA, pointing out that it is a label for a specific type of research (experiments) rather than a field of study (Bertelli & Riccucci, 2022). Maybe there is room for both. PSM has been shown to influence day-to-day personnel management; BPA seems to be mainly an academic pursuit.

Human resource management is concerned with developing and administering policies that (1) identify and employ high-quality personnel who have career opportunities, (2) regulate employment relations to assure that all employees are treated fairly and equally, and (3) advance the representativeness of public organizations. Personnel management is often centralized at the higher levels of the organization. As a staff function, personnel management is not directly involved with providing goods or services to the public. Instead, it offers other services for line and staff units, including training and development, benefits administration, personnel records management, position classification, and compensation.

Personnel management comes from two very different traditions. In the "harder" workforce planning tradition, the personnel management function focuses on determining potential employees' knowledge, skills, and abilities (KSAs). It also focuses on developing techniques to determine the best job candidate, evaluate employee performance, and ensure the organization retains qualified workers.

In this tradition, an effort is made to standardize the rules and techniques applied to personnel management. Indeed, standards and labor relations were so important in the first half of the twentieth century that the emphasis was more on rules than results (Sayre, 1991 [1948]). The heavy reliance on standards dominated scholarly literature until the late 1940s and everyday practice until the 1960s.

The "softer" human relations tradition is in stark contrast since it focuses on the employee in the organizational and environmental context (Condrey, 1998). This approach emphasizes the development of the professional capacities of employees and makes the workplace enjoyable so that employees' needs are satisfied, and they are motivated to work hard. It views employees as being as much, if not more, driven by an appreciation for a job well done and a client or citizen happy with their help as they are by a salary and benefits.

Workforce planning focuses on resource management or ensuring organizational inputs, such as assigning employees to different job categories, are used most efficiently. On the other hand, the human relations tradition is more concerned with identifying and developing human resources or ensuring that employees have a desirable working environment that promotes increased productivity (Legge, 1995).

Labels assigned to the unit charged with personnel management have changed significantly over time, reflecting a new focus. What was initially called personnel management, which emphasized organizational needs, became human resource management in the 1970s, denoting more emphasis on employee needs. In the 1990s, many organizations changed the label to *human capital management*, focusing on the individual employee as an investment. Also, human capital management seeks to balance organizational with employee needs. Table 10.1 outlines the differences between the three labels for the function tasked with managing the government's human assets.

How Has Human Resource Management Evolved?

The development of the human resource management function is closely related to the growth in the number of personnel working in public organizations since the late nineteenth century. Before this time, most civil servants were hired based on patronage. They got a job because they supported people elected to public office or were related to them as constituents, friends, or even family members. Hiring based on political support did not require any systematic testing of knowledge, skills, and abilities.

Table 10.1 Features of three personnel management labels

	Personnel management (PM)	*Human resource management (HRM)*	*Human capital management (HCM)*
General approach	Personnel management as a toolbox of instruments; emphasis on technique over purpose; legalistic focus on efficiency	Less a toolbox, more focus on empowerment, productivity, and legality + democracy	An integrated management system that connects strategic workforce planning, recruitment and hiring, pay issues, benefits, and development of skills
Organization level	Top-down management: machine bureaucracy, personnel unit as subordinate staff; rule-driven; centralized personnel management; reform for efficiency, hiring is filling vacancies, compliance with laws and rules; McGregor's Theory X	A mix of top-down and bottom-up; professional bureaucracy; personnel unit part of the management team; business orientation, reform for service quality, hiring is filling vacancies with an eye for future potential; McGregor's Theory Y	A mix of top-down and bottom-up; bureaucracy of mutual relationships; balancing short- and long-term needs; strategic workforce planning, hiring is filling vacancies with an eye for long-term needs
Employee level	Emphasis on duties, training for specific skills, salary is the only incentive	Focus on rights and duties, education for skills and learning why, pay, and other incentives	Improve pay for performance, improve government benefits and quality of work-life initiatives, competency management

Source: Lane, L. M., Wolf, J. F., and Woodard, C. A. (2002). Reassessing the human resource crisis in the public service, 1987–2002. *The American Review of Public Administration*, 33(2), 123–145. The remaining table content is by the authors

Indeed, public organizations had no personnel management units before the 1880s. Personnel management did not emerge as a separate staff function until public sector jobs were considered professional positions that required expertise. To understand the development of public personnel management, we need to look at the development of the civil service. The example outlined in Table 10.2 is that of civil service development in the United States. We will pay attention to it because this has been a well-established study area in American public administration. In addition, we will provide comparative comments based on an international research project.

Implementation of civil service reforms often face two main challenges and, as a result, do not change civil service employment immediately or entirely. The first challenge is how to balance the interaction between administration and politics. The second is maintaining a professionally trained civil service. In view of rapid government growth from the late nineteenth century on, it was then that the study of public personnel administration emerged.

The first challenge, separating politics from administration, was met by introducing a personnel system where the recruitment of civil servants was not dependent upon political influence. Initially, in the United States, only 10% of all federal positions were subject to the authority of the Civil Service Commission, which was created by the Pendleton Act (1883) to oversee merit

Table 10.2 Phases of civil service development in the United States

Period	Features
Guardian period: 1789–1829	Government by Gentlemen: focus on the appointment of people of character, ethical conduct, and competence; power concentrated among the gentry Signal event: Washington elected president
Spoils period: 1829–1883	Government by the Common Man: focus on the accessibility of government to and for all Signal event: Andrew Jackson elected president
Reform period: 1883–1906	Government by the Good: focus on assuring a professional civil service through training and separation from politics Signal event: the Pendleton Act
Scientific period: 1906–1948	Government by the Efficient: focus on the discovery of universal organizational principles; first handbooks of personnel management in the 1910s Signal event: New York Bureau of Municipal Research established
HRM period: 1948–1970	Government by Administrators: increased focus on employee needs and organizational concerns specific to the public sector Signal event: Waldo's *The Administrative State*
Professional period: 1970–present	Government by Professionals: focus on training specialist professionals (lawyers, doctors, etc.) in the career civil service for higher-level generalist management positions Signal event: National Associations of School of Public Affairs and Administration (NASPAA) created (1970)

Source: Based in part on Mosher, F. C. (1982). *Democracy and the public service* (2nd ed., Chapter 3). Oxford University Press

appointments. By the time Theodore Roosevelt headed the Commission, this number had expanded to 25%. At the beginning of Roosevelt's presidency in 1901, it rose to 46%. When Theodore Roosevelt left office, 66% of all positions were within the Civil Service Commission's purview (White, 2000).

The second challenge, creating a professional civil service, initially focused on getting employees with liberal arts backgrounds. It was thought this would give them a broader perspective on societal challenges and needs (Hoffman, 2002). The commonly held notion was that anything related to the personnel function could be systematized and standardized. After all, efficient personnel management was a challenge for all organizations. Since business management practices served as the shining example for government reform, the first personnel management handbook described for-profit sector activities and assumed that principles of standardization would uniformly apply to organizations in all sectors (Tead & Metcalf, 1920).

In the 1930s, attention shifted to uncovering organizational and managerial principles (e.g., POSDCORB). Personnel management started to rationalize procedures to improve productivity using this mechanistic view of organizations. At the same time, the attention on personnel management slowly shifted from a focus on standardization to a concern with employee needs and career development. This *human relations approach* emphasizes employee learning rather than job-related training. It also seeks to provide enhanced employee benefits to meet various individual needs. Under the human relations approach, employees are encouraged to provide input on how to improve operations since they are the subject matter experts doing the task.

This attitude represents a humanistic view of the organization, where all employees are essential for organizational achievement. From the humanistic perspective, increased attention is paid to employee needs and potential. Simultaneously, there is an increase in the methods used to measure employee performance. You could say that personnel management starts to view employees as humans during this time and becomes increasingly objectified in its operations by establishing performance standards to ensure equitable treatment of similar employees.

In the final period of civil service development, the personnel function became concerned with the academic training, development, and nurturing of experts for effective management in generalist positions. The signal event of this time was the creation of the National Association of Schools of Public Affairs and Administration (NASPAA) in 1970, which, among other things, accredits American and international public administration and public policy programs that provide professional training for mid-career professionals who aspire to higher-level positions. Recognizing the need for public administration program standards, Mosher et al. (1950) observed that:

> Almost all future public administrators will be college graduates, and within two or three decades, most of them will have graduate degrees. Rising proportions of public administrators are returning to graduate schools for refresher courses,

mid-career training, and higher degrees. These trends suggest that university faculties will be responsible for preparing and developing public servants in technical specialties and broader social skills. (p. 219)

Mosher reiterated this on the last page of his 1968 book (Mosher, 1982). Indeed, this observation has proven correct. Public administration programs have boomed since the early 1970s. They appeal to mid-career civil servants who need a professional degree in public administration to advance to higher public service ranks.

What Mosher predicted would happen in the American public service has also happened in other countries. Everywhere, the great challenge in public personnel management has been balancing efficiency, effectiveness, and economy with the equally important desire to safeguard democracy, fairness, equity, and due process.

Professionalization of the civil service has been a global phenomenon affecting civil service careers. In Europe and North America, professionalization was achieved by developing public administration programs in higher education in the late nineteenth century. So, it was entry-level education. In the past 30–50 years, attention has come to include the need for administrative leadership education for middle- and upper-level personnel. People are initially hired for their educational background and training. Once they climb in rank, their educational expertise becomes less critical and often old-fashioned in the natural and technical sciences. It becomes more critical to understanding the challenges of administrative leadership, budgeting, program evaluation, communicating information within the organization and to the citizenry, evaluating personnel, developing a strategic management plan, etc.

That professionalization happened everywhere is not contested, but how it unfolded is often country-specific (for various country cases, see Verheijen, 1999; Bekke & van der Meer, 2000; Burns & Bowornwathana, 2001; Halligan, 2003; Van der Meer et al., 2015). What is also country-specific is the extent of attention for public personnel administration in the study of public administration. Personnel management (and budgeting) are considered topics for higher vocational programs in several continental European countries, not part of a university curriculum. In contrast, many public administration curricula consider personnel and financial management critical topics. Professionalization is visible in expert and managerial education, vocational training, and personnel managers' roles over time.

What Are Different Types of Personnel Managers?

Personnel managers oversee all government employees' human resources functions except elected officials and political appointees. The role of the personnel manager has changed significantly over time. However, most agree that there still is no one best managerial style. There are, however, three general operating styles of human resource or personnel managers (Legge, 1995). The clerk of works personnel manager is subordinate to line managers, provides routine services, and processes the proper hiring and payroll documentation for employees. The manager operates on a short-time horizon and with very little discretion. Hiring is done only to fill a vacancy. The contract manager monitors personnel policies and has substantial discretion in developing and interpreting procedures, agreements, and contracts. This manager uses a middle-range planning horizon and holds a senior position with reasonable discretion. Finally, the architect is, first and foremost, a business manager who happens to be responsible for personnel. This type of manager operates with a long-term horizon. It has excellent discretion for employee training and development, workforce composition, and succession planning.

The clerk type of personnel manager is no longer considered to meet the demands of a modern, significant personnel function. Instead, the architect type has come to the forefront. This type of personnel manager is part of the executive management team. The architect role was advocated decades ago, but it has only been in the past three decades that it has been used heavily in public and for-profit sector organizations. You can see how important it is in any job description for a Human Resources Manager. The personnel manager as an architect is as much a part of an organization's management team as the Chief Executive Office, the Chief Financial Officer, and the Chief of Staff.

What Are the Core Functions of Human Resource Management?

There are various ways to categorize personnel management's core functions. We have clustered them into six categories. Four of these follow the stages of the hiring-firing cycle; the last two deal with external influences on personnel management in government. Dede (2002) gives an overview of the six functions.

Job Description, Position Classification, and Compensation

The first function includes activities that must be done before a position is advertised and covers activities such as job and career planning, job description, position classification, and compensation. In many large organizations, expected job promotions are identified on a career map from the time one enters the organization. In a closed career-line system, you cannot be promoted unless you have come through the ranks and spent a certain number of years in each rank. Good examples are the uniformed officers in front-line positions in the military, police, and fire organizations.

Job and career planning is focused on outlining career lines for employees. Using career-line positions allows the organization to create short-term, middle-range, and long-term strategies for replacing personnel. It also allows the organization to anticipate how employees will move up through the system based on years of service.

Creating a job description is an activity to develop a profile for specific jobs stating what KSA's position holders must have. This will typically include job title, duties, responsibilities, education and experience requirements, grade level, and pay ranges. A good job description also indicates how performance will be evaluated.

Position classification is the activity where, for each job, a determination is made about the needed level of KSAs, and the appropriate salary range is indicated. Position classification originated in the early twentieth century. Initially, position classification systems were very detailed; they contained many job levels. However, in the past two decades, there has been a tendency in various countries to combine different job levels and to reduce and simplify the number of occupational categories distinguished, called job banding or *broad banding*.

Compensation is based on the job's difficulty, the level of responsibility (for instance, supervisory tasks), and the cost of living for the area in which one works. An adjustment for a higher cost of living in some geographical regions of the nation is included in the pay range. That means that the average salary for each of the geographical areas varies. Thus, federal civil servants can expect cost-of-living adjustments in the United States when moving from Montana to Washington D.C., where housing prices are much higher on average.

Recruitment and Selection

The second function includes the activities of the hiring process, which are recruitment and selection. Recruitment is the activity through which an organization attempts to fill a vacancy. Organizations can recruit internally or externally. Internal recruitment is the preferred route for many organizational positions because the organization wants employees to know they can advance. This is a significant incentive to have high performance and stay with the organization. Positions filled through internal recruitment generally represent a promotion of a highly valued employee. External recruitment is the only way to fill entry-level positions. Still, it can also be used for filling high-level positions. Hiring employees from outside the organization is expected when a significant change in organizational direction or operations is desired. It brings in new ideas at the top. Also, since there are few positions at the top, external recruiting can alleviate the conflict that might result from the selection and promotion of one internal candidate over others.

The recruitment process involves creating an advertisement announcing the position (required for internal and external recruitment), designing a selection procedure, forming a selection committee, and determining the appropriate examinations for the job candidates. In addition, potential employees must usually provide letters of recommendation and resumes and attend one or more interviews. They may also be asked to take an exam, complete personality tests, agree to a background investigation, and have a physical.

Generally, you can say that the higher the position you apply for, the more elaborate and lengthier the selection process and requirements for supporting documentation will be. Once all these pieces of information are gathered, each applicant is given a score based on their education and experience. Then, the pool of applications is ranked ordered by number for hiring purposes.

Employee Training, Learning, and Job Modifications

The third function considers how employees can be motivated to stay with the organization. It includes activities such as employee training, education, and job modification. Training is generally focused on the development of specific job-related skills. It can be done through on-the-job training or short-term seminars provided or paid for by the employer. An example would be a weekend training course in a new computer program the organization will be using. On-the-job training can also be hands-on training provided by other employees.

Learning is concerned with the overall intellectual development of employees. Someone outside the organization typically provides it. It covers a broader range of topics than the specific skills needed to perform in the current position. It also takes longer to complete this type of training. An example of learning is the civil servant who studies for a Master of Public Administration degree to advance her career prospects.

Another way to motivate employees is through minor or major job modifications. Small changes do not generally change how the work for a specific position is performed. Instead, the employee can learn other positions through job rotation or work on a project or task force. Major job modifications to the employee's work include job enrichment, where a subordinate assumes some of the supervisor's tasks; job sharing, where two or more people hold one job; and flextime or remote working, where employees have the freedom to determine the work location and hours.

During the COVID-19 global pandemic, many offices and businesses closed, hoping to stem the virus's spread. One significant job modification that developed in response was working from home. For example, many classes at secondary- and higher-level educational institutions shifted from in-class delivery to an online mode of teaching. Another significant change is that many meetings during that time were conducted via online virtual technology platforms that allowed participants to see each other conduct business remotely. One challenge for the future is to strike the right, or at least a reasonable, balance between working remotely and working at an office.

Performance Appraisal, Promotion, Discipline, and Termination

The fourth function concerns managing employees already in the personnel system and includes performance appraisal, promotion, retention, and termination. In most organizations, each employee is evaluated annually. This performance appraisal can reward high performers, while low performers can be counseled. Evaluations can also be conducted to distinguish between those who deserve a promotion, raise, or bonus, and those who do not.

Promotion is a change in an employee's job position as they move up the career path in an organization. Traditionally, this was based only on seniority, but that is generally not the case today, where performance, education, and experience are more significant considerations. However, seniority remains an essential criterion for promotion in closed career systems. This is especially the case in uniformed personnel systems.

Another critical area of public personnel management today is retaining qualified personnel. Not only is retention concerned with finding ways to keep high-performing employees, but it is essential during downsizing or rightsizing to decide who will be leaving the organization. Unfortunately, in the past 40 years, these activities have negatively influenced employee morale, the attractiveness of public sector jobs, and the ability to recruit people (Light, 2019).

Discipline is the formal process of notifying employees when their performance is unsatisfactory and determining what must be changed to make performance satisfactory. Progressive employee discipline systems start with verbal counseling, advance to an oral and a written warning, then become more intense with a performance improvement plan (PIP), leave without pay, and even firing the employee. Termination is also called separation and can be categorized as voluntary or involuntary. Voluntary termination occurs when the employee quits or retires. Involuntary termination results from layoff due to economic necessity, for instance, on a massive scale during the COVID-19 global pandemic or discharge due to poor employee performance, misconduct, or illegal behaviors.

Unionization and Collective Bargaining

Unionization and collective bargaining have become increasingly important to the public sector. These activities are the fifth functional area. Unionization occurs when employees become labor union members to advance their collective interests. Unionization is prevalent for lower-level and blue-collar positions. The most significant degree of unionization is among teachers, nurses, police officers, and firefighters in the public sector.

Unionization started in the mid-nineteenth century and was instrumental in protecting workers' rights in the industrial sector. Union membership in the for-profit sector started to decline after World War II, while at the same time it started to climb in the public sector. However, union membership in the private sector has declined in most developed countries, but differences exist. In Iceland, almost 92% of the total workforce is unionized. Look at the percentage of union membership for some other countries: Sweden 67%, Italy 37%, Canada, 26.5%, the United Kingdom almost 25%, Germany close to 18%,

Japan a little above 17%, Australia at 17%, France a little above 12%, and the United States at 10.6% (OECD, 2017). What do these numbers tell you?

What about union membership in the public sector? This has been increasing since the 1950s in most Western countries (Reder, 1988). In the United States, and according to National Public Radio, unionization has grown in the public sector in the past 40 years from around 10% in the 1960s to nearly 34% of all civil servants nowadays. In the for-profit sector, unionization has declined significantly from 35% in the 1950s to about 6% nowadays (Berman et al., 2001; Reiff, 2020). Public school teachers, police officers, and fire personnel are most likely to be unionized in the public sector. Any contract negotiated between the union and a government organization is subject to approval by the jurisdiction's legislative body. Unlike for-profit sector unions that focus on salary and benefit increases, the primary motive of public sector collective bargaining is to establish the equitable treatment of employees (Klingner & Nalbandian, 1998).

Collective bargaining is where representatives from management and labor negotiate a labor contract. Usually, when collective bargaining occurs, there is a conflict of interest between management and employees about job conditions, salary, or benefits that can only be solved through the intervention of an outside actor, namely a union. For the for-profit sector organizing activities, if a certain percentage of the workforce signs a petition, a union can represent workers to management. In the public sector, unions often have a different status where they cannot force management to an agreement during collective bargaining or threaten a shutdown. Instead, they can only meet and confer with no obligation for change on the part of the public organization.

Collective bargaining in the public sector is very different from the for-profit sector. One difference is that negotiations in the public sector focus on non-wage issues such as work hours, caseload ceilings for social workers and nurses, job entry standards, and assignment and transfer rules. In the for-profit sector, negotiations also include salary and benefits. In the public sector, anything that has to do with wages is ultimately taxpayers' money, not profit. Thus, wage changes through public sector bargaining are infrequent.

Representativeness and Diversity

The last function concerns the emancipatory personnel management function and dates to the 1960s. Following the massive entry of women into the public sector workforce since the 1940s, there have been calls for representative bureaucracy so that government reflects the demographic diversity found in society. The most recent is the attention to diversity, equity, and inclusion (DEI) both in public administration programs as well as in hiring practices (Gooden, 2015), on the one hand, and for systemic racism and discrimination, on the other (Ray, 2019). These DEI-initiatives that support representativeness is the topic of the next section.

Why Is Creating a Representative Bureaucracy Necessary?

Based upon the perception that the government was biased in its hiring and promotion criteria, most attention is given to passive representation (Andersen, 2017), which attempts to assure that the composition of the public workforce mirrors that of society at large. This seeks to ensure that the composition of the workforce is like the population in terms of demographic characteristics and considers factors such as gender, race, ethnicity, religion, political affiliation, sexual orientation, age, or physical and mental disability. Discrimination based on any of these categories is prohibited by law. There are notable efforts to hire women and minorities: for example, Indians in the United Kingdom, Turks and Moroccans in northwestern Europe, and Africans in European countries, African Americans and Hispanics in the United States, senior citizens and physically or mentally disabled people in pretty much all Western countries.

The government, and especially the military, clearly has led the way in making its workforce more representative of the composition of the population. *Active representation* is a policy that seeks to advance the interests of a group in society through preferential hiring of members of that group. The assumption is that they will serve as a voice for that interest within the government. The problem is that such interest representation conflicts with the political representation system because the elected representatives should represent the people's interests. Likewise, bringing in employees because they represent an interest also clashes with the political representation system. This is because political representation includes all people in society, while employees hired for their representativeness of a population do not.

One example of active representation is a preference for specific categories of persons, such as veterans or disabled persons. It is an example of active representation because the hiring targets specific individuals as group representatives. It is not active representation in that neither veterans nor disabled persons are expected to defend the interest of veterans and disabled persons once employed. Job candidates from both categories must pass a general examination like everyone else. Still, then their score is increased by adding preference points. In practice, veterans applying for positions have priority over other job candidates, even when others are better qualified.

Finally, there is symbolic representation where the civil servant is not expected to change behavior but where the client's behavior toward the civil servant is influenced by shared social identities (Xu & Meier, 2022). This may lead to increased trust, co-production, and perceiving the civil servant as a role model.

Affirmative action (AA) and *equal employment opportunity (EEO)* are policies that address issues of representativeness. AA specifically aims at rectifying past inequalities through positive measures to include underrepresented groups in the workplace. EEO aims to prevent future discrimination in the hiring of personnel. Together they have been quite effective in reducing the hiring biases of the past. Both are motivated by correcting past injustices (Shafritz et al., 2001). Another development in this area is diversity management, where individual differences are recognized, used, and welcomed as an asset to the organization (Riccucci et al., 1978).

How do we balance a need for a *representative bureaucracy* with a need to have a well-qualified workforce? Even though the education gap between certain groups has decreased, it still exists. Personnel managers must ensure that the KSAs of the people they hire are equal to that of other applicants. Some have even gone so far as to argue that, in the workforce, minorities have a significantly better chance of being hired than white males. This concern with representative bureaucracy is shifting to focus on the executive levels of organizations, given that women and some minorities are now over-represented in lower-level positions in the public sector workforce. As they get promoted, the representation in higher civil service levels will better mimic those in society.

This assumes no hindrance to vertical mobility or moving up in the organization through promotion. At middle and upper levels in the career civil service, women and minorities are represented better and better in the United States at the GS-14 and GS-15 levels and the *Senior Executive Service* (SES). The number of women is 38% of the total. The number of minorities in the SES stands at 28% (Anestaki et al., 2016). Assuming no change in the trends occur, it is expected that the proportions of females and minorities will not change in the foreseeable future.

The choices faced by today's personnel managers can be divided into two main categories: internally and externally motivated choices. Internal choices mainly concern streamlining personnel practices to balance organizational and employee needs. Few citizens outside the organization will be aware of these choices. A critical internal choice concerns job promotion opportunities for women and minority ethnic groups who face equal pay and promotion barriers. A distinction is made between three types of barriers. Glass ceilings are invisible barriers to mobility. A sticky floor describes a situation where one can hardly escape a low-wage job. A trapdoor is a situation where women or minorities who have broken through the glass ceiling face closer scrutiny of their performance. In the real world, we make choices that limit some job mobility and, thus, create the impression that others are favored.

Externally motivated choices are much more focused on choices that concern equality of opportunity. One choice here concerns the active or passive pursuit of equal pay. While the gender gap has decreased significantly since 1967, in the United States, from $0.62 to $0.83 today, meaning that a woman earns 17 cents per dollar less than a man in the same position, according to the 2020 U.S. Census. The same can be said for the racial gap, which has been harder to reduce from $0.70 in 1967 to $0.76 in 2020 statistics for African Americans and 0.75 cents for Hispanics. An individual personnel manager or organization director can do little to change this. After all, elected officials establish the pay schedule and annual salary increases. Furthermore, public sector salaries are financed out of taxes, and taxpayers may not desire tax increases to improve public sector pay.

Concerning the wage disparities experienced by women, some of the usual explanations for the gender gap include that they are over-represented in traditionally female jobs. These are generally lower paid than positions held by men. Women also leave the workforce to raise children and re-enter the labor market at the price of lower-earning potential, or women with children more frequently work part-time. While some advocate more aggressive measures to assure equal pay and close the gender gap, others point out that, for instance, childless females between the ages of 27 and 33 earn 98% of the male salary. Concerning the gender pay gap, this is a challenge and a choice. The United States lags all Western European countries in this regard (Bok, 1996). Are we inadvertently creating a mommy gap in addition to the gender gap?

In managing the human assets of government, public administrators face unique choices when determining how to balance organizational and employee needs. For example, how would you select between the following three candidates: a candidate with advanced education and prior experience who is also a white male, a person of color with less experience but the same education, or a veteran with lesser education and experience than the other two? Hiring the first serves efficiency since you will not have to spend as much on on-the-job training; hiring the second person helps representativeness, while hiring the third person upholds the equal employment opportunity and affirmative action laws.

Civil servants must make similar irreconcilable choices daily when making decisions about promotion, discipline, evaluation, etc. These decisions are partially subject to internal guidelines and external restrictions and regulations. It is seldom possible to satisfy these conflicting values in managing human assets and the public sector.

This first section examined the management of human capital in government. The wages for government workers constitute one of the most significant expenditures in the annual budget for the government at any level. We considered how the function for managing people has evolved and how the labels reflect changes in perceptions of the human assets of government. Even though the labels have changed, the core functions remain the same, as described in the third section. Lastly, the characteristics of and need for a representative bureaucracy were described. Next, we turn to how these workers can improve the organizations they serve.

How Do We Encourage Innovation?

The design of implementation activities is arguably the best time to conduct benchmarking and best-practice research and to consider adopting innovative and novel ways of conducting the organization's activities. The concept of innovation was first introduced in the for-profit sector; however, it rapidly gained importance in the public sector (Abramson & Littman, 2002). There has been much debate about the proper definition (Altshuler & Behn, 1997). Still, we define *innovation* as novel approaches or changes to an organization's activities caused by a need to be responsive and adapt to changes in the external operating environment.

Innovation activities often improve service quality or provide cost reductions. Through innovation, a desire for change can respond to a crisis, but there is often frustration with the status quo. There can also be a focus on results or an emphasis on prevention, the introduction of new technology, or a moral imperative to serve values other than cost-efficiency. One such value, doing the right thing, was the driving factor in San Diego's Trauma Intervention Services changes. The innovation was to send a volunteer to the scene of workplace incidents or traffic accidents alongside emergency personnel. The task of the volunteer was to offer emotional support to survivors (Walters, 2002). Before this innovation, public safety and emergency personnel, who were more concerned with returning the scene to an operational condition and attending to physical injuries rather than emotional traumas, were the only public officials present. Nowadays in the United States, and possibly elsewhere, law enforcement responding to a traumatic call is frequently accompanied by behavioral health professionals. This has proven very helpful in, for instance, dealing with people on the autism spectrum disorder.

Innovations, such as San Diego's initiative, are often necessary when gaps between what the organization currently does and what it should be doing, or wants to do in the future, are identified through strategic planning. Gaps suggest that the organization needs to modify or reorganize its processes to adapt to changes in the operating environment.

Gap analysis compares current performance against something else. The comparison could be either past performance, expected performance, desired or potential performance, competitors' performance, or industry standards. This quote, attributed to John Elway, provides a great illustration of gap analysis: "With 2:30 left in the game, the Denver Broncos were down by 9 points to the Cleveland Browns. 'All we need is a touchdown and a field goal, boys—no problem'" (as cited in Formisano, 2004, p. 140). Isn't it amazing how simply John Elway analyzed and articulated the gap?

More formally, a gap exists when there is a difference between the current performance level and that desired. Anastasiadou (2018) studied student satisfaction in Greek University services. It was discovered that there were differences in attitudes with adverse reports related to obstacles to getting services. Positive attitudes were related to other qualities such as reliability, responsiveness, empathy, and accessibility. Knowing the differences allowed for strategies to reduce harm and build positive attitudes.

The first step in gap analysis is finding out how large the gap is. The next step involves finding out why performance is having different results than expected. The third step is identifying ways to improve performance. Finally, it is necessary to identify critical success factors to overcome performance differences (Formisano, 2004). Critical success factors influence the success of processes and practices specific to one organization.

The gap can be significant for underused services. For example, in a study of transit users' opinions on the quality of services and what could be done to attract new users, different preferences and varying levels of willingness to pay for changes were discovered between potential and current users (Bellizzi et al., 2020). In this case, multiple performance gaps were identified, and models combining the desired levels of service, quality, and cost were created as strategies to close the gap.

People are the ones who propose and carry out innovations. For this reason, managers and supervisors need to promote innovativeness in employees rather than merely expecting innovation to happen. They should also attempt to identify factors critical to organizational success. Encouraging people to be innovative can be done in various ways, including supporting mistakes, using strategic planning to direct work behavior, broadening or enlarging jobs, rewarding team success, and reporting innovation success (Behn, 1995). Innovation leverages organizational strengths to take advantage of opportunities or to mitigate threats. It is most successful in large organizations that have abundant resources. In addition, government organizations that work closely with for-profit sector organizations are more likely to embrace innovations (Berry, 1994). Finally, since it is a new way of doing things, innovation depends on risk-taking inside and outside the organization (Moore, 1995).

Innovation can also be enhanced by identifying and encouraging employees who are likely to be innovative. Characteristics common to innovators include higher education and social standing, enhanced receptivity to change and risk, strong interpersonal communication skills, actively seeking and boundary-spanning attitudes, and membership in professional associations. People with these characteristics think creatively about problems and solutions. Instead of tinkering with how things are currently done, innovators often view the problem with fresh eyes or "start with a blank sheet of paper" (also called blue sky thinking in non-governmental organizations) to diagnose the problem and identify a range of solutions, no matter how absurd.

Ideas for innovation can also occur when people engage in collaborative problem-solving. This is done by explaining the problem to group members, describing what has happened in the past, identifying factors contributing to the problem, and what actions could be taken in response. Then, group members are tasked to develop a creative solution by bouncing ideas off each other, no matter how crazy they seem, until an innovative solution is uncovered.

When people with different perspectives are brought together for collaborative problem-solving, conflict can occur because of different ideas, perceptions, or ways of processing and judging information. It can be as simple as the process owner (the person responsible for doing that portion of the job) being resistant to suggestions for change since they perceive this as criticism of their performance. But when this conflict is managed, it can lead to creative abrasion where novel approaches are identified, and innovation occurs (Leonard & Straus, 1998).

Innovation outcomes depend primarily on the availability of knowledge related to organizational processes. The success of innovation activities can be improved when analysis determines that savings can be realized and activities can be carried out with current resources. Additional resources must be secured before change plans are established if resources are insufficient. Also, innovation success is more likely if there is no attempt to take away benefits, even if it will cut costs. Taking away benefits can create resistance to the changes required by innovation. Any change strategy that can enhance success is one of building on a series of small stages of change. This provides flexibility to address and adapt the implementation when unanticipated problems occur.

Can Organizations Document and Manage Employee Knowledge?

Increasingly, organizations are discovering how important it is to manage their knowledge. Knowledge can be defined as the comprehension and understanding that comes from acquiring and organizing information (Starling, 2002). Knowledge comes from people. Managing this knowledge involves assessing how information flows between users and how best to capture knowledge and make it accessible to others (Drucker, 1998). The organization can develop processes that document processes and employee knowledge by collecting and organizing this information and then distributing the knowledge in accessible and user-friendly ways. When this is done, the organization has increased its intellectual capital or the agreed-on facts, problem definitions, shared information, and mutual understandings that provide a basis for coordinated action (Bardach & Patashnik, 2019).

Well-documented information is a form of intellectual capital. It supports the organization's efforts to improve its competencies or knowledge resources and strengthens unique know-how knowledge (Mouritsen et al., 2005). Knowledge management has been called the new wealth of organizations because it taps into intangible but vital assets such as employee talents, customer loyalty, and the value of copyrights and patents.

As you may guess from this definition, helpful knowledge is both "hard" and "soft" and can come from qualitative as well as quantitative data (Nonaka, 1998). Quantitative data is typically presented as objectively gathered numbers, but do not forget that the data collected cannot reveal the choices made by those who decide what information to collect and how to collect, measure, and analyze the data. The subjective choices made that underlie quantitative data are not so visible.

Qualitative data is more visibly subjective and can come from personal insights, perceptions, and relationships with others necessary to do the job. Qualitative data about relationships are necessary since they influence centrality, or the number and importance of ties one person has with others working in a policy network as a form of partisan analysis (Lindblom & Woodhouse, 1993). By identifying those employees with high centrality levels, data on processes and procedures established through these relationships can easily be captured (Kingsley & Melkers, 2001). Qualitative data can also include tacit knowledge, which evolves through experience that employees may not explain but that employees apply based on situational contingencies. For instance, an experienced tennis player will not think of length about how to hit a ball approaching at a speed of 120 miles an hour (Nelson & Winter, 1982).

An example of using *tacit knowledge* occurs in the manufacture of aircraft engines. Even though there are very detailed guidelines and exacting specifications about how an engine is to be assembled to assure high-quality performance, when workers on an assembly line inspect aircraft engines, they often adjust based on the sounds they hear when they tap the engine in different places with a hammer before it goes off the assembly line. When an observer asks why they do it or how they know where to tap, it is not unusual for the worker to say something like, "I do not know, it just does not sound right, so I hit it until it sounds normal." There is no manual to guide these employees when they tap, listen, and adjust. Instead, they use their knowledge and experience with aircraft engines to guide their actions.

Knowledge management involves capturing what workers know and putting this knowledge to work for the organization. Often it is a systematic process of documenting tacit knowledge and making it available to other employees or tapping into the organization's institutional memory. Since knowledge management deals with employees and encourages employee interactions to share knowledge, it is a responsibility shared by line-unit supervisors, managers, and executives throughout the organization as they seek to capture the professional intellect of every worker (Franklin et al., 2017).

Professional intellect comprises four components: (1) professional knowledge one learned to do the job, (2) advanced skills that adapt professional knowledge to real-world situations, (3) an understanding of cause-and-effect relationships that enable the individual to anticipate unintended consequences, and (4) self-motivated creativity (Quinn et al., 1996). These four components are labeled respectively as know-what, know-how, know-why, and care-why knowledge. It is more than capturing what your employees need to know and how they do their job; it also facilitates the flow of information and employee learning to improve their and the organization's performance.

We have found that writing a textbook uses the four components of professional intellect. First, researching what has been written about the different topics in this book uses "know-what" knowledge. Second, cross-walking research and including information from our comparative and practitioner experiences to explain what happens in today's organizations is "know-how" knowledge. Third, designing a book that uses different techniques to assist student learning, such as outlines, definitions of keywords, and case examples, is an example of know-why knowledge. Finally, arranging the topics according to four levels—Governance, Government, Public Administration, and Public Management, because we think they reflect fundamental principles of democratic government—is an example of care-why knowledge.

We want to introduce you to public administration and make what we know available in a usable format so that you do not have to start learning everything from scratch. We all "stand on the shoulders of giants when writing or studying," as Sir Isaac Newton reminded us. Suppose we have successfully presented knowledge in this book. In that case, you are already intellectually "taller" because we encouraged you to stand on our shoulders and those of many colleagues and have presented knowledge learned through literature reviews, research, publication, experiences, and interactions with other academic and practitioner professionals to assist you in your own knowledge development.

Knowledge management encourages innovation since it creates opening and transparency in the organization's operations and collaborates with internal stakeholders (Chaurasia et al., 2020). Furthermore, with the transition to knowledge workers in government and creative society, knowledge management can also build social capital (Mayasari & Chandra, 2020) and trust in government.

Chapter Summary

The management of human assets for organizations in all sectors has undergone an almost continual transformation as we moved from a bureaucratic lens of viewing workers as replaceable cogs in a machine to attending to the development of government workers so that they can achieve their full potential. We have also come to recognize that government programs and services should serve a full range of values beyond the traditional managerial values of being fast and at the cheapest price. Now we also value active representation, fostering employee innovation to provide world-class service that meets client and stakeholder expectations, and leveraging the knowledge of our employees to improve our goods and services.

In Chap. 11, we turn to managing the government's financial assets. The quality and integrity of the government's stewardship of "the people's money" is critical since, in most cases, the money used to run government is not voluntarily given for the desired service. Further, those who pay for the government may not be the recipients, so they want to know that the government is spending the money as authorized and that expected outcomes are being achieved.

Practical Applications

1. What is human resource management? Is it trust-building by leaders? Is it managing employees' KSAs? Does it encourage productivity, yes or no? Elaborate your answer.

2. What are the core functions of human resource management? How does that inform employee motivation? What additional factors influence motivation?
3. Why is creating a representative bureaucracy necessary? What role do diversity and power play in creating an inclusive and equitable workplace?

In-Class Instructional Suggestions

1. Describe the development of the career in civil service in your country, both in terms of size as well as in terms of professionalization. Encourage students to consider how universal the professionalization of civil servants has been.
2. Job descriptions have changed significantly in the past 150 years. Collect job advertisements for civil servants from newspapers for the past century and compare their content. How have they changed? You can also focus on job descriptions for personnel managers over time. How have these changed?
3. Levels of unionization vary between countries and between the public and the for-profit sectors. How has the level of public sector unionization developed in your country?

REFERENCES

Abramson, M. A., & Littman, I. D. (Eds.). (2002). *Innovation*. Rowman and Littlefield.

Altshuler, A. A., & Behn, R. D. (1997). *Innovation in American government: Challenges, opportunities, and dilemmas*. Brookings Institution Press.

Anastasiadou, S. (2018). Gap analysis between perceived and expected service quality in Greek Tertiary Education. In *EDULEARN18 Proceedings* (pp. 8373–8382). IATED.

Andersen, S. C. (2017). From passive to active representation—Experimental evidence on the role of normative values in shaping white and minority bureaucrats' policy attitudes. *Journal of Public Administration Research and Theory, 27*(3), 400–414.

Anestaki, A., Sabharwal, M., Connelly, K., & Cayer, N. J. (2016). During Clinton, Bush, and Obama administrations, race and gender representation in presidential appointments, SES, and GS levels. *Administration and Society, 51*(2), 197–228.

Bardach, E., & Patashnik, E. M. (2019). *A Practical Guide for Policy Analysis: The eightfold path to more effective problem solving*. CQ Press.

Behn, R. D. (1995). Creating an innovative organization: Ten hints for involving front-line workers. *State and Local Government Review, 27*, 221–234.

Bekke, A. J. G. M., & van der Meer, F. M. (Eds.). (2000). *Civil service systems in Western Europe*. Edward Elgar.

Bellizzi, M. G., dell'Olio, L., Eboli, L., & Mazzulla, G. (2020). Heterogeneity in desired bus service quality from users' and potential users' perspective. *Transportation Research Part A: Policy and Practice, 132*, 365–377.

Berman, E. M., Bowman, J. S., West, J. P., & Van Wart, M. (2001). *Human resource management in the public service*. Sage.

Berry, F. S. (1994). Innovation in public management: The adoption of strategic planning. *Public Administration Review, 54*(4), 322–330.

Bertelli, A. M., & Riccucci, N. M. (2022). What is behavioral public administration good for? *Public Administration Review, 82*(1), 179–183.

Bok, D. (1996). *The state of the nation: Government and the quest for a better society.* Harvard University Press.

Bozeman, B., & Su, X. (2015). Public service motivation concepts and theory: A critique. *Public Administration Review, 75*(5), 700–710.

Burns, J. P., & Bowornwathana, B. (Eds.). (2001). *Civil service systems in Asia.* Edward Elgar.

Chaurasia, S. S., Kaul, N., Yadav, B., & Shukla, D. (2020). Open innovation for sustainability through creating shared value-role of knowledge management system, openness and organizational structure. *Journal of Knowledge Management, 24,* 2491–2511.

Condrey, S. E. (Ed.). (1998). *Handbook of human resource management in government.* San Jossey Bass.

Dede, M. J. (2002). Building a public personnel system for the City of Freedonia: A new approach to teaching human resources management in an MPA program. *Journal of Public Affairs Education, 8*(4), 275–285.

Drucker, P. F. (1998). The coming of the new organization. In *Harvard Business Review on Knowledge Management* (pp. 1–19). Harvard Business School Publishing.

Formisano, R. A. (2004). *Manager's guide to strategy.* McGraw Hill.

Franklin, A. L., Le, J., Grossman, A., & Shafer, M. (2017). Knowledge management and research production: The Oklahoma climate science case. *Oklahoma Politics, 27,* 103–138.

Gooden, S. T. (2015). *Race and social equity: A nervous area of government.* M.E. Sharpe.

Halligan, J. (Ed.). (2003). *Civil service systems in Anglo-American countries.* Edward Elgar.

Hoffman, M. C. (2002). Paradigm lost: Public administration at Johns Hopkins University, 1884–1896. *Public Administration Review, 62*(1), 12–23.

Kingsley, G., & Melkers, J. (2001). The art of partnering across sectors: The influence of centrality strategies of state R and D projects. In J. L. Brudney, L. J. O'Toole Jr., & H. G. Rainey (Eds.), *Advancing public management. New developments in theory, methods, and practice* (pp. 97–108). Georgetown University Press.

Klingner, D. F., & Nalbandian, J. (1998). *Public personnel management. Contexts and strategies.* Prentice-Hall.

Lane, L. M., Wolf, J. F., & Woodard, C. A. (2002). Reassessing the human resource crisis in the public service, 1987–2002. *The American Review of Public Administration, 33*(2), 123–145.

Legge, K. (1995). *Human resource management: Rhetorics and realities.* Palgrave.

Leonard, D., & Straus, S. (1998). Putting your company's whole brain to work. In *Harvard Business Review on knowledge management* (pp. 109–136). Harvard Business School Publishing.

Light, P. (2019). *The government-industrial complex: The true size of the federal government, 1984–2018.* Oxford University Press.

Lindblom, C., & Woodhouse, E. (1993). *The policymaking process* (3rd ed.). Prentice-Hall.

Mayasari, Y., & Chandra, T. (2020). Social capital for knowledge management system of the creative industry. *Journal of Enterprising Communities: People and Places in the Global Economy, 14*(4), 481–494.

Moore, M. H. (1995). *Creating public value: Strategic management in government.* Harvard University Press.

Mosher, F. C. (1982 [1968]). *Democracy and the public service* (2nd ed.). Oxford University Press.

Mosher, W. E., Kingsley, J. D., & Stahl, O. G. (1950). *Public personnel administration.* Harper and Brothers Publishers.

Mouritsen, J. H., Thorsgaard, L., & Bukh, P. N. (2005). Dealing with the knowledge economy: Intellectual capital versus balanced scorecard. *Journal of Intellectual Capital, 6*(1), 8–27.

Nelson, R. R., & Winter, S. G. (1982). *An evolutionary theory of economic change.* The Belknap Press of Harvard University Press.

Nonaka, I. N. (1998). The knowledge-creating company. In *Harvard Business Review on knowledge management* (pp. 21–45). Harvard Business School Publishing.

OECD. (2017). *OECD Employment Outlook 2017.*

Perry, J. L. (1996). Measuring public service motivation: An assessment of construct reliability and validity. *Journal of Public Administration Research and Theory, 6*(1), 5–22.

Perry, J. L., & Wise, L. R. (1990). The motivational bases of public service. *Public Administration Review, 50*(3), 367–373.

Quinn, J. B., Anderson, P., & Finkelstein, S. (1996). Managing professional intellect: Making the most of the best. *Harvard Business Review, 74*(2), 71–80.

Raadschelders, J. C. N. (2020). Impartial, skilled, respect for the law: The ancient ideals of civil servants at the root of eastern and western traditions. *Korean Journal of Policy Studies, 35*(1), 1–27.

Ray, V. (2019). A theory of racialized organizations. *American Sociological Review, 84*(1), 26–53.

Reder, M. W. (1988). The rise and fall of unions: The public sector and the private. *Journal of Economic Perspectives, 2*(2), 89–110.

Reiff, M. R. (2020). *In the name of liberty: The argument for universal unionization.* Cambridge University Press.

Riccucci, N. M., Naff, K. C., Shafritz, J. M., & Rosenbloom, D. H. (1978). *Personnel management in government. Politics and process.* CSC Press.

Sayre, W. S. (1991 [1948]). The triumph of techniques over purpose. In F. J. Thompson (Ed.), *Classics of public personnel policy* (pp. 154–159). Wadsworth Publishing Company.

Shafritz, J. M., Rosenbloom, D. H., Riccucci, N. M., Naff, K. C., & Hyde, A. C. (2001). *Personnel management in government. Politics and process.* Marcel Dekker.

Starling, G. (2002). *Managing the public sector* (6th ed.). Harcourt College Publishers.

Tead, P., & Metcalf, H. C. (1920). *Personnel administration: Its principles and practice.* McGraw-Hill.

Tummers, L. (2020). *Behavioral public administration.* Oxford Research Encyclopedias, Politics (online).

Van der Meer, F. M., Raadschelders, J. C. N., & Toonen, Th.A.J (Ed.). (2015). *Comparative civil service systems in the 21st century.* Palgrave Macmillan.

Vandenabeele, W., & Schott, C. (2020). *A moral theory of public service motivation.* Oxford Research Encyclopedias, Politics (online).

Verheijen, T. (Ed.). (1999). *Civil service systems in Central and Eastern Europe*. Edward Elgar.
Walters, J. (2002). Understanding innovation. In M. A. Abramson & I. D. Littman (Eds.), *Innovation* (pp. 13–58). Rowman and Littlefield.
Wang, T.-M., van Witteloostuijn, A., & Heine, F. (2020). A moral theory of public service motivation. *Frontiers in Psychology, 11*(1), 1–15.
White, R. D. (2000). Theodore Roosevelt as civil service commissioner: Linking the influence and development of a modern administrative President. *Administrative Theory and Praxis, 22*(4), 696–713.
Xu, X., & Meier, K. J. (2022). Separating symbolic and active representation: A mixed methods study of gender and education in China. *Public Management Review, 24*(9), 1429–1451.

CHAPTER 11

Managing the Financial Assets of Government

Overseeing its financial assets, including money, property, buildings, and equipment, is an essential function of government. This chapter examines how we hold government organizations and the employees working for those organizations accountable for the use and protection of the financial assets necessary for providing goods and services. Financial management is based on the prudent person concept, which means individuals use the government's financial assets wisely by exercising good judgment and following the law (Willoughby, 2014). In the first section of this chapter, the budget function is described. In the second section, we consider how to improve budgeting processes. The third section explains capital projects and funding. The final section introduces financial management functions.

WHAT IS THE BUDGETING FUNCTION?

Government finances are typically reported in such large numbers, with so many zeros, that they are nearly incomprehensible to the average citizen. As one political commentator observed: "[B]udgets are such abstract things—add a little here, cut some there, all produced by the Department of Great Big Numbers—it is hard to see what they mean to real people's lives" (Ivins, 2005 p. A4). Yet, this is one of the most important activities of government and one that consumes much of elected officials' and civil servants' time. The importance of budgeting can be understood by reviewing historical data. As a percentage of Gross Domestic Product, public spending worldwide increased remarkably in the twentieth century as the government started spending more resources on social protection, education, and health care (Ortiz-Ospina & Roser, 2016).

When dealing with so much money, the people who decide how much revenue to raise and how to pay for programs citizens desire must develop a plan to match value creation with the cost of government. Decisions about how much money comes to the government and how that money is spent are determined through the budgeting process. The decisions from this political process are detailed in the budget which carries the force of law.

Budgeting is the process by which public officials allocate the government's available resources among competing interests to achieve society's objectives and the highest public value. The concept "competing interests" underscores a dilemma for government officials embedded in this definition: resources are scarce, and many alternative uses are proposed for those limited resources (Robbins, 2007). The budget has been described as an instrument of democracy, a means for correlating legislative and executive intent with administrative action, and a tool for securing administrative efficiency and economy as well as the central and controlling feature of financial administration (Willoughby, 2004 [1918]).

One of the perennial questions posed in budgeting is, "Who gets how much, for what purpose, and who pays for it?" (Mikesell, 2017, p. 6). When allocating government resources, decisions involve politics and political wrestling as much as they do financial calculations (Wildavsky & Caiden, 2004). This definition of budgeting can be broken down into several parts. First, it is a plan to provide services and programs to achieve objectives and goals within a specified time and dollar amount. In thinking about this definition, do not be fooled into thinking it is merely a technocratic exercise that results in an official document. It is also a mechanism for setting the course of government. Finally, it represents a political process to decide what results can be accomplished within certain financial constraints.

Budgeting is a complex topic. In this section, we introduce several concepts in budgeting to give you a working familiarity with the terminology and the things commonly discussed in budgeting and financial management classes. Next are Cliff Notes for how this section is arranged.

- Level of Analysis—budgets can be analyzed based on the macro or societal level or micro or organization/program level.
- Types of Budgets—the budget that funds organizations that will provide the typical goods and services of government in the budget period is called the *operational budget*. There are also *capital budgets* for large projects, plus particular revenue funds/budgets for restricted programs. A last type of budget is off-budget for funds that elected officials do not appropriate because they are funded by a different level of government or an external funder with its own rules about spending.
- Revenue Sources—money is segregated into different funds based on their sources. These funds have usage limits. Typically, each government has one general revenue fund which is unrestricted and funds the government's annual operations. There can be many additional funds based on restricted sources or uses. Budgets are created for these as well.

- Purpose of Budget—there are four orientations (planning, management, control, and policy). Different formats are used for each to achieve the purpose desired by each.

When people talk about a budget, they can talk about its macro-level effects on financial systems. However, they can also be speaking of micro-level budget decisions that determine organizational- or program-level spending. It is necessary to understand the differences to understand the nature of the issues being considered. *Macro-level*—budget decisions reflect collective preferences for how government influences policy in three general categories:

Fiscal policy—the operations of government
Economic policy—the influence of government on the economy
Monetary policy—the control over the money in circulation

Micro-level—budget decisions determine where government revenues will come from and the allowable use of these funds.

The macro-level refers to a whole level of government and can include economic, fiscal, and monetary policy decisions. *Economic policy* examines how government activities impact the economy and financial markets. Government policymakers often stimulate the economy by varying government spending and tax levels. For example, some economists advocate more government in recession to boost the national economy. Others favor tax cuts during recessions to stimulate the economy. *Fiscal policy* is related to the taxing and spending policies of the government. It can also refer to the government's tax policies on individuals and organizations. *Monetary policy* describes government policies in terms of the money supply. These policies concern the amount of money printed in circulation and government borrowing through issuing Treasury notes, bills, bonds, and interest rates.

The national level of government is primarily engaged in economic, fiscal, and monetary policies. Subnational governments cannot affect monetary policy and seldom have significant influence over economic policy in their jurisdiction. They do, however, change fiscal policy through the budget. The micro-level considers levels of revenues and expenditures for individual government organizations and programs. These decisions are aggregated and reported at the macro-level.

Like the budget decisions for a typical household, two main decisions are made about government budgets. First, how much money will be received and from what sources? Second, what will this money be spent on, or how will money be used to achieve financial goals? In government, we use *revenues* to talk about the sources of income and *expenditures* to talk about spending. Decision-makers consider both where the money comes from and how it will be spent.

There are three primary revenue sources for the government. The first source, which comprises most government budgets, is taxes. This can include personal and corporate income, sales, and property taxes. Elected officials hesitate to use the "T" word (taxes) since most citizens have negative tax attitudes. However, in Kenya, Byaro and Kinyondo (2020) found that citizens will be more willing to support tax policy changes when trust in government is high and services are perceived as high quality. In addition, minor changes to the tax collection process—gathering taxpayer preferences, connecting taxes to benefits, making payment easy, and appealing to social norms—reduce negative attitudes and increase compliance (Sussman & White, 2018).

The projected *tax compliance* level is an essential consideration for any revenue source. Tax compliance compares the amount that is owed according to tax laws and the amount that is collected. The difference is tax avoidance. In the European Community, the international integration and liberalization of capital markets have complicated the collection of personal taxes on capital income earned by residents within a nation (Tanzi & Bovenberg, 2019). As a result, higher levels of tax avoidance and lower compliance (which may be caused by a lack of taxpayer understanding) are predicted. *Tax harmonization*, an agreement between neighboring jurisdictions to adopt the shared tax rules and rates, is one way to increase tax collection efficiency and tax compliance rates.

A second government revenue source includes special taxes, fees, or charges for government services or specific items people consume, such as tobacco. Tobacco sales and the sale of other things that members of society may consider as "sinful" activities (such as marijuana and other drugs, prostitution, and alcohol) are often subject to special taxes. Different objectives drive the assessment of these taxes: reduce consumption, raise revenues, and reduce illegal activity (Abbas & Park, 2018). The simultaneous existence of legal and illegal activities complicates the anticipated tax effect: higher taxes can decrease "legal" consumption by stimulating illegal sales. This conclusion was relevant in the Canadian context, where illegal sales are estimated to be up to 20% of total consumption (Anonymous, 2016).

A third common revenue source for government organizations is funds borrowed or received through transfers from others. This category can include debt, money loaned to/from individuals, and other organizations to the government. It can also include intergovernmental transfers or money that may or may not have to be repaid to the government providing the funds.

The sources of revenue vary dramatically based on the level of government. The national government often relies primarily on personal and corporate income taxes. The subnational government generally collects income, property, sales taxes, and grants from the national government. Municipal governments rely on sales and property taxes and intergovernmental grants. In addition, all levels of government can have dedicated revenue sources such as user fees, fines, licenses, and enterprise activities for their jurisdiction.

Over time there has been a change in the composition of government revenues. In earlier days, revenues came from corporate income tax, sales and gross receipt taxes, and other taxes such as property tax. From the beginning of the twentieth century, however, personal income tax has slowly become the most critical source of revenue at the national level. At the subnational, sales and gross receipt taxes are the largest sources of revenue. In contrast, property tax is the most significant source of income for local governments.

The mix of revenue sources for the government is an important policy decision. The revenue allocation to special funds dedicated for a specific purpose can indirectly affect the government's *financial sufficiency*. One example of the need to carefully consider revenue allocation is special funds for capital expenditures in Indonesia. Suratno (2020) concludes that local governments must understand the source and sufficiency of revenue from existing resources before new capital projects are undertaken. The question of revenue sufficiency applies to all governments. Small local governments in Slovenia tend to under-tax or avoid taxing completely (Brajnik et al., 2022). The most probable explanation for this practice is that elected officials' closeness to the electorate creates a reluctance to tax and a lack of administrative capacity to manage tax collections. A strategy of under-taxing can hurt financial sufficiency, especially for long-term sustainability considerations.

Decisions about government spending have been characterized as answering this question: "On what basis shall it be decided to allocate X dollars to Activity A instead of activity B?" (Key, 1940, p. 118). The main categories used for spending are direct expenditures, transfer payments, transfers, and funds borrowed. *Direct expenditures* include wages and benefits for government personnel and purchasing the equipment, materials, and supplies necessary to provide government goods and services. *Transfer payments*, as the name suggests, reflect direct payments to individuals. Transfers are also the intergovernmental funds received by one level of government from another level of government. Finally, *funds borrowed* refers to money raised by a government through the sale of securities such as Treasury notes, bills, and bonds.

Expenditures are grouped within specific pre-established categories described in a *chart of accounts*, which is a listing of all the accounting categories used to record government spending. In the chart of accounts, there are major spending categories. Within each, multiple subcategories, called *objects of expenditure*, provide greater detail about purchases made with public funds. Each government entity creates a chart of accounts. However, there are exceptions to this. For example, in the Philippines (Ebdon & Franklin, 2020), a higher level of government has laws governing the significant objects of expenditures used by other governmental units in its jurisdiction.

Government decision-makers generally establish the source and level of revenues available before determining expenditure levels. Some funds are put into a *general revenue fund* which can be used for any purpose. In contrast, other funds are kept in separate accounts with specific funding sources and can only be used for purposes identified when the fund was created. Limits on revenue sources and uses means they receive special treatment in the budget process.

Capital budgets are for infrequent and irregular purchases of land, buildings, and expensive equipment and government assets' maintenance, upkeep, and replacement. Each of these items is called a "big ticket" item. These items are expected to be used for one or more years. They are expensive, with the costs often paid off over a long time (although a few governments pay off the expense in the year the item is purchased). In most cases, the government cannot generate sufficient funds to pay for these items within the short-term operating budget. Capital budgets typically involve government borrowing, usually through long-term government bonds. This practice is known as *PAYUSE* (pay as you use) since you pay for the project every year that you use it. However, some governments have adopted an approach where work on the project is funded each year and no borrowing is done. This is known as *PAYGO* (pay as you go) and is a way to avoid long-term borrowing.

A last type of budget is for entities called *off-budget* and relies on non-appropriated funds. They typically receive less consideration since they represent the activities of quasi-government organizations for which funds are not appropriated like other fund sources. These include public enterprises, public authorities, special districts, and government corporations. Non-appropriated funds increase flexibility because they do not have the same restrictions as other funds (Franklin & Douglas, 2003).

Because of the segregation necessary for different funds, government entities typically adopt more than one budget. The most typical budgets are an *operating budget* for the current year's normal operations and a *capital budget* for large, infrequent purchases repaid over more than one year. It is not unusual for other budgets, such as those for special, enterprise and intergovernmental funds, to be adopted. No matter how many or what types of budgets are authorized, each budget is considered separately, and legislation (such as appropriations bill(s) or ordinances) must be enacted before collecting revenues or making expenditures. The desired budget is one that is balanced, meaning that anticipated expenditures cannot exceed forecasted revenues. However, the balanced budget requirement can be misleading since the definition and timing of balance differ. We return to the balanced budget requirement in the section on budgetary reform.

What Are the Purposes of Budgets?

Thurmaier and Willoughby (2001) identified four different purposes for the budget: control, planning, management, and policymaking. Decision-makers may prefer one over another depending on government spending and activities. Next, we describe what influences decision-makers' orientations toward budgeting.

When you have a *control orientation*, decision-makers attempt to constrain organizations to operate programs and spend government funds the way they prefer. Early attempts to control budgets were designed to assure that the fund-granting authority was approved in an official document, that spending did not exceed revenue estimates, and that there were standard means for recording and reporting expenditures (Willoughby, 2004 [1918]). The line-item budget format, which authorizes expenditures based on specific categories in the chart of accounts, is an example of a budget format emphasizing control. This format focuses on inputs and controlling types and levels of expenditures.

A *management orientation* emphasizes efficiency and effectiveness in budget execution. The goal is to improve government processes to achieve enhanced levels of performance. A management orientation favors using the performance budget, where a specific expected level of performance is specified in exchange for a certain level of funding. The performance budget focuses on inputs and outputs and encourages using assets efficiently in an organization's activities.

A *planning orientation* emphasizes establishing goals for government programs and allocating resources to achieve these goals. A program budget format estimates the direct service provision costs and capital and administrative staff costs. Funds are often allocated in a lump sum allowing flexibility to shift resources to where they can best be used to achieve goals. The program budget format focuses on inputs, outputs, and effects, emphasizing attaining a certain level of results. This approach often considers ratios that compare costs and outputs to reach objectives (Grizzle, 1986).

The budget is often described as a tool for policy decision-making because the budget reflects agreement on policies and financial limits that are considered politically realistic (Bunch & Straussman, 1993). A *policy orientation* focuses on coordinating activities within the government system to achieve policy objectives and create public value. For example, budget deliberations may be about where to cut government services, promote interorganization cooperation for similar programs in a specific policy area, and redirect service provision responsibilities to other levels of government or even organizations in different sectors. When used as a policy tool, the budget can decide controversies over desired public programs, goods, and services (Bland & Rubin, 1997). Zero-based budgeting and top-down budgets are examples of budget formats used in a policy orientation.

A *zero-based budget* is advantageous when budget cuts are anticipated. In theory, each organization must start from scratch when preparing the budget. No incremental requests are allowed (Taylor, 1977). Instead of requesting funds by line-item or program, the organization creates decision packages reflecting activities performed and ranks them in order of importance. Only those above an established cut-off point are funded. So, as a program manager, if you must cut funds by 10%, only those packages you ranked as in the top 90% of the most important activities will be funded. The emphasis is on cost-effectiveness and forcing choices in service delivery priorities. *Top-down budgets* feature instructions to agencies about allowable items in budget requests. Frequently, requests are justified based on the degree to which the item contributes to achieving system-wide policy goals.

The Fiscal Year

Many governments do not operate on a calendar year. Instead, they use a fiscal year for financial management activities. The start of the fiscal year is established in law and is any period that is one year long. The importance of the fiscal year for budgeting and financial management is that spending authorized in the appropriations bills is only for that period. This is not always one year since there are some governments that adopt a biennial budget, meaning two years' worth of spending is authorized. If the funds are not spent within the time allowed, they are no longer available for spending and revert, or must be returned, to the original revenue account.

There are, however, circumstances where spending can continue after the fiscal year. An example is when the government signed a purchase contract before the end of the fiscal year and the contract has not been completed or the vendor has not been paid. In this case, an encumbrance, which is a reserve for the remaining amount owed, must be placed on funds for that fiscal year. This means that spending can occur after the end of the fiscal year since the government has authorized payment and reserved funds for that payment.

Budget Stages and Calendars

Although activities vary across government units, four stages are typically used to describe the budget process, as shown in Table 11.1.

The stages in a budget cycle overlap, meaning budgeting work in one year is being done on budgets for multiple years. During preparation and approval, we are developing the budget for the next fiscal year. While we are doing this, we are executing the budget approved for the current fiscal year and can also be making sure the money was properly spent for the previous fiscal year(s). For this reason, there is a significant time lag in the entire cycle of preparation, approval, execution, and auditing. In practice, it is not unusual for an organization to be working on all four budgeting stages simultaneously.

Table 11.1 Stages of budgeting

- *Budget Preparation* involves the development of expenditure estimates and the forecasting of available revenues. It is done by agencies and central office staff 15–18 months before the budget year begins.
- *Budget Approval* includes review by elected officials and their staff with decisions made on the macro- and micro-level of the budget to authorize expenditure limits through appropriation. It occurs three to nine months before the budget year begins.
- *Budget Execution* involves implementing what has been approved in the budget and monitoring the implementation to ensure spending follows the law represented by the appropriations bill throughout the budget year.
- *Budget Evaluation* involves auditing expenditures to comply with legal requirements and determining performance levels to see if the public value has been produced. It occurs 0–18 months after the budget year ends.

Why Is Budgeting So Complicated?

Government budgeting often seems haphazard and fragmented, partly because of timing of the budget stages and the fiscal year. We usually do not know how much money is available for the upcoming year until we determine the revertments (unspent funds to be returned to the general fund) for the current and previous fiscal years. This makes budgeting difficult since the budget must be approved long before the current fiscal year ends. Plus, as noted above, *encumbrances* may not be spent for up to 18 months after the end of a fiscal year.

Fragmentation in budgeting also makes budgeting complicated. Fragmentation occurs because there are many different decision-making arenas. Various legislative committees make new laws that have fiscal impacts—meaning revenues will be generated or government spending will be required. There are also multiple committees who make decisions about specific parts of the budget. Aggregation of all the individual budget decisions seldom occurs until right before the final budget is approved. If all budgeted items are not included in the budget, there is a possibility that balance may not be achieved, increasing the haphazard nature of budgeting.

How Could Government Budget Processes Be Reformed?

The budget process is perhaps the administrative process most subject to reform. Reforms are championed to rationalize the process and make budgeting more comprehensive, balance the budgets, and address the uncontrollable drivers of the budget. When thinking about budget reform, important institutional factors to consider are the degree and longevity of political support, the availability of analytic staff, familiarity with performance levels achieved and expected, and the role and power of the budget authorities within the government (Ho, 2019; Melkers & Willoughby, 2005).

Alfred Ho (2019) organized budget reforms emphasizing the need to increase performance into six theoretical perspectives. We note below illustrative countries from his case studies. Budget reform is viewed as

- an organizational change process (Indonesia);
- a policy diffusion process (the Netherlands, Mexico);
- a political process (Chile, Afghanistan);
- a communicative process (Kenya, Tunisia);
- a principal-agent challenge (Australia); and
- an institutional change (the Netherlands, the United States).

Many reform efforts attempt to rationalize the process. The best examples are recurring efforts to adopt multi-year budgets, use program budgets, or zero-based budgeting techniques (Schick, 1966). *Multi-year budgets* make budgeting more rational because they encourage longer-term planning instead of political partisanship each year (Rubin, 1990). *Program budgets* make budgeting more rational because they include all the costs for program operations and consider outcomes. The program budget format had some successful applications in the military. Still, most government agencies did not have the staff expertise or technological capacity. As a result, they spent more time creating information, but the information was not perceived as credible and did not get used. *Zero-based budgets* are rational for reducing budgets during lean fiscal times by prioritizing expenditures. Alternatively, rationality may be reduced since they start from an unreasonable assumption, thinking that programs will not receive any money unless they justify their request. Instead, it is more realistic to begin with a reduced budget level, say 80% or 90%, and then to justify and prioritize the remaining request.

A significant challenge in budgeting is determining what is included and what is outside the general budget. Historically, there has been a preference for *back-door spending* or making monetary commitments for government agencies outside of the regular appropriations process in the U.S. national budget (Bowsher, 1985). Reform attempts to make the budget comprehensive often seek to reduce or eliminate the number of items treated off-budget and bring them into the regular budgeting process (Staats, 2002).

There are other ways government organizations can get more money than what appears in the budget bill (Schultze, 1968). They may do this through borrowing authority like student loan guarantees, contract authority for defense weapons development, and permanent or non-lapsing appropriations. Recent reforms have attempted to make the budget deliberation process more comprehensive by requiring the reporting of budgets for all government funds, connecting operating and capital budgets, and linking strategic plans and performance reports with budgeting decisions. Yet, this is not a uniform practice.

A perpetual challenge that different rounds of reform have attempted to address is the proper balance of control and flexibility. Effective operations must strike a balance between two extremes: too much control and insufficient control (Rautenstrauch & Villers, 1950). Further, the focus of the controls must be considered. It appears that reforms have the desired effects when they shift the focus of legislative controls from inputs to outputs. By making appropriations' formats less restrictive, the managers have discretion regarding how to achieve the desired output level and the flexibility to allocate resources to their best use (Franklin, 2002). This provides control and flexibility since elected officials control results and future resources to be allocated.

Reformers tout a *balanced budget requirement* for all levels of government to ensure a structural balance between revenues and expenditures. Most governments must operate under some type of balanced budget requirements. This means that the anticipated revenues in the approved budget must always exceed the anticipated expenditures. The balance is then carried forward into future fiscal years as available revenue. This ending balance, often referred to as a reserve, could be the same or different from a rainy day or budget stabilization fund. This type of fund requires that a certain percentage of the budget be segregated into a particular account for use in severe fiscal conditions where revenue shortfalls may occur. National governments may not have a balanced budget requirement. Many argue that this is appropriate because the national government can issue debt to cover spending gaps as a form of economic policymaking. Reformers say this is irresponsible fiscal management since there is no full accounting for government spending or the overall deficit.

Another budgeting challenge is treating *uncontrollable spending* (on programs driven by statutory mandate) and *unfunded mandates* (orders from a higher level of government without providing funding to the lower level of government). Expenditures for uncontrollable spending and unfunded mandates depend on the number of clients eligible for services; generally, this is driven by those in entitlement programs like old-age pensions and national public health programs. These kinds of programs often have long-term growth trajectories and have resisted attempts to control spending (Wildavsky & Caiden, 2004). Other uncontrollable expenditures represent commitments for spending that have already occurred. These include repaying the interest due on debt and fulfilling contracts for multi-year spending (Caiden, 1993). As the expenditure levels rise in these programs, the amount left over for discretionary spending on other government programs shrinks.

Budget reforms have also attempted to address the power relationships between government actors and the people for whom the budgets are being made. For example, *participatory budgeting* (PB) was explicitly introduced to align citizens' preferences with the elected officials' budget allocations. Originating in the 1980s in Brazil, by 2019, it was estimated that more than 3000 governments had implemented participatory budgets around the world (Franco & Assis, 2019). These were championed as a way to open up government through direct citizen engagement, which increases government transparency. Like gender-responsive budgeting reform efforts (Chowdhury, 2020; Rubin & Bartle, 2022), PB has been perceived by some as providing a more equitable distribution of public resources that enhance social well-being and provide critical societal outcomes such as reducing infant and child mortality (Touchton & Wampler, 2014).

Like Brazil, Poland enacted national legislation for participatory budgeting and encouraged local community flexibility by using community funds allocated via citizen participation (Szescilo & Wilk, 2018). This form of collaboration encourages co-production which is an acknowledged partnership between the government and those who provide services to coordinate their efforts and resources to improve socially desired outcomes (Gonçalves, 2014). This collaboration often leads to public service reform (Escobar, 2021). In Bangladesh, focusing on co-production with non-governmental organizations improved local-level planning and encouraged women's participation in budgeting to achieve more equitable outcomes through budgeting reforms.

What Are Different Intergovernmental Funding Relationships?

One concern in intergovernmental relations is determining which level of government can secure revenues and which level can best provide program services. Shifting decision-making and executing responsibilities from a higher to a lower level of government is called *devolution* or decentralization. Advocates of devolution claim that it puts service delivery closer to the people, increases efficiency, enhances innovation, and custom-tailors programs to meet local circumstances. However, critics claim that while devolution is a way of mandating national social policy, it is also a way to pass the buck regarding who bears the cost through unfunded mandates.

There are many ways of passing the buck through intergovernmental funding. First, *grants-in-aid* are used to transfer money between levels of government to support policy or program implementation. Second, a *formula grant* provides funding based on a pre-established formula for each person in a jurisdiction who meets some criteria. Third, the *project grant* gives money to applications for pre-specified types of projects. Fourth, a *block grant* provides money for use in broad program areas such as law enforcement, social services, and community development. Finally, the *general revenue sharing grant* transfers funds between levels without strings, limiting allowable spending on certain items.

Grants offered by governments at all levels may have conditions regarding who can receive the money. In some cases, it is a government unit; in other cases, the recipients are organizations or individuals. Or the recipients can be mixed. It is not unusual for regional governments to receive federal funds and transfer them to lower government levels responsible for service delivery. Under this agreement, the regional government retains responsibility for statewide program administration. In other grant programs, federal money passes through a subnational government and is paid to a contracting non-governmental organization that is directly providing services for government programs. This pass-through contracting approach is common in child welfare and protection programs.

There are also differences in the recipient's level of discretion for spending the funds. For some grants, there are no restrictions. For others, the allowable categories of expenses are specified and restricted to target spending for specific purposes. The use of categories can result from interest group activism to earmark funds, a certain level of distrust by the grantor of whether the funds will be used as intended, and the desire for a standardized social policy through the encouragement of funding of certain types of activities (ACIR, 1988).

Monetary transfers from the national government are often used to foster equity between regional or municipal government by establishing a certain minimum level of services or equalizing resources available for assistance throughout the nation. Usually, there are strings attached, such as conditions that must be met before the funds can be spent. Alternately, there have been program directives by higher levels of government to lower levels without any funding transfers (Peters, 1991). Studying intergovernmental financial arrangements in China, Ma (1997) found that these directives often stabilize and equalize fiscal policies. Still, they can have unintended effects on interregional trade, capital flow, and market competition.

Dissatisfaction with directives and unfunded mandates from the national government voiced by subnational government officials to members of the U.S. Congress resulted in the Unfunded Mandates Reform Act of 1995. This Act required estimating the costs and benefits of both existing and proposed regulations. The Act also made it easier to stop passing bills that included unfunded mandates. However, impact analysis indicates little has changed in enacting or repealing unfunded mandates (Congressional Research Service, 2020; Gullo & Kelly, 1988; Posner, 1997).

One possible approach to overcoming the challenges associated with intergovernmental transfers is improving the information being reported to decision-makers. For example, financial reports can highlight different results and explain varying performance levels through the reported data. With this data, the efficacy of transferring funds to subnational levels for service delivery can be established.

What Are Capital Projects?

Capital budgets are used to build or buy buildings for operating government programs, construct or maintain public infrastructures, buy equipment, and carry out the capital improvements program (CIP). Governments have many capital projects, such as stadiums, parks, recreation facilities, airports, bridges, military, and law enforcement equipment, and even business improvement districts or community redevelopment zones. What is shared across all these projects is that they require large amounts of funding and are projects with a useful life of many years. In some cases, they will generate revenues during the period the asset can be used, called the asset's useful life.

A capital expenditure is defined as a project: (1) with an essential public purpose, (2) with a long, useful life, (3) which is purchased infrequently and expensive, (4) which is related to other government functions, and (5) which is regarded as government's responsibility to provide (Robinson, 1991). Because they are large, stretch over multiple years, and are nonrecurring, they are described as lumpy and require careful planning (Ebdon, 2003).

Capital asset management is vital because it is based on plans to purchase and replace or restore large items used for organizational operations over multiple years. *Capital asset management* provides an inventory of government assets, indicating their value and condition. Capital asset management is essential when considering how to pay for capital items and match debt maturity with valuable life. Lastly, a capital management function provides continuity in planning and asset management when there are changes in elected and appointed officials (Bowsher, 1985).

The World Economic Forum's Global Competitiveness Report ranks infrastructure as a critical pillar of competitiveness. Four of the top ten capital asset management countries in the 2017–2018 report were from Asia. These countries had long-term trends showing steady improvement patterns suggesting a commitment to best practices in capital infrastructure monitoring and management. The capital asset management function has become increasingly important as countries identify and develop critical infrastructure resilience. Many, such as the OECD, argue that new approaches, such as public-private partnerships, will be needed to maintain and upgrade critical infrastructures.

One component of the capital asset management function that is funded through the capital budget is the *capital improvements program*, generally referred to as the CIP. The Capital Improvement Plan is a multi-year plan that ranks the capital projects to be funded to maintain the government's capital assets. To create the plan, it is first necessary to inventory all government assets and determine their current condition and performance. The CIP can be updated annually but generally sets a multi-year prioritization for large projects. This is because not all can be undertaken and funded in the same fiscal year. The CIP plans to improve or replace government assets and estimate the necessary funding and debt financing. After updating the CIP, the projects to be funded in the current year become the capital budget amount.

Government officials often must decide on what commitments they will make to new building projects or contract purchases that will cost millions, billions, and even trillions. One option, the pay-as-you-go approach (PAYGO), requires paying the project costs each year and not borrowing any money. The advantage of this approach is that it can be covered in your operating budget with no other actions required. Still, of course, you will not have a completed project for quite some time.

A second option would be to search for money from other sources, such as grants or issuing debt. Issuing debt is referred to as pay as you use (PAYUSE). There are advantages to using debt. It (1) provides sufficient current revenues to pay for some large projects, (2) avoids large fluctuations in tax rates when the government faces major nonrecurring expenditures, (3) allows the government to undertake revenue-producing projects (sports complex), and (4) improves equity: those who benefit from the project should pay for it (user fees).

But there are also disadvantages to using debt. It may (1) overextend government, (2) impose restrictions on future residents/generations, (3) limit fund uses that could have been used for other worthy purposes, (4) create less flexibility in the operating budget, (5) minimize capacity to borrow in the future, (6) be abused, for example when debt is used to balance the budget.

Some basic rules to consider when using debt financing for capital projects exist. First, the debt maturity, or the date when the loan will be paid off, should be equal to or less than the capital project's useful life so that you are not paying for an asset that can no longer be used (Franklin, 2012). This is the problem that people have when they are "upside-down" in their house or car payments and owe more than the house or car is currently worth. About homes, this is what can happen when a housing "bubble" exists. In this condition, housing prices rise at historic rates based on low mortgage rates. As a result, housing becomes less and less affordable to low- and middle-income wage workers, pricing them out of the homeownership market.

Second, the revenues generated from the capital project should come from the people who will benefit from the project. This is a concern in metropolitan areas where people live in the suburbs and outside city limits and commute into the center to work but do not pay the property taxes used to finance capital projects. An alternate approach is to use employment or sales taxes or user fees so those who benefit cannot avoid paying.

A third concern is to make sure that there is *intergenerational equity*. When the government borrows money for 30 years, the current and future taxpayers are responsible for repaying the loan. This is because the obligation to repay loans extends years into the future. To assure equity, you need to finance only those items that future taxpayers will also be able to use or from which they will receive benefits. All current and future users need to pay their fair share during the period they benefit from the capital asset. Other good practices for managing government finances are presented next.

How Do We Manage the Finances of Government?

Financial management ensures that the government's monetary assets are used wisely. Most financial management activities are carried out inside the public organization, away from the political arena. However, it is not unusual for the Director of Finance and the Director of Budgeting (often in separate units) to be political appointees. It is argued that this is necessary so that someone under the control of elected officials can more readily carry out government's financial policies.

The main areas of responsibility when managing the government's financial assets are establishing and maintaining internal control systems. These systems are necessary for complying with laws, rules, regulations, and policies, assuring accurate financial data, and promoting operating efficiency (Heeschen & Sawyer, 1984). These tasks should be carried out while considering the prudent person standard, meaning someone who strives to be a good financial steward and avoids the appearance and the reality of waste, fraud, and abuse.

Many different functions are performed within financial management. In addition to budgeting and capital management, there are an estimated 22 finance functions (Petersen et al., 1986). Of these functions, we introduce the following activities: accounting, cash management, procurement, contract monitoring, debt management, risk management, and pension administration.

Accounting

The accounting function of a finance organization is the primary means for assuring prudent financial management in any organization. When combined, it has been said that the accounting and financial reporting functions form the informational infrastructure of public finance (Gauthier, 1991). The accounting function records, analyzes, summarizes, and reports financial data, receipts, investments, and disbursements. This information is then aggregated into reports describing the overall financial condition of the government. These reports are necessary to make informed decisions about budgeting and financial transactions.

Every transaction of government involving any amount of money, no matter how small, must be recorded appropriately through documents such as a purchase order or petty cash vouchers for small dollar amounts, a shipping receipt, or an expenditure voucher. The financial impact of each one of these transactions is then entered into the appropriate accounts in the accounting system. There will be at least two accounts for all transactions, a debit and a credit account, to show where the money came from or went out in exchange for some good or service. This double entry accounting system is done to document money flow to ensure no improper spending of government funds (Reed & Swain, 1997).

Information from the accounting system can be used for planning, management, and policy purposes. However, accounting emphasizes the control orientation of budgeting since we use it to track actual expenditures and compare them to what was authorized in the budget. Spending public monies in ways not authorized by the budget is equivalent to thumbing your nose at the legislative intent of elected officials. A well-functioning accounting organization helps ensure that the control desired in prudent financial management is present.

Cash Management

The "cash" that is being managed refers to any money in any form (paper, check, electronic, etc.) that is received or paid out by an organization. In this financial management function, we are concerned with three primary activities: (1) processing receipts in a timely and efficient manner, (2) paying bills when they are due, not before or after, and (3) investing funds for a reasonable return while meeting cash needs and minimizing risk on the money that is invested (Finkler, 2000). Or, stated in reverse, the cash management practices of government need to be designed to avoid three dangers: (1) failing to collect what is owed to the government, (2) not having sufficient cash on hand to pay the bills and not using idle funds, or (3) holding money that is not needed or will not be spent for a while, to make your money work for you (Mikesell, 2017). There are three general rules for cash management: (1) get revenues into banking accounts as quickly as possible, (2) pay bills at the last moment you can without a penalty, and (3) invest idle cash in prudent investments that balance returns with safety and liquidity needs.

Purchasing, Procurement, Contracting

The third area of concern in financial management is purchasing goods and services for the government. Sometimes, purchases will be tangible items such as a snowplow, copy paper, or a desktop computer. We call the process of getting goods or services procurement. In other cases, the purchase may be made through a contract with a for-profit or non-profit service provider. It has been argued that privatization contracts, where governments' goods and services are devolved to and provided by non-governmental organizations, have become the dominant form of state government contracting (MacManus, 1992).

There are three main activities in the purchasing function. The first is planning and scheduling the future purchases of the organization and the timing of these purchases. The second is vendor selection, done by determining different suppliers, soliciting and evaluating offers, and awarding contracts. The third, contract administration, occurs after the vendor is selected. It ensures that the right good or service is provided at the agreed-upon price and that all contract requirements are met.

There are very detailed rules and regulations to guide the purchasing process in a government organization. As the cost of the item increases, there are often requirements for a bidding process where any vendor can submit a proposal to provide the item. The process for requesting and reviewing proposals and awarding a contract is highly controlled to assure fair and equitable treatment of competing bids. These rules and procedures balance the most appropriate and highest quality goods or services with the least possible cost (Reed & Swain, 1997). Over time, governments have come to rely much more on collaborative networks of government agencies working with for-profit and non-profit organizations via contracting-out (also referred to as co-production, public-private partnership, collaborative government) to deliver a variety of public services (Durant, 2020).

It has become clear that there are severe limits to contracting practices. Contracting can create a hollow state of government (Kettl, 2000). This condition leads to a danger that government could not provide the goods or services if the collaborative arrangements were to cease or if there was malfeasance by a contracted non-governmental service provider. No matter how carefully the budgeting process is designed, the quality of that process stands or falls with the people in charge of that process. There are many other reasons why contracting is being reconsidered. First, it is challenging to supervise contractors effectively and avoid exceeding the proposed budget (Brown et al., 2013). Second, contracting may superficially keep government size small, but it may not make a difference in the cost of government. After all, the taxpayer still must pay, and government workers must supervise the contractors. Third, it is difficult to supervise, for instance, private security contractors who may exceed the public safety function by having four times more workers (Etzioni, 2019). Can sworn law enforcement officers effectively supervise private police and security forces? And what about private military contractors such as Blackwater or Halliburton? During the war in Afghanistan, it proved very difficult, if not impossible, to hold these companies accountable for the services they were supposed to provide (Etzioni, 2019, pp. 38–43). Indeed, it has been said that contracting and privatization activities may well threaten democracy when unchecked (Verkuil, 2007). While financial management may appear to be a technical process, this discussion about the promise and perils of contracting for services should clarify that it is also a political process.

Debt Management

Debt is a term that refers to the amount of money the government has borrowed or what is owed by the government to be repaid in the future. It is argued that government borrowing "is one of the most potent and profound activities undertaken in government finance" (Peterson & McLoughlin, 1991, p. 263). Public debt is issued to make purchases when there are revenue shortfalls, finance the capital budget, or manage the national economy. The national government issues most debt. Subnational governments also issue debt, although this practice is more restrictive than for the national government.

The management of debt is critical because government needs to ensure there are funds available to repay the funds that have been borrowed (Denison et al., 2012). Debt levels and the amount of debt worldwide are significant and grew from $20 trillion to $69 trillion in 20 years. For 2021, the International Monetary Fund calculated the global debt to Gross Domestic Product ratio as 82%—the highest level in human history. Who will pay for all this debt? It is unlikely that it will be repaid in our lifetimes, meaning we will leave a legacy of debt for our children. Unfortunately, intergenerational equity, which means not burdening future generations with debt incurred today, does not seem to be prioritized in today's budgeting decisions.

Risk Management

Risk management is a systematic effort to identify, eliminate, or reduce conditions that harm employees or customers or threaten the overall operations in an adverse event. For example, if you have ever moved your child's bicycle away from the sidewalk or taken their toys off the stairs, you have practiced risk management. Organizations, like homeowners, are at risk if someone comes onto their property and is injured due to the owner's failure to remove identifiable risks. Similarly, all organizations in all sectors seek to provide a safe and secure environment for workers and clients.

There are four main areas of risk to consider: (1) liability in operating activities, (2) loss of income caused by property loss, (3) injury to personnel, and (4) damage to property (Reed & Swain, 1997). When analyzing risk, knowing the severity and the expected frequency of an adverse event can help determine the appropriate action an organization should take.

To effectively manage all the different types of risk, organizations develop a risk management program to identify where risk exists, and suggest strategies to take in response. Risk managers are responsible for determining the appropriate type and amount of necessary insurance coverage. Then, arrangements to purchase insurance may be made. Sometimes government establishes a fund where the money is set aside to pay for adverse events. This is called self-insurance. Or individual governments, mainly at the municipal level, combine their insurance coverage with other governments in an insurance pool. However, the typical option the government uses is to purchase insurance from an insurance agent, the same as you do for your car or home. Ensuring that the organization is protected is essential in a litigious society where the government does not always enjoy immunity from civil and class action lawsuits and can face damage awards that range in the millions!

Pension Administration

Pensions are a type of retirement plan employers offer in all organizational sectors. Some form of a pension plan covers nearly all government employees. Government retirees depend on these benefits for income after retirement. Since there are many public employees, the amounts in these funds are significant.

Some pension plans are fully funded by the employer, meaning employers make all the contributions. However, most pension plans require a matching contribution from the employee with a certain percentage of their wages. The employer collects the contribution through a payroll deduction. Individual employees typically receive a part, or all, of their pension funds when they retire or leave employment under defined contribution plans where the funds for each employee are separate from those for other employees. In defined benefit plans, the amount of the pension fund benefit is determined by a calculation that considers the age and the number of years of employment at the time of separation from the employer. Defined benefit plans do not consider whether the amount of employer and employee's contributions during employment is sufficient to pay retirement benefits to eligible employees.

Until an employee leaves the organization, the employer has responsibility for safeguarding pension assets by managing them to invest in ways that increase their value under defined benefit plans. Pension funds are typically administered by an externally appointed Board of Trustees, a system administrator (equivalent to an organization executive) who is usually a political appointee, and technical consultants who are civil servants (Zorn, 1991). The members of the Board of Trustees act as fiduciaries for the beneficiaries and the public. They set policies about the investment of pension funds and benefits. The system administrator is responsible for managing the day-to-day activities of the pension fund. Technical consultants can include a variety of professional experts such as legal counsel, actuaries, investment advisers, auditors, and fund custodians responsible for carrying out day-to-day activities. Combined, these different internal and external actors have an enormous policy and administrative responsibility for safeguarding public financial resources.

Some public employee pension plans are in financial distress because the contributions collected are insufficient to pay expected retirement benefits (Peng, 2008). This situation is called an unfunded pension liability and is often caused by longer life expectancies of retirees (Swope, 2005 [2003]), reduced earnings on the investment of pension funds, and insufficient annual contributions to cover the shortfall. Strategies, such as changing the retirement age, limiting retiree insurance benefits, changing from a defined benefit to a defined contribution plan, and changing the investment rules for pension funds, are being explored by many governments to address anticipated future shortfalls.

The overarching purpose of financial management is to safeguard government assets. Safeguarding assets involves having adequately trained personnel, segregating and rotating job responsibilities and functions, requiring multiple levels of authorizations for spending, recording transactions properly, assuring limited access to assets, and periodic testing, measurement, and reconciliation (Mikesell, 2017). A significant retrospective safeguard is the periodic reporting and analysis of variances (Finkler, 2000). The financial management function requires expertise in each of the areas being managed.

In all financial management functions, you can find parallel applications in your personal life. Your checkbook serves as the primary tool of your accounting system. You must manage your revenues and expenses, determine what purchases should be made and when to make them, make suitable investments for your future financial needs, and minimize the risk that could cause a loss of assets. The primary difference between you and the government professionals is the number of zeros that must be considered as decisions are made about safeguarding and effectively using financial assets!

Chapter Summary

This chapter introduced the significant activities associated with managing the government's financial assets. Starting with the budget, decisions influence macroeconomic policy and social outcomes. Simultaneously, the decisions have micro-level impacts, such as determining how much revenue to collect from individuals and how the money will be spent to improve the condition of all persons living in the collective society. The discussion presented the stages and actors in the budget cycle and described different formats for presenting budgeting information for decision-making. Many efforts to change the budget process and format have occurred over the years. The decisions on these issues reflect community preferences, and there is no one "right way" to do budgeting. The operating budget is for regular expenses of operating government programs and providing public goods and services. An entirely separate budget process occurs for capital projects, including spending on roads, sewers, airports, and public buildings such as libraries and fire stations. The last topic in this chapter examined how we manage the money that comes into government to keep it safe and make sure it is used only for allowable purposes. Doing this creates accountability for the public's money.

Chapter 12 describes other control activities that occur in government to make sure that (1) money is used as legislated; (2) people who are being paid are working and have satisfactory evaluations; (3) programs are providing the desired outputs, outcomes, and impacts; and (4) we evaluate programs to look not just at performance but to see if the operating environment has changed and a new course for government should be set through the policymaking process. When adequate controls exist for monitoring, evaluating, and feeding information about budget implementation and program performance to elected officials for the next round of policymaking, trust in government is likely to increase.

Practical Applications

1. How can residents in your community provide input into budget decisions? What reforms might be possible to align community preferences with budget decisions better?
2. How have government budget processes been reformed at the national level? Identify two ways these reforms have caused changes at the subnational government levels.
3. What information would you need to determine the long-term sustainability of capital project commitments? Is this adequately reflected in the capital project prioritization criteria?
4. How could shifting public opinion about government fees or taxes influence the future programs and services government can offer? Identify one example from a recent budget discussion in your community.

In-Class Instructional Suggestions

1. Describe the impetus experiences, positive and negative, of budget reforms in your community.
2. Identify a current tension related to perceived unfunded mandates between governmental levels.
3. Review the capital project prioritization criteria commonly used in your jurisdiction.
4. Share information about the history of special taxes and fees local governments have chosen.

REFERENCES

Abbas, A., & Park, G. (2018). *Tariffs and taxes versus labor regulation: Analyzing which government policies help and hurt domestic economies.* Georgia Institute of Technology.

American Council for Intergovernmental Relations (ACIR). (1988). *The organization of public economies.* ACIR.

Anonymous. (2016). Commenting on Ian Irvine and William Sims, The simple analytics of tobacco taxation with illegal supply (2014) 47:4 *Canadian Journal of Economics* 1153–72. *Canadian Tax Journal*, 551–552.

Bland, R. L., & Rubin, I. S. (1997). *Budgeting a guide for local governments.* ICMA.

Bowsher, C. A. (1985). Governmental financial management at the crossroads: Reactive and proactive financial management is the choice. *Public Budgeting and Finance, 5*(2), 9–22.

Brajnik, I. B., Prebilič, V., & Kronegger, L. (2022). Explaining strategies in setting own local taxes in Slovenia. *Lex Localis-Journal of Local Self-Government, 20*(1), 239–257.

Brown, T. L., Potoski, M., & Van Slyke, D. M. (2013). *Complex contracting. Government purchasing in the wake of the US Coast Guard's Deepwater program.* Cambridge University Press.

Bunch, B. S., & Straussman, J. D. (1993). State budgetary processes: The two faces of theory. *Public Budgeting and Financial Management, 5*(1), 9–36.

Byaro, M., & Kinyondo, A. (2020). Citizens' trust in government and their greater willingness to pay taxes in Tanzania: A case study of Mtwara, Lindi, and Dar es Salaam Regions. *Poverty and Public Policy, 12*(1), 73–83.

Caiden, N. (1993). Processes, policies, and power: Budget reform. *The Public Manager, 22*(1), 13–17.

Chowdhury, S. (2020). Resistances to gender mainstreaming: An analysis of the trend of women engagement in participatory gender-responsive budgeting in Bangladesh. *Journal of Contemporary Governance and Public Policy, 1*(2), 53–66.

Congressional Research Service. (2020). *Unfunded mandates reform Act: History, impact and issues.* Government Printing Office.

Denison, D. V., Jepsen, C., Gibson, B., Wallace, C., & Kreis, D. (2012). Development of performance measures and revenue projections for state highway transportation systems. uknowledge.uky.edu

Durant, R. F. (2020). *Building the compensatory state: An intellectual history and theory of American administrative reform.* Routledge.

Ebdon, C. (2003). Capital management. In K. Alan (Ed.), *Paths to state and local government performance: Final report from the Maxwell School* (pp. 71–100). Syracuse University, Campbell Public Affairs Institute.

Ebdon, C., & Franklin, A. L. (2020). The effects of participatory budgeting in the Philippines. Invited submission to Participatory Budgeting symposium. *Chinese Journal of Public Administration, 11*(1), 60–74.

Escobar, O. (2021). Transforming lives, communities and systems? Co-production through participatory budgeting. In *The Palgrave handbook of co-production of public services and outcomes* (pp. 285–309). Palgrave Macmillan.

Etzioni, A. (2019). *Law and society in a populist age: Balancing individual rights and the common good.* Bristol University Press.

Finkler, S. A. (2000). *Financial management for public, health, and not-for-profit organizations* (1st ed.). Prentice-Hall.

Franco, S. H. R., & Assis, W. F. T. (2019). Participatory budgeting and transformative development in Brazil. *Geoforum, 103,* 85–94.

Franklin, A. L. (2002). An examination of the impact of budget reform on Arizona and Texas. *Public Budgeting and Finance, 22*(3), 26–45.

Franklin, A. L. (2012). Chapter 7: Budgeting. In J. Bartle, B. Hildreth, & J. Marlow (Eds.), *ICMA management policies in local government finance* (6th ed.). International City/County Management Association Press.

Franklin, A. L., & Douglas, J. W. (2003). Revolving funds as budgeting tools: An examination of Oklahoma state agencies. *State and Local Government Review, 35*(2), 90–101.

Gauthier, S. J. (1991). Accounting and financial reporting. In J. E. Petersen & D. R. Strachota (Eds.), *Local government finance: Concepts and practices* (pp. 221–240). Government Finance Officers Association.

Gonçalves, S. (2014). The effects of participatory budgeting on municipal expenditures and infant mortality in Brazil. *World Development, 53*(1), 94–110.

Grizzle, G. (1986). Does budget format really govern the actions of budgetmakers? *Public Budgeting and Finance, 6*(1), 60–70.

Gullo, T. A., & Kelly, J. M. (1988). Federal unfunded mandate reform: A first-year retrospective. *Public Administration Review, 58*(5), 370–387.

Heeschen, P. E., & Sawyer, L. B. (1984). *Internal auditors handbook*. Institute of Internal Auditors.

Ho, A. T. K. (2019). Six theoretical perspectives on performance budgeting reform. In *Performance budgeting reform* (pp. 13–27). Routledge.

Ivins, M. (2005, February 18). Budget shows who gets screwed. *The Norman Transcript*, A4.

Kettl, D. (2000). Public administration at the Millennium: The state of the field. *Journal of Public Administration Research and Theory: J-PART, 10*(1), 7–34.

Key, V. O., Jr. (1940). The lack of a budgetary theory. *American Political Science Review, 34*(6), 1137–1144.

Ma, J. (1997). *Intergovernmental relations and economic management in China*. The World Bank.

MacManus, S. A. (1992). *Doing business with the government*. Paragon House.

Melkers, J., & Willoughby, K. (2005). Models of performance-measurement use in local governments: Understanding budgeting, communication, and lasting effects. *Public Administration Review, 65*(2), 180–190.

Mikesell, J. L. (2017). *Fiscal administration: Analysis and applications for the public sector* (10th ed.). Wadsworth/Thomson Learning.

Ortiz-Ospina, E., & Roser, M. (2016). Government spending. *Our World in Data*. Retrieved November 26, 2021, from https://ourworldindata.org/government-spending

Peng, J. (2008). *State and local pension fund management*. Routledge.

Peters, G. B. (1991). *The politics of taxation: A comparative perspective*. Blackwell.

Petersen, E., Watt, P., & Zorn, P. (1986). *Organization and compensation in local government finance*. Government Finance Officers Association.

Peterson, J. E., & McLoughlin, T. (1991). Debt policies and procedures. In J. E. Petersen & D. R. Strachota (Eds.), *Local government finance: Concepts and practices* (pp. 263–290). Government Finance Officers Association.

Posner, P. L. (1997). Unfunded Mandates Reform Act: 1996 and beyond. *Publius, 27*, 7–16.

Rautenstrauch, W., & Villers, R. (1950). *Budgetary control*. Funk and Wagnalls.

Reed, B. J., & Swain, J. W. (1997). *Public finance administration* (2nd ed.). Sage.

Robbins, L. (2007). *An essay on the nature and significance of economic science.* Ludwig Von Mises Institute.

Robinson, S. G. (1991). Capital planning and budgeting. In J. E. Petersen & D. R. Strachota (Eds.), *Local government finance: Concepts and practices* (pp. 65–84). Government Finance Officers Association.

Rubin, I. S. (1990). Budget theory and budget practice: How good the fit? *Public Administration Review, 50*(2), 179–189.

Rubin, M. M., & Bartle, J. R. (2022). Gender-responsive budgeting: A global perspective. In *Handbook on gender and public administration.* Edward Elgar Publishing.

Schick, A. (1966). The road to PPB: The stages of budget reform. *Public Administration Review, 26*(4), 243–258.

Schultze, C. L. (1968). *The politics and economics of public spending.* The Brookings Institution.

Staats, E. B. (2002). The continuing need for budget reform. Reprinted in A. C. Hyde (Ed.), *Government budgeting: Theory, process, politics* (3rd ed., pp. 69–76). The Brookings Institute.

Suratno, J. M. V. (2020). Taxes, revenues, and capital expenditure as determinants of financial sufficiency of regional government. *International Journal of Economics and Business Administration, VIII*(2), 283–290.

Sussman, A. B., & White, S. M. (2018). Negative responses to taxes: Causes and mitigation. *Policy Insights from the Behavioral and Brain Sciences, 5*(2), 224–231.

Swope, C. (2005 [2003]). Payout planning. In A. Ehrenhalt (Ed.), *Governing: Issues and applications from the front lines of government* (2nd ed., pp. 49–51). CQ Press.

Szescilo, D., & Wilk, B. (2018). Can top-down participatory budgeting work? The case of Polish Community Fund. *Central European Public Administration Review, 16,* 179.

Tanzi, V., & Bovenberg, A. L. (2019). *Is there a need for harmonizing capital income taxes within EC countries?* (pp. 171–208). Routledge.

Taylor, G. M. (1977). Introduction to zero-base budgeting. *The Bureaucrat, 6*(1), 33–55.

Thurmaier, K. M., & Willoughby, K. G. (2001). *Policy and politics in state budgeting.* M.E. Sharpe.

Touchton, M., & Wampler, B. (2014). Improving social well-being through new democratic institutions. *Comparative Political Studies, 47*(10), 1442–1469.

Verkuil, P. R. (2007). *Outsourcing sovereignty: Why privatization of government functions threatens democracy and what we can do about it.* Cambridge University Press.

Wildavsky, A., & Caiden, N. (2004). *The new politics of the budgetary process* (5th ed.). Pearson Education.

Willoughby, W. F. (2004 [1918]). The movement for budgetary reform in the States. In J. M. Shafritz, A. C. Hyde, & S. J. Parkes (Eds.), *Classics of public administration* (5th ed., pp. 46–49). Thomson, Wadsworth Learning.

Willoughby, K. G. (2014). *Public budgeting in context: Structure, law, reform and results.* John Wiley & Sons.

Zorn, W. P. (1991). Public employee retirement systems and benefits. In J. E. Petersen & D. R. Strachota (Eds.), *Local government finance: Concepts and practices* (pp. 375–3776). Government Finance Officers Association.

CHAPTER 12

Controlling the Activities of Government

Chapter 11 introduced the concept of the stewardship duty for government's financial resources and the necessity of transparency and accountability in all government taxing and spending actions. The topic of this chapter is the need to control the activities of government workers and assess performance outcomes from government-funded programs and services. There are many control activities used to understand performance and establish accountability.

Many activities designed to control and assess the activities of government are initiated or conducted by people who may not work in the program being assessed. In the mid-1990s, elected officials and scholars worldwide advocated for government reinvention that included active citizen participation (Box, 1998). Citizen participation in performance system design was promoted to strengthen governance systems and control government activities so that what was being does aligned with what was important to government's clients, including citizens. Unfortunately, neither clients nor citizens are commonly invited to participate in developing or reviewing the performance measures of government programs. Program administrators suggest this is often the case because, while citizens are the beneficiaries of government policies, they may not have experience with the program that is sufficient to evaluate performance. However, involving external actors is helpful since it reveals how people outside government evaluate government's overall performance. In the (paraphrased) words of John Dewey (1954, p. 207): "The shoemaker (expert) may know how to make and fix shoes (policies), but the citizen knows if/where the shoe pinches and where she wants to go wearing the shoe." There is more accountability for societal outcomes when citizens are involved in performance evaluation (deLancer Julnes, 2001).

To better understand expectations about performance accountability, citizens, elected officials, and city staff in nine cities were tasked with jointly developing performance measures (Ho & Coates, 2004). Public advertisements and invitations sent to citizen advisory board members and neighborhood organization leaders drew community participants. Over a series of meetings, citizens were asked to identify essential elements of public service. For example, when asked about the police department, residents suggested that legal knowledge and compliance, the adequacy of police officer training, response time, and professionalism were critically important when interacting with citizens. Department staff then collected performance data and incorporated these measures into strategic plans and resource allocation decisions.

Through these activities, researchers documented how citizens' perceptions of accountability vary when compared to elected officials, government staff, or professional organizations (Ho & Coates, 2004). For example, citizens think the police department is accountable when officers are perceived as competent in citizen interactions. Elected officials believe accountability is ensured when citizen satisfaction surveys reflect positively on their leadership. On the other hand, government administrators think of accountability more in terms of their officers' level of professional training and the response times for emergency calls. With better knowledge about community members' values, departmental practices, policies, and procedures can be modified to align what is measured with citizens' performance expectations.

Building relationships and communicating regularly with stakeholders were factors critical for developing sustainable performance indicators in the Mekong Delta in Vietnam (Huy & Phuc, 2020). Researchers there concluded that there can be as many different perspectives on what is considered "good performance" for a government agency as there are people providing feedback. From the perspective of reporting accountability in meaningful ways, a study in Finland found that it is essential to analyze the different legitimacy priorities of various stakeholder groups, such as politicians and entrepreneurs (Mättö et al., 2019), since there may be different conceptions of the priorities of government programs.

Which perspective is correct? Rather than conclude that one perspective is appropriate and others are wrong, it is crucial to design performance measures that are perceived as credible indicators of results by all actors, thereby increasing the likelihood that the information will be used and accountability will be enhanced. Is it possible to arrive at standard criteria for government accountability? This chapter tackles this and other questions about using performance measures and internal and external controls to ensure accountability.

How Do Performance Measures Promote Accountability?

For government organizations, *performance measurement* has been defined as "a method of measuring the progress of a public organization or [provision of] public goods or services in achieving the results or outcomes that clients, customers, or stakeholders expect" (Center for Accountability and Performance

"CAP," 1999, p. 5). As noted in this definition there are many different audiences for performance measures. Performance measures are a signal of what activities are essential since "what gets measured, gets done." For internal management, they can be a diagnostic tool for identifying problem areas, problem-solving, and continuous improvement. Performance measures also allow comparison to the processes and outcomes of other organizations providing similar goods and services. For external audiences, they describe work performed and results achieved. This can foster accountability as well as inform planning efforts to allocate resources and establish future levels of performance. They can also provide a means for comparing different policy alternatives for future service delivery.

This section describes different measures and the criteria for selecting a few to report. After that, the types of comparisons and analyses that can be done with performance measures are described. The creation of performance monitoring systems is explained at the close of this section.

What can be measured? There are several ways to measure what a government organization does and why that matters. Many labels are used to describe performance measures. For simplicity, we describe three types: inputs, outputs, and results (outcomes and impacts).

Inputs identify the number of resources that come into an organization. These resources are used to provide a good or service. An example is money budgeted for the service or the number of employees in the organization. They can also measure service demand, like the number of clients or requests for service. Inputs are easy and straightforward to count. However, organizations have little control over the inputs they receive.

Outputs measure what the organization produces or the services it provides. These measures report the number of services delivered or goods provided. They may tell how many clients were served or the amount of time it took to process each service request. Output measures are within the control of the organization. However, output measures, by themselves, do not reveal whether these results were good or bad or if they contributed to goal achievement.

Results measures indicate what has been accomplished because a good or service was provided. Outcomes describe short-, intermediate-, and long-term changes in a client or condition caused by government interventions. They can include things such as the ability of clients to live independently, the health of the population, or the number of natural resources (air, water, land) that meet or exceed the desired condition.

A second kind of measure of results indicates how well the work was done. They can report on efficiency of service, such as the ratio of inputs to outputs, the cost per unit of service, completion rates as a percentage of some desired level of performance. They can also be indicators of the quality-of-service delivery in terms of accuracy, courtesy, and responsiveness; the percentage of goods or services that meet or exceed standards; and customer satisfaction.

Outcomes allow for assessment of the public value created because an organization exists. They are a change in a client's state or status. Impacts, on the other hand, measure change in the human condition. Impacts are indicators important for assessing our societal condition. A common example is the level of recidivism or the number of incarcerated people who are released after their sentence is served and do not commit another crime within a certain time period. However, it is hard to hold someone, or some organization, responsible for performance levels on impact measures because organizations have little control over others whose cooperation (co-production) is necessary to achieve some outcome.

Think about a prisoner. The government agency that oversees prisons cannot be solely responsible for assuring someone does not return to prison; the prisoner's behavior plays a significant role in recidivism. We cannot hold a prison warden or the government executive in charge of all prisons responsible for released prisoners committing crimes and returning to the criminal justice system. However, as a collective, we need to know recidivism rates to decide if our justice and incarceration policies are successful. So, government information reporting recidivism within its jurisdiction is vital to policymaking as well as program implementation.

Not all results can be measured quickly or at a reasonable cost (Starling, 2002). It may take several years to see any measurable change in an impact measure. In addition, it may be very difficult or costly to gather this information because of the time involved. Think about how difficult it would be to measure this assumption: if people can read and write, they will get better jobs. In addition, we would have to track people throughout their lifetime to compare their earnings based on literacy levels. We do have tests for student literacy. However, it is difficult and costly to follow each student over time to determine how much money they are making.

For these reasons, we often rely on proxy measures which are things we think have a causal connection to the desired results. What could we measure instead? A proxy measure could be the percentage of high school graduates who can read and write at a 12th grade level. As a society, we are interested in the general trend in terms of the reading levels of all students. If the 12th grade literacy levels are improving, this is a proxy for two measures of results. First, it tells us that our schools are providing a solid education. Second, it tells us that people in society have the basic skills necessary to hold a job and be self-sufficient. We also know that, over their lifetimes, students who get a high school diploma are more likely to go into higher education. Getting a bachelor's degree will allow them to earn more than those with a high school diploma. So, we could use the percentage of people in the country who can read at the 12th grade level as a proxy measure for the likelihood that fewer social services will be required. Plus, if a greater percentage of the population go to college or university, arguably even fewer would need public assistance in the future.

What Are Performance Management Systems?

One of the biggest challenges when measuring performance and developing a system for reporting organizational results is determining what to measure. As we suggested above, there are different kinds of measures, including inputs, outputs, and outcomes, and they can be used both to improve organizations as well as to establish accountability for results. Studies of performance measures developed and reported by over 800 government organizations in Arizona found a heavy reliance on input and output measures in the early rounds of performance measurement (Franklin, 1999). This makes it hard to know what has been accomplished in each situation. What would be preferred is to report a mix of productivity and results to provide a more robust picture of organizational performance and the organization's impacts in society. Table 12.1 presents other criteria that should be considered when creating useful performance.

When selecting performance measures, the users and setting where performance data will be used should be considered. For example, internal stakeholders highly value measures that describe the efficiency of converting inputs to outputs to improve the organization's services. On the other hand, external stakeholders value outcome and impact measures to know that government organizations are improving the social conditions in our society. These data can inform policy decisions. They suggest what services are needed and how and by whom they should be delivered.

Another benefit of performance measures is that they can be used for comparison. For example, you can compare current performance to past performance, expected performance, desired performance, industry performance standards, the performance of similar organizations, or even the performance of the best-practice organizations. These comparisons allow us to identify variances requiring corrective action, reward exceptional performance, improve internal and external communication, create accountability, identify successful best practices, and set targets for organizational activities (Morley et al., 2001). In addition, we can compare performance levels for different types of products

Table 12.1 Performance measure characteristics

Meaningful—directly related to the vision, mission, and goals.
Responsibility linked—reported by the responsible unit.
Results-oriented and organizationally accepted.
Customer and stakeholder focused.
Timely—collected frequently enough to give useful information.
Responsive to users' needs.
Accurate and reliable—should be credible and measured each time similarly.
Cost-effective—automate data collection as much as possible.
Comparable—to others and over time.
Simple—easy to calculate and easy to interpret.
Balanced—to include several types of measures.
Comprehensive—include all critical aspects of organizational performance.

or sub-populations of service recipients, geographical areas, or even time-adjusted historical performance. Finally, comparisons between organizations can help assess the relative level of performance.

When performance information is compared, we need to ensure that the measures actually measure items or performance levels that are alike. We say this comparison is apples to apples and not apples to oranges. To make sure you are comparing like items, you need to make sure performance measures are standardized (Meier & Brudney, 2002).

Performance monitoring systems are created to document organizational performance at set intervals. Different types of measures may be gathered at different time intervals. For example, inputs and outputs may be collected routinely, such as monthly or weekly, or in some cases, even daily. On the other hand, outcome data and measures of long-term impact might only be collected or calculated annually. The frequency for tracking needs to be periodic, based on when information is required and considering the amount of time necessary to measure meaningful changes in the condition.

To set up a monitoring system, you must know what performance measures will be used. You also will need information on how the data is collected and from what sources, knowledge of who has responsibility for data collection and reporting, and who gets the information and how and when it will be reported (remember: knowledge management systems in Chap. 9). It is also helpful if performance monitoring systems include details on past, current, and future expected performance levels for comparison and planning purposes. To the extent possible, the performance monitoring system should be set up to have automatic data collection through information technology systems. Doing this can reduce time spent on measurement, making more time available for organizational activities. Automation can also reduce the risk of human error or manipulation when reporting performance. Performance monitoring can indicate where management action is needed when performance falls outside what is desired or a large amount of variance is noted (Wholey et al., 1994). You can design custom-tailored corrective actions to remedy the problem with this diagnostic information.

What Challenges Are There in Performance Monitoring?

A significant emphasis in our evaluation of government performance is determining the efficiency of operations. We all want to ensure that we are getting our money's worth. In this case, a comparison with the performance of for-profit sector organizations is often inevitable. These organizations are evaluated on profits, sales, and return on investment (Morgan & England, 1999). Yet, assessing government performance based on the cost per unit of service provided, or the timeliness of service provision, is often unrealistic because these benefits are difficult to convert into everyday currency. Also, the government tackles problems that are very difficult to solve, usually because no market exists to resolve societal issues. And finally, government clients have different needs that are, in many situations, harder to serve quickly or at a low cost.

For these reasons, one must realize that we do not always want government to provide the cheapest or fastest services. In some cases, we want government to pursue values other than efficiency, such as equity or effectiveness. Equity can be defined in at least three ways: (1) making sure everyone receives the same service, (2) making sure everyone pays a proportional amount, or (3) making sure that everyone has the same results (Levy et al., 1974; Stone, 2001). These equity concerns are common when we talk about public schools' performance. For example, equity can mean that every classroom has a low student-to-teacher ratio. Equity can also mean the same amount of money is spent on each student. Or equity can mean that all students are helped until they reach a certain minimum achievement level. The definition of equity one will have implications for measuring performance. It will also influence the resources necessary to achieve the desired result. Malta et al. (2019) found this to be the case in the impact of anti-discriminatory legislation on sexual and gender minorities' rights in Latin America and the Caribbean. The laws existed, but there was no effective mechanism to enforce them, causing people to leave their home countries.

Similar concerns exist when we talk about the delivery of any government service. Effectiveness is a measure of how well the desired outcomes are achieved. Therefore, it seems reasonable to assume that high outcomes, stated as a percent of successes compared to all cases processed, would be a good measure of government performance. When performance changes, a twist on how to determine effectiveness is raised. If the felony crimes per 100,000 person statistics for the police department worsen, does this mean that officers are not doing their job?

When a situation like this occurs, we should determine what the data mean (Lipsky, 1980). What is the appropriate response to this situation? Should we take punitive action and reduce the law enforcement agency's budget and personnel? Or is this a signal that they do not have enough money and people to do an adequate job? Concerns like these call into question our ability to decide upon the success or failure of organizations based on how performance is reported. To ensure the reported data are valid, the accuracy of the information must be double-checked. Where possible, a comparison of data from two or more different indicators should be compared (Carter, 1994). One way to do this would be to compare quantitative and qualitative performance measures. For example, we could survey people to find out if crimes go unreported for the crime rate (e.g., sexual violence and human trafficking cases). If there are, we need to find out why this happens. Alternatively, increasing the sample size of the data collected can be one way to assure high data validity.

Unfortunately, identifying "good" performance measures is not enough. We must also find ways to explain why certain performance levels occur; often, this will reveal the importance of organizational differences. For example, the performance of government organizations is often heavily criticized as not equal to what can be done by for-profit organizations. The government is held responsible for the percentage of cases that were not "successful." One explanation for why the government may not do as well as organizations in other sectors is the phenomenon of *creaming*. Creaming, which comes from taking the richest milk (the cream) off the top, is serving the most accessible clients first so that you can report high levels of success. Doing this means that the most challenging clients may not get adequate attention or sufficient services.

One example where there is potential for creaming to occur is job training programs, especially those contracted out through a performance-based contract. Contracts like this are often paid based on the number of successful job placements. To make the most money, employees in the contracting organization may try to minimize the time and resources spent on client placements and suggest jobs that have low potential for future salary increases. But the government cannot pick and choose. They must serve everyone eligible.

Creaming is a paradox since government organizations are charged with helping everyone and serving the clients who will have the most challenging time achieving self-sufficiency by their very nature. Yet, if government employees skim off only the easy clients, how will government ever be genuinely successful in ameliorating social conditions like persistent unemployment, illiteracy, or poverty?

An analogy closer to home occurs every term in the classroom. Even though we, as instructors, maintain that everyone can learn the material and get a high grade, the sad fact is that some students will fail. Should we target our classes to intelligent students and measure our success by the number of A's and B's handed out? Can we safely assume that instructors are responsible for students' success if we do this? Or do some instructors just luck out and get intelligent students who are more likely to get A's and B's? And, what obligation do instructors, specifically those in public education institutions, generally have for assuring the success of all students? Is more public value created when instructors work intensively with a D student to learn the material, and, as a result, the student receives a B? Or is value created when the percentage of students achieving high grades increases? This potential for creating perverse incentives, where short-term outcomes are more important than long-term impacts, is a perplexing problem with no commonly agreed-upon solution.

There are other ways where performance measurement may lead to unexpected results. Government employees face situations where sharing information with other offices may not be advantageous since the employees who received the information may improve their performance. If this happens, the original office sharing the secrets of their success may lose their high position in the ranking of organizations. Or there may be incentives to "cheat" when reporting performance results to gain a higher ranking.

To what extent can performance measurement rankings supplant the goal of providing the best possible service to the clients? A study in Canada examined this issue in the context of a shift to remote work during the pandemic. The concern was how employees could securely share information for a client who needed services from workers in multiple agencies. They found that access to information systems remotely offered the potential to electronically track the time spent working on each case for each employee. Realizing that time spent using a database was not necessarily equivalent to time spent serving the client they put in place privacy protections for a digitally connected workforce (Charbonneau & Doberstein, 2020).

This example can be applied to your situation when taking a class. If your school uses an online learning system, the instructor most likely knows how often you go to the class website, how much time you spend on the class website, and what areas of the class website you are accessing. Would these performance measures be a reasonable proxy for the grade you are expected to receive in the class? Certainly, they would not. Learning is more than a function of time—even though one could argue that devoting more time to your studies is likely to increase your grade, there are other factors that matter more. This potential misunderstanding of the relationship between effort and performance, like what was learned in the Canadian study, reflects a growing awareness that a thoughtful and more complete understanding of performance measures as well as performance monitoring system is beneficial.

Performance measurement and monitoring systems in place are vital to understanding if and how well organizational processes and performance achieve specific standards and meet expectations. Some claim this is a way to maintain respect, trust, and confidence in government. But this can also result in higher expectations of public officials (Goodsell, 2004, 2014). Higher expectations can encourage activities to achieve one specified result but may reduce achievement on other values we expect from government such as responsiveness, fairness, flexibility, honesty, accountability, and competence. They can also create a fear of change among public sector workers. Finding creative ways to alleviate these fears is the responsibility of public administrators. Studying public organizations in Sweden, Finland, and Norway, it was determined that a lack of efficiency and ineffectiveness could be overcome by a performance-driven leadership, reporting, and discussing performance, and offering a reward system that reinforces the positive results of change (Kotková Stříteská & Sein, 2021).

What Are Organizational Controls?

Controls are organized, systematic, and rational ways to achieve some desired state. They strive to "automate" processes or behaviors to safeguard the organization's assets (Finkler, 2000). There are many different types of controls. Some are imposed by external actors such as performance measures identified by elected officials and citizens. These are more informal controls since measuring different kinds of performance is suggested but not mandated. Other controls are more formal and often mandated by law, such as evaluating an organization before it can be legally reauthorized.

Some controls are prospective, meaning they are put in place before some event occurs, such as limiting spending authority through the budget. Others are retrospective, such as looking back to see if performance was at the level desired. An example is a financial audit of the organization's operations to determine if they have complied with generally accepted accounting practices. In Kosovo, implementing rules and procedures for monitoring systems combined with requirements for annual reporting created a positive link between prospective and retrospective controls that enhance the transparency, efficiency, and effectiveness of financial management (Ujkani & Vokshi, 2019).

We review five controls typically used in government organizations: evaluations, audits, financial reports, termination reviews, and elected official oversight activities. These controls can be implemented by a combination of internal and external actors who gather, analyze, and report on the organization's effectiveness. The first three are formal controls that generally conform to professionally established standards of good practices. Termination reviews and elected official oversight activities can be formal, informal, or a combination.

Evaluation

Evaluation is the systematic assessment of the processes or results of an organization to determine performance. Like performance measures, evaluations can serve many purposes. For example, evaluations can: (1) determine the extent of program utilization by eligible recipients, (2) analyze an organization's costs and benefits, (3) establish the quality and efficiency of the organization's processes, (4) measure client satisfaction, (5) identify unintended outcomes of the organization's services, (6) measure the public value that is being produced, and (7) allow for comparisons.

As Table 12.2 shows, the evaluation function has many different names, but the activities are generally the same. The differences between them are the focus and when the evaluation is conducted. The first set of evaluations occurs during the program design stage. These can be useful for determining organization theory or logic models and estimating the need for a government organization. The second set of evaluations looks at what happens inside a government organization. These evaluations seek ways to improve the processes or outputs of an existing organization in the implementation stage. The third set of evaluations is helpful for monitoring and accountability. It assesses

Table 12.2 Three classes of evaluation and the life cycle of an organization

Organization design	Implementation	Results
Formative	Process	Outcome or summative
Needs assessment	Fine-tuning	Impact

how well an organization meets its objectives or measures organizational impacts or long-term changes in a social condition requiring public action. There are many potential evaluators, as well. Most common are government workers in the organization. However, external evaluators with no ties to the organization can also conduct any of the evaluations noted in Table 12.2.

Outcome monitoring

One big challenge to conducting any type of evaluation is determining the counterfactual, or what would have happened if no one nor any organization had been performing these activities. For example, government officials, doctors, and hospitals encourage people to get a flu vaccine yearly. But not everyone in the population does. How would the number of people who get the flu change if no one got a flu shot? The value of public health outcomes related to the promotion of getting a flu shot could be established by considering the counterfactual results for people who did not get the flu shot. To establish the counterfactual for public interventions, well-designed experimental techniques can be used, like drug and medical testing that divides participants into groups receiving varying treatment levels (Dennis, 1994). These evaluations estimate how results differ under varying conditions and how much change is attributable to the organization's activities.

In a comparative study of health care systems in seven countries in Eastern Europe (Torkayesh et al., 2021), using multiple performance indicators in a hybrid weighted system of evaluation provided a more direct comparison of the outcomes of different health care system practices. The areas of best practices were communicated widely which informed the adaptation and implementation to other settings which then improved their client outcomes.

Evaluation Barriers

No matter which type, evaluations are challenging to do for various reasons. First, it takes time, money, and skilled personnel to conduct the evaluation. Second, the organization's logic model (Mohr, 1988) may not exist, or the organization's goals may not be clearly defined. When this is the case, it is more difficult to establish a relationship between the organizations' activities and its outcomes and impacts. Third, sufficient quality information on the organization's performance may not be available. Fourth, there is often an unwillingness to change the organization (Wholey, 1994). And a fifth difficulty encountered is that there is no guarantee that the results will get used even after the evaluation is completed. Rossi and Freeman (2003) present several reasons for the low use of evaluation results, including uncertainty over goals, intended use, official resistance, inability to impact current operations, other factors driving decisions more than the evaluation results. There are also considerations related to ability to identify cause and effect, and to gather usable data that demonstrates change over time.

One thing that can be done to improve the likelihood that evaluation results will be used is to pay careful attention to the design of the evaluation. An evaluation designed with input from internal and external stakeholders can help ensure that information desired by the intended users of the evaluation results is gathered. Evaluation utilization can also be improved by taking these actions: (1) beginning with an evaluability assessment, (2) prioritizing evaluation studies to assure that the most critical information needs are met promptly, (3) including recommendations that focus on organization improvement, and (4) creating triggers that guarantee use by different stakeholders (Carter, 1994).

However, the most significant contributor to a lack of use is resistance. This often comes from fear: of investigation, of innovation, that the organization may be terminated, that the evaluation information will be misused, that a mix of quantitative and qualitative measures will not be used to gain a complete picture of performance within a specific context, and that employees will lose control of the organization. Finding ways to mitigate these bases of fear and the resistance associated with these fears is an integral part of the evaluation design.

Auditing

An audit determines if the organization operates consistently with generally accepted professional principles and practices. It is a process of reviewing and evaluating what has been done to determine if accurate records have been kept, internal controls are in place, legal requirements are upheld, and plans are fulfilled (Reed & Swain, 1997). Audits are valuable for preventing and detecting fraud and theft and discovering weaknesses in internal controls. If these are uncovered, corrective actions are taken to avoid future wrongdoing.

An auditor can be an employee of an organization. Still, most organization activities are also reviewed by external auditors, often on an annual basis. There is often a central audit agency for an entire level of government for public organizations, such as an Inspector General or a Legislative Auditor. Or external audits can be provided by contract from for-profit consulting firms. Doing this can assure independence in the findings. In Indonesia, the independence of the auditor was found to improve control and signal ethical leadership as a good governance practice (Sari, 2018)

An auditor's responsibility is to "independently and objectively analyze, review, and evaluate existing procedures and activities; to report on conditions found; and, whenever necessary, to recommend changes or other actions for management and operating officials to consider" (Pomeranz et al., 1976, p. 68). To fulfill these responsibilities, the auditor follows standards established by professional organizations. These standards prescribe the process for collecting evidence on internal controls, the accounting system, and the accuracy of procedures. Then, auditors test the evidence gathered to see how well it meets the standards. When weaknesses are uncovered, the auditor will determine if they are reportable or material. Reportable weaknesses go to the organization's management, and material weaknesses go into the audit findings and become part of the public record. In the Kingdom of Bahrain, a study found that implementing the recommendations through the support of the executive is an essential way to reinforce stewardship and the rule of law (Alqooti, 2020).

There are four areas an audit can investigate (Reed & Swain, 1997). The first and most common is the *financial audit* which examines transactions in the organization's financial accounts. Second, a *compliance audit* determines if the organization follows appropriate laws and regulations. The third, an *audit of economy and efficiency*, looks at the use of resources to examine how things are done and if they can be improved to reduce inefficiencies. The fourth, a *performance audit*, evaluates the organization's results to see if goals and objectives are achieved. This type of audit is like an outcome evaluation, but it usually is done by someone outside the organization.

No matter which type of audit is conducted, or if an internal or external auditor is used, the auditor is not supplying the data, only reviewing the transactions. The auditor judges the factual nature of assertions made by management. By doing this, auditors can assess the claim that all data in the financial statement are accurate. However, because samples of transactions and documents are reviewed, the auditor can only be reasonably sure there is no material misstatement. The opinion issued by the auditor is a statement about their assessment of the likelihood of irregularities based on the sample of transactions that the auditor reviewed.

Unlike an evaluation that looks at how well an organization performs and, perhaps, how operations can be improved, an audit tests conformance with generally accepted standards and practices (Davis, 1990). Audits only say something is or is not happening. They do not explore the reasons for what contributed to the achievement (or lack of achievement) of results. Auditing is also different from outcome monitoring because auditing is a normative activity that compares what should be with what was to examine how well we wanted to occur happened (Chelimsky, 1985). Monitoring measures what has occurred, detects variance, and suggests when corrective action, such as the creation of a fraud prevention program in Malaysia after an audit documented fraudulent reporting (Kamaliah et al., 2018), is necessary. Monitoring can also help discern when new trends are emerging so the organization can proactively make changes. The audit function is an essential organizational control; when combined with financial reporting, it was found to improve the sustainability of Kenyan organizations (Oluoch et al., 2021). The following section provides more details on financial reporting.

Financial Reporting

Financial reports contain details to assess the extent to which the budgetary plan has been achieved; the report also describes the government's financial position. Like audits, laws, regulations, and professional standards prescribe the format and content of financial reports (Ho, 2003). Most financial reports are prepared inside the organization and certified by an independent reviewer or auditor.

There are three main sections in a financial report. The first section provides information about the most recent fiscal year's operations through three typical statements. The first statement depicts assets, liabilities, and net assets, or what the government owns and owes at the end of the fiscal year. Annual revenues and expenditures and the operating surplus or deficit at the end of the fiscal year are shown in the second statement. Other financing activities such as transfers, debt issued, capital assets sold, and fund balances will also be noted.

The second section of an annual financial report contains the Notes to the Financial Statements. These are management's statements describing how the organization operates and explaining deviations from generally accepted practices. There is also information about exceptional circumstances for the organization, such as pending lawsuits, for which the outcome may impact operations and financial conditions in future years.

The last section of the financial report provides multi-year statistical data on various financial and economic factors. These data are useful for analyzing historical trends that may impact future financial conditions. The final section of the financial report often gives information about major employers in the area, the amount of taxes they pay, local population demographics, debt levels compared to legal limits, and taxes charged by nearby governments.

The analysis of financial reports can help identify existing or emerging problems and any changes in the operating environment that may impact the organization's finances. They are also helpful for comparing performance with other organizations, against prior performance, and to legal or economic limits. The use of the report often depends on the user. Financial reports have many different users. Managers inside the organization use them to assess operations and look for areas for improvement. Bond-rating agencies use financial reports as part of their evaluation of the organization's financial condition and to assign a rating for publicly traded government bonds. Investors review financial reports to independently assess the organization's solvency. Other organizations, groups, and citizens review financial reports to gain insight into the organization's financial condition and operations.

Termination Reviews

Termination reviews are deliberate, and usually timing-specific actions, to decide whether to end or terminate specific government functions, programs, policies, or organizations (Brewer & deLeon, 1983). Some high-profile events can cause the termination of public activities, like when organizations provide similar or even overlapping services or apparent policy failures (Lambright & Sapolsky, 1976). However, termination reviews do not always represent deliberate, prospective decisions to stop some activity. Policy termination sometimes occurs based on political activity based on values and ideology rather than decision-making based on administrative analyses of efficiency and effectiveness (deLeon, 1987).

It has been suggested that policy and organization termination is extraordinarily tricky in government and seldom occurs (Daniels, 2001). Kaufman (1976) even wrote a book titled *Are Government Organizations Immortal?* in which he concluded that once a policy is adopted and a program established to carry out the policy, it is difficult to terminate either one. Part of this explanation is that clientele and advocacy groups have been established and can quickly mobilize support when termination is threatened. In addition, the act of termination has been shown to have a strong negative connotation that government is failing in most societies, causing a psychological reactance to this action (deLeon, 1978).

Not everyone sees termination as a negative thing. Advocates claim that a specific policy or organization need not live forever. If the objectives are reached, the continued relevance of the activity should be reconsidered. Or, if there are redundancies with other government activities, termination could be a reasonable action. Policies and organizations most in danger of termination are new and unproven. Conventional wisdom suggests that if an organization makes it through a couple of rounds of reauthorization in the budget process, its future is virtually assured.

Sunset reviews can be scheduled for a specific time in the future or upon request to purposefully ask whether a government organization should be terminated (in which case the sun would set on the organization). Sunset laws automatically terminate an organization unless it is determined that sufficient public value is being created and the organization should be reauthorized. Sunset laws also require periodic evaluations to ensure government accountability (Kearney, 1990).

Sunset reviews can balance the power distribution between the executive and legislative branches. Some argue that they are an important control mechanism for the oversight of government agency activities (Thompson & Jones, 1982). Others question the value of the time and resources necessary to conduct sunset review when the evidence suggests that few government organizations are terminated. The possible outcomes of sunset reviews are not just termination or re-authorization. In some cases, programs within an organization may lose funding, but the organization survives. There are also high rates of procedural changes and increased oversight mechanisms and requirements.

Elected Official Oversight

A final type of control mechanism is oversight activities by public officials. Elected officials have many different mechanisms for assessing and controlling government organizations and their service delivery activities. Oversight is often accomplished through constituent casework, a term that describes what happens when individuals appeal to their elected officials from their political jurisdiction for intervention related to an unsatisfactory government service or a service request that has not been approved by a government program (Anderson, 2000). Second are committee hearings to investigate the operations of a specific organization, primarily when they are held as part of the appropriations process. The third is the approval of executive appointments to administrative positions, which offers organization control, as does the request for legislative staff studies.

The oversight mechanisms available to elected officials vary in the degree of formalness, ranging from official legislative and executive activities to informal interactions between elected officials, their staff, and civil servants. They can be directed toward an organization's operations or investigate a specific decision regarding an individual service recipient.

How Can We Design Adequate Controls?

Even though control mechanisms can help assure accountability, there are challenges in gathering the data needed about organization activities and performance that can be used for control purposes. Common challenges are the subjectivity of data selection, issues concerning data validity, and the difficulty of measuring effects caused by extenuating circumstances as well as establishing the counterfactual. Each presents a challenge to control and accountability since, without valid and reliable information, overseers of government organizations will not have a credible picture of performance upon which to base their actions.

Subjectivity in the selection of performance data is unavoidable and a threat that makes is difficult to design adequate controls. One example of how this can occur is when deciding whether to measure performance at an aggregated or disaggregated level. The choice can lead to very different conclusions about performance. For example, attendance at national parks can vary based on seasonal visitation rates. As the national park manager, do you report the annual number of visitors? Or would it be better to compare visitation by season, especially since your park had the initiative to increase the number of winter visitors? Or, if you are the director of a job training organization in an area with a large rural population, do you report the wages of clients getting jobs as an average? Or do you break it down to show differences in wages for urban and rural workers since rural workers usually earn much less than those employed in urban areas?

Problems with the face validity of the data is another common performance measurement challenge. For example, a government tax agency's tax form distribution center may report a customer satisfaction rate of 68%. This may sound low, but it may be artificially low because the organization has only surveyed customers who received their forms through the mail. It does not include those who used electronic resources such as websites and tax preparation software to get their forms. The satisfaction levels of these other types of customers may differ. They may perhaps be higher since they got quicker service when they wanted it—rather than waiting for the mail delivery.

Here's another example that suggests why face validity is an important issue. A standard performance measure for an auto emissions testing center is when customers must wait to perform their emissions test. What if the government required a new test in addition to those already being performed, but no additional machines or workers were provided with this unfunded mandate? Then, we could expect that people would have to wait longer to test their emissions. As a manager for the organization, do you feel comfortable showing results that have gotten worse? Is it valid to say that your organization is doing worse, or is it just a reflection of the additional workload required by the government with no additional resources?

Changes in operating conditions beyond the organization's control are another source of performance measurement problems. The COVID-19 infection rate significantly dropped in early 2022, with many claiming this was due to rising vaccination rates and the omicron variant having run its course. However, these data could be misleading. Concurrent with this drop in the infection rate, there has also been a dramatic increase in self-testing at home rather than testing by public-health-related organizations. No official reporting is required for self-testing. Could an alternate explanation for the drop in infection be that those with COVID-19 stay home and recover without ever having visited a medical provider who would officially report the infection?

Despite these challenges, there remains a demand for performance information to ensure accountability (Radin, 2000). One observer notes: "Spreadsheet-based performance is now a primary instrument for assessing government effectiveness as well as holding public officials accountable" (Fredrickson, 2004, p. 11). How can we ensure that expanded knowledge about performance improves policymaking and government management? One way to do this is to integrate management functions for accountability.

There need to be strong connections between different management functions to assure that controls are well-designed and executed in ways that provide useful information for assessing the transparency, performance, and accountability of government programs, services, and providers. Performance measures can link several management functions inside an organization together to do this. In addition, performance measures are essential in strategic planning and budgeting since they link resource allocations to strategies designed to provide specific performance levels. Plus, performance measures can also link the personnel management function to organization implementation since a comparison of the current level of performance with expected performance levels can be documented in annual employee evaluations. Third, they link the budget allocation to organization implementation since budgets signal expectations regarding resource use. Fourth, they link implementation and evaluation activities by telling how outputs relate to results achieved. Finally, information about results identified through evaluation activities is helpful in the planning process to set performance expectations for the future.

Chapter Summary

The effectiveness of organizational controls, such as performance measurement, audits, financial reporting, termination, and sunset reviews, and elected official oversight can be enhanced through laws, rules, and policies that require them to be conducted combined purposeful administrative efforts to communicate the value of these activities. Organizations would be well advised to use multiple kinds of controls, before, during and after implementation, to emphasize the importance of performance and to foster a results-oriented culture (van der Kolk, 2019).

Chapter 13 is the concluding substantive topic chapter in our presentation of public administration at three different levels: conceptual—as a mechanism for civil society; institutional—as an official regime that serves multiple values favored by the collective; and as policymaking and administrative functions that deliver the programs, goods, and services for which a perfect market does not exist. In the next (and last) chapter of this book, we revisit the question of what makes public administrative, as a field of study, so challenging.

Practical Applications

1. A forum at Suffolk University offers several ideas for driving change and action through data. Can these ideas have the same results for government, for-profit, and non-profit organizations?
2. Research and develop a set of performance indicators to assess the level of social equity and the impact of social justice initiatives. In what ways are these more challenging to measure than crime-rate statistics?
3. Imagine you are an auditor for the old-age pension system. What controls would be the most important to have? Justify your conclusion.
4. Look up what government organization is responsible for occupational licensing. Identify potential circumstances for an occupational licensing organization to be terminated during sunset review.

In-Class Instructional Suggestions

1. Suggest how organizations in different sectors promote accountability.
2. Engage in a class discussion about the difficulty of holding the government accountable for social equity and justice improvements.
3. Describe standard controls used for the old-age pension and health organizations.
4. Share information on laws or regulations for sunset reviews.

References

Alqooti, A. A. (2020). Public governance in the public sector: A literature review. *International Journal of Business Ethics and Governance, 3*(3), 14–25.

Anderson, J. E. (2000). *Public policymaking: An introduction* (4th ed.). Houghton Mifflin Company.

Box, R. (1998). *Citizen governance*. Sage.

Brewer, G., & deLeon, P. (1983). *The foundations of policy analysis*. Dorsey Press.

Carter, R. (1994). Maximizing the use of evaluation results. In J. S. Wholey, H. P. Hatry, & K. E. Newcomer (Eds.), *Handbook of practical organization evaluation* (pp. 576–589). Jossey-Bass.

Center for Accountability and Performance (CAP). (1999). *Performance measurement: Concepts and techniques* (2nd ed.). American Society for Public Administration.

Charbonneau, É., & Doberstein, C. (2020). An empirical assessment of the intrusiveness and reasonableness of emerging work surveillance technologies in the public sector. *Public Administration Review, 80*(5), 780–791. Canada.

Chelimsky, E. (1985). Comparing and contrasting auditing and evaluation. *Evaluation Review, 9*(4), 483–503.

Daniels, M. R. (2001). Policy and organizational termination. *International Journal of Public Administration, 24*(3), 301–315.

Davis, D. F. (1990). Do you want a performance audit or an organization evaluation? *Public Administration Review, 50*(1), 35–41.

deLancer Julnes, P. (2001). Does participation increase perceptions of usefulness? An evaluation of a participatory approach to the development of performance measures. *Public Performance and Management Review, 24*(4), 403–418.

deLeon, P. (1978). Public policy termination: An end and a beginning. *Policy Analysis, 4*(3), 369–392.

deLeon, P. (1987). Policy termination as a political phenomenon. In D. Palumbo (Ed.), *The politics of organization evaluation* (pp. 173–189). Sage.

Dennis, M. L. (1994). Ethical and practical randomized field experiments. In J. S. Wholey, H. P. Hatry, & K. E. Newcomer (Eds.), *Handbook of practical organization evaluation* (pp. 155–197). Jossey-Bass.

Dewey, J. (1954 [1927]). *The public and its problems*. Henry Holt.

Finkler, S. A. (2000). *Financial management for public, health, and not-for-profit organizations*. Prentice-Hall.

Franklin, A. L. (1999). Managing for results in Arizona: A 5th-year report card. *Public Productivity and Management Review, 23*(2), 194–209.

Fredrickson, H. G. (2004). Spreadsheets, management, and the challenges of public sector performance. *PA Times, 27*, 7.

Goodsell, C. T. (2004). *The case for bureaucracy: A public administration polemic*. CQ Press.

Goodsell, C. T. (2014). *The new case for bureaucracy: A public administration polemic*. CQ Press.

Ho, A., & Coates, P. (2004). Citizen-initiated performance assessment: The initial Iowa experience. *Public Performance and Management Review, 27*(3), 29–50.

Huy, P. Q., & Phuc, V. K. (2020). The impact of public sector scorecard adoption on the effectiveness of accounting information systems towards sustainable performance in the public sector. *Cogent Business and Management, 7*(1), 1717718.

Kamaliah, K., Marjuni, N. S., Mohamed, N., Mohd-Sanusi, Z., & Anugerah, R. (2018). Effectiveness of monitoring mechanisms and mitigation of fraud incidents in the public sector. *Administratie si Management Public, 30,* 82–95.

Kaufman, H. (1976). *Are government organizations immortal?* Brookings Institution Press.

Kearney, R. C. (1990). Sunset: A survey and analysis of the state experience. *Public Administration Review, 50*(1), 49–57.

Kotková Stříteská, M., & Sein, Y. Y. (2021). Performance driven culture in the public sector: The case of Nordic countries. *Administrative Sciences, 11*(1), 4.

Lambright, W. H., & Sapolsky, H. M. (1976). Terminating federal research and development organizations. *Policy Science, 7*(2), 199–213.

Levy, F., Meltsner, A., & Wildavsky, A. (1974). *Urban outcomes: Schools, streets, and libraries.* University of California Press.

Lipsky, M. (1980). *Street-level bureaucracy: Dilemmas of the individual in public services.* Russell Sage Foundation.

Malta, M., Cardoso, R., Montenegro, L., de Jesus, J. G., Seixas, M., Benevides, B., ... Whetten, K. (2019). Sexual and gender minorities rights in Latin America and the Caribbean: A multi-country evaluation. *BMC International Health and Human Rights, 19*(1), 1–16.

Mättö, T., Anttonen, J., Järvenpää, M., & Rautiainen, A. (2019). Legitimacy and relevance of a performance measurement system in a Finnish public-sector case. *Qualitative Research in Accounting and Management, 17*(2), 177–199.

Meier, K. J., & Brudney, J. D. (2002). *Applied statistics for public administration* (5th ed.). Thomson-Wadsworth.

Mohr, L. (1988). *Impact analysis for program evaluation.* Dorsey Press.

Morgan, D. R., & England, R. E. (1999). *Managing urban America* (5th ed.).

Morley, E., Bryant, S. P., & Hatry, H. P. (2001). *Comparative performance measurement.* The Urban Institute Press.

Oluoch, F. O., K'Aol, G., & Koshal, J. (2021). Influence of balanced organizational controls on financial sustainability of NGOs in Kenya. *The University Journal, 3*(1), 45–58.

Pomeranz, F., Cancellieri, A. J., Stevens, J. B., & Savage, J. L. (1976). *Auditing in the public sector: Efficiency, economy and organization results.* Warren, Gorham, and Lamont.

Radin, B. A. (2000). *Beyond Machiavelli: Policy analysis comes of age.* Georgetown University Press.

Reed, B. J., & Swain, J. W. (1997). *Public finance administration* (2nd ed.).

Rossi, P. H., & Freeman, M. W. (2003). *Evaluation: A systematic approach* (7th ed.).

Sari, W. I. (2018). *The influence of organizational commitment, auditor independence, internal control, and ethical leadership in good governance and organizational performance.* Indonesia. Proceedings of the 2017 Mulawarman International Conference on Economics and Business.

Starling, G. (2002). *Managing the public sector* (6th ed.). Harcourt College Publishers.

Stone, D. (2001). *Policy paradox.* W. W. Norton and Company.

Thompson, F. L., & Jones, L. R. (1982). *Regulatory policy and practices: Regulating better and regulating less.* Praeger.

Torkayesh, A. E., Pamucar, D., Ecer, F., & Chatterjee, P. (2021). An integrated BWM-LBWA-CoCoSo framework for evaluation of healthcare sectors in Eastern Europe. *Socio-Economic Planning Sciences, 78,* 101052.

Ujkani, S., & Vokshi, N. B. (2019). An overview on the development of internal control in public sector entities: Evidence from Kosovo. *The International Journal of Economics and Business Administration, 7*(4), 320–335.

van der Kolk, B. (2019). Management control packages: A literature review and guidelines for public sector research. *Public Money and Management, 39*(7), 512–520.

Wholey, J. S. (1994). Assessing the feasibility and likely usefulness of evaluation. In J. S. Wholey, H. P. Hatry, & K. E. Newcomer (Eds.), *Handbook of practical organization evaluation* (pp. 15–39). Jossey-Bass.

Wholey, J. S., Hatry, H. P., & Newcomer, K. E. (Eds.). (1994). *Handbook of practical organization evaluation.* Jossey-Bass Publishers.

CHAPTER 13

What Is Public Administration? The Nature of the Study

We ended Chap. 12 by discussing how we control organizations and determine their effectiveness. Effectiveness, as we noted, can be measured using three different levels of conceptualization of public administration: conceptual, institutional, and policymaking/administration. In this chapter, we return to the question, "What is Public Administration?" A simple answer is that there are so many ways it can be (and is) studied, for example, as a mechanism, an institution, and as policymaking and administrative functions. A more nuanced answer captures how the *transdisciplinarity* of the specializations studied in public administration has grown continuously since the dawn of civilization. Further, the ideas and theories of the natural, physical, social sciences, and the humanities have become embedded in the study of government—much the same as the government is present in nearly every aspect of our private and public life spheres.

We hope this book and the readings prescribed for your class gave you an image of public administration as something you want to know more about. Perhaps you are even considering it as a major. This sounds like a great choice! Millions of public sector jobs require knowledge of public administration. In addition, millions more jobs in all sectors would benefit from employees with general knowledge about government and specific knowledge about government budgeting, grants, contracts, stakeholder relations, and lobbying.

Suppose a friend asks you about your major, and you respond that you are studying public administration. She asks: What is public administration? How would you answer?

There are different possible answers. You can focus on *what the government does* and say that public administration studies how government provides a wide range of services and regulates human interaction in the broadest sense through laws. Thus, public administration examines how these services are provided in programs and delivered by line and staff units.

You could also focus on *how government operates* and mention that public administration studies the functioning of government organizations, which includes attention to policy implementation, strategic management, budgeting, human resource management, and so on.

Or your answer can focus on the role and position of government organizations (also referred to as the bureaucracy) within and across the three branches of government. In that case, you would point out that public administration *studies the interactions between elected officials, civil servants, and citizens.* Each of these answers is correct.

Next, your friend asks you: Why public administration? Why not law, engineering, regional and city planning, or business administration? After all, bureaucracy has a bad name, and you can make much more money in other professions. How would you respond? You could say that in every country worldwide, many government employees are lawyers, and many civil engineering and planning specialists who provide sustainable living spaces work in government or conduct government-sponsored research. People who choose to work in government often see "public service as a public trust." You, too, may find it appealing to serve the public interest.

Your friend may also point out that public administration is not an exact science. So why not study something with a clear body of knowledge, a collection of knowledge exclusively belonging to that field of study? That is perceived to be the case with such "hard" sciences as mathematics, physics, and chemistry; language studies; social sciences such as economics and psychology; and humanities studies like theology, philosophy, and history.

Public administration is an inclusive social science as it relies on multiple bodies of knowledge. It only has an object of knowledge, which is government. Governance and government are topics of interest to scholars in public administration, as well as to many social sciences and the humanities. What is the body of knowledge that public administration "claims"? We use quotation marks here on purpose since public administration does not claim a body of knowledge so much as it "claims" an object of knowledge. It is the only academic study solely concerned with governance and the relations between citizens and their government. Scholars in other disciplines study aspects of government.

Public administration scholars draw as much upon the insights of professional psychologists, sociologists, historians, economists, philosophers, and physical and natural scientists as they do upon theories developed in their study. It was recently shown that public administration scholars are increasingly "giving back" concepts and theories to the studies and disciplines they draw upon.

Public administration has been called the "Israel of academic disciplines" (Rodgers & Rodgers, 2000) because some scholarship has come from people in different academic disciplines while other scholars have come to study public administration to complement their understanding of government. This final chapter is different from previous chapters since it is not concerned with summarizing the study of public administration. Instead, this chapter assesses the academic and disciplinary nature of the study and provides an intellectual history. It tells you where the study is now and where it came from.

WHY IS PUBLIC ADMINISTRATION A SCIENCE, A CRAFT, AND AN ART?

When you consider public administration as a *science*, the scholarship aims to develop theories and methods specific to it. This is a pursuit of knowledge for the sake of knowledge itself, for the growth of knowledge. The ultimate objective is to elevate the study of public administration to the level and rigor achieved in the natural sciences through developing and testing theories. This approach to seeking knowledge for its own sake is characteristic of pure academia.

Viewed through the lens of a scientific approach, public administration has done quite poorly. According to one of its harshest critics, public administration and management books are generally embarrassing when viewed through the norms of science (Simon et al., 1981). This criticism comes from a view that public administration scholarship is not theory-driven in the same way as the natural sciences, partly because public administration does not have methods specific to its study. These methods must be developed first to include mathematical formulae as their primary language in its most robust expression. More common are sophisticated statistical analysis techniques. If you decide to study public administration, you will become versed in this type of scholarship. In Chaps. 7 and 9 you will find examples of a scientific approach to setting the course of government and designing government organizations.

From the beginning to the present, many scholars regarded the study of public administration as a *craft*. Scholars provide civil servants with usable or applied knowledge. While scientific knowledge is tailored to academics' interests, applied knowledge seeks to help practitioners. Science solves knowledge problems; applied knowledge strives to address social issues and challenges. Its methods can be quantitative-statistical but also are often case-study, best-practices comparisons, and descriptions of skills and techniques. Several chapters in this book are an example of that approach. Just think of all the techniques involved in structuring organizations, policy and decision-making and planning, budgeting and financial management, human resource management, and auditing and evaluation.

Finally, the study is also interested in the *art* of governing; in that sense, public administration is an art. Art can be taught up to a point; that is, you can learn how paint can be applied, how a chisel can be used best, and what materials can be welded together. In other words, art requires knowledge of techniques and experience with using those techniques. Examples include the art of statecraft discussed in Chap. 3 and the interactions between citizens, elected officials, and career civil servants in Chap. 5. However, art cannot teach creativity, developing a novel idea of how to paint, sculpt, and design: art relies heavily upon the natural talents of its practitioners.

The same is the case with those who have completed a degree in public administration. You will know about various theories and will have learned various techniques relevant to the job, but no one can teach you how to govern. What helps is to know and understand the role and position of government in society. This helps you know better what is expected of you. Doing this requires knowledge of the nation's governance regime and structure of government, the size of government, government culture and climate, how public servants and citizens can and do interact, the relationship between politics and administration, and ethics and integrity.

As is clear from the above, the quality of public administration as an academic study cannot only be judged by its epistemological and methodological rigor. It should also be assessed by the extent to which it can provide practitioners with usable knowledge and the extent to which it provides students with insight and understanding about the position and role of government in society. Unfortunately, when scholars focus only on the scientific aspect, they focus on evidence-based knowledge, that is, empirical knowledge generated through sophisticated analytical techniques. This often leads to relatively narrow research, publishable in journal-length articles, which leaves the "big questions" aside that can only be addressed in book-length studies (Raadschelders, 2019). Those big questions include how government emerged and developed in human societies and how today's government in democratic political systems differs from totalitarian or dictatorial systems (Raadschelders, 2020).

What Are Public Administration's Wide-Ranging Interests?

There is a second reason why public administration borrows from such a wide range of theories and specializations. Traditional public administration emerged as a study that desired to help the fast-growing government organizations be more effective and efficient in their service delivery. The need for practical knowledge was great. Government services increased rapidly, and as a result, the complexity of government organizations increased sharply. Public administration started as a study to help government work better. The focus was on the organization of managerial practices in government. The central object of interest was administration. This situation changed for two reasons: the need for specialists in government and the growth of specializations in academia.

Until the 1860s, the government often employed people with a law degree to serve at higher administrative levels. After all, the main task of government was writing laws and regulations, and who could do that better than someone trained in the law? Once the laws were in place, hiring subject matter experts for the organization became necessary. For example, in an agricultural agency, experts in chemistry, botany, entomology, animal science, and other natural sciences were necessary. As government services and policies expanded and modernized, the government needed more and more specialists. Nowadays, we can safely conclude that every kind of academic degree has graduates working in government.

Because government provides services and policies in very different fields, it needs specialists trained in these areas. But, since government organizations have become so complicated and pervasive, it also needs specialists in budgeting, personnel management, evaluation, and so forth. Also, sound policymaking usually requires specialists trained in using theories and techniques of their specialization to coordinate their activities.

A good example is developing a policy for approving COVID-19 immunizations and treatments. All around the world, government officials and heads of regulatory agencies were identifying experts inside and outside of government in the medical and pharmaceutical industries who could participate in the formulation of public health precautions and the medical interventions. These were necessary for protecting the population during a pandemic as well as to determine which vaccines and treatments were safe and highly effective in stopping the spread of the virus and treating people who were seriously ill.

Medical doctors investigated the benefits of using antiviral medicines to restore dysfunctional body parts (the craft approach). Microbiologists described how important it was to push further the boundaries of knowledge about the SARS vaccine for translation to the COVID-19 virus and its variants (the science approach). Finally, ethicists were consulted on the problematic issue of using mRNA medical interventions and how differing opinions in society about this issue could be navigated (the art approach). This is but one example; we would argue that government provides or regulates, no good, service or policy where the input of one specialization is sufficient.

Why Do We Have Principles for the Study of Public Administration?

The modern study of public administration goes back to the late nineteenth century. Woodrow Wilson's article, "The Study of Administration" (Wilson, 2005[1887]), is often listed as one of those starting points. But, as noted earlier, the study's modern appearance was significantly advanced and pursued by local administrators. Since the early seventeenth century, there has been quite a bit of academic attention to government and public administration in Germany, France, Italy, the Netherlands, and the United Kingdom. However, even in these *demand-side theories* earlier times, practitioners crossed the bridge between the academe and practice to better align the ideas in theories with the results achieved through practice.

Wilson's article provided a general rationale for and principles of an independent study or public administration. In the words of Wilson (2005 [1887]):

- practical statesmanship: a focus on how to do things,
- to make government less like a business,
- a distinction between constitutional and administrative questions,
- training for an educated and self-sufficient civil service,
- training for a trustworthy public service, and
- an administration of governments within governments in service of the community.

We discuss each of these briefly, using Wilson's wording in his article.

Public administration should serve the immediate needs of communities and not focus on theories and doctrines only. Practical experience is regarded as essential. Public administration is also a study that can learn from practices and arrangements in business management. Government organizations and processes might benefit from applying a more operating for-profit-type attitude, for instance, regarding appointments and promotions solely based on merit. This relates to Wilson's distinction between constitutional functions, which are matters of politics and policy, and administrative functions, mainly instrumental, applied actions. Public administration, he argues, should be considered the systematic implementation of public law, nothing more, nothing less.

The detailed execution of law and political desire was left to a cultured (meaning educated) and self-sufficient civil service. The "cultured" aspect was to be served by competitive examination in various liberal arts. At the same time, the "self-sufficient" side would be determined based on technical knowledge tests. The study of public administration was intended to train technically proficient civil servants. It also required civil servants to be sensitive to public opinion so that their actions would neither be arbitrary nor inspired by class spirit. This combination of technical skill and cultural understanding would create a trustworthy civil service whose motives, objects, policy, and standards were bureaucratic and did not favor anyone or any group. Finally, public administration had to serve government agencies across all levels of government. This was so important to Wilson that he devoted the last section of his article to the equal role that national and regional governments played in serving everyday public purposes.

A fundamental distinction between institutions and actors can be made between structures and actions. At the level of ideas, we look at the foundation of governance as a collective endeavor. That includes attention to why people want government and why the government needs people and looks at society's legal and moral foundations. What values are considered central to society? Some are expressed in law, and many others simply as unspoken rules, customs, and habits. For instance, no law says individualism is a citizen's protected right. Still, there are quite a few laws that protect individual rights.

To protect and advance the interests of individual citizens and society's values at large, government organizations, goods, and services are developed and operate in the context of a political system, be it a constitutional democracy, an authoritarian system, or anything in between. Institutional arrangements are put in place at the societal level to define the government's role and position in society.

Turning to the actor level, actors make decisions. The heads of government agencies are organizational actors. The head of the agency and the executive in charge of administration are individual actors. At the organizational level, public administration is concerned with serving public values and how to carry out public policy. The actor level is focused on the groups of people involved in running the business of government.

Combined, these government institutions and actors within these institutions form the identity of the study of public administration. Taken together, they determine the functions government provide and specify a broader perspective about individuals and the government's role and position in society. In addition, they educate people about what it means to be good citizens who know and practice their civil rights and public duties in support of the government. That is the next topic.

What Is the Nature of the Study of Public Administration?

The new study of public administration's immediate goals was to help a growing government become efficient, professional, fair, and responsive. Efficiency and professionalism were served by improving techniques, standardizing procedures, and creating benchmarks to assess performance outcomes. Fairness and responsiveness were served by enhancing citizen participation and securing an impartial administration. These were the ultimate purposes: an efficient and non-corrupt civil service. Of course, both values are still important today, but they must be constantly refined to fit a society and its citizens who were quite different from when governments were created.

People in early society knew and understood the importance of civic duty and citizens' rights. Presently, citizens in democratically governed countries live in a society that advances civil rights and is less concerned with civic duty but is possibly rediscovering its importance. In more authoritarian systems, people are expected to know their civic duty. However, their civil rights are often constrained.

There is also an inverse relationship for public servants. In democratically governed countries, public servants are trained as generalists and develop skills as specialists over time. In an authoritarian system, public servants typically need generalist training—even at the highest levels. The ultimate purpose of public administration in this time and context is very different. If anything, public administration must educate people to be sensitive to the needs of the times. For our time, this is a needed for strengthening a sense of civic duty, upholding civil rights, and balancing generalist and specialist civil servants.

How Does Public Administration Promote Civic Duty and Trusteeship?

Constitutional democracy is probably the only political system where all citizens have access to fundamental civil rights, such as voting, associating, and participating in public policy and decision-making. These are civil rights because the citizenry is sovereign (see Chap. 3) and that conception is well captured in *Government is Us* (King & Stivers, 1998). It is a government by, for, and through the people; it is a government that serves rather than commands. However, a constitutional democracy that protects our civil rights will not survive for long when its citizens are unaware or unfamiliar with their civic duties. The rise of right-wing and populist parties in various Western countries is testimony to the extent to which citizens are increasingly ill-informed about their rights and duties (Etzioni, 2019). Voting is not only a right; it is also a duty. We have the right to be protected if we also feel the duty to defend our country. We are entitled to excellent education for our children but must be willing to help with their homework and contribute time to the parent-teacher associations in public schools. We have a right to expect the law to help settle our differences, but we also must know and uphold the law ourselves.

Constitutional democracy today is a political system forced to walk a fine line between individual rights and collective needs. When should the individual's rights be sacrificed for society's needs? When should individual rights override the needs of the collective? These questions are essential in societies with multi-cultural and multi-ethnic populations. We no longer live in a small tribe where differences can be settled personally. Instead, we live in a *supertribe* (Morris, 1996 [1969]), in an *imagined community* (Anderson, 2006), where the only role that we genuinely share is that of a citizen. We are all citizens, irrespective of gender, race, education, and wealth. The big question is, of course, what kind of citizen we wish to be.

There are two extreme options. First, one can emphasize individual responsibility, which translates into a small and efficient government. This is a strong tradition in America. It was voiced 200 years ago in Thomas Jefferson's "the best government is that which governs least." Or the emphasis can be on running government like a business, which is the argument of New Public Management and government reformers. Second, one can point to a community's needs, which often come with a big or bigger government. This has been more common in continental Europe. Each new vision of an imagined community contributed to advancing the rights of the disadvantaged, such as the unemployed, senior citizens, women, and African, Hispanic, and Asian, and indigenous peoples. As you can expect, the best governance structure is one where individual rights and community needs are constantly weighed and (re)balanced. And, whether we like it or not, a robust governance structure must also be efficient, professional, responsive, and fair. It may not be trendy to say that we need less governance and more bureaucracy consisting of ethical civil servants. Still, the fact of the matter is that the kind of government we take for granted is not possible without civil servants working within a bureaucracy.

What kind of public servant does this require? For the answer, we can start with two observations. The first is by Thomas Jefferson: "When a man assumes a public trust, he should consider himself public property." The second is from Grover Cleveland: "Public office is a public trust." Elected officials and civil servants are guardians, stewards, or public trustees. When they take an oath of office, they pledge to uphold the law and commit to protecting and advancing the needs and interests of all citizens. Once an individual accepts a public office through election or appointment, they become a trustee of the public and for the public.

What does it mean to be a public trustee? First, citizens rely upon the competent performance of civil servants, which includes serving the public good. Second, citizens should expect that the trustee is careful in dealing with public resources (water, land, air, and atmosphere) and money (taxes). Third, citizens should trust that the authority and power invested in a public official are not abused. Fourth, citizens should expect the trustee to work with an eye for the long-term benefits rather than the short-term gains. Indeed, a reliable civil servant is prudent. The word "prudent" is derived from the Latin word *prudentia*, which means "to see ahead" or "foreseeing." In other words, public servants do, and ought not only, govern to serve the needs of the "here and now" but also to serve the needs of future generations. But, again, what kind of public servant does this require? And, yet, what does it take to be a public trustee?

Naturally, you ask: How can you educate me about this? In all fairness, public administration scholars know no better than anyone who says: practice, practice, practice, study, learn, reflect, and build upon experiences. Could it be that a good public servant is like a concert pianist? They just close their eyes and play the piece with all the passion they have? Well, yes and no. The solo concert pianist has played the same piece so often in solitary practice that playing it on stage only requires concentration and passion. That type of commitment and lots of practice should also be expected from a public servant. The pianist is not just a servant of the muse but also a servant of the audience. The civil servant serves the elected political leaders, appointed administrative leaders, and citizens. Both the pianist and civil servant must match technical proficiency with audience-oriented performance. A technically superior performance may not carry the passion that convinces an audience to clap after the concert. The big difference between a pianist and a public servant is that governing does not consist of just one musical piece or technique. The public servant we need today is someone who can be a specialist and a generalist, with the ability to subordinate specialization to higher demand and set aside personal convictions for the larger good.

Why Is Studying Public Administration Challenging?

The first challenge is that the study of public administration constantly refines itself to respond to the constantly changing social, economic, and political environments. Its object of interest, government, is also constantly subject to change. Therefore, the study must embrace various approaches. It cannot "settle" for one approach since no single study or theory can claim the ability to study government in its entirety. Moreover, the study of public administration does not have the luxury of studying something guided by universal laws, as in physics or mathematics. What society and its citizens find essential now will not necessarily be the same ten years from now. Consequentially, public administration's object of knowledge regarding government changes over time and with context.

The second challenge is that the study is expected to provide practical, usable knowledge. Citizens and political officeholders have a right to ask for something that works, for techniques, policies, and standards that solve a problem. Make no mistake, public administration includes much usable knowledge. Just think of the techniques for budgeting, human resource management, strategic management, program evaluation, and so on. Still, it also includes attention to social equity and fairness issues. It is not too difficult to judge a government's efficiency. You simply measure. Judging government action regarding social equity and fairness is far more challenging. For example, how can we measure the value of a decent health care system that guarantees care for everyone? Not just by counting patients, operations, or the number of medical doctors but also by assessing the quality of life of our citizens. This challenge has to do with balancing the need for efficiency with the needs of society.

The third challenge is that the government is often expected to provide immediate solutions to problems. In some cases, that is possible. When a bridge collapses after a flood, it can be repaired in a specified amount of time and at a specific cost. But there are many areas of government activity where such immediate problem-solving is simply impossible and the funding may not be available. In the words of one scholar,

> Certain fields of human endeavor display an orderliness that lends itself to scientific precision and measurement, and the development of rules, laws, and principles [...]. Other fields of human endeavor, while not random, are much less orderly and, therefore, less amenable to scientific precision and management. There is simply no question that building more freeways is much easier than figuring out how to improve inner-city public education. (Frederickson, 2003, p. 53)

How can the study of public administration help government provide solutions to both tame and wicked problems? Some things can be solved quickly. Others take time. Many policies are nothing more than the product of incremental steps over time, accumulating into something big. The political distribution of power between parties and branches of government, combined with the short electoral cycle, demands quick solutions. Civil servants provide a counterweight. They may warn against hasty measures and point out that past policies cannot be discarded easily. This is necessary because people expect the government to live up to its promises. And, as they say, you do not want to throw the baby out with the bathwater. We cannot easily change the baby, but cold and dirty bathwater can easily be replaced by something better. Specialists and generalist civil servants have the knowledge and experience to recognize the need for change and advise on what can be done to improve society for the future.

What Are the Ways We Can Improve Public Administration?

At the beginning of this chapter, we noted that public administration can be and ought to be perceived as a science, a craft, and an art. We need scholars who study public administration from their scientific desire to expand knowledge. Still, we also need scholars who develop new ways of doing things and new techniques that help save money or help do things faster and better, just like the craftsmen so many years ago. And finally, we also need scholars who raise the so-called big questions about the role and position of government in society and think about different forms of government similar to the way an artist creates.

The first improvement is for academics and civil servants to recognize that public administration must dare to be a generalist's study without discarding specialization. Also, it must show how the day-to-day administrative and operational choices and techniques are related to the level of analysis. Civil servants cannot work in isolation from society or people's values. Instead, they must be attuned to subtle and sudden social, political, and economic changes. They must work with both the techniques of a specialist and the intuition of a generalist.

The second improvement public administration can make is no longer searching for an identity. Public administration has an identity because it is the only study that studies government in all its aspects (Raadschelders, 2011, 2020). While it is true that many other disciplines study elements of government as far as these are relevant to their main object of study, does that mean that public administration has no domain? Quite the contrary, public administration scholars seek to integrate the knowledge and insights generated by scholars in other disciplines and studies. The choice is to embrace the idea that different approaches to government study are equally relevant to understanding government. Any approach that limits this goal is not good enough. This also means that a hierarchy of knowledge does not exist in the study of public administration. For example, some scholars hold that science is better than craft or art. But does that not depend on what you want to do with it? Can we afford to close our eyes to the approaches that may not be as scientific but might be very helpful in understanding what government does, how it does it, who does it, and why it does it?

Finally, the study must combine attention to traditional public administration functions (organizational structure and processes, policy, and management) and asking hard, value-laden questions about the purposes and processes of government. For example, a budgeteer may know everything about budgeting. The study of public administration offers excellent classes that teach budgeting techniques. But the civil servant must also learn about the politics of budgeting, about who gets what, when, and how. A budget reflects choices, which must be presented and defended in terms of values people recognize (Franklin & Raadschelders, 2004). This improvement also requires public administration scholars and practitioners to rediscover the usefulness of comparative and historical perspectives. Indeed, this is a lesson learned by many government officials visiting other countries to learn about best practices elsewhere and why they work and to what extent they can be applied in their own country.

Chapter Summary

We cannot understand the position of government in contemporary society, nor the role that government plays in contemporary society, without (a) drawing upon the works of literature in other studies and disciplines, (b) comparing the position and role of a nation's government to that of governments elsewhere, and (c) considering how and why a nation's government became what it is today so that we can see where we can improve. The study of public administration is a transdisciplinary study indispensable for understanding and steering the ship of state into the future. You may not always like it, but in our densely populated, increasingly diverse, and globally interconnected society, we cannot do without our governance regimes and government institutions nor with the organizations and public administrators that serve the needs of the collective.

In-Class Instructional Suggestions

1. While the government is a global phenomenon, most textbooks are written in a specific national context. Thus, there are "Introductions to Public Administration" textbooks in Australia, Brazil, France, Germany, India, the Netherlands, South Africa, and South Korea.
2. When was the first textbook in public administration published in your country?
3. Compare the table of contents of that first textbook with a much more recent text.
4. What are the differences and similarities?

REFERENCES

Anderson, B. (2006). *Imagined communities: Reflections on the origin and spread of nationalism* (3rd ed.). Verso.

Etzioni, A. (2019). *Law and society in a populist age: Balancing individual rights and the common good.* Bristol University Press.

Franklin, A. L., & Raadschelders, J. C. N. (2004). Ethics in local government budgeting: Is there a gap between theory and practice? *Public Administration Quarterly, 27*(4), 456–490.

Frederickson, H. G. (2003). Look, public administration ain't rocket science. *PA Times, 26*(9), 11.

King, C. S., & Stivers, C. (1998). *Government is us: Public administration in an anti-government era.* Sage.

Morris, D. (1996 [1969]). *The human zoo: A zoologist's classic study of the urban animal.* Kodansha International.

Raadschelders, J. C. N. (2011). *Public administration: The interdisciplinary study of government.* Oxford University Press.

Raadschelders, J. C. N. (2019). The state of theory in the study of public administration in the United States: Balancing evidence-based, usable knowledge, and conceptual understanding. *Administrative Theory and Praxis, 41*(1), 79–98.

Raadschelders, J. C. N. (2020). *The three ages of government: From the personal to the group, to the world.* University of Michigan Press.

Rodgers, R., & Rodgers, N. (2000). Defining the boundaries of public administration: Undisciplined mongrels versus disciplined purists. *Public Administration Review, 60*(5), 435–445.

Simon, H. A., Langley, P. W., & Bradshaw, G. L. (1981). Scientific discovery as problem-solving. *Synthese, 47*, 1–27.

Wilson, W. (2005 [1887]). The study of administration. In R. J. Stillman, II (Ed.), *Public administration: Concepts and cases* (pp. 6–15). Houghton Mifflin.

Concept List

The concepts and theories in this list are alphabetically organized, with the chapter in which the concept or theory is discussed in parentheses. The concepts and theories in this list are highlighted in italics in the main text. The entries in the glossary provide a brief definition, reference to the lead theorist (if relevant), and some considerations about how the concept or theory relates to practice. This not only refers to government practice in general, but also to unique practices in different settings. For example, how does this concept or theory help describe and understand developments in one's community? In this element, the instructor is invited to link the main text to the experiences of students to the geographical area where they study respectively grew up.

The concepts and theories we have selected are central to the study of public administration. The reader may find that some concepts are missing while others should not have been included. The instructor can augment this listing with any concepts and theories relevant to their course or context.

Accountability (Ch.12)

The feature in any organization of expecting the employees' best possible performance; if performance is under par, an individual can be held accountable by receiving a warning or even a performance improvement plan. Accountability is also applied to the organization and its performance and goal achievement.

Accounting (Ch.11)

A management function that records, classifies, analyzes, summarizes, and reports financial data and receipts, investments, and disbursements. This information is then aggregated into reports describing the overall financial condition of government.

Active Representation (Ch.10)

The effort to recruit people from various portions of the population in the hope they will advance the interests of the group to which they belong.

280 CONCEPT LIST

Adjudication (Ch.7)
The process where a court, independent regulatory agency, or a designated third party applies existing laws or rules to individual cases to determine if the correct action was taken.

Administrative Discretion (Ch.7)
The situation under which career civil servants, in their role as an expert (i.e., especially *policy bureaucrats*), have the responsibility to interpret and flesh out ambiguous legislation.

Administrative Procedures Act (Ch.6)
The APA became law in 1946 to govern how federal departments and agencies propose regulations and grants.

Administrative State (Ch.1)
A condition where government bureaucracies offer a wide range of services, regulations, and policies for almost all areas of people's life.

Advocacy Coalition Framework (Ch.7)
An approach to policy and decision-making that recognizes and acknowledge the influence of actors other than government upon the content and substance of decisions and policies. Additional actors are mainly interest groups that provide information about the preferences of their members to influence decision-makers' preferences. The focus is on the competition between opposing viewpoints and how information is given to decision-makers supporting these multiple viewpoints. This approach is associated with political scientists Paul Sabatier and is often referred to as the ACF or Coalition Advocacy Framework.

Affirmative Action (AA) (Ch.10)
These are efforts to increase representation in government of those portions of the population previously discriminated.

Agency-fication (Ch.5)
These are efforts to split off a coherent set of activities and services from a government department and organize it in a separate agency. This is often done at the federal level in the hope that it will give the Executive better control of the bureaucracy by directly appointing agency heads.

Auditing (Ch.12)
A process of reviewing and evaluating what has been done to determine if accurate records have been kept, internal controls are in place, legal requirements are upheld, and plans are fulfilled. Four types of audits are distinguished:

a) the *financial audit* that examines transactions in the organization's financial accounts,
b) a *compliance audit* determines if the organization is following appropriate laws and regulations,
c) an *audit of economy and efficiency* looks at the use of resources to examine how things are done and if they can be improved to reduce inefficiencies, and

d) a *performance audit* that evaluates the organization's results to see if goals and objectives are being achieved.

Authoritarian Regime (Ch.3)
A political system controlled by a wealthy elite class closely related to the ruling class or the military. Authoritarian regimes have little tolerance for the opposition, and political and civil rights are often suppressed.

Authoritative Allocation of Values (Ch.2)
This is a characterization of the policy- and decision-making process that political scientist David Easton developed. It concerns the fact that any policy involves the use of scarce resources. For instance, money spent on health care cannot be spent on defense. Ultimately, any decision made by policymakers, whether in elected office or as a career civil servant, is an expression of what is considered necessary, that is, valuable, in and to society at large.

Backward Mapping (Ch.8)
An approach to policymaking where the end objective is identified first, after which the policymaker backtracks the various steps that will lead to reaching the end objective. Education scholar Richard Elmore coined the term (see also *forward mapping*).

Balanced Budget Requirement (Ch.11)
The requirement at state and local levels of government that anticipated revenues in the approved budget must equal or exceed anticipated expenditures.

Benchmarking (Ch.8)
Actions an organization takes to find out what other organizations are doing and whether some of their practices can be adapted to and adopted in one's organization. Also known as best-practices research.

Bounded Rationality (Ch.7)
The situation when people have limited information processing and storage capabilities. The term was coined by the interdisciplinary scholar Herbert Simon.

Broad Banding (Ch.10)
The effort to categorize a variety of jobs in one large category to simplify the job category structure and thus the pay structure.

Budgeting (Ch.11)
The process by which public officials allocate the available resources of government among competing interests to achieve society's objectives and the highest public value.

Bureaucracy (Ch.6)
According to Max Weber, bureaucracy is both a type of organizational structure and a type of personnel system. Organizational structure is characterized by, among other things, unity of command, hierarchy, formal rules, and written communication. As a personnel system, it is one where employees are appointed based on relevant educational background and merit.

Bureaucracy-Internal Theories (of government growth) (Ch.6)
These include a range of ideas that explain the growth of government in terms of negative or unavoidable reasons. Negative is the notion that

power-hungry bureaucratic officeholders seek to grow their office and maximize their responsibilities via the growth of subordinates and budget. Unavoidable reasons for the growth of government include the growth of personnel size that prompts a further vertical and horizontal differentiation of organizational structure.

Capital Asset Management (Ch.11)
This begins with an inventory of government assets, indicating their value and condition, and periodically assesses, evaluates, and plans for the purchase and replacement of large items used for organizational operations over multiple years.

Capital Budget (Ch.11)
Money set aside for special projects to build or purchase assets the government will use for many years. As a result, the money for purchasing these costly assets is often financed over multiple years, sometimes decades.

Capital Expenditure (Ch.11)
This is defined as a project: 1) with an essential public purpose, 2) with a long, useful life, 3) which is purchased infrequently and expensive, 4) which is related to other government functions, and 5) which is regarded as government's responsibility to provide.

Capital Improvements Plan (CIP) (Ch.11)
A multi-year plan that rank orders the capital projects that will be completed each year to maintain the government's capital assets (see also *Capital Asset Management*).

Casework (Ch.12)
Efforts by an intermediary, who can be an individual (such as an elected official) or an organization (such as a law firm), to change the actions or outcomes for an individual that are determined by a government program.

Cash Management (Ch.11)
A managerial function for processing receipts in a timely and efficient manner, for paying bills when they are due—not before or after–and investing funds for a reasonable return while meeting cash needs and minimizing risk on the money invested.

Centralization (Ch.9)
The transfer of tasks and decision-making authority from a lower level of an organization to a higher level.

Citizen Functionaries (Ch.5)
All those who serve voluntarily in specific government-let operations or committees. These can be regarded as public servants, but they have no work contract with the government level where they serve. Citizen functionaries are usually found in local government, for instance, as members of the Parks and Recreation Board, the Library Board, etc.

Civic Engagement (Ch.7)
Individual and collective actions designed to identify and address issues of public concern. Civic engagement can take many forms, from individual voluntarism to organizational involvement to electoral participation. It can include

efforts to address an issue directly, work with others in a community to solve a problem, or interact with the institutions of representative democracy.

Civil Servants (Ch.1)
All those working in the public sector who are appointed to a position based on merit. Merit includes relevant educational background, expertise, and professional experience.

Civil Servants (Ch.1)
All those directly employed in a government department or agency at the local, state, or federal level. They can also be referred to as Public Servants.

Collective Bargaining (Ch.10)
An activity where representatives from management and labor (through labor unions) negotiate a labor contract. In the public sector, collective bargaining occurs in unionized jobs, such as police officers, school teachers, and firefighters.

Command-and-Control (Ch.5)
A style of management and leadership that is hierarchical and where subordinates are expected to obey the directives of their superiors.

Common Pool Resources (Ch.3)
Common pool resources (CPR) are shared governance systems that manage natural or human-made resources (such as an alpine meadow for grazing, a lake for fisheries, and a system of irrigation canals for agriculture), not owned or used exclusively by one person or organization. Instead, all people living nearby and dependent upon the resources govern it as a collective to assure that everyone can benefit and everyone will pay a fair share to maintain the CPR.

Confederacy (Ch.3)
A loose association or league of independent, sovereign states that have decided to operate together in some policy areas. Most notably, confederacies are formed in response to military threats. Examples include the Dutch Republic (1581–1798), formed to defend against the military attacks of the Spanish monarchy.

Constitutional Democracy (Ch.12)
A system of government where people have the right to vote (active representation) and be elected to political office (passive representation).

Controls (Ch.12)
Organized, systematic, and rational ways of doing things to achieve some desired state. They often strive to "automate" processes or behaviors to safeguard the organization's assets.

Co-Production (Ch.9)
Collaboration between a public organization and non-profit or private partners for producing and delivering a good or service.

Cost-Benefit Analysis (Ch.7)
A policymaking tool that seeks to identify the costs and benefits of alternative policy choices. The alternative where the benefits are more significant than the costs is recommended as the preferred alternative.

Cost-Effectiveness Analysis (CEA) (Ch.7)
A policy instrument that seeks to relate the cost of an alternative to how well it will meet pre-specified goals and provide the desired outcomes (without considering the costs of the alternative).

Creaming (Ch.12)
Taking the richest milk (the cream) off the top, that is, serving the easiest clients first so that you can report high levels of success. Doing this means that the most challenging clients may not get adequate attention or sufficient services.

Debt (Ch.11)
A term that refers to the amount of money government has borrowed or what is owed by government to be repaid in the future.

Decentralization (Ch.9)
The transfer of decision and policymaking authority for government tasks and services from a higher to a lower level of government (see also *unfunded mandate*).

Deconcentrated Organizations (Ch.3)
The transfer of tasks from a higher level of government to a lower level, but without the transfer of decision and policymaking authority.

Delphi Method (Ch.7)
A policy and decision-making process that invites subject matter experts to brainstorm various alternatives without critiquing any particular alternative. Discussion continues until consensus about the best possible solution is achieved.

Demand-Side Theory (of government growth) (Ch.6)
A group of theories that explain government growth in terms of environmental influences that create a living situation unfavorable or even detrimental to people and thus prompt people to request government intervention and action.

Developmental Policy (Ch.6)
This involves intergovernmental transfers of financial and other resources for a particular community's economic and infrastructural development.

Direct expenditures (Ch.11)
The amount spent for personnel and the purchase of the equipment, materials, and supplies necessary to provide government goods and services.

Discipline (Ch.10)
The process of notifying an employee when their performance is unsatisfactory and determining what must be changed to make performance satisfactory. Sometimes these changes are formalized in a performance improvement plan (PIP).

Distributive Policy (Ch.5)
Public policies where there are no eligibility criteria and benefits are distributed equally to all persons.

eGovernment (Ch.8)
Using electronic means to provide information and deliver government services. An example of eGovernment for information provision is a local government's website. An example of a service is that citizens can submit their tax information electronically.

Enabling Act (Ch.9)
A piece of legislation creating a new department or agency.

Entrepreneurial Organization (Ch.8)
A government organization that operates like a business and thus sells its goods or services. Examples include the National Parks Service and the National Forest Service. Another example would be toll roads when they are government owned.

Equal Employment Opportunity (EEO) (Ch.10)
A personnel hiring policy that aims at seeking to limit and even avoid future discrimination.

Executive Order (Ch.4)
A decision made by the head of the executive (president, governor) for which no legislative approval is required. Through it, the head of the executive manages the executive branch.

Federalism (Ch.7)
A system of government where sovereignty is shared between national and regional governments.

Federal Register (Ch.6)
A daily publication of the adopted rules, proposed rules, and notices of federal government agencies and organizations, as well as executive orders and other governmental documents.

Financial Management (Ch.11)
The managerial activity that assures the best possible use of government revenues and monetary assets.

Fiscal Policy (Ch.11)
This is reflected in the decisions about the taxing and spending policies of government and may also refer to the regulatory policies that government imposes on individuals and businesses that have financial implications.

Fiscal Year (Ch.11)
The period of time in which the government collects revenues and authorizes the spending of government funds. The fiscal year does not have to be the calendar year. Many organizations have fiscal years that are different from the calendar year.

For-Profit Organizaions (Ch.1)
The family, households, and organizations that are non-governmental and have the authority to make and carry out decisions about how they will function. These organizations are often referred to as the Private Sector.

Forward Mapping (Ch.8)
A common approach to policymaking that seeks to identify which steps must be taken to achieve a particular (set of) end goal(s). The term was coined by education scholar Richard Elmore (see also **backward mapping**).

Funds Borrowed (Ch.11)
Money raised by a government through the sale of securities such as Treasury notes, bills, and bonds, as well as state and municipal bonds.

Gang Planking (Ch.9)
Situations where employees from different units at the same hierarchical level communicate directly with one another about courses of action without consulting their respective immediate supervisors.

General Purpose Government (Ch.6)
A unit of government that provides a wide range of services characteristic for those identified with the *nightwatch state* plus those that are generally considered part of the *welfare state*.

General Schedule (GS) (Ch.10)
A position classification system that divides all the jobs for that government into pay ranges that feature a range of wages, which often increase based on educational qualifications or years of service.

Governance (Ch.1)
The system and process of government that applies to all organizations and institutions that play a role in structuring, steering, and organizing society. However, that definition obscures the fact that government has an authority (i.e., making binding decisions for all) that no other social actors (church, labor unions, business, interest groups, etc.) have.

Government (Ch.1)
All the structural institutional arrangements that operate under the rule of law and are identified as the "public sector."

Government Institutions (Ch.2)
Rules of the game in society; they help determine how people can and should interact with one another. Government as a whole is an institution that consists of many organizations that include the political, judicial, government and social spheres. The highest court in a nation is both an institution and an organization. An environmental protection agency is an organization but not an institution. Also referred to as Institutions of Government.

Grants-in-Aid (Ch.11)
Transfers of money from the federal or national government to lower-level government in support of policy or program implementation.

Human Capital Management (Ch.10)
An approach to personnel management that regards the individual employee as an investment. In helping to develop an employee's skills, knowledge, and abilities, the organization seeks to meet both employee and organizational objectives and desires.

Human Relations Approach or Tradition (Ch.10)
An approach to personnel management that places primary importance on employee learning; in contrast, *scientific management* stresses skills-based learning. The human relations approach became popular in the 1930s due to the Hawthorne studies that showed how employees performed better when supervisors paid attention to and showed appreciation for their work.

Human Resource Management (Ch.10)
The organizational activity and unit responsible for all personnel policies, including recruitment and selection, promotion, performance evaluation, and termination. It is one of the core staff functions in any organization.

Imagined Community (Ch.2)
A group of people who live together in the same geographical area but are so numerous in size that they no longer know one another on a personal level. This concept can be contrasted with the notion of a physical community of people where the members know one another well. An imagined community is similar to what the mathematician and philosopher Bertrand Russell called "artificial communities."

Incremental Model (Ch.7)
A policy and decision-making process where change is made in incremental, that is, in small steps from the previous level based on the new resources that are available. Incrementalism is most associated with some of the work by political scientist Charles Lindblom.

Independent Regulatory Board or Commission (Ch.7)
An organization that operates outside the executive branch of government which is often governed via a collegial structure with the members selected by the legislative or executive branch and serving staggered terms. A director or administrator usually leads these organizations.

Innovation (Ch.10)
Novel approaches or changes to an organization's activities are caused by a need to be responsive and adapt to external operating environments.

Intergenerational Equity (Ch.11)
Taking action to assure that today's decision recognizes the need to wisely use current resources so that future generations have similar resources available to them for the benefit of the collective.

Intergovernmental Management (Ch.2)
All activities of the public administrators charged with carrying out the day-to-day activities of public programs involving multiple governments.

Intergovernmental Relations (Ch.2)
The interactions and relationships that exist between levels of government. The relationships are necessary to coordinate the funding and delivery of services and regulatory relationships between levels of government.

Jurisdiction (Ch.6)
A territorially defined area in which a specific governmental unit has the authority to make decisions about and implement government programs.

Kaldor-Hicks Analysis (Ch.7)
The analysis of costs (who pays) and benefits (who gains) under each different policy alternative and whether the winners will benefit enough to compensate the losers.

Knowledge Management (Ch.8)
A system in which an organization systematically identifies its employees' skills, knowledge, and capabilities and determines how these can be shared with everyone in the organization and put to best use for the organization.

Line Unit (Ch.9)
The units in an organization directly responsible for delivering the good or service for which the organization was created.

Logic Model (Ch.8)
An approach to policy and decision-making that focuses on identifying (a) outcomes as desired in organizational vision and mission statements and (b) as viable in terms of financial and personnel resources. Also referred to as the Theory of Change.

Matrix Organization (Ch.9)
A type of organizational structure where an employee has two supervisors: one from the standing organization and one from a project in which the employee participates.

Merit System (Ch.1)
Merit is a praiseworthy quality, a mark of excellence. Merit pay is based on relevant educational background and job experience. In a merit system, people are generally appointed based on merit, not because of kinship or friendship ties.

Mixed Scanning (Ch.7)
An approach to policy and decision-making that combines some of the features of the rational-comprehensive and the incremental models. Advocated by political scientist Amitai Etzioni, this approach assumes that sometimes policies proceed in big steps (which he calls contextuating decisions) and at other times in small steps (which he calls bit-by-bit decisions).

Monarch (Ch.3)
A crowned head of state (e.g., queen, king, empress, emperor, prince, archduke) who occupies the office, usually based on heredity.

Monetary Policy (Ch.11)
All government policies concerning money supply, including the amount of money printed and in circulation, determining the levels of government borrowing held in Treasury notes, bills, and bonds, and setting the interest rate.

Monitoring Systems (Ch.12)
The effort to measure what has happened, detect variance, and suggest when corrective action is necessary. Monitoring can also help to discern when new trends are emerging so that the organization can proactively craft changes in response to the change.

Mutual Adaptation (Ch.8)
The process where organizations make changes and adjustments to a policy during the implementation phase based on the realities and changes present in the operating environment.

Nation (Ch.3)
Either a homogenous group of people defined by shared culture, language, customs, and so forth; or, in the past two centuries, a group of people, heterogeneous in geographical origin but living in the same sovereign country.

Night-Watch State (Ch.6)
A type of state and government where public services and policies are limited to protecting order and safety through military, police officers, and judiciary.

Non-Constitutional Branches (Ch.3)
In most nations, there are three constitutional branches of government: legislative, executive, and judicial. Three other branches mentioned in the literature that substantially influence public policymaking are bureaucracy as the fourth branch, the media as the fifth, and interest groups as the sixth.

Non-Profit Organizations (Ch.3)
These are organizations that encourage participation by "leveling the playing field" through education about government and how input works, as well as by facilitation of community dialogue and deliberation forums to bring government officials and stakeholders who are least likely to participate together. An example is the Kettering Foundation and its collaboration with the National Issues Forums about pressing policy issues. See also third-party intermediary organizations.

Non-State Actors (Ch.3)
Influential organizations that influence a government due to the resources and subject matter expertise they can provide to the government. While non-state actors do not have the authority to force collective actions, governments are increasingly influenced by actions and decisions taken by the many non-state actors in the world. Examples of non-state actors are the United Nations, the World Bank, and the International Monetary Fund.

Off-Budget and **Non-Appropriated Funds** (Ch.11)
Funds that are created for the activities of quasi-government organizations for which funds are not appropriated like other fund sources. These include public enterprises, public authorities, special districts, and government corporations. These funds increase flexibility since they do not have the same restrictions as other funds do.

Operational Budget (Ch.11)
The revenues and expenditures authorized to operate government programs within the budget cycle (typically one fiscal year).

Organic View of Government (Ch.1)
A view that everyone in society contributes to the common good. It is based on Woodrow Wilson's idea of society as a beehive where all survive since all work together.

Organizational Culture (Ch.4)
This is defined by the underlying assumptions held by members of an organization about how the world operates and how we understand human nature, the universe, and relationships such as those in the political system. An organization's culture can be evidenced in the shared norms about what is considered unique to the organization and the visible elements of culture evidenced in logos, mottos, dress codes and uniforms, mottos, and songs.

Organization Charts (Ch.9)
A visualization of an organization's structure. The levels and groupings in the organizational chart suggest hierarchical relationships and the types of work conducted within units.

Oversight Mechanisms (Ch.12)
Formal policies and informal practices used by elected officials to guide the actions of government programs and workers in a program. They can be directed toward an organization's entire operations or a specific decision made for an individual seeking government services.

Pendleton Act (Ch.10)
Legislation passed in 1883 to establish a Civil Service Commission (CSC) that would oversee the appointment of civil servants based on merit. This Act was designed to eliminate the *spoils system*, which gave jobs based on relationships rather than merit.

Pensions (Ch.11)
A type of retirement plan that may be offered by employers in all organizational sectors designed to provide adequate income after retirement.

Performance Measurement (Ch.12)
The effort to assess via measurable indicators what progress a public organization makes with delivering public goods or services in achieving the results or outcomes that clients, customers, or stakeholders hope for and expect. This is both a tool for internal management (i.e., assessing who lives up to expectations) and external management (i.e., showing citizens that they receive value for money).

Political Appointees (Ch.2)
Public servants who the executive selects to lead a department or agency. Many of these appointments require legislative branch approval.

Political Culture (Ch.4)
A set of views and normative judgment citizens have about their political system and form of government. Political scientist Daniel Elazar distinguished three types: individualist, moralist, and traditionalist political cultures.

Political Officeholders (Ch.2)
Those elected to public office to serve either in the legislative or executive branch or to be the elected leader of standalone government organizations such as the Superintendent of Public Instruction or a School Board Member.

Politics—Administration Dichotomy (Ch.5)
The idea, and later theory, that politicians should concern themselves with determining policy, while administrators would focus on executing and

implementing such policy. Advanced as an ideal situation by the legal scholar Frank Goodnow, he acknowledged politics and administration could not be but intertwined in practice.

Policy Analysis (Ch.7)

The systematic investigation of alternative courses of public action using evidence for and against each option and introducing these into the discussion before a decision is made.

Policy Bureaucrats (Ch.5)

Career civil servants whose work mainly or exclusively concerns the development and writing of policies and regulations. They account for about 30% of the public sector workforce. The term was first coined by political scientists Page and Jenkins (2005).

Policy Field (Ch.2)

A visual presentation of the various public, non-profit, and private actors involved in delivering services or developing policy in a particular area. Policy fields provide insight into the extent to which actors at all levels are intertwined in the development of policy and the delivery of services.

Policy Implementation (Ch.8)

The activity that seeks to execute policy decisions. This involves interpreting statutory language to determine feasible actions and guidelines, designing or redesigning a program's operational structure, and providing goods or services.

POSDCORB (Ch.1)

One of the most well-known acronyms in public administration that describes core managerial activities: planning, organizing, staffing, directing, coordinating, reporting, and budgeting. Luther Gulick coined the acronym in the 1930s.

Position Classification (Ch.10)

The activity where, for each job, a determination is made about the needed level of knowledge, skills, and abilities (KSA), and the appropriate salary range is indicated.

Primary Legislation (Ch.6)

This includes all regulations debated and passed into law by the legislative branch.

Public Management (Ch.9)

Ideas that guide the day-to-day operations and activities of government. It includes decisions about how to provide public services (directly by government or through contracts with non-government organizations) and how to determine the performance and effectiveness of these programs.

Project Organization (Ch.9)

A temporary, ad hoc organizational arrangement where employees from different units are brought together to help resolve a particular challenge or problem. Once the project is completed, the employees return to their standing organization.

Public Personnel Management (Ch.10)

See Human Resource Management.

Public Sector (Ch.1)
A label to describe everything in society that occurs outside the family, household and private organizations. Since the late eighteenth century, everything has been considered governmental and concerns society's protection, safety, and advancement.

Rational-Comprehensive Model (Ch.7)
A decision and policymaking theory that assumes that a decision-maker has complete information about all alternative policy directions. It is also assumed that the decision-maker will arrive at a decision objectively, that is, based on facts only.

Recruitment (Ch.10)
The process through which a vacancy or a new position is filled.

Redistributive Policy (Ch.5)
Policies that seek to advance the interests of vulnerable or historically disadvantaged populations through government programs that gather revenue from many but provide services to only a few who meet pre-established criteria.

Regionalization (Ch.3)
A process where parts of a territorial state desire to split off and become autonomous. Regionalization can also happen via direct interactions between subnational governments and supranational or international organizations. The best example is the Europe of the Regions in the European Union.

Regulatory Policy (Ch.6)
Policies aimed at regulating citizen behavior and the activities of private corporations.

Representative Bureaucracy (Ch.10)
The notion that the composition of the public workforce, especially of the career civil service, reflects the composition of the population. This is also known as passive representation or representative government (see also *active representation*).

Risk Management (Ch.11)
The systematic effort to identify, eliminate, or reduce conditions that may harm employees or customers or threaten the overall operations in an adverse event.

Rule of Law (Ch.2)
The situation where all people in a sovereign state are subject to the same laws, and no one is considered to be above the law, including kings, presidents, and other high-level rulers. This term is closely related to constitutionalism and Rechtsstaat and thus refers to a specific political situation and not a particular legal rule.

Safeguarding Assets (Ch.11)
This involves having adequately trained personnel, segregating and rotating job responsibilities and functions, requiring multiple levels of authorizations, recording transactions properly, assuring limited access to assets, and periodic testing, measurement, and reconciliation.

Satisficing (Ch.7)
A decision and policymaking theory that assumes that decision-makers make a decision based on existing information and under acceptance of bounded rationality once they identify the first feasible solution rather than devoting additional time to research all possible alternatives before deciding. For his work on bounded rationality, the interdisciplinary scholar Herbert Simon received the Nobel Prize in Economics in 1978.

Scientific Management (Ch.1)
An approach to managing work that carefully establishes how much time and what kind of actions are needed to accomplish a specific task. This approach, also known as time-and-motion studies, was championed by mechanical engineer Frederick Winslow Taylor in the early twentieth century to improve industrial production. His ideas became very popular and were also applied to the public sector. In the late twentieth and early twenty-first centuries, ideas about increasing efficiency returned under New Public Management.

Secondary Legislation (Ch.6)
All regulation that has the force of law but is developed and passed into law by government departments and agencies through delegated authority.

Senior Executive Service (SES) (Ch.10)
A personnel system that provides advancement opportunities to career civil servants at the highest level of a government organization.

Social Capital (Ch.1)
This is developed through the social networks or associations that create imaginary bridges to connect people of different backgrounds (i.e., religion, politics, race, gender, income level, class, etc.), as well as to bond, or connect like-minded people irrespective of their backgrounds (i.e., relatives, church groups, sports clubs, etc.). Combined, the bridging and bonding that occur support us as well as with connections to accomplish our goals and make society function better. Many scholars have written about social capital, most notably sociologist Robert Putnam.

Social Culture (Ch.3)
This is present in the entirety of values, norms, goals, and expectations in a given society.

Sovereignty (Ch.2)
The ultimate power and authority in society, especially concerning the political power in society and the state's boundaries in the international arena of territorial states. The domestic dimension of sovereignty concerns the government's authority in society; the international dimension concerns the relations between states.

Span of Control (Ch.9)
The number of people (ideally 6–12) one can effectively supervise. For routine-type tasks and activities, the span of control can be pretty large; for specialized tasks and activities, it is much smaller.

Specialization (Ch.9)
The effort to structure a specific set of interrelated tasks into one position or organizational unit.

Special Purpose Entity (Ch.7)
A public sector organization that only provides one specific service. The best example is independent school districts that only provide education. Also referred to as a special purpose government.

Spoils System (Ch.5)
A personnel system where recruitment for public office is based on kinship and friendship relations rather than merit.

Staff Unit (Ch.9)
Units that provide internal services within an organization to help service delivery programs function efficiently. They include human resources, finance, evaluation, facilities management such as a restaurant, cleaning, planning, information technology support, etc.

Stakeholder (Ch.5)
Any group or individual who can affect or is affected by the activities of an organization.

State (Ch.2)
A territorially defined and independent country, usually with a political system. Also known as a *territorial state* (see also *sovereignty*).

Strategic Plan Elements (Ch.8)
The components of a planning process often include the development of a vision, mission, internal/external assessment, goals, and actions plans.

Strategic Planning (Ch.7)
Disciplined decision-making guiding an organization to what it wants to do by asking where it is now and where it wants to be.

Street-Level Bureaucrats (Ch.5)
Career civil servants who come in direct contact with citizens as they fulfill their duties.

Sunset reviews (Ch.12)
Planned inquiries to determine if a government organization should be terminated (in which case the sun would set on the organization).

Supply-Side Theories (of government growth) (Ch.6)
A group of theories explaining government growth caused by the availability of resources.

Third-Party Interest or Lobbying Organizations (Ch.3)
Non-governmental organizations that mobilize the needs, concerns, and interests of people who are least likely to participate or organize their voices. Also referred to as third-party intermediaries. See also *non-profit organizations*.

Totalitarian Regime (Ch.3)
A political system characterized by a lack of political liberties and human rights. An official state ideology touches every aspect of life through a single political party, state control of the media, state control of the economy, and secret police.

Transdisciplinarity (Ch.13)
A practice of bringing together experts in many disciplines and a wide variety of knowledge sources to address complex problems in natural and human systems synergistically.

Transfer Payments (Ch.11)
Direct payments to individuals (e.g., unemployment benefits), as well as the allocation of funds from one level of government to another.

Uncontrollable Spending (Ch.11)
Government payments made to everyone eligible for a public program. Administrators cannot limit the program spending by the amount of money available. The only way to reduce the program spending is to legally change the eligibility requirements or reduce the amount each eligible program recipient can receive.

Unfunded Mandate (Ch.7)
A phenomenon where a higher level of government transfers tasks and responsibilities to a lower level of government without providing the funding necessary to perform the tasks.

Unfunded Pension Liability (Ch.11)
A situation where the public employee contributions to pension plans are not sufficient to pay expected retirement benefits. The longer life expectancies of retirees often cause this situation.

Unity of Command (Ch.9)
An organizational structure in which an employee is answerable to only one supervisor.

Unionization (Ch.10)
This occurs when categories of employees become members of a labor union to advance their interests. Unionization is prevalent for lower-level and blue-collar positions. The most extensive degree of unionization in the public sector is among teachers, nurses, police officers, and firefighters.

Virtual Organization (Ch.9)
Self-organizing structures that involve multiple, interdependent organizations, often from different sectors, where one unit is not superior or subordinate to the others.

Welfare State (Ch.2)
A state that provides both repressive and protective services such as defense, policing, and justice, as well as preventative and caring services in the areas of education, health care, housing, zoning, etc.

Zero-Base Budgeting (Ch.11)
The situation where each department and agency starts developing a budget from scratch. This means that every activity and related spending must be justified and reauthorized, rather than assuming that current activities and related funding levels will be continued in the next year.

Index[1]

A
Accountability, 239, 252
Accounting, 234
Active representation, 207
Adjudication, 144
Administrative discretion, 146
Administrative Procedures Act, 142
Administrative state, 7
Advocacy coalition framework, 139
Affirmative action (AA), 207
Agency-ification, 94
Auditing, 226, 254–255
Authoritarian regime, 41
Authoritative allocation of values, 18

B
Backward mapping, 166
Balanced budget, 228
Benchmarking, 162
Bounded rationality, 138
Broad banding
Budgeting, 201
Bureaucracy, 47, 85, 99
Bureaucracy-internal theories (of government growth), 115

C
Capital asset management, 231
Capital budget, 220
Capital expenditure, 231
Capital Improvement Plan (CIP), 232
Casework, 46
Cash management, 234
Centralization, 179
Citizen functionaries, 86
Civic engagement, 129
Civil servants, 47, 58, 59, 68, 71, 72, 74–78
Collective bargaining, 206
Command-and-control, 92
Common pool resources (CPR), 31
Confederacy, 42
Constitutional democracy, 271
Controls, 221, 224, 225, 228, 229, 233, 234, 239, 243
Co-production, 159, 168, 186
Cost-benefit analysis, 135
Cost-effectiveness analysis (CEA), 137
Creaming, 250

[1] Note: Page numbers followed by 'n' refer to notes.

D

Debt, 222
Decentralization, 179
Deconcentrated organizations, 36
Delphi method, 140
Demand-side theory (of government growth), 115
Developmental policy, 114
Direct expenditures, 223
Discipline, 177
Distributive policy, 101

E

eGovernment, 168
Enabling act, 175
Entrepreneurial organization, 185
Equal employment opportunity (EEO), 207
Executive Order, 74, 76, 77
Externality, 5

F

Federalism, 129
Federal Register, 122
Financial management, 201
Fiscal policy, 221
Fiscal year, 226
Forward mapping, 166
Funds borrowed, 223

G

Gang planking, 180
General-purpose government, 109
General Schedule (GS), 208
Governance, 11–31
Government, 11–31
Grants-in-aid, 230

H

Human capital management, 198
Human relations approach/tradition, 200
Human resource management, 196

I

Imagined community, 23
Incremental model, 138
Independent regulatory board/commission, 143
Innovation, 185, 188–190
Institutions of government, 12
Intergenerational equity, 233
Intergovernmental management, 16
Intergovernmental relations, 127, 129–133, 148

J

Jurisdiction, 109

K

Kaldor-Hicks Analysis, 135
Knowledge management, 167

L

Line unit, 177
Logic model, 160

M

Matrix organization, 176
Merit system, 2
Mixed scanning, 139
Monarch, 35
Monetary policy, 221
Monitoring, 245, 248–252, 255
Mutual adaptation, 167

N

Nation, 23, 29
Night watch State, 102
Non-constitutional branches, 47
Non-profit organizations, 24
Non-state actors, 50

O

Off-budget and Non-appropriated funds, 224

Operational budget, 220
Organic view of government, 4
Organizational culture, 60
Organization charts, 166, 177
Oversight mechanisms, 257, 258

P
Pendleton Act, 199
Pensions, 237
Performance measurement, 244
Planning elements, 161
Policy analysis, 134
Policy bureaucrats, 98
Policy field, 15
Policy implementation, 148, 163
Political appointees, 79
Political culture, 59, 68–69
Political officeholders, 17
Politics-administration dichotomy, 89
POSDCORB, 5
Position classification, 5
Primary legislation, 122
Private sector, 5n1
Project organization, 176
Public management, vii, 182
Public personnel management, 196
Public sector, 7, 8
Public servants, 58, 72–77

R
Rational-comprehensive model, 138
Recruitment, 203
Redistributive policy, 101
Regionalization, 47
Regulatory policy, 112
Representative government/bureaucracy, 185
Risk management, 236
Rule of law, 21

S
Safeguarding assets, 238
Satisficing, 138

Scientific Management, 4
Secondary legislation, 122–124
Senior Executive Service (SES), 208
Social capital, 24–25
Social culture, 60
Sovereignty, 16, 18, 20, 30
Span of control, 182
Specialization, 176, 180–183
Special purpose entity, 130
Spoils system, 87
Staff unit, 177
Stakeholder, 92, 145
State, 13, 15, 16, 20, 30
Strategic planning, 140–141
Street-level bureaucrats, 97, 128
Sunset reviews, 257
Supply-side theories (of government growth), 115

T
Third-party intermediary organizations, 53
Totalitarian regime, 41
Transdisciplinarity, 265
Transfer payments, 223

U
Uncontrollable spending, 229
Unfunded mandate, 130
Unfunded pension liability, 238
Unionization, 205
Unity of command, 177

V
Virtual organization, 185

W
Welfare state, 30

Z
Zero-base budgeting, 225